THE FRENCH REVOLUTION

consulting editor
Eugene Rice
Columbia University

second edition

THE FRENCH REVOLUTION
Conflicting Interpretations

selected & edited by

Frank A. Kafker
James M. Laux

University of Cincinnati

 Random House
New York

Second Edition
9 8 7 6 5 4 3 2
Copyright © 1968, 1976 by Random House, Inc.

Kafker, Frank A   comp.
   The French Revolution.

   Bibliography: p.
   1.   France—History—Revolution, 1789–1799—Addresses, essays, lectures.
I.   Laux, James Michael, 1927–   joint comp.   II.   Title.
DC142.K3   1976   944.04   75-35676
ISBN: 0-394-31073-X

Manufactured in the United States of America

Text Design: Meryl Sussman Levavi
Cover: Leibert Studios

Preface

This anthology stresses variety rather than consensus. One of its primary aims is to acquaint readers with the work of many of the leading historians of the French Revolution—the great names of the past as well as present-day scholars. We have not sought to give special prominence to any one view or school of revolutionary studies; instead we have tried to include selections by historians of different countries, different political persuasions, different religious beliefs, and different historical methodologies. All we have asked is that they present their points of view with knowledge and clarity. And in our search for such selections, we have not limited ourselves to those easily accessible or already in English. Eleven of the selections, for example, are our own translations from the French.

We have also tried to organize the readings around some of the most important historical problems of the Revolution and the conflicting interpretations of them. In so doing, we have chosen selections that are long enough to show not only the authors' viewpoints, but also the main arguments they use to support them; and we have not confined ourselves to two contrasting interpretations when others might be considered equally cogent. We hope that students will see that some of the explanations and analyses offered here have more validity than others and that they can arrive at preliminary conclusions on at least some of the historical problems presented.

Of course, some noted historians are not represented and some major problems are not discussed. But, we believe, these gaps can be filled. For example, issues such as the long-range causes of the Revolution or the relation between the French Revolution and other revolutions of the eighteenth century have been treated elsewhere in single paperback editions. In any event, given the vast historical literature on the French Revolution—an embarrassment of riches—gaps are inevitable. Some indication of this literature can be found in the bibliography.

In the second edition we have revised the introductions to the historical problems, the biographical sketches of historians, and the bibliography. Most important, we have added eleven selections—three of them translated by us—and two new chapters—"The Revolutionary Common People of Paris" and "Who Benefited from the Revolution?" These additions fill some of the gaps in the first edition and illustrate recent research.

The spelling, capitalization, and punctuation of the individual authors have been retained. When we as editors have added explanatory material to any piece, such additions have been enclosed in brackets. To distinguish these brackets from the authors' brackets in the original text, we have italicized the contents of the authors' brackets.

We are very happy to acknowledge the help of Kornel Huvos, our colleague at the University of Cincinnati, who has been generous with his time and learning.

F. A. K.

J. M. L.

Contents

THE FRENCH REVOLUTION

1

The Outbreak
of the Revolution
(1787-1789)

WHO led the overthrow of the Old Regime in France? Although every July 14 the French celebrate the victory of "the conquerors of the Bastille," historians long ago decided that the story was much more complicated. Many of them have accepted an interpretation popularized by Georges Lefebvre in his *Coming of the French Revolution*: "The first act of the Revolution, in 1788, consisted in a triumph of the aristocracy. . . . But, after having paralyzed the royal power which upheld its own social preeminence, the aristocracy opened the way to the bourgeois revolution, then to the popular revolution in the cities, and finally to the revolution of the peasants—and found itself buried under the ruins of the Old Regime."[1] Thus, the outbreak of the Revolution occurred in four stages; it was carried out by four different social classes; and it was dominated by class conflict. We include here a short version of Lefebvre's interpretation, that contained in his survey *The French Revolution*. The three selections that follow it may be read as tests of Lefebvre's thesis.

Jean Égret's article deals with what Lefebvre calls the "aristocratic revolt," especially with the part played by the parlements, the chief law courts of France. Égret studies the extremely varied social backgrounds of the judges. As a result, the word "aristocratic" takes on many shades

[1] Georges Lefebvre, *The Coming of the French Revolution*, trans. Robert R. Palmer (Princeton, N.J.: Princeton University Press, 1947), p. 3.

of meaning. Does his article simply add nuance to Lefebvre's account, or does it undermine it?

Elizabeth Eisenstein's article concerning the "bourgeois revolt" directly challenges Lefebvre. She finds that the leaders of revolutionary reform in 1788–1789 were a loose-knit coalition of such aristocrats as the Marquis de Lafayette, such clergymen as the Abbé Sieyès, and such commoners as Target, liberals drawn from all three estates. Consequently, she thinks Lefebvre's term "bourgeois revolt" is inaccurate.

Finally, Jacques Godechot considers the "popular revolt" in Paris. He sees the storming of the Bastille as part of a national uprising, not as a plot by small groups or as a riot by Parisians alone. In the course of his discussion, he examines the social background of the "conquerors." Does the evidence presented support the idea that these rioters were people from any one particular class or that the disturbance was largely class-inspired?

In judging the Lefebvre interpretation as a whole, one may also ask the following: if it be true that the leaders of these four stages in the coming of the Revolution were formed primarily by their class backgrounds, how is one's class determined? Marxists stress a person's relation to the means of production—whether, for example, he works the land or owns it, whether he is a laborer in the city or a capitalist. Others believe that such factors as family ancestry, occupation, and education must also be taken into account. What criteria does Lefebvre use when he divides eighteenth-century society into aristocrats, bourgeois, city masses, and peasants? Are these classifications too imprecise, too simple?

Moreover, does he exaggerate the importance of class to the neglect of the individual? In all times, men from similar social backgrounds have chosen different political routes. For example, some aristocrats supported the king in 1788 and many Parisian workers did not riot on July 14. Were such cases exceptional or common, inconsequential or momentous? The answers to these questions have an importance far beyond the study of the French Revolution, for they would illuminate to what extent man is a creature of his class and to what extent he is a free agent, a power in his own right.

$\mathcal{A}$ Series of Class Revolts

GEORGES LEFEBVRE

Georges Lefebvre (1874–1959) is generally considered the foremost twentieth-century historian of the French Revolution. Born in the north of France, the child of poor parents, he attended local public schools and the University of Lille. For the next twenty-five years he taught at provincial and Parisian secondary schools. At first he did research on medieval history, but after several years he turned to the study of the Revolution. In 1924, at the age of fifty, he presented his four-volume doctoral thesis on the peasants of the Department of the Nord during the French Revolution. This pioneering study of the life of the common people during the Revolution made his reputation. He then taught at various universities and published volume after volume on such topics as the outbreak of the Revolution and the revolutionary mentality, as well as highly regarded surveys of the revolutionary and Napoleonic epochs. In 1932 he succeeded Albert Mathiez as editor of the *Annales historiques de la Révolution française*, and in 1937 he was appointed to the Chair in the History of the French Revolution at the University of Paris. Although he retired in 1945, his formidable energy, intelligence, and devotion to the studies of the French Revolution continued to the end of his life.

The Aristocratic Revolution, 1787–1788

The French Revolution was started and led to victory in its first phase by the aristocracy. This fact is of primary importance, but for differing reasons both the

From Georges Lefebvre, *The French Revolution from Its Origins to 1793*, trans. Elizabeth Moss Evanson (New York: Columbia University Press, 1962), pp. 97–130. Copyright © 1962 Columbia University Press. Reprinted with some minor changes in translation by permission of Columbia University Press, Inc., and Routledge & Kegan Paul, Ltd.

Third Estate and the aristocracy took pains to thrust it into the background. The immediate cause of the Revolution was a financial crisis originating with the war in America. Necker [the Finance Minister] had financed the war by borrowing, and his successor, Calonne, had used the same method to pay off arrears. The deficit grew to such proportions that on August 20, 1786, Calonne sent Louis XVI a note declaring state reform imperative.

Calonne and the Notables

The fiscal administration was so confused that the situation can be described only roughly. A statement of financial expectations drawn up in March, 1788, the first—and last—budget of the Old Regime, estimated expenditures at 629 million livres and receipts at 503 million, leaving a deficit of 126 million, or 20 per cent. Contemporaries attributed the deficit to court wastefulness and financiers' profits. Some economies could be and were made, but servicing the debt alone required 318 million, more than half of expenditures. The government could have reduced expenses only by repudiating the debt; raising taxes seemed out of the question, as taxes were already considered too high. At any rate there was one resource left. Certain provinces paid very little in taxes; the bourgeoisie less than the peasantry, the nobility and clergy least of all. From a technical point of view, the crisis could be easily resolved: equality of taxation would provide enough funds.

Calonne did not prove bold enough for fiscal equality, but he at least proposed to extend the [government's] salt and tobacco monopolies through the whole kingdom and to replace the *capitation* and twentieths[1] by a direct land tax, a "territorial subvention," to be levied without exception upon all landowners. At the same time he planned to stimulate economic activity and consequently swell treasury receipts by freeing the grain trade from all controls, by abolishing internal customs barriers, and by suppressing certain indirect taxes. Going even further, he intended to give responsibility for apportioning taxes to provincial assemblies elected by landowners without distinction as to order, and to relieve the clergy of its own debt by selling the Church's manorial rights [chiefly, its right to collect dues on land worked by others]. Financial stability would strengthen royal power, reducing opposition from the parlements to insignificance. Unity of the kingdom would be advanced. The bourgeoisie would be permitted to take part in government administration.

Although the sacrifices required of privileged groups were modest—they would still be exempt from the *taille* and from the tax which Calonne proposed to substitute for road-service obligations (the *corvée des routes*)—he entertained no illusions as to how the parlements would receive his plans. He might have attacked them openly had he been able to count upon the king's support, but the fate of Turgot and Necker[2] gave him no encouragement. Moreover, although royalty still

[1] [The *capitation* and the twentieth *(vingtième)*, as well as the *taille*, were direct taxes levied by the Crown. During the course of the eighteenth century they came to fall most heavily on the peasants, while the privileged groups were able to avoid paying much of their share.—Eds.]

[2] [Both of these ministers had proposed reform programs which aroused opposition. Louis XVI had

carried prestige, Louis personally had none. He was devoted to the hunt and liked to work with his hands; he drank and ate to excess; he liked neither high society, gambling, nor dancing; he was the laughing-stock of his courtiers; and rumours of the queen's conduct made him appear ridiculous. Marie Antoinette had gained the reputation of a Messalina and had lost face in the Diamond Necklace Affair of 1785. Calonne was therefore resigned to practise indirect methods. He thought out a plan to convoke an assembly of notables consisting primarily of various noble elements. By selecting them himself, and banking on administrative influence plus respect due the king, he expected that they would prove amenable and that their acquiescence would in turn impress the parlements. But the calling of an assembly was an initial surrender: the king was consulting his aristocracy rather than notifying it of his will.

When they convened on February 22, 1787, the notables were angered by the proposal to elect provincial assemblies without distinction as to order, by the restriction of their powers, and by the attack on the clergy's manorial rights. As could be expected, they censured the direct land tax and asked that they first be given a treasury report. They declared themselves desirous of contributing to the welfare of the state—but they intended to dictate their own terms. Louis saw that Calonne would get nowhere with the assembly, and dismissed him on April 8.

Brienne and the Parlements

At the head of those who opposed Calonne stood Loménie de Brienne, archbishop of Toulouse, who wanted to become [a government] minister and did so without delay. To soothe the notables he submitted the treasury accounts to them, promised to retain the three orders in the provincial assemblies and to leave the clergy's manorial rights alone. But he took over the plan for a territorial subvention and to it added an increase of the stamp duty. The notables replied that it was not within their power to consent to taxes, an allusion to the Estates-General. On May 25 their assembly was dissolved. Calonne's device had failed; it was obvious that Brienne had next to proceed to the parlements.[3]

The Parlement of Paris made no protest over registering freedom of the grain trade, commutation of the *corvée des routes*, and institution of provincial assemblies. But it drafted remonstrances against the stamp tax and rejected the territorial subvention, openly referring this to an Estates-General. A *lit de justice* was held on August 6; the parlement declared it null and void, then started proceedings against Calonne, who fled to England. On August 14 the magistrates were exiled to

given neither of them wholehearted support. Turgot was dismissed in 1776; Necker resigned in 1781.—Eds.]

[3] [During the reign of Louis XVI, an edict often became a law in the following manner: the royal administration prepared the edict, which was then sent to the leading law court of France, the Parlement of Paris. If the Parlement accepted the edict, it was registered. If it objected to parts of the edict, it drafted remonstrances. The king could override these objections by a *lit de justice*, that is, he could appear before Parlement in person or by proxy, sit on a pile of cushions (a *lit*), and order the registration. Then, according to the king, the edict had the force of law, but the Parlement frequently did not accept this interpretation.—Eds.]

Troyes. Other sovereign courts supported them. Brienne quickly retreated, and on September 19 the reinstated parlement recorded restoration of the old taxes.

Brienne fell back on loans, but the same problem faced him: he had to have consent of the parlements to borrow. A few members agreed to negotiate and did not hesitate to set their decisive condition—that the government should promise to convoke the Estates-General. Brienne asked for 120 million livres to be raised over a five-year period, at the end of which—in 1792—the Estates-General would be convened. But, uncertain of a majority, he suddenly had an edict presented by the king himself on November 18 in a "royal session," that is, a *lit de justice* in which traditional ceremonies of convocation had not been observed. The duc d'Orléans protested and the registering of the edict was declared void. Louis retaliated by exiling the duke and two councillors [members of the Parlement]. The parlement came to their defence, condemning *lettres de cachet* and demanding that royal subjects be given personal freedom. To ward off an attack by force, on May 3, 1788, it published a declaration of fundamental laws of the kingdom, stating that the monarchy was hereditary, that the right to vote subsidies belonged to the Estates-General, that Frenchmen could not be arbitrarily arrested and detained, that their judges were irremovable, the customs and privileges of provinces inviolable.

The government had evidently resolved to imitate Maupeou.[4] On May 5 armed soldiers took up posts around the Palais de Justice until two members of the parlement who had been placed under arrest gave themselves up. On May 8 Louis succeeded in registering six edicts drawn up by Lamoignon, keeper of the seals [Minister of Justice]. According to them the power of registration was transferred to a "plenary court" composed of princes and crown officers, and at the same time the judiciary was reformed at the expense of the parlements—without, however, abolishing venality [the sale of government offices]. The *question préalable*—torture preceding the execution of criminals—was abolished (the *question préparatoire*, used to extract evidence during a judicial inquiry, had ended in 1780). Last of all, a fresh blow was dealt the aristocracy: a litigant could now refuse to accept the ruling of a manorial court by referring his case to royal tribunals.

This time resistance was more widespread and more violent. The provincial parlements and most of the lower tribunals protested. The assembly of the clergy, already annoyed by a recent edict granting Protestants a civil status, criticized the reforms and offered only a small contribution as its "free gift" [the Church's periodic grant of money to the government]. Riots broke out in Paris and several other cities. On June 7 the citizens of Grenoble rose and rained missiles upon the garrison from the rooftops in what was known as the "Day of Tiles." The provincial assemblies set up at the end of 1787 satisfied no one; several provinces clamoured for their old estates vested with the right to vote taxes. In the Dauphiné nobility and bourgeoisie met together at the château of Vizille on July 21, 1788, to convoke the Estates on their own authority. Brienne gave way.

The treasury was now empty. Pensions had had to be cut. Stockholders [owners of government securities] received nothing and notes from the Bank of Discount were made legal tender. Having no money, Louis had to leave it to the Prussians to

---

[4] [A minister of Louis XV from 1768 to 1774, who had attempted to tame the parlements.—Eds.]

invade Holland and support the Stadholder against his burghers. The Stadholder broke his alliance with France and joined with the English. Brienne yielded again, this occasion being the last: the Estates were to convene on May 1, 1789. He resigned on August 24, 1788. The king recalled Necker, whose first act was to dismiss Lamoignon and reinstate the Parlement of Paris. On September 23 the parlement hastened to stipulate that the Estates-General would consist of three orders, as in 1614. Each order would have the same number of representatives, would make its decisions separately, and would have a veto over the others. The nobility and clergy were made masters of the assembly. This was the aristocracy's victory.

During these events privileged groups—especially those in Brittany—had acted together in forming propaganda and resistance organizations to protest royal authority; they had intimidated and sometimes won over the intendants and army leaders; occasionally they had roused sharecroppers and domestics. These revolutionary precedents were not to be forgotten. The parlements above all had taught a lesson: the Third Estate would duplicate their tactics when the Estates-General met. They had even presumed to indict a minister, making Calonne the first émigré.

The Bourgeois Revolution

To annoy the ministers a number of commoners, notably lawyers, had favoured the revolt of the nobility. Many others, such as the Rolands, expecting nothing, remained neutral. The summer of 1788 brought no evidence that bourgeois would take part in events. But news that an Estates-General was to be convened sent a tremor of excitement through the bourgeoisie: the king was authorizing them to plead their case. In this early stage accord with the aristocracy was not out of the question: the example set by the Dauphiné, where nobles granted commoners vote by head and equality of taxation, was welcomed enthusiastically. The atmosphere changed abruptly when the Parlement of Paris showed its true colours on September 23. Suddenly the popularity of the magistrates vanished. A clamour arose throughout the kingdom. "Public debate has assumed a different character," [the journalist] Mallet du Pan stated in January of 1789. "King, despotism, and constitution have become only secondary questions. Now it is war between the Third Estate and the other two orders."

Formation of the Patriot Party

The rupture was still not complete. Some of the liberal great lords joined the upper bourgeoisie to form the "National," or "Patriot," party. The "Committee of Thirty," which seems to have exerted considerable influence within the party, counted among its members the duc de La Rochefoucauld-Liancourt, the marquis de Lafayette, and the marquis de Condorcet, along with Talleyrand, bishop of Autun, and the abbé Sieyes. Mirabeau also appeared at its meetings. Sieyes and Mirabeau were in contact with the duc d'Orléans, who had at his disposal a large sum of money and who wielded unquestionable influence within his extensive appanage. Personal connections as well as bonds created by the many associations that had sprung up in the eighteenth century—academies, agricultural societies, philanthropic groups, reading circles, Masonic lodges—were utilized in the provinces as in Paris. Some have attributed to the Masonic Grand Orient, whose grand master was the duc d'Orléans, a decisive role. But the duc de Luxembourg, its administrator-general, remained devoted to the aristocratic cause, and the lodges were full of nobles. It is difficult to imagine that Masonry could have sided with the Third Estate without being split by conflicts, of which we have no evidence.

Although propaganda of the Patriots provoked counterarguments, the government raised no objection to controversy: the king had invited his subjects to air their thoughts and viewpoints concerning the Estates-General. Under pretext of replying to his appeal, a flood of pamphlets appeared, and their authors slipped into them whatever they wanted to say. The Patriots none the less used brochures with cautious skill—they limited themselves to requesting as many representatives for the Third Estate as for the nobility and clergy combined, invoking the example of the provincial assemblies and the Estates of the Dauphiné. The order of the day was to overwhelm the government with petitions, for which the municipalities assumed, willingly or not, full responsibility. Actually, all were counting on Necker.

Necker and the Doubling of the Third Estate

The minister of finance took care of the most urgent fiscal needs by drawing upon the Bank of Discount and by granting financiers, as security for their advances, "anticipations" on future tax receipts. He did this only to gain time until the Estates assembled, since he expected them to abolish fiscal privileges. If the nobility dominated the Estates the government would be at its mercy. Necker was therefore inclined to favour the Third Estate without being under its power. By doubling that order, and by limiting the vote by head to financial questions, all could be reconciled: equality of taxation would be adopted, while constitutional reform would bring conflict and require arbitration by the king. There can be no doubt about Necker's own view concerning the type of government to be instituted. He admired the British system—a House of Lords would soothe the aristocracy; admission to public office regardless of distinction by birth would satisfy the bourgeoisie.

He had no intention of revealing these plans. As an upstart financier, a foreigner, a Protestant, he had always been suspect in the eyes of the aristocracy, the court, and the king. Several of his colleagues—especially Barentin, the new keeper of the seals—opposed him. Determined above all else to preserve his power, he advanced with measured step. Like Calonne he hoped to persuade the notables to approve doubling of the Third. To this end he again convened them on November 6, 1788, but they disappointed him. On December 12 the royal princes sent Louis an entreaty which, by virtue of its clarity and moving tone, can be considered the manifesto of the aristocracy.

> The State is in danger . . . a revolution of governmental principles is brewing . . . soon the rights of property will be attacked, inequality of wealth will be presented as an object of reform: already the suppression of feudal rights has been proposed. . . . Could

Your Majesty resolve to sacrifice, to humiliate, his brave, his ancient, his respectable nobility? . . . Let the Third Estate cease attacking the rights of the first two orders . . . let it confine itself to asking a reduction of the taxes with which it is perhaps overburdened; then the first two orders, recognizing in the third citizens dear to them, may renounce, in the generosity of their feelings, the prerogatives relating to pecuniary matters, and consent to bear public obligations in the most perfect equality.

But Necker went further and with the support of a few colleagues won the day—probably because Brienne's fall had displeased the queen and the nobility's rebellion had antagonized the king. An "Order of the Council" of December 27 granted doubling of the Third Estate. Louis XVI has since been criticized for not specifying the voting method at that time. This reproach is groundless, for in his report Necker mentioned that voting by order was to be the rule. But the decree failed to record this, and the minister had already hinted that the Estates-General might consider it appropriate to vote by head on tax questions.

The Third Estate cried victory and affected to consider the vote by head won. The nobility denied this interpretation and in Poitou, Franche-Comté, and Provence violently protested the doubling which had given rise to that conclusion. In Brittany class struggle degenerated into civil war; at Rennes fights broke out at the end of January, 1789. The Third Estate, annoyed, moved towards radical solutions. In a famous pamphlet issued in February, "What Is the Third Estate?" Sieyes described with cool rancour the hatred and scorn inspired in him by the nobility: "This class is assuredly foreign to the nation because of its do-nothing idleness." At the same time Mirabeau, in a speech which he had planned to deliver to the Estates of Provence, praised Marius "for having exterminated the aristocracy and the nobility in Rome." Fearful words, heralding civil war.

The Elections and the Cahiers

The electoral rules could have handicapped the bourgeoisie either by giving existing provincial estates the right to appoint deputies or by reserving a proportion of seats in the Third Estate to provincial delegates. Some of the nobles recommended these devices; Necker brushed them aside.

The method of election varied considerably, but the ruling of January 24, 1789, generally prevailed. It designated bailiwicks *(bailliages)* and seneschalsies *(séné-chaussées)* as electoral districts, even though these judicial areas were unevenly populated and differed widely in size. Contrary to precedent, whether or not he possessed a fief every noble was summoned to appear in the assembly of his order, but those ennobled by personal [nonhereditary] title only were relegated to the Third Estate—an error, for it wounded their pride. To elect clerical deputies, all parish priests met with the bishops, whereas [groups of] monks and canons were merely allowed to send representatives. Most parish priests were of the Third Estate and, commanding a majority, often neglected to elect their aristocratic bishops as delegates. The electors who chose the Third Estate's deputies assembled in bailiwick meetings after themselves being named by tax-paying heads of families within villages and parishes. They were elected directly in the villages, by two stages in the large towns. In each of the small bailiwicks designated "secondary" electoral districts, the meeting was allowed only to draw up a *cahier de doléances,* or list of grievances, and send one-quarter of its members to the assembly in the "principal" bailiwick to which it was attached. Peasants outnumbered all others at these meetings, but, lacking education, were incapable of expressing their opinions and were all the more intimidated because the meetings began with discussion of what should be included in the *cahiers.* They almost invariably elected bourgeois deputies.

Among the representatives elected by clergy and nobility were able men who opposed reform, such as Cazalès and the abbé Maury, but owing to circumstances only the liberals—Duport, Alexandre de Lameth, and notably Lafayette—took a leading role. Deputies of the Third Estate were for the most part mature, often rich or well-to-do, educated, industrious, and honest men. Sometimes they had received special distinction—Bailly and Target were members of the Académie Française— but more often they had earned a reputation in their particular province. Mounier and Barnave were well known in the Dauphiné, Lanjuinais and Le Chapelier in Brittany, Thouret and Buzot in Normandy, Merlin de Douai in Flanders, Robespierre in Artois. A telling characteristic of the bourgeoisie was that it had long idolized the marquis de Lafayette, noble deputy from Riom, and that the most celebrated of its own deputies, Sieyes and Mirabeau, came from the privileged classes. This foretells what position the nobility could have assumed in a reformed society by siding with the bourgeoisie.

Sieyes and Mirabeau were both from Provence. Sieyes, the son of a notary in Fréjus, had become canon of Chartres and was elected deputy from Paris. He guided the Third Estate during the early weeks. His pamphlets earned him a reputation as an oracle. It was he who developed the theory of "constituent power," declaring that sovereignty resided in the nation alone and that representatives of the nation were to be invested with dictatorial power until a constitution could be written and put into effect. He was the loyal interpreter of the bourgeoisie and later made the significant distinction between "active" and "passive" citizens. But, lacking application or special talent as an orator, he quickly shut himself off in isolation. Mirabeau, on the other hand, possessed the realistic foresight of a statesman, knew how to handle men, and was unexcelled in eloquent oratory. Unfortunately his scandalous youth and cynical venality made it impossible to respect him; no one doubted that the court could buy him at will. Neither he nor Sieyes could direct the Third Estate. Its work remained a collective achievement.

Necker could have exerted considerable influence over the drafting of the *cahiers de doléances.* Malouet, an official in the naval ministry and a deputy of the Third Estate from Riom, pointed out to him that he must draw up a royal programme to guide public opinion, impress the nobility, and—most important— restrain the enthusiasm of the Third Estate. Necker very likely sensed the wisdom of this suggestion, but he had already been soundly criticized for permitting the doubling and was now inclined to consider his moves carefully. He rejected this additional risk, content with having persuaded the king to remain neutral.

The bourgeois were therefore free to participate in drafting lists of grievances from the parishes. Some model *cahiers* were sent out from Paris or were drawn up regionally; lawyers and parish priests sometimes set pen to paper for the cause. A number of *cahiers* were nevertheless original: indifferent to constitutional reform, they were content to criticize the overwhelming burdens laid upon the populace. But these should not necessarily be taken as an accurate reflection of what the lower classes felt most deeply, for in the presence of a manorial judge peasants were not always likely to say what they thought. Moreover, the proletarians rarely participated in deliberations. Grievances sent out from the bailiwicks are even less representative, since bourgeois members simply eliminated from the original lists those demands which displeased or did not interest them. The popular classes of town and countryside were concerned not only with attaining fiscal equality and tax reduction, but with suppressing the tithe, manorial rights, and seigneurial authority, with gaining observance of collective usage [of common land in rural communities], regulating the grain market, and instituting controls to curb capitalist expansion. The people threatened aristocratic property along with aristocratic privileges, and bourgeois aspirations as well. But since the populace did not have access to the Estates-General, king, aristocrats and bourgeois were left alone to settle their triangular conflict.

In their *cahiers* the nobles and bourgeois were of one accord in expressing devotion to the monarchy, but they also agreed upon the need to replace absolutism with rule of law accepted by representatives of the nation; with reasonable freedom of the press and guarantees of personal liberty against arbitrary administrative and judicial ruling; with reform of various branches of the administration, including ecclesiastic reorganization. To the desire for national unity was joined a keen desire for regional and communal autonomy which would end ministerial despotism by loosening the grip of a centralized administration. Both classes agreed to religious toleration, but secularization of the state stopped at this point: they wished to leave the privilege of public worship to the Catholic Church and did not consider abolishing religious instruction or Church poor relief, nor did they deny clerics the right to register births, marriages, and deaths. The clergy was not satisfied with this much: it would not allow criticism of its doctrines through the press or the same treatment for heretics as for true believers. Even a recent edict granting legal status to Protestants had provoked protest. Except for these qualifications, not inconsiderable in themselves, the clergy agreed with the other two orders. More or less generally conceived, liberty was a national desire.

Class conflict was none the less evident. The privileged classes resigned themselves to financial sacrifices—with strong reservations as to the extent and method of contributions demanded of them—but they were generally opposed to the vote by head and expressly stipulated that the orders be preserved and honorific prerogatives and manorial rights be retained, whereas for the Third Estate equality of rights was inseparable from liberty.

But this did not mean that royal arbitration was destined to fail. No one challenged the king's right to approve legislation or the need to leave executive power intact. By renouncing the exercise of arbitrary will and by governing in accord with the Estates-General, the Capetian dynasty would only emphasize its national character; royal authority would not be lessened if reformed. There were many men among the aristocracy and bourgeoisie who, whether they actively desired it or not, might have leaned towards compromise. Among the nobles obedience to the princely will might have quelled opposition. Such bourgeois as Malouet and Mounier wanted above all to end despotism and judged that wrangling among the orders would perpetuate it. With little concern for the peasants, they were willing to respect the manorial authority and honorific primacy of the noble. Among each of the orders fear of civil war, already perceptible, secretly pleaded for conciliation.

A great king or a great minister might have taken the initiative towards a settlement. But Louis XVI was not Henry IV; Necker was clearsighted, but his background paralysed him. The nation was left to itself.

The Victory of the Bourgeoisie

Far from thinking of compromise, the court tried to get rid of Necker. The Parlement of Paris, repentant, gladly offered its assistance. In April rumour had it that a new cabinet would be formed and would promptly adjourn the Estates-General *sine die*. The issue of verifying powers aroused contention among the ministers: Barentin held that precedent accorded power of verification to the Council of State [the king's Cabinet]; Necker objected. Louis ended by supporting Necker, thereby averting a palace revolution but leaving the question of who was qualified to verify powers undecided. This conflict probably accounts for the postponement of the opening of the Estates from April 27 to May 5.

Prudence advised that the deputies should assemble far from Paris, but Versailles was the preferred choice—by the king so he could hunt; by the queen and her entourage for their own pleasures. The court also acted unwisely in clinging to a protocol that humiliated the Third Estate. Each order was assigned a particular dress, and they were segregated for presentation to the king on May 2. In the procession of the Holy Ghost, on May 4, they paraded in separate groups from Notre Dame to Saint Louis. Representatives of the Third, dressed in black, were indistinguishable except for the commanding ugliness of Mirabeau, but were applauded confidently by an immense crowd. The nobles were decked and plumed. The dark mass of parish priests came next, then the king's musicians, then bishops dressed in dazzling robes. This war of ceremony lasted until July 14: in royal sessions the Third affected to dress like the privileged orders; Bailly gave notice that deputations he led to the king would not kneel before the royal presence.

The Hôtel des Menus-Plaisirs on the Avenue de Paris, actually an ordinary storehouse, had been prepared for the meetings of clergy and nobility. Behind it, on the Rue des Chantiers, a room built for the notables was enlarged and redecorated for plenary sessions, which were presided over by the king. But because nothing else was large enough to hold the Third Estate, this "national hall" was turned over to it on ordinary occasions. Spectators sat on the speakers' platforms, thronged in and out, and were allowed to join in discussions, a habit which persisted until the end of the Convention [1795]. This careless arrangement increased the importance of the Third Estate and subjected the more timid to pressures of intransigent and rash opinions.

Louis opened the meeting on May 5. His brief address was applauded. Barentin, who could not be heard, followed. Then Necker, with the aid of an acting official who relieved him from time to time, harangued the anxious deputies. His listeners were soon disappointed and seriously annoyed. For three hours the minister of finance explained the detailed situation of the Treasury and the proposed improvements, made no allusion to constitutional reform, expressed confidence in the generosity of the privileged classes, then repeated the method of voting which had been announced in December. On the following day the nobility and clergy began to verify their powers separately. The Third Estate refused to follow suit. The Estates-General was paralysed.

Deputies from Brittany and the Dauphiné favoured outright refusal to vote by order, but that would have been an infringement of legality, and the politicians did not want to take chances so early in the game. The representatives were not yet familiar with one another, and no one knew how far each would agree to advance. Some found the ardour of the Bretons alarming. A delaying tactic was necessary, and Necker's refusal to grant the Council of State power of verification provided an escape. The Third Estate alleged that each order had to establish whether the two other orders were legally constituted, and that powers should therefore be inspected in common session. During this stalemate the Third refused to constitute itself as a separate order: no minutes were taken, no rules established; not even a steering committee was set up. They consented only to choose a "dean," who after June 3 was Bailly. At the beginning the Third had taken the name Commons *(communes)* for itself. Although no one other than a few of the more erudite knew exactly what the medieval communes were, the word evoked a vague memory of popular resistance to feudal lords, an idea strengthened by what knowledge they had of English history. To the Third Estate the name meant refusal to recognize a social hierarchy that had relegated it to third rank.

This attitude had its drawbacks. The people were told that the Third Estate was responsible for delaying the abolition of fiscal privileges. When Malouet tried to negotiate by offering to guarantee the rights and property of the aristocracy he was roundly criticized. Everyone, however, sensed the need for some new tactical issue, and it was the clergy which furnished them with just that. The nobility, in no way perturbed, on May 11 announced itself constituted as a separate order. Because a large proportion of the parish priests supported the Commons, the clergy instead proposed that designated members of the three orders meet in conference. To humour the other order, the Third Estate agreed. But the discussions of May 23 and 25 came to nothing: the nobles retreated behind precedents which the Third Estate either challenged or fought with arguments of reason and natural right. They next tried to get the clergy to agree that the three orders should be fused. The bishops sensed imminent defection from the parish priests and asked the king to intervene. On May 28 Louis asked that the conferences be resumed in the presence of his ministers, and on June 4 Necker drafted a conciliatory proposal: each order should first verify the powers of its own members, then announce the results to the others and consider any objections that were raised. If no agreement could be reached, the king was to deliver a final decision. Once more the Third found itself in a difficult position. This time it was the nobility that came to its rescue by rejecting royal arbitration except for the "complete" delegations—those which, as in the Dauphiné and in several bailiwicks, had been chosen in common by the three orders. This was the signal for revolutionary action.

On June 10 the Third Estate followed a proposal from Sieyes and invited the privileged members to join it. Those who did not appear to answer a roll call would be considered to have defaulted. The roll was begun on June 12 and finished on the 14th: several parish priests had responded, but not one noble. After two days' debate the Third Estate on June 17 conferred the title "National Assembly" upon the combined and enrolled orders. It immediately arrogated to itself the power to consent to taxation, confirming existing taxes provisionally. Had sovereignty passed to the nation? Not exactly. On June 20 Bailly acknowledged that these revolutionary resolutions required the king's approval.

Louis had no intention of approving them. The Dauphin had died on June 4, and the king had withdrawn to Marly, where the queen and royal princes instructed him. The nobility finally abdicated in favour of the throne and begged the king to make the Third Estate return to the path of duty. On June 19 the majority of the clergy declared itself in favour of fusing the three orders. The bishops hastily called for assistance. Royal ministers and even Necker agreed that intervention was necessary. The Council of State announced that a royal session would be held on June 22. But what would the king declare then? With the support of [the ministers] Montmorin and Saint-Priest, Necker hoped to manage the Commons by simply ignoring their decrees rather than by overriding them. At last he came out into the open, proposing to establish equality of taxation, to admit all Frenchmen to public office, and to authorize the vote by head in constituting future Estates-General, stipulating that the king would agree to this only if the Estates met as two houses and if he were granted full executive power with a legislative veto. Necker protected aristocratic prerogatives and property with the vote by order [in future Estates-General], but Barentin objected: did this mean they were to adopt the British system of government? Louis hesitated, postponing the decision. The royal session was put off until June 23.

On June 20 the Third Estate discovered its hall closed without notice or warning. It finally found asylum in a neighbouring tennis court, where, because there was talk of retiring to Paris and seeking the protection of the people, Mounier stepped in and proposed the famous oath, that they remain united until a constitution was established. A threatened *lit de justice* had provoked enough indignation to incite the deputies, with few exceptions, to sign the oath. The Third Estate, like the Parlement of Paris, rebelled in advance against the royal will.

On June 21 Louis admitted his brothers to the Council and, finally, withdrew his support from Necker, whose programme was defeated the next day. On the 23rd an impressive show of armed force surrounded the Hôtel des Menus-Plaisirs, from which the public was excluded. Received in silence, Louis had Barentin read two declarations of capital interest in that they revealed quite clearly what was at stake in the struggle. They granted the Estates-General power to consent to taxes and loans and to various budget allocations, including the funds set aside for upkeep of the court. Personal liberty and freedom of the press would be guaranteed; decentralization would be carried out through the provincial estates; an extensive programme of reforms would be studied by the Estates-General. In sum, the proposals meant that a constitutional system, civil liberty, and achievement of national unity were to be the common inheritance of monarch and nation. Louis made an exception only for the clergy: its special consent was required for everything touching upon ecclesiastic organization and religious matters. Furthermore, he appeared as arbiter among the orders—if the Third Estate's decrees were overridden, so were the binding mandates that the privileged orders had invoked to compel voting by order and to postpone equality of taxation. Verification of powers would follow the system proposed on June 4. The orders were authorized to meet together to deliberate matters of general interest. The king strongly hoped that the clergy and nobility would agree to assume their share of public burdens.

But Louis failed to impose equal taxation and remained silent upon the question of admittance to public office; he expressly retained the orders and excluded vote by head from such matters as organization of future Estates-General, the manorial system, and honorific privileges. The throne thereby committed itself to preservation of the traditional social hierarchy and aristocratic pre-eminence. As a result of this decision, the Revolution was to mean conquest of equality of rights.

The king concluded by ordering the Estates to separate into orders and by giving them to understand that he would dissolve the assembly if its members did not obey. He then departed, followed by the nobility and most of the clergy. The Third Estate did not stir. Brezé, grand master of ceremonies, repeated his sovereign's command, to which Bailly replied: "The assembled nation cannot receive orders." Sieyes declared: "You are today what you were yesterday." Ignoring, as the Parlement of Paris had done previously, the existence of a royal session, the Third Estate confirmed its own decrees and declared its members inviolable. The expressive and significant statements made by Bailly and by Sieyes deserve to be those remembered by posterity, but Mirabeau's epigraph has proved more popular: "We will not stir from our seats unless forced by bayonets." The Commons could not have carried out this challenge, but the court thought itself in no position to find out, as agitation had already reached menacing proportions. After this point, resistance to the Third Estate disintegrated: a majority of the clergy and forty-seven nobles joined the Commons; on June 27 the king asked the others to follow suit.

The legal, peaceful revolution of the bourgeoisie, achieved by lawyers who borrowed their methods from the Parlement of Paris, was to all appearances victorious. On July 7 the Assembly appointed a committee on the constitution and two days later Mounier delivered its first report. From that day, and for history, the Assembly was the Constituent Assembly. On July 11 Lafayette submitted his draft for a declaration of human rights.

Appeal to Armed Force

The Third Estate did not lose its composure. Dictatorship of the constituent power, advocated by Sieyes, was not instituted. Royal approval was still considered necessary. The modern idea that a constitution creates its own powers before it regulates them had not yet been formulated; instead, Louis XVI, invested with his own power rooted in history, would contract with the nation. On the other hand, although the Third Estate fused the three orders, it did not proclaim their disappearance within the nation, nor did it call for election of a new assembly: the bourgeoisie therefore did not aspire to class dictatorship. On the contrary, it seemed possible that a moderate majority would be formed: the clergy, the liberal nobility, and a segment of the Commons favoured a party of the middle. Most of the nobles, however, made it known that they by no means considered the matter settled, and when troops were seen thronging around Paris and Versailles the king was suspected of preparing a show of force. He had excuses: agitation was growing; hunger multiplied disturbances; at the end of June disorderly conduct of the French Guards [a regiment of royal troops] caused a riot in Paris.

The court had not yet fixed a plan of action. To draw one up, it had to get rid of Necker and his friends. The maréchal de Broglie and the baron de Breteuil had been called in. Wisdom commanded that a cabinet be formed secretly, ready to appear when sufficient forces were on hand. This was a game with fearful consequences. We can understand that the king regarded deputies of the Third Estate as rebels and that the nobility considered surrender a humiliation. But if a show of arms failed, the blood spilled would stain both king and aristocracy. Nevertheless, on July 11 Necker was hastily dismissed and banished from the kingdom; his friends were replaced by Breteuil and his cohorts. No further steps were taken. But the Assembly expected the worst, and the bourgeois revolution seemed lost. They were saved by popular force.

The Popular Revolution

Resort to arms transformed the struggle of social orders into civil war which, abruptly changing the character of the Revolution, gave it a scope that far surpassed what the bourgeoisie had intended or expected. Popular intervention, which provoked the sudden collapse of the social system of the Old Regime, issued from progressive mobilization of the masses [caused] by the simultaneous influences of the economic crisis and the convocation of the Estates-General. These two causes fused to create a mentality of insurrection.

The Economic Crisis

Starting in 1778, the surge in production which had followed the Seven Years War and which is known as the splendour of Louis XV, was checked by difficulties rooted in agricultural fluctuations, a continual problem of the old economy. These setbacks became established in cyclical depressions and caused what their historian[5] called the decline of Louis XVI. First, unusually heavy grape harvests provoked a dreadful slump in the wine market. Prices fell by as much as 50 per cent. They rose

[5] [C.-E. Labrousse, *Esquisse du mouvement des prix et des revenus en France au XVIIIᵉ siècle* (Paris: Dalloz, 1933) and *La Crise de l'économie française à la fin de l'ancien régime et au début de la Révolution* (Paris: Presses Universitaires de France, 1943).—Eds.]

somewhat after 1781 because of scarcity, but short supply then meant that the wine sector could not recoup its losses. Wine-growing was still practised in almost every part of the kingdom and for many peasants was the most profitable market product. They suffered cruelly; those who were sharecroppers found their income reduced to nothing. Grain prices were the next to fall, remaining relatively low until 1787. Finally, a drought in 1785 killed off much of the livestock.

Rural inhabitants constituted the majority of consumers, and because their purchasing power was reduced industrial production was in turn threatened after 1786. Traditional interpretation has laid primary blame for industry's troubles upon the commercial treaty with Britain [the Eden Treaty of 1786]. Although this was not the most important cause, it certainly did obstruct industry temporarily, since production had to modernize if it was to withstand foreign competition. Unemployment spread. The countryside, where domestic industry had developed, suffered as much as the cities.

The lower classes therefore had no reserves left when they faced the brutal prospect of famine after grain crops failed in 1788. The price of bread rose steadily. At the beginning of July, 1789, a pound of bread sold for four sous in Paris—where the government nevertheless sold its imported grains at a loss—and twice as much in some provinces. At that time wage earners considered two sous per pound the highest price they could possibly pay and still subsist, for bread was their staple food and average daily consumption ranged from one and a half pounds per person to two or three for an adult manual labourer. Necker ordered large purchases from abroad, and, as usual, labour centres [ateliers de charité, or public workshops] opened up, while measures were taken for distributing soup and rice. The previous winter had been severe, and the cruel effects of high prices did not lessen as the harvest season drew near. For over a half-century we have known, chiefly from the works of Jaurès, that the prosperity of the kingdom of France was responsible for the growing power of the bourgeoisie, and in this sense it is with reason that [the historian] Michelet's interpretation has been attacked, for the Revolution broke out in a society in the midst of development, not one crippled and seemingly threatened with collapse by nature's Providential shortages. But the social importance of this enrichment should not deceive us. Since colonial profits were realized mainly through re-exportation, the nation's labour force did not benefit as much as we might think, and, while a long-term rise in prices swelled the income of large landowners and bourgeoisie, wages failed to keep pace. We now know that production was dislocated and curtailed in the last decade before the Revolution, and we can justifiably state that the living standard of the masses was steadily declining. Famine, when it came, overwhelmed the populace.

"The people" (artisans, shopkeepers, hired help) as well as proletarians ("the populace"), peasants—small proprietors and sharecroppers who did not raise enough to support themselves or wine-growers who did not raise any grain—as well as townsmen unanimously agreed that the government and upper classes were responsible for these afflictions. Income declined but taxes did not. Tolls and duties on consumption became more hateful in times of high prices. If the wine market was restricted it was because excises limited consumption. There was no bread because Brienne removed controls on grain exports and shipments in 1787. True, Necker had stopped exports, subsidized imports, and reinstituted market sales. But he was too late. "Hoarders" had gone to work. Anyone in authority, all government agents, were suspected of participating in hoarding. The "famine plot" was thought to be more than a myth. Tithe collectors and lords were just as odious—they were hoarders because their levies cut into a poor harvest and consumed the peasants' supplies. The final blow was that collectors and lords profited even more from the high prices that increased poverty. And, finally, the solidarity of the Third Estate was shaken: the grain merchant, the baker, and the miller were all threatened; the bourgeois, partisan of economic freedom, clashed with popular hostility towards capitalism, since the people by nature favoured requisitions and controls. In April Necker authorized requisitions to replenish the markets, but the intendants and municipal officials rarely used this power.

As the months of 1789 passed, riots kept the tired and frightened officials in a constant state of alert. On April 28 Parisian workers from the faubourg [district] Saint-Antoine sacked the manufactories of Réveillon and Henriot. Throughout the kingdom markets were the scenes of disturbances. Grain shipments, forced by milling and transportation conditions to use roads and rivers in plain view of famished hordes, were sometimes halted. The army and constabulary exhausted themselves rushing from one place to another, but were not inclined to deal harshly towards rebels whose privations they shared and unconsciously began to feel a common sympathy with them. The armour of the Old Regime was rapidly disintegrating.

Agitation was especially pronounced in the countryside. There the tax burden was crushing; tithes and manorial dues drove the peasants to desperation. Sentiment in the peasant community was divided among journeymen, sharecroppers, small proprietors, and large-scale tenant farmers, but on all matters of taxation it was solidly opposed to royal authority and the aristocracy. Tremors of agrarian revolt could be felt well before July 14—in Provence at the end of March, around Gap in April, in Cambrésis and Picardy in May. Near Versailles and Paris game had been exterminated, forests cleaned out. Moreover, the people were afraid of each other because begging, a regional trouble, spread before their eyes. Many journeymen and small landowners became mendicants. The poor left their villages to crowd into towns or else became vagabonds, forming groups which coursed through the country. They invaded farms even at night, forced themselves in by the fear of burning and of attacks on livestock, trees, the crops that were just beginning to grow, or by threatening to pillage everything. Officials had their own reasons for worrying about the crops and let the villagers arm themselves for protection. As fear of brigandage spread, panics broke out. The slightest incident was enough to put a timid person to flight, convinced that brigands had arrived, sowing fear wherever he fled.

The "Good News" and the Great Hope

But we cannot be sure that economic crisis would have driven the people to aid the bourgeoisie if the calling of the Estates-General had not deeply moved the populace. The goals appropriated by the bourgeois they elected scarcely concerned the lower classes, but an event so foreign was welcomed as "a good piece of news" presaging a miraculous change in men's fates. It awoke hopes both dazzling and vague of a future when all would enjoy a better life—hopes shared by the bourgeoisie. This vision of the future united the heterogeneous elements of the Third Estate and became a dynamic source of revolutionary idealism. Among the common people it gave to the Revolution a character that can be called mythical, if myth is taken to mean a complex of ideas concerning the future which generate energy and initiative. In this sense the Revolution in its early stages can be compared to certain religious movements in nascent form, when the poor gladly discern a return to paradise on earth.

Arthur Young [the British traveller and agricultural reformer] has recorded that on July 12, while walking up a hill near Les Islettes, in the Argonne Forest, he met a poor woman who described her misery to him. " 'Something was to be done by some great folk for such poor ones,' but she did not know who nor how, 'but God send us better, *car les tailles et les droits nous écrasent*' " (for the *taille* and [*manorial*] rights are crushing us).

Since the king consulted his people, he pitied their plight. What could he do if not remove their burdens—taxes, tithes, fees? He would therefore be content if they went ahead and helped him: after the elections aristocratic cries of alarm arose on all sides, for the peasants openly declared that they would pay no more.

At the same time this great hope inflamed fearful passions, from which the bourgeoisie was not exempt. The revolutionary mentality was imbued with them; the history of the period bears their deep imprint.

The Aristocratic Conspiracy and the Revolutionary Mentality

The Third Estate was at once convinced that the nobles would stubbornly defend their privileges. This expectation, soon confirmed by aristocratic opposition to the doubling and then to the vote by head, aroused suspicions that with little difficulty hardened into convictions. The nobles would use any means to "crush" the villagers; they would outwit their well-intentioned king to obtain dissolution of the Estates-General. They would take up arms, bar themselves in their châteaux, and enlist brigands to wage civil war just as the king's agents enlisted the poverty-stricken. Prisoners would be released and recruited. Nobles who had already hoarded grain to starve the Third Estate would willingly see the harvest ruined. Fear of the aristocracy was everywhere rapidly linked with fear of brigands, a connection that fused the results of the calling of the Estates with those of the economic crisis. Moreover, foreign powers would be called on to help. The comte d'Artois was going to emigrate and win over his father-in-law (the king of Sardinia), the Spanish and Neapolitan Bourbons, and the emperor, brother of the queen. France, like Holland, would be invaded by the Prussians. Collusion with foreign powers, which weighed heavily in the history of the Revolution, was assumed from the beginning, and in July an invasion was feared imminently. The whole Third Estate believed in an "aristocratic conspiracy."

The burden of royal centralization and the conflict of orders dominated the Third Estate's view of the crisis. Neglecting to accuse natural forces and incapable of analysing the total economic situation, the Third laid responsibility upon royal power and the aristocracy. An incomplete picture perhaps, but not inexact. The freeing of the grain trade, which Brienne had decreed, did favour speculators; to the argument that this would increase production the people replied that it would profit the aristocracy and bourgeoisie first, while they had to bear the costs. Similarly, if the Third Estate falsely imputed Machiavellian qualities to the aristocracy, it was true that the court, in agreement with the nobles, thought to punish the deputies for their insubordination; and it was true that the aristocratic conspiracy, although denounced prematurely, was soon to become a reality. In any case the mind of the Third Estate is of capital interest in showing the historian that events have their immediate roots not in their antecedents but in the men who intervene by interpreting those events.

If aristocratic conspiracy and "brigands" instilled many with enough fear to cause occasional panics, there were others who, although frightened, remained rational and faced danger resolutely. Consequently the labels "fears" and "Great Fear" unjustly imply that the whole Third Estate was struck dumb with terror. Actually the revolutionary mentality was capable of countering unrest with vigorous defensive reaction. The Third was kept informed by letters from its deputies and in turn encouraged its representatives with innumerable appeals. The bourgeoisie would gladly have pushed further: it wanted to take municipal control from the petty oligarchy made up of those who owned offices, many of whom had acquired noble titles. At Paris the electors who had chosen deputies organized a secret municipal council in the Hôtel de Ville at the end of June. Notables hoped to set up a "national militia" [soon to be called the National Guard]. This was proposed by Parisian electors to the Constituent Assembly, but deputies did not dare authorize it. A double purpose lay behind the desire to organize a militia: to resist royal troops should the occasion rise, and to hold the people in check. Meanwhile efforts were made to win over the army, not without success, since lower-ranking officers had no hope of advancement and the soldiers, who had to pay for part of their subsistence, were affected by high prices. The French Guards fraternized with crowds at the Palais Royal; at the end of June the people freed prisoners at the Abbaye [jail]. Several men are known to have distributed money among the soldiers or to have paid the July insurgents. Beyond doubt the agents of the duc d'Orléans did as much.

Finally, along with the defensive reaction there existed a punitive will either to cripple the aristocratic conspiracy, hoarders, and all enemies of the people, or to punish those enemies. From July on this took the form of imprisonments, acts of brutality, and popular massacres.

These three aspects of the revolutionary mentality—fear, defensive reaction, and punitive will—together constitute one of the keys to the unfolding narrative of the French Revolution. The conspiracy was to all appearances halted by the end of 1789, and repression slackened. The plot later reappeared, cloaked with many of the characteristics given it in advance, and foreign powers came to its aid. The resulting defensive reaction first stimulated the volunteers who poured in and then was responsible for the mass levy [military conscription]. Punitive will provoked the massacres of 1792 and, when danger again loomed in 1793, the Convention warded off further perils only by setting up the Terror. Fear and its accompaniments died out only, and gradually, after the uncontested triumph of the Revolution.

The Parisian Revolution

Against this background, Necker's dismissal was a torch set to a powder keg: it was taken as evidence that the aristocratic conspiracy had begun to act. News of the event circulated in Paris on Sunday, July 12. The weather was good and a crowd gathered at the Palais Royal, whose garden and arcades, recently opened by the duc d'Orléans, had become a centre of amusement. Groups clustered about extemporaneous orators; only one, Camille Desmoulins,[6] do we know by name. Soon processions of demonstrators reached the boulevards, then the Rue Saint-Honoré. The cavalry undertook to make them disperse and charged the crowd at the Place Louis XV. The French Guards in return attacked the cavalry. The baron de Besenval, military commander, mustered his whole following on the Champ de Mars that evening.

The Parisians did not think of rallying to the aid of the Assembly; they saved it, but only indirectly. They were concerned with their own fate, convinced that their city, surrounded by royal troops and brigands, would first be bombarded from Montmartre and the Bastille and then would be pillaged. Panics erupted continually during these "days," Act One of the Great Fear. The police were gone. Toll gates were burned. [The monastery of] Saint-Lazare was sacked. Person and property were seemingly endangered. Fright hovered over the capital, abandoned to its own resources.

A defensive reaction followed immediately. Barricades arose in the streets, and gunsmiths' stores were wiped clean. The electors appointed a permanent committee and set up a militia. To arm their forces, they took 32,000 guns from the Invalides[7] on the morning of July 14. In search of more, they went to the Bastille. Its governor, de Launay, parleyed. Commanding only a small garrison, he had ordered the outer courts evacuated. They were quickly filled by the crowd. Behind walls ninety feet high, surrounded by a water-filled ditch seventy-five feet wide, he had no cause to fear an attack. But he lost his nerve and opened fire. Several men fell; others drew back in disorder, crying treason, convinced that they had been permitted to advance only to offer better aim. Shots rang out from those who were armed, and battle was engaged, but on an entirely unequal basis: the assailants lost a hundred men, whereas one sole member of the garrison was hit. A census was later taken among the "conquerors of the Bastille," so we know a good number of the attackers. All classes of society were represented among them, but most were artisans from the faubourg Saint-Antoine.

The tide of battle was still uncertain when the French and National Guards arrived from the Hôtel de Ville. Led by a former non-commissioned officer named Hulin and by Lieutenant Élie, they entered the courtyard of the Bastille and under heavy fire aimed their cannons at the gate. De Launay took fright and offered to give himself up. Élie accepted, but the attackers protested—No surrender! Amid total confusion the governor had the drawbridge lowered, and the crowd rushed

---

[6] [At that time a penniless young lawyer and writer, he was soon to become a polemical revolutionary journalist. By 1794 he was a supporter of Danton and was executed with other Dantonists on April 5, 1794.—Eds.]

[7] [A large public building housing elderly war veterans and military equipment.—Eds.]

across into the fortress. Efforts to save most of the defenders were successful, but three officers and three men were massacred. De Launay was with difficulty led to the doors of the Hôtel de Ville, where he lost his life. Shortly after, Flesselles, provost of the merchants [chief municipal official of Paris], was also killed. Their heads were paraded through the city on pikes.

Besenval ordered a retreat to Saint-Cloud. The electors took over municipal control, appointed Bailly mayor, and offered command of the National Guard to Lafayette, who soon afterwards gave the Guard a cockade of red and blue, the colours of Paris, between which he placed a white band, the king's colour. Through Lafayette the tricoloured flag, emblem of the Revolution, joined old France with the new.

No one considered the Bastille the stakes of the struggle, and at first no one thought that its fall would determine the outcome. Panics continued. But seizure of the Bastille, of mediocre importance in itself, broke the court's resistance. The forces Versailles had on hand were not enough to take Paris, especially since the loyalty of the troops was not certain. Louis hesitated. Would he try to flee? Against the urgings of the comte d'Artois he decided to give in. On July 15 he yielded to the Assembly and announced the dismissal of his troops. The next day he recalled Necker. On the 17th he went to Paris and accepted the cockade.

Few concluded from this that the aristocracy had laid down its arms, and wild rumours continued to circulate. The comte d'Artois and many others emigrated; according to one story an English squadron lay in wait off the coast of Brest. The permanent committee searched the edges of Paris for brigands. Finding only vagabonds, it sent them back where they had come from. The suburbs feared that they would be overrun with such wanderers, and panic spread. Bertier de Sauvigny, the intendant of Paris, his father-in-law, Foullon de Doué, and Besenval himself were arrested. Massacres began again: on July 22 Sauvigny and Doué were hanged at the Place de Grève; Necker returned just in time to save Besenval on July 30. These murders provoked strong protest, but now part of the bourgeoisie, roused by the obvious danger, joined the people in their fury—"Is this blood then so pure?" cried Barnave before the Constituent Assembly. Nevertheless, they could hardly deny that summary executions ought to cease. On July 23 a notary from the Rue de Richelieu proposed, in the name of his district, that a popular tribunal be set up; and on the 30th Bailly made a similar request. The Assembly paid no heed. Only in October did it institute prosecution for crimes of lèse-nation [treason against the people], to be handled by the Châtelet of Paris—an ordinary court. In July the Assembly did at least establish a "committee of investigation," prototype of the Committee of General Security; and the municipality of Paris organized another which was the first revolutionary committee. While debating the issue of privacy of correspondence during the summer, deputies of all representation, from the marquis de Gouy d'Arsy and Target, member of the Académie Française, to Barnave and Robespierre, firmly maintained that one could not govern in time of war and revolution as in time of peace—in other words, that the rights they were proposing to grant to all citizens depended upon circumstances. This was to become the doctrine of the revolutionary government.

The Municipal Revolution

In the provinces, too, Necker's dismissal provoked strong feeling and an immediate reaction. The populace was no longer content only to send addresses, now often menacing, to its representatives. In several towns the public coffers were broken open and arsenals or military storehouses looted. One committee undertook to set up a militia and issued an appeal to neighbouring communes, even to the peasants. The governor of Dijon was arrested; nobles and priests were confined to their dwellings—this was the first example of detention of suspects. At Rennes the townsmen persuaded the garrison to desert and then rose up. The military commander fled.

When news came of the fall of the Bastille and of the king's visit to Paris—an event celebrated in some places—the bourgeoisie took heart and laid hands on the instruments of control in almost every area. The "municipal revolution," as it is known, was in most cases a peaceable one: the municipal councils of the Old Regime took on notables or stepped down for the electors.[8] Very often they had to create, or permit the formation of, a permanent committee. It was charged initially with organization of the National Guard, but gradually absorbed the whole administrative apparatus. Nevertheless, the people, having taken part in bourgeois demonstrations, demanded that bread prices be lowered. If this was not soon granted riots broke out, the houses of officials and those known as hoarders were sacked, and often the former municipal councils were ousted.

The municipal revolution thus differed from place to place and was often arrested half way. In every instance, however, the only orders obeyed were those of the National Assembly. The king no longer commanded authority. Centralization, too, was weakened: each municipality wielded absolute power within its own confines and over surrounding districts as well. From August on, towns started to conclude mutual-assistance pacts, spontaneously transforming France into a federation of communes. Local autonomy opened the field of action to a small group of resolute men who, without waiting for instructions from Paris, passed what measures they considered necessary to secure public safety. This was a basic stimulant to revolutionary defence.

Yet the other side of the coin was immediately visible. The Constituent Assembly enjoyed a prestige accorded none of its successors, but the populace observed only such decrees as suited it. What did the people want above all else? Tax reform, abolition of indirect levies, institution of controls over the grain trade. Tax collection was suspended; the salt tax, excises, and municipal tolls were suppressed; exchange of grains was either forbidden or continually thwarted. Proclamations and decrees against this had no effect. At Paris the populace went even further. Within the districts—divisions established for elections to the Estates-General—assembled citizens, like the electors before them, claimed to supervise the municipal authority they set up to replace the electors. In their eyes national sovereignty entailed direct democracy, an idea that would remain dear to the sans-culottes.

---

[8] [The electors were those in the cities and towns who had chosen deputies to the Third Estate. Often the electors had remained organized.—Eds.]

The Peasant Revolution and the Great Fear

The countryside had joined the towns, but revolution in Paris had even greater effect on rural areas. Agrarian revolt broke out in several regions. In the woodlands of Normandy, in the Hainaut and Upper Alsace, châteaux or abbeys were attacked by those seeking to burn archives and force surrender of manorial rights. In Franche-Comté and the Mâconnais peasants set fire to many châteaux, sometimes laying them waste. The bourgeoisie was not always spared: they, too, had to pay. In Alsace the Jews suffered. On the other hand, there was clear evidence of rural hostility towards a menacing capitalism whose instrument had become the manorial reaction: free pasturage was reclaimed, enclosures destroyed, forests invaded, commons taken back or demanded for the first time—the peasant revolution was a double-edged sword. Faced with this threat, the notables drew closer together. Urban militias were used to restore order. In the Mâconnais the bourgeoisie set up extraordinary tribunals beside the old provost courts, and thirty-three peasants were hanged. Revolt fired men's minds. Even more important, however, was a passive resistance which everywhere interfered with collection of the tithe or the *champart*[9] demanded from crops harvested. Only those who wished to pay did so. The Great Fear gave irresistible force to this movement.

Events in Paris strengthened fear of the aristocratic conspiracy, of foreign invasion which could carry it out, of recruitment of brigands for its service. Brigands were the source of even greater fear now that the wheat was ripe, and Paris, along with other large towns, was expelling beggars and vagabonds. Grain riots and agrarian revolts heightened tension. So did forays by National Guards who left towns to pillage châteaux or demand grain. The Great Fear grew out of six localized incidents no different from those which had unloosed so many panics, but this time they set off currents which were fed along the way by new outbreaks acting as relay reinforcements. Some of these can be traced for hundreds of miles, with branches that covered entire provinces. This extraordinary diffusion in a chain reaction gives the Great Fear its distinctive character and illuminates the mentality that made it possible.

A "disturbance" at Nantes alarmed Poitou. At Estrées-Saint-Denis, in the Beauvais, another spread fright in all directions. A third in southern Champagne sowed terror through the Gâtinais, Bourbonnais, and Burgundy. A fourth, originating near the Montmirail forest, close to La Ferté-Bernard, alerted Maine, Normandy, Anjou, and the Touraine. From the edge of the Chizé forest fear struck Angoulême, spread into Berry and the central mountains, alarmed Aquitaine as far as the Pyrenees. In the east, agrarian revolts in Franche-Comté and the Mâconnais drove fear to the shores of the Mediterranean.

Revolutionaries and aristocrats accused one another of having contrived the Great Fear. The enemies of the Revolution, charged the revolutionaries, sowed anarchy in an effort to paralyse the National Assembly. The bourgeoisie, replied the aristocrats, alarmed the people to make them take up arms and rebel just when the lower classes desired to remain at peace. This last version met with success because the Great Fear provoked a defensive reaction which turned upon the aristocracy.

---

[9] [A manorial rent payable in kind by the peasant to the lord.—Eds.]

Near Le Mans and in Vivarais three nobles were put to death, and peasants in the Dauphiné provided a formidable relay station for panic by burning châteaux.

It was therefore repeated afterwards that fear had broken out everywhere and at once, spread by mysterious messengers and engendering agrarian revolt. It did not, in fact, cover the whole kingdom: Brittany, Lorraine, lower Languedoc, among other areas, were unaffected. The Great Fear lasted from July 20 to August 6. Documents show that some propagated it in good faith, and one significant fact is that it never touched the districts which had previously witnessed insurrection. Only in the Dauphiné did it provoke a *jacquerie* [large-scale peasant revolt]. If it encouraged the revolution of the peasants it did not cause it. They were already on their feet.

The Night of August 4 and the Declaration
of the Rights of Man and the Citizen

While popular revolution spread, the Assembly's debates dragged on ineffectively. Was this the appropriate moment to publish a declaration of rights? Would it not be better to postpone any such action until the constitution was drawn up, so that the two could be reconciled? Arguments of a general nature were voiced with no mention of the reasons behind opposing views: the existence of orders and the privileges, both of which would be suppressed by the principles to be proclaimed. Aristocrats therefore favoured postponement, hoping to preserve a few of their prerogatives, while the Patriots, growing impatient, accused the nobles of undue obstruction, and the more clairvoyant suspected that privileges held by provinces and towns gave the nobility secret supporters within the Third Estate. On the morning of August 4 the Assembly ruled that it would begin by voting the declaration. But its members could expect discussion to provoke new resistance.

On the other hand, the popular revolution had to be resolved. The Assembly, which it had saved, had no choice but to endorse it, yet order had to be re-established, since the people were quietly waiting for the reforms their representatives would deem appropriate. The bourgeoisie in all probability could control townsmen, but the peasants were a different matter. They were destroying the manorial regime without concerning themselves about the Assembly. What course should be taken? If it resorted to the army and provost courts, the Assembly would break with the people and place itself at the mercy of king and aristocracy. The alternative was to grant satisfaction to the rebels—but then how would the parish priests and liberal nobles react? And it was their support which had assured the Third Estate's victory.

The terms of the decision and the tactics to carry it out were decreed during the night of August 3–4 by a hundred deputies meeting at the Café Amaury as a "Breton Club," which dated back to the end of April, when deputies from Brittany had, as soon as they arrived in town, adopted the custom of concerting their moves and had immediately opened their debates to colleagues from other provinces. They resolved to sway the Assembly by "a kind of magic." In matters involving the feudal system, the duc d'Aiguillon was to take the lead.

But on the evening of August 4 it was the vicomte de Noailles who made the first move, and there was no alternative but to support him. Without debate the Assembly enthusiastically adopted equality of taxation and redemption of all manorial rights except for those involving personal servitude—which were to be abolished without indemnification. Other proposals followed with the same success: equality of legal punishment, admission of all to public office, abolition of venality in office, conversion of the tithe into payments subject to redemption, freedom of worship, prohibition of plural holding of benefices, suppression of annates (the year's income owed the pope by a bishop upon investiture). Privileges of provinces and towns were offered as a last sacrifice. Nevertheless, the "magic" had worked its powers.

These resolutions had to be written up formally, so the debate opened again the next day and lasted until August 11. The final decree began: "The National Assembly destroys the feudal regime in its entirety." This was far from exact: they retained the law of primogeniture and honorific prerogatives, while requirement of an indemnity promised a long life to manorial fees. The tithe was suppressed without indemnity, but, just as fees could be collected until the method of redemption was determined, the tithe could be exacted until a law on public worship was passed.

Despite these qualifications, on the night of August 4 the Assembly achieved in principle the legal unity of the nation. It destroyed the feudal system and aristocratic domination over rural areas; it launched fiscal and ecclesiastical reform. The way was paved for discussion of a declaration of rights. This started on August 20 and continued without intermission until the 26th. Proclaiming liberty, equality, and national sovereignty, the text was in effect the "act of decease" of the Old Regime, which had been put to death by the popular revolution.

Was the "Aristocratic Revolt" Aristocratic?

JEAN ÉGRET

Jean Égret (1902–   ), a postmaster's son, grew up in Lyon. After teaching at various secondary schools, he was Professor of Modern History at the University of Poitiers from 1945 until his recent retirement. An authority on the law courts of eighteenth-century France and on the early years of the Revolution, he has published much on these topics. Two of his works are *Louis XV et l'opposition parlementaire* (1970), a judicious defense of the law courts in their battles with the royal administration, and *La Pré-Révolution française (1787–1788)* (1962), a standard historical narrative showing the complexity of politics in those years.

The importance of the role played by the parlements of France in the last crisis of the Old Regime has never been ignored, and the revolt of these sovereign courts[1] in 1787–1788 has often been described. We are less fully informed on the social class of these magistrates, whose uprising opened the way for the French Revolution. Detailed studies devoted to this matter are rare,[2] and general accounts not always reliable.[3]

From Jean Égret, "L'Aristocratie parlementaire française à la fin de l'ancien régime," *Revue historique*, CCVIII (July–September 1952), 1–14. The entire article is printed here except for some footnotes. Printed by permission of the author, the editor of *Revue historique*, and Presses Universitaires de France. Editors' translation.

[1] [The sovereign courts included the thirteen parlements, two sovereign councils very similar in functions to parlements, and some fifteen additional specialized high courts. These latter included several chambres des comptes and cours des aides, which dealt primarily with royal financial and fiscal matters.

[In the parlements, the first president was at the top of the hierarchy, followed by the présidents à mortier. Other officials were the procureurs-généraux and avocats-généraux, who represented the royal interests, and the councilors—the large majority of the members of the parlements—who were the deliberative mass of the court. Specialized branches within the parlements included the chambres des requêtes and the chambres des enquêtes.—Eds.]

[2] Of particular value are A. Colombet, *Les Parlementaires bourguignons à la fin du XVIII⁵ siècle* (Dijon, 1937); E. Michel, *Biographie du Parlement de Metz* (Metz, 1853); F. Saulnier, *Le Parlement de Bretagne* (Rennes, 1908); A. de Mahuet, *Biographie de la Cour souveraine de Lorraine et Barrois et du Parlement de Nancy (1641–1790)* (Nancy, 1911); A. Duboul, *La Fin du Parlement de Toulouse* (Toulouse, 1890).

[3] H. Carré, *La Fin des Parlements (1788–1790)* (Paris, 1912), includes useful information, but the lists of

A recently published collection of documents offers at least a partial answer to the historian's curiosity.[4] The information it presents, together with what we already know, sheds new light on the backgrounds of the members of the French parlements who held office at the end of the Old Regime.

Article VIII of the Edict of December 1770 had required those who obtained governmental posts conferring nobility to pay, in addition to the usual marc d'or [gold mark] that was due from all recipients of a royal pardon, favor, mission, or position, a supplementary fee equivalent to that paid for letters patent of nobility. If the candidate already was a nobleman, he was exempted from paying this marc d'or of nobility by furnishing proof of his rank to the king's Cabinet. A collection of the Orders of Exemption granted by the Cabinet has just been published.

Dealing exclusively with nobles who were candidates for positions conferring nobility, the Orders, as one would expect, concern primarily the highest positions in the robe [mainly the judicial hierarchy]. In practice these positions did not confer nobility, because the candidates for them already possessed it. Actually, this collection of Orders exempting payment of the marc d'or of nobility provides us with some first-class documentary evidence. From it we learn the family origins of most of the twelve first presidents (of fifteen in office in 1790), of the ten procureurs-généraux (of fifteen in office), of the fifty-nine présidents à mortier (of ninety-five in office), of the sixteen presidents of chambres des enquêtes and chambres des requêtes (of twenty-eight in office), of the twenty-six avocats-généraux (of thirty-three in office), and of the 426 lay [nonclergy] councilors (of 757 in office) admitted to the thirteen parlements and to the two Sovereign Councils of Colmar and Perpignan. All this information has to do with the period after the courts were reestablished [1774] and concerns those magistrates who obtained their offices from 1774 to 1789 and who still occupied them in 1790.

Among the parlementary positions, it is best to deal separately with those which were neither purchasable nor hereditary, but which derived solely from the king, that is, the positions of first president and procureur-général, for they were filled by officials specifically representing the monarch within each court.

The first president was above all the agent of the king, who personally swore him into office. His primary function—a delicate and formidable one in a period of crisis—was to maintain relations between the king and the company [the particular court in which he served]. One would expect that the monarch would select him, without any restrictions, on the basis of his loyalty and his ability, and that he would preferably come from a province and a court different from those in which he was to carry out his duties. In fact, at the end of the Old Regime, only four first presidents were new to the companies over which they presided and to which they had been appointed by royal favor alone: Hocquart de Mony at Metz, Cœurderoy at Nancy, Malartic at Perpignan, and Baron de Spon at Colmar, all courts of secondary

---

members of the parlements given in the appendix are incomplete and contain errors. . . .

[4] A. de Roton, *Les Arrêts du Grand Conseil portant dispense du marc d'or de noblesse*, annotated and completed by J. de La Trollière and R. de Montmort (Paris, 1951). . . .

importance. Only Baron de Spon was, by his origins, a stranger to the sovereign courts; the other three belonged to the parlementary aristocracy. And this background, somewhat alarming for an agent of the king, even more strongly characterized all the other heads of the parlements in France.

In some courts, there were veritable dynasties of first presidents, so that the agents of the king, whatever their distant origin, became, as time went on, men of the local province. At Grenoble, Pierre-Albert de Bérulle was the fourth in his family line to be first president. During the eighteenth century, two ancestors had already preceded Camus de Pontcarré at Rouen and Pollinchove at Douai. The same development occurred at Aix-en-Provence, where Gallois de la Tour, like his father before him, was both the intendant of the province and first president of the parlement; and again at Besançon and at Bordeaux, where Perreney de Grosbois and Le Berthon directly succeeded their fathers as first presidents. Is it surprising to see First President Le Berthon disregard his role as an intermediary, identify himself with a company that he should have dominated, and do this "with a perseverance that came close to obstinacy"? [5]

Still more amazing is the appointment of one of the présidents à mortier as first president of the very same parlement, thereby crowning an industrious career. As a matter of fact, the king's choice was narrowly limited in such a case, and the agent of the king really became the man of the company. In this way the Second President Lefebvre d'Ormesson, who died in January 1789, and then the Third President Bochard de Saron were successively chosen for the highest position in the Paris Parlement, after First President d'Aligre retired in October 1788. In the provinces the local parlementary aristocracy conquered the first presidency in the persons of Présidents à Mortier Le Gouz de Saint-Seine at Dijon (1777), Merdy de Catuélan at Rennes (1777), Cambon at Toulouse (1787), and Casamajor de Charitte at Pau (1789).

A procureur-général had less influence than a first president, since he did not take part in the assemblies of the chambers [special plenary sessions of the several chambers of a parlement]; nevertheless he was, in the words of one of them, "an agent acting in His Majesty's name, working with the men who administer the royal courts. He pleads cases and he is a party in cases—that is his career. . . . When he is not an interested party, he oversees and points out to the king and the representatives of royal justice everything that deserves attention. . . ." [6]

Obviously, dynasties arose from the inheritance of these positions, even though at the end of the eighteenth century they could no longer be purchased. At Besançon, Doroz was the third procureur-général in his family. At Paris, Guillaume-François-Louis Joly de Fleury filled—without any distinction—the position made famous by his father. At Rennes, the Marquis de Caradeuc succeeded his father, Louis-René de la Chalotais, although his talents were known to be very inferior. When the famous Le Blanc de Castillon retired in 1787, he left to his forty-six-year-old son the position of procureur-général at the Parlement of Aix.

---

[5] C.-B.-F. Boscheron des Portes, *Histoire du Parlement de Bordeaux* (Bordeaux, 1878), II, 331.
[6] Berger de Moydieu of Grenoble, in a letter to a minister (Archives des Affaires Étrangères, MS 1563, fol. 142).

Before the age of thirty, the sons of Dudon of Bordeaux and of Godart de Belbœuf of Rouen were accepted as procureurs-généraux *en survivance*[7] and were in line to succeed their fathers, who were reaching their declining years.

Those who had not depended on their fathers to raise them to the highest ranks of the robe magistrature were former avocats-généraux, or more often former councilors, who had filled these positions for many years in the very same parlements where they became the *representatives* of the Crown, showing a loyalty that we may presume to be rather hesitant. Did not almost all of them belong to the local parlementary aristocracy? The list of procureurs-généraux at the end of the eighteenth century provides only two exceptions to this rule: Herman, who was procureur-général of Colmar and a former royal praetor [a municipal official] at Sélestat in Alsace; and Pierre de Bordenave, the son of an ennobled army officer, who began as a councilor and owed his unusual promotion to the post of procureur-général of the Parlement of Pau to the outstanding services that he had performed for this court.

Below the first president, every court had "several leaders [présidents à mortier] subordinate to the first president, but equal among themselves. They were ranked only by seniority. . . . On formal occasions they wore ermine on the standard red gown of the simple councilor. They also carried a round cap of black velvet trimmed with two stripes of gold braid; the first president had three stripes on his cap. . . ."[8]

Forty-three of the fifty-nine présidents à mortier admitted to office in the years 1774 to 1789 came from parlementary families. Those of Paris bore names already long illustrious in the Parlement and the Council of State. At Bordeaux, where earlier there had been a stubborn and ultimately successful opposition to the promotion of Avocat-Général Dupaty to the post of président à mortier (he did not possess all the requirements for noble rank), the three presidents admitted were all sons of presidents. At Pau, Grenoble, Besançon, and Toulouse, those newly promoted could all point to fathers and often to several ancestors who had served in the same court. The parlementary aristocracy still enjoyed an overwhelming preponderance in the recruitment of présidents à mortier at Rennes, Douai, Aix, and Rouen. Only the parlements of Nancy, Dijon, and Metz appear less exclusive.

For the less exalted positions of presidents of the chambres des enquêtes and the chambres des requêtes, which existed in only some of the parlements, and for the positions of avocats-généraux, where the younger members of the high robe aristocracy often served their *novitiate*,[9] the members of the parlementary aristocracy numbered half of the magistrates admitted.

The 426 positions of lay councilor, held in 1790 by judges appointed in the last fifteen years of the Old Regime, were divided unequally—the parlementary aristocracy totaled 160 representatives; the *new men*, 266. This numerical superiority of new men among those who filled the lower ranking positions in the

---

[7] [One who has the right to succeed the present incumbent in office.—Eds.]

[8] S.-N.-H. Linguet, *Annales politiques, civiles et littéraires du XVIIIᵉ siècle* (London and Paris, 1777–1792), IV, 187.

[9] This expression is used by Linguet in the article just cited.

high magistracy is one of the most interesting things we learn from the collection published by M. de Roton. It goes counter, in fact, to a generally accepted view—that which asserts that during the last period of their history the parlements always recruited from the same families, who were destined in time-honored fashion to the same positions. The collection of Orders of Exemption also gives us rather precise information on the diverse origins of these new men.

In theory, one might expect wealthy commoners to have been tempted by parlementary positions, all of which sooner or later conferred hereditary nobility on their holders. In reality, most positions gave only *gradual nobility (patre et avo consulibus)*, that is, father and son in succession had to fill the position for twenty years each or die in office before hereditary nobility could be acquired by the third generation. In some privileged parlements, those of Paris, Besançon, Douai, Metz, and Grenoble, the positions gave *hereditary nobility in the first degree*, that is, after twenty years' service by a single magistrate.

Actually, and Jacques Necker pointed this out in his *Treatise on the Administration of Public Finance*, a "large number" of parlementary positions "do not serve as a source of new nobles. Since the kingdom is teeming with nobles, several sovereign courts hesitate to admit into their membership bourgeois families who have not yet gained a footing in the nobility." [10] Inspired by aristocratic pride and careful of their composition, several parlements demanded a fully acquired nobility for those candidates who were not the sons of judges. The Parlement of Rennes, by its regulation of January 2, 1732, appears to have led the way. The royal government recognized the uncompromising stand of the Parlement of Rennes in this matter, for by an Order of Council dated September 6, 1775, the Crown gave up the requirement of the marc d'or of nobility due from magistrates admitted by the sovereign court of Rennes, since they were sure to be noble already. In the second half of the century several other parlements—Nancy, Grenoble, Aix, and Toulouse—took similar resolutions, but the government did not, in their cases, give them official consecration. Although the principle was not established so categorically everywhere, the tendency appears to have been rather general. The Orders of Exemption prove that the majority of the new men admitted to all the parlements during the reign of Louis XVI were noblemen already. But even so, a closer study reveals some very important differences among the courts.

In the last quarter of the eighteenth century, all the parlements of France admitted nobles whose forebears did not owe their nobility to judicial service, but whose families could prove at least a century of noble rank. To gain exemption from the marc d'or of nobility, it was not unusual, after 1781, to see these noble gentlemen submit certificates from the genealogist Chérin proving that they possessed the nobility required for a position as second lieutenant in the royal army. This seems to suggest that these young men hesitated when choosing between two equally honorable careers. This recruitment of magistrates from the old nobility was flattering to the sovereign courts: it ratified the fusion of the two nobilities. This

[10] J. Necker, *De l'administration des finances de la France* (Paris, 1784), III, 90–91.

fusion was complete in the Parlement of Rennes, where all the new men, without exception, were *noblemen of long standing*; but everywhere else only a minority of the newcomers were.

Several families whose members entered the parlements during the reign of Louis XVI had achieved nobility in the course of the century by filling positions in the chambres des comptes and the cours des aides, where they served for a time. The Chambre des Comptes of Dôle sent several men who had been ennobled there to the Parlements of Besançon and Dijon. At Aix, Grenoble, and Dijon, there were both chambres des comptes and parlements; the first was often a stepping stone to the second. At Paris, two streams carried families from the chambre des comptes and the cour des aides to the Parlement. Somewhat lower positions conferring noble rank, such as those in the bureaus of finance, also led some families to their first positions in the robe magistrature; and the Parlement of Toulouse received two councilors whose grandfathers had earned noble rank as city alder-men.

There were other more expensive but easier ways to acquire nobility and to hasten the slow and regular ascent of a family. The position of secretary of the king, which was expensive but required only unimportant duties fully compatible with other activities, conferred nobility in the first degree. Necker denounced these hasty grants of nobility, which were not a reward for service.[11] A Councilor in the Parlement of Normandy, Gressent, in his private journal, deplored this practice, "I am not a nobleman by birth, and it always injures my pride to see some loutish fellow whose father had been a secretary of the king enjoy all the advantages of nobility. . . ."[12] Indeed, during the reign of Louis XVI, it was a rare parlement which did not admit some sons or grandsons of secretaries of the king. The number of these wealthy parvenus was important at Paris, where they added up to more than a third of the new men. And in the persons of the Présidents à Mortier Bruny de La Tour d'Aigues, Micault, and Lassalle, they gained, at the outset, the highest judicial positions at Aix, Dijon, and Metz.

In this way the barriers that some courts tried to erect in order to bar candidates of lowly birth could be surmounted. The ease with which nobility might be achieved allowed the aristocratic parlements to keep commoners out without halting the recruitment of new members and without completely eroding the already declining value of these offices. The Orders of Exemption from the marc d'or of nobility, which were obtained by nearly all the new magistrates at Nancy, Grenoble, Aix, and Toulouse, show that in these courts the policy of excluding commoners was effective.

In the other parlements, however, many councilors do not seem to have obtained an Order of Exemption. This was true of all the new members admitted at Colmar; about two-thirds of those at Perpignan and Metz; more than half of those at Pau, Douai, and Bordeaux; a third of those at Dijon and Rouen; and a quarter of those at Besançon. It is possible that some of those presumed to be commoners

---

[11] *Ibid.*, III, 91–92.
[12] Comte d'Estaintot, *Notes manuscrites d'un conseiller au Parlement de Normandie, 1769–1789* (Rouen, 1889), p. 12.

already possessed at least a *noblesse commencée.*[13] Others, of course, were able to take advantage of useful connections that further research would reveal. In any event, it can no longer be said that all the parlements of France were closed to commoners at the end of the Old Regime and that it was impossible for sons of lawyers or lower ranking judges to take their seats on the *fleurs-de-lis* [a contemporary expression for the higher courts].

Thus there can be no doubt of the heterogeneous composition of parlementary circles in France at that time.

Contemporaries noticed this extreme diversity, and it inspired comparisons and sarcastic comments. The Parlement of Rennes gloried in its unusual recruitment, and the Breton magistrates called themselves *The Robe's Knights of Malta.*[14] The Parlement of Paris was less highly esteemed. Besenval said its members were "of a different nature from what are called men of high society." [15] And Vitrolles, the son of a councilor of the Parlement of Aix, commented that the first court of France was much more poorly constituted than that of Provence: "Almost all the members of the Parlement of Paris came from provincial families or from big business—from the Rue Saint-Denis, as one said then." [16]

Within each parlement, the councilors of high birth noted the distance separating them from the others. Chancellor Pasquier's remarks in his memoirs that recall his earliest days in the Parlement of Paris, in 1787, still breathe the disdain of the old robe families for the new men of common birth, who were so numerous in the court of the capital: "Of 150 magistrates," wrote Pasquier, "half, at the most, belonged to families that had served in high judicial positions for generations; the other half had come rather recently from the families of lower ranking judges and from financial circles." [17] At Dijon, both of the double doors of the assembly hall of the chambers were opened when the councilors entered; but when it was the turn of the commissaires aux requêtes (almost all commoners) to enter, one of the doors was closed.

In each parlement, the group of présidents à mortier—recruited almost entirely from the parlementary aristocracy—personified the traditional outlook of the higher robe nobility. We have seen that it succeeded in exerting its authority over the king's representatives—the first presidents and procureurs-généraux. Pasquier tells us that at Paris, "the high bench, where the présidents à mortier sat, was still occupied by the illustrious names of the judiciary; they exemplified the most admirable virtues, but they included no men of outstanding ability and especially none with any talent for oratory." [18] Talent was not so scarce among the presidents

---

[13] [The status of a person who had started but had not yet completed all the formalities required to gain noble rank.—Eds.]

[14] This was the expression of the Breton Councilor Desnos des Fossés, writing in the middle of the eighteenth century (cited by Saulnier, p. lxi).

[15] Pierre Besenval, *Mémoires* (Paris, 1882 edition), p. 327. [Besenval commanded the royal troops in Paris in 1789; his memoirs were first published in 1805–1807.—Eds.]

[16] E. de Vitrolles, *Mémoires* (Paris, 1950 edition), p. 40.

[17] *Mémoires du Chancelier Pasquier* (Paris, 1893–1895), I, 25.

[18] *Ibid.,* I, 24.

of the provincial parlements: Mareschal de Vezet at Besançon, Joly de Bévy at Dijon, and La Croix de Sayve d'Ornacieux at Grenoble expressed with eloquence and authority the venerable claims to which Montesquieu's *Spirit of the Laws* had recently given a new form.

Could the old nobility count on the support of men recently ennobled, who were so numerous in some of the courts, who had hardly emerged from the Third Estate, who—as a liberal noble of Dauphiny put it—"still had relatives, friends, and all manner of ties and associations there," [19] men whom the old nobility would always distrust? Could they even count on the complete loyalty of the very young councilors (who dominated some courts at the end of Louis XVI's reign), even though they belonged to their own class?

The Orders of Exemption from the marc d'or of nobility, which inform us about the family backgrounds of the judges admitted from 1775 to 1789, also indicate their ages. They prove that the clause of the Edict of November 1683, which required a minimum age of twenty-five years for new councilors, was rarely applied. The entry of very young councilors into a court did not have serious consequences when the turnover of the court's personnel was slow enough so that there was still a preponderance of old and experienced councilors. The Parlement of Toulouse, from a total membership of seventy-five, admitted only twenty-seven new lay councilors from 1775 to 1789; and so, in 1790, this parlement had only seventeen councilors under thirty-five years of age.

In other courts—Besançon, Douai, and Metz—where new councilors numbered more than half the total, but where the prejudices of the nobility, less intransigent than elsewhere, did not bar the admission of competent commoners, mature men still clearly comprised the majority.

This majority was weaker in the aristocratic Parlements of Aix and Grenoble, which had to admit the very young sons of families whose fathers were always in a hurry *to find them positions*.[20] It became a very slender majority in the Parlement of Rennes, where fifty-two of the sixty-five councilors in office in 1790 had been admitted during the reign of Louis XVI. Finally, in the courts of Dijon and Paris, where the turnover was especially rapid during this last phase of their existence, the lay councilors under thirty-five held an absolute majority in the assembly of the chambers on the eve of the Revolution.

All the contemporary memoirs outdo each other in insisting that this majority of young men exerted a decisive influence on the debates of the principal parlement of France [Paris] in 1787 and 1788. The First President of the Paris Cour des Aides, Barentin, deplored "their headlong and rash actions";[21] and a witness who was also a participant, the ex-councilor Sallier, reported that they "came to the assemblies of

---

[19] The Chevalier du Bouchage, in a letter to the Marquis de Viennois, September 27, 1788 (Archives of the Marquis d'Albon).

[20] The expression of Reynaud, Procureur-Général of Grenoble, in a letter to the Minister of Justice Lamoignon, July 18, 1787 (Municipal Library of Grenoble, Q 6, fol. 86). . . .

[21] C.-L.-F. de Paule de Barentin, *Mémoire autographe sur les derniers Conseils du roi Louis XVI* (Paris, 1844), p. 86.

the chambers as if they were marching to battle. . . ." [22] Councilor Ferrand, an upholder of the old tradition, pointed out to them how the very existence of the sovereign courts was endangered by their thoughtless enthusiasm for the convocation of the Estates-General, an enthusiasm described by Pasquier, who, with Sallier, lived through those feverish times: "From the moment when it became clear that our interests were at stake, we saw nothing more beautiful than to sacrifice them to what we believed to be the public good." [23]

Although one may question the recollections written many years later by Chancellor Pasquier, the conclusive value of the letters of the Parisian Councilor De Pont cannot be denied. He also was a member of the parlementary aristocracy. The son of the Intendant of Metz, he had discovered England and its institutions in 1786, when he was eighteen, and he wrote to Edmund Burke on November 6, 1789, that he would never forget that it was while listening to Burke speak "that his heart first beat in the name of liberty." [24]

At the end of the Old Regime the parlementary aristocracy was not a caste closed to new men and new ideas. Only the Parlement of Rennes was restricted to noblemen of long standing. Along with the Provincial Estates of Brittany, it was a fortress of the Breton nobility. Bésenval's opinion on the provincial parlements, which were—unlike the Parlement of Paris—"composed almost entirely of nobles . . . and which formed, in a manner of speaking, a great family, to which all members were linked by sentiment and by interests," [25] was true for Brittany. But the Parlement of Rennes was an exception. Most of the others welcomed, not only the parlementary nobility and some nobles of long standing, but also, with varying warmth, noblemen of recent date and even commoners. At a time of crucial decisions, it was difficult to establish a close collaboration, a sincere *union of classes*, among courts of such varied composition. Within each of them, who could stop the same jealousies from echoing the same scorn?

Differences in ages provoked other divisions. Several parlements had a majority of mature and cautious men; but in others youth triumphed. At Paris the chambres des enquêtes approved the boldness that the grand' chambre censured.[26]

Here, no doubt, we see the explanation of the hesitations, the contradictions, and the inconsistencies in the parlementary agitation of the years 1787–1788, an agitation which was the principal expression of what we usually call the *Aristocratic Revolution*.

---

[22] G.-M. Sallier-Chaumont de La Roche, *Annales françaises, 1774 à 1789* (Paris, 1813), p. 79.

[23] *Mémoires*, I, 28.

[24] Letter published with three others, all written by C.-J.-F. De Pont to Burke between 1776 and 1790, edited by H. V. F. Somerset, *Annales historiques de la Révolution française*, XXIII (1951), 365. [Burke's *Reflections on the Revolution in France* was written in the form of a letter addressed to De Pont.—Eds.]

[25] Bésenval, p. 427.

[26] [The grand' chambre was composed of the leading members of the Parlement, those of the highest rank.—Eds.]

Was the "Bourgeois Revolt" Bourgeois?

ELIZABETH L. EISENSTEIN

Elizabeth L. Eisenstein (1923–   ) received her Ph.D. from Radcliffe in 1953. Named to the Alice Freeman Palmer Chair of History at the University of Michigan in 1975, she has written a biography, *The First Professional Revolutionist: Filippo Michele Buonarroti, 1761–1837* (1959), in addition to several pioneering studies concerning the impact of printing on Western European thought and culture.

This paper is concerned with discrepancies in Georges Lefebvre's presentation of the point at which, "strictly speaking, the Revolution of 1789 began" [1]—more precisely with how the author locates revolutionary initiative at this point. . . . The point at issue comes, according to the author's scheme, when the Paris Parlement on September 23, 1788, ruled that the Estates-General should be constituted according to the precedent set in 1614. Up to this point the "aristocratic revolution" was proceeding without intervention from other social sectors and appeared to be successful in accomplishing its purpose. The Bourbon monarchy had been forced to concede constitutional limitations upon royal power, and, crippled by bankruptcy, forced to act in accordance with this concession: by reinstating the Paris Parlement and agreeing to convoke an Estates-General to determine fiscal policy. In prior decades, since the era of the *Fronde* [the civil strife in France from 1648 to 1653], the political prerogatives of the intermediary orders had been weakened, those of the crown extended. A reversal of this trend after so long an interval of time may be appropriately classified as a "revolution." Major alterations in an unwritten constitution were being made. But one should note that this sort of revolution was not unprecedented. Prolonged experience, at home and abroad, could account for the behavior of the contestants in the struggle. As the author

Excerpts from Elizabeth L. Eisenstein, "Who Intervened in 1788? A Commentary on *The Coming of the French Revolution*," *The American Historical Review*, LXXI (October 1965), 77–103. Reprinted by permission of the author, who has prepared this abridgment.

[1] Georges Lefebvre, *The Coming of the French Revolution*, trans. R. R. Palmer [*from* Quatre-Vingt-Neuf, *1st ed., Paris, 1939*] (Princeton, N.J., 1947), 37. [*Hereafter page references to this book are given by numbers in parentheses following citations.*]

himself points out, these particular "beginnings of the Revolution" may be viewed as "the last offensive of the aristocracy." They represented, he says, "merely the crowning effort" of this class, the culmination of a struggle that had begun with the first Capetian kings (16). Similarly, earlier "times of troubles" had seen not only the co-incidence of empty royal treasuries with noble sedition but also widespread out-breaks of urban *émeutes* [riots], peasant uprisings, and even municipal insurrections.

If we agree with Lefebvre that the Revolution of 1789 begins "strictly speaking" with an orchestrated wave of protest over the issue of representation at the Estates-General, it is because this is the first large-scale response to the prolonged political and financial crisis that differentiates it from all preceding "times of troubles." The organization of this protest movement could not have been anticipated since it had no precedents in the annals of French statecraft. Its effectiveness in throwing the authorities off balance owed much to its coming from no familiar centers of sedition, no duly constituted groups in particular, but from many different amorphous groups who seemed to be at large. As the author notes, as late as "the summer of 1788 there was no reason to anticipate that the bourgeoisie would intervene in the name of the whole Third Estate in the conflict between the royal power and the aristocracy" (51).

It is this unanticipated intervention in the fall of 1788, made in the name of the whole Third Estate, that seems to lie at the heart of the question: "Who started the French Revolution?" Who was responsible for this intervention? What scanty evidence the author supplies, relating to the social composition of the groups who intervened, does not bear out his implication that initiative passed from one class to another. This appears to be true however loosely or widely one cares to define the term "bourgeoisie" or even the much larger residual category "Third Estate." His evidence, to the contrary, suggests that a loose coalition of men drawn from all three estates provided the initial impetus for the protest movement and steered it through to obtain what is described as "The First Victory of the Bourgeoisie." On his own showing, intervention came from persistently undefined members of a shadowy "patriot party" led by a "Committee of Thirty," only nine of whose members are named. Not one of those named could be characterized as "bourgeois" or as members of the Third Estate.[2] When leaders other than those belonging to this committee are mentioned, moreover, a sizable proportion turn out also to belong to the first two estates. In every passage describing political action the names of the real men who initiated this action are presented to the reader. . . . But the blank-faced visage of the bourgeoisie is invariably substituted in analyzing the significance of this action, introducing it, summing it up, or generalizing about it.

Thus we are told about the first moves made to protest the Parlement's ruling: "In aligning themselves against the privileged classes, the bourgeoisie took the name hitherto claimed in common by all who opposed the royal power. *They* formed the 'national' or 'Patriot' party [*italics mine*]" (52). Who are *the real people* who took the initiative to form this more exclusive, class-oriented party?

> . . . great noblemen, the duc de La Rochefoucauld-Liancourt, the marquis de La Fayette, the marquis de Condorcet, and certain members of the Parliament, Adrien du

[2] For the names see the following page.

Port, Hérault de Séchelles, Le Pelletier de Saint-Fargeau. These men, to take the lead of the movement, joined with bankers like the Labordes,[3] academicians like the lawyer Target[4] and jurists and writers of note, such as Bergasse and Lacretelle, Servan and Volney. The party organized itself for propaganda. Like the Parliaments and the Breton nobility before them, each man made use of his personal connections. Correspondents in the depths of the provinces did the same. . . . The general staff of the new party met in certain drawing rooms like that of Mme. de Tessé, soon to be Mounier's Egeria. Journalists harangued in the cafés . . . (52–53).

The phrase "to take the lead of the movement" is misleading. There was no "bourgeois" movement in the summer of 1788 organized by bankers, academicians, jurists, and writers for some great noblemen to join or to lead. There was no party to organize itself. None of those who "took the lead" could be depicted as "fellow travelers," climbing on a bandwagon that was already rolling. All of them were planning how to beat the drums and wave the banners in order to attract a procession, as they did by the winter's end. Although he sums the matter up—"the bourgeoisie from the first move showed shrewd political sense" (55)—the author, instead, describes how nonbourgeois leaders made the first moves, employed shrewd political tactics, utilized extensive personal connections, and expended much printer's ink in order to mobilize and organize resistance over the issue of "doubling the Third."

The question is whether a central intelligence directed this orchestra of protest. . . . A directing role can apparently be attributed only to the Committee of Thirty of which unfortunately we know very little. It met especially at the house of Adrien du Port and its membership is said to have included the duc de La Rochefoucauld-Liancourt, La Fayette, Condorcet, the duc d'Aiguillon[5] . . . Sieyès . . . and Talleyrand. . . . Mirabeau also came to the meetings. This committee inspired pamphlets, circulated models for the petitions of grievances, supported candidacies and dispatched agents to the provinces. . . . But the influence of the Committee of Thirty . . . would be greatly exaggerated were we to imagine that everything done in every town was merely in execution of its orders. The state of communications allowed no such strict control. If the movement prospered it was because the local bourgeoisie proved its initiative . . . (53–54).

Possibly the local bourgeoisie did prove its initiative in the provinces, although one

[3] The earlier description of the aristocracy tells us (13) that a daughter of the banker Laborde became the Comtesse de Noailles, thus linking the Labordes with La Fayette's family circle. This sort of alliance of great nobles with the *haute bourgeoisie* points to the fallacy of dividing revolutionary leadership into aristocratic and bourgeois elements. It should be noted that financial connections linking both groups are not as significant as and do not necessarily correlate with social, familial, or personal affinities. Thus business associates may be excluded or snubbed—even down to the present—by aristocrats who prefer the company of members of their own class. D'Artois' investment in the Javel works (13) thus tells us nothing at all about his political or social orientation.

[4] On the important continuous role played by this academician, see numerous references to Target in the index of Lefebvre's book.

[5] The duc d'Aiguillon, a prime mover along with Target, La Fayette, and the latter's son-in-law, the Vicomte de Noailles, in the night of August 4, 1789, is later described as "one of the greatest landowners in France" (161).

wonders about the social composition of those correspondents in its depths. Certainly it was not the Parisian bourgeoisie that took the initiative in their home town, but rather a socially heterogeneous, ideologically homogeneous collection of notables and nobodies drawn from the three estates. All that the Parisian leaders seem to have shared in common was that their private social circles overlapped and that they "unreservedly adopted the new ideas" (52). The point is not that everything done everywhere was done on the basis of orders from the Committee of Thirty. It is rather that, as the author tells us, what central organization the state of communications permitted *was* provided by this group. On the basis of what happened in Paris and judging from the other evidence provided it seems plausible that where local initiative did come, it came from similarly heterogeneous provincial groups. . . .

We had earlier been informed, in the first act of the drama, that

> the aristocratic class developed an organization for political action, exchanging correspondence and passing instructions from town to town. The Committee of Thirty, which was soon to take over the leadership of the Third Estate, seems to have originated as a center of parliamentary resistance (33).[6]

If Parisian leadership of the Third Estate emerged from an organization developed by "the aristocratic class" (by heterogeneous groups of "notables" might be more accurate), why should not local initiative have emerged from a similar source? In fact, precedents established both by the royal ministers Calonne and Brienne, experimenting with newly formed provincial assemblies (24, 32), and by the "aristocratic revolution" in defense of old provincial estates, provided those who pressed the issue of "doubling the Third" with their main arguments. The case of the Vizille assembly—when "the aristocracy of Dauphiny got out of hand" (32) and after successfully defying the royal minister conceded "double representation to the Third Estate, vote by head and fiscal equality" (51)—is twice cited in this connection (51, 55).[7]

We are told also how the program to press double representation was executed:

[6] The author does not account for the apparent contradiction involved in a center of parliamentary resistance that becomes a center of resistance to parliamentary authority. This is only one of many puzzles obscured by the very clarity of his scheme. Since one-half of the puzzle belongs to the first act, the other to the second, the reader, like the author, is apt to forget that the pieces belong together. Thus the Breton Third Estate is, on pages 18–19, represented by nobles and privileged persons. On pages 60–61 this same privileged body defies the nobles and clergy until fiscal equality long demanded by it is granted. The fact that municipal oligarchs did have different interests than the hereditary nobles would, in this case, solve the puzzle created by overdramatizing the solid front composed of privileged status groups in the first act. But no such simple solution of the first-mentioned puzzle occurs to me.

[7] Nowhere is the analysis more puzzling than in the account (32) of this action by the Dauphiny aristocracy. "Still . . . dissatisfied, *because* Brienne . . . had granted double representation [*italics mine*]" and vote by head to the new provincial assemblies, this aristocracy demanded the return of their old estates. They defied his refusal to grant this request, "obtained the support of the bourgeoisie," and then at Vizille granted the very forms of representation that had, we were told, provoked their original defiance. By considering the issue of Versailles versus the provinces rather than that of aristocrats versus commoners this affair might seem less puzzling. Regional rivalries that crisscrossed social cleavages tend to find no place in the book, but they were of equal importance in determining the forms of conflict that set the stage for the coming of the Revolution.

The scheme was to overwhelm the government with a flood of petitions for which the municipalities whether willing or not were obliged to take responsibility during the autumn of 1788. At Dijon, for example, the matter was put through as follows: Some twenty "notables" [8] met and decided to submit to their respective guilds and corporate bodies the questions of doubling the Third and of vote by head (56).

Favorable response from roughly twenty out of fifty guilds, resistance from the municipal authorities overcome by an invasion of the town hall, and a petition sent to the King in the name of the Dijon Third Estate followed. Similar action occurred in the other towns of Burgundy. Who devised this "scheme," suggested to the original twenty notables in Dijon, elsewhere in Burgundy, and presumably throughout many other provinces in the vast realm of France that they canvass the guilds and force, by direct action, the signing of similar petitions by municipalities? "A directing role can apparently be attributed only to the Committee of Thirty" (53). In the one example offered we see that the burghers of Dijon were by no means unanimous in their response to the issue pressed upon them. Thirty or so guilds did not respond. Violence was required to force urban oligarchs to sign and send the petitions.

Evidence drawn from countless such towns, located in all the French provinces, would be required to determine precisely how members of the Third Estate divided on this issue. One would like to know, in the one example given, why some burghers and guildsmen (in particular the local lawyers' guild) responded favorably while others did not. But despite the evidence, bourgeois solidarity is blandly taken for granted. According to the author's scheme, in fact, the bourgeoisie moved to the center of the stage just as soon as the Paris Parlement pronounced its verdict.

A wave of excitement passed over the bourgeoisie at the news that the Estates-General were to be convoked. For the first time since 1614 the king was authorizing the bourgeoisie to speak. At first no struggle was foreseen. . . . The assembly at Vizille had left a deep impression by conceding double representation to the Third Estate. . . . Agreement seemed by no means impossible.[9]

But the outlook changed abruptly when the Parliament of Paris . . . ruled that the Estates-General should be constituted as in 1614. A clamor rose from one end of the kingdom to the other. Between night and morning the popularity of the Parliament vanished (51).

---

[8] As always, when specific examples come in the narrative, the blank-faced bourgeoisie disappears. In dealing with the issue of revolutionary initiative, social nomenclature which is vague appears to be more accurate than that which is precise. The closer one gets to the real men involved the further one is from clearly polarized class divisions. It should be noted that even craftsmen in some cases "counted as notables" (44), along with urban oligarchs, academicians, magistrates, and aristocrats.

[9] To suggest that agreement about representation seemed possible before the Parlement's ruling conveys a prior preoccupation with this issue before it was posed. The issues over which men might agree or disagree were still invisible during the two and a half months from July 5 to September 23, 1788, when the wave of excitement rippled over literate sectors of the public. It seems likely that no one, bourgeois or not, knew quite what to expect after learning an Estates-General would meet, that all sorts of vague hopes and plans were encouraged rather than specific expectations about how the orders would be represented.

The state of communications, which did not permit Parisian organization to penetrate the provinces and left matters to local initiative, apparently proved more efficient in transmitting news of the Parlement's ruling. The question of who transmitted this news and how it was transmitted is, however, by-passed. The length of the interval between night and morning is not discussed. On how the news was received, we are offered some undated comments by Weber and Brissot, told that Mme. Roland and Rabaut-Saint-Étienne "now took passionately to public affairs," and informed of Mallet du Pan's remark: "The controversy has completely changed. King, despotism and constitution are now minor questions. The war is between the Third Estate and the other two orders" (52).[10] Mallet's remarks are dated. They came in January 1789, after three or more months of canvassing and campaigning on the issue of doubling the Third.

It seems to have been this canvassing and campaigning, accompanied by an outpouring of pamphlets that "astonished contemporaries" by their number (54), that accounted for the way hitherto quiescent subjects took passionately to public affairs in the winter of 1788–1789. But disappointment at the Parlement's ruling and immediate action designed to reverse it came first of all from groups who had already been active in the first act of the drama. Indignation, defiance, and effective action from such quarters are, however, muffled by the author and detached from the public storm of protest.

> As was to be expected, some of the privileged were inclined to grant the Third Estate a certain satisfaction of its pride. On December 5, 1788, the "nationals" in the Parliament of Paris prevailed on that body to declare, by formal order, that it had no intention of prejudging the number of deputies in the Estates-General, and that the number was not fixed by law (58–59).

"In private," we are also told, "some of the privileged expressed themselves definitely in favor of the Third Estate" (59). Presumably public expressions of such an attitude were not becoming to aristocrats. Yet something more than the tepid inclination to grant commoners "a certain satisfaction" is conveyed by a letter cited from one aristocrat to another.

> Some think the non-privileged, who are the base and pillar of the State, should be without sufficient representatives in an Assembly which is to regulate their destiny. This is really too insulting and will not work. In any case the thing has been seen through. It will be best to be careful of what is done. . . . But I perceive my dear count that I am repeating to you what you know and think (59).

This was, to be sure, a private letter. But the convictions contained in it were implemented by public action coming from the same privileged social strata, resulting not only in the Parlement's reversal of its ruling but also in the official decree of December 27 granting double representation to the Third Estate.

These moves did not occur without considerable opposition from many

---

[10] Eighteenth-century journalists, however intelligent, were less well informed than their modern counterparts and just as inaccurate. In fact, the war between the Third Estate and the other two orders saw the clergy split on the issue.

aristocrats, whose resistance, we are told, led "many bourgeois to become more radical in their ideas" (61). Along with the later behavior of the Breton deputies and a shift in Rabaut-Saint-Étienne's views, two illustrations of this change in bourgeois attitudes are offered. One is a famous pamphlet by Abbé Sieyès: *What Is the Third Estate?* The other is a famous printed speech by Count Mirabeau, eulogizing Marius for exterminating the order of the nobility (61–62). It is typically difficult to describe the social position of both authors in terms of conventional social nomenclature. Mirabeau was a "deserter from the nobility" who "had lived by his pen in the service of Calonne and Calonne's enemies" (71). Sieyès was a frustrated member of the Second Estate barred from a bishopric as a commoner whose "pamphlets made him an oracle" (69). In their service to the Committee of Thirty both "were certainly in contact with the Duc d'Orléans" (54). As publicists drawn from the first two estates who were ultimately elected to represent the Third, they are ill-adapted to illustrate changes in attitudes on the part of a single social class. They seem better suited to illustrate the more amorphous social strata to which "men of letters" (a formidable pressure group in its own right) belonged, and from which the attack on both despotism and privilege, the thoroughgoing assault on all the traditional ruling elites first came.

On the evidence provided then, sensitivity to a ruling that was taken as an insult to the nonprivileged was not confined to the bourgeoisie. The canvassing, pamphleteering, and circulating of petitions to reverse this ruling were neither initiated nor directed by the bourgeoisie. What precedents existed for a contrary ruling and what action was taken to obtain a reversal from the Parlement did not come from the bourgeoisie. Yet all of these measures receive the same treatment as the scheme that was put through in the fall of 1788:

> By such means, the *bourgeoisie* set the "nation" into motion. *Its* maneuver was denounced then, and has been ever since. But the aristocracy, shortly before, had acted no differently. Every political movement naturally has its instigators and leaders.[11] No one has ever dared to maintain that *the Third Estate*, invited to appear in the Estates-General, could have thought it natural to leave the aristocracy supreme in the assembly. Hence, what *the leaders of the patriot party* are blamed for is simply to have roused *the nation* to shake off *its* torpor and organize *itself* to defend *its* cause [*italics mine*] (56).[12]

One must bear in mind that what is meant by "torpor" is the political passivity of quiescent subjects accustomed for hundreds of years to leave decisions pertaining to affairs of state to others. Otherwise one is apt to overlook the necessity of explaining how that torpor was shaken off. There was as yet no "nation" to be set in motion or, a more problematic issue, to rouse or organize itself. Since no evidence is presented concerning "maneuvers" by the blank-faced bourgeoisie—since scattered

---

[11] The presumption is that movements give rise to instigators and leaders. Some movements do, but, in my view, the reverse was the case with regard to the point at issue.

[12] The italics are employed to suggest ambiguity concerning the group whose behavior is involved, who set whom into motion, and who defended whose cause. At least four, possibly five or six collective terms are used: the bourgeoisie, the leaders of the patriot party, the Third Estate, the "nation," the instigators and leaders.

unorganized commoners were not in a position to undertake such maneuvers—one is at a loss concerning the means by which they set "the nation" in motion. As already noted, the maneuvers of the leaders of the patriot party may be examined. It is not surprising that they appear similar to those employed by "the aristocracy, shortly before." For most of these leaders are the very same men whose tactics the author had described "shortly before"—in connection with aristocratic political organization—before he had them "range themselves" on the same side as the bourgeoisie. In fact, he shows them choosing sides before lines had been drawn, setting the terms of the debate, and canvassing opinion on it. How could they range themselves on the same side as men who had yet to be heard from? . . .

"No one has ever dared to suggest that the Third Estate could have thought it natural to leave the aristocracy supreme in the Assembly." The author himself shows that had the orders not been kept separate, it was feared that many members of the Third Estate would vote to be represented by aristocrats (55). What men thought "natural" before the French Revolution needs to be distinguished from what historians view as "natural" thereafter. Certainly few of the customs of the *ancien régime* appeared natural to men steeped in Enlightenment thought. But most of them probably appeared natural enough to men who were not. Both groups confronted what appeared by the late eighteenth century to be an "unnatural" vagueness about numerical representation in earlier meetings of the Estates-General. For, as antiquarians scouring the records discovered, the Third Estate, although officially summoned to send one delegate for each sent by the other two orders, had in fact sent many more than its share of delegates, outnumbering the clergy on one hand and the nobility on the other by different numbers which varied in each case[13] (and which made little difference since there was also an unnatural agreement about consistently voting by order[14]). To follow the precedent of 1614 precisely was in this regard impossible. When the Estates-General had to be resurrected, after its demise more than a century and a half before, such vagueness concerning quantitative representation no longer came naturally to any party concerned. The fact that some eighteenth-century provincial estates had already doubled the Third and were voting by head suggests what France suffered by letting the Estates-General atrophy during the seventeenth and eighteenth centuries. In place of a relatively flexible institution that could accommodate social change, Frenchmen confronted only a brittle precedent that had to be either artificially reconstructed or deliberately broken. No one could escape this either-or issue. Every notable had to rethink and make explicit his view of how the body politic should be constituted. The resulting division of opinion involved conflicting

[13] This is not discussed by Lefebvre; I have taken it from J. M. Thompson, *The French Revolution* (New York, 1945), 4.

[14] Lefebvre points to the shrewdness of pressing the issue of doubling the Third while leaving open that of voting by head (55, 59–60). Indirectly he shows how the postponement of this latter issue was politically indispensable for the patriots. But he never makes clear that when propagandists *did* stipulate "voting by head" or when, as in the Dijon case, the municipal authorities balked on this issue (56), the separation of the orders was taken for granted by *everyone* as far as the elections to the Estates-General went. Voting by head referred *only* to the procedure to be followed at Versailles—after the doubled Third had arrived there.

concepts of a well-ordered commonwealth, incompatible opinions about how it should be governed, and rival ambitions about who should govern it.

Was this division congruent with the division between the first two estates and the Third? Did it not first of all divide those who had just emerged victorious in their long struggle with the crown and expected to exploit this victory to the full? Should we not look to the "liberal" aristocracy, even before turning to the bourgeoisie, for a "full consciousness of historic mission" shaped by "the thought of eighteenth century writers" (50)? At least the men who thought it unnatural to leave the aristocracy supreme in the Assembly, who at any rate posed the issue in this way to their fellow countrymen happened—many of them—to be marquis, counts, bishops, *abbés,* in short, members of the first two estates. Why did *they* think it unnatural to follow, as best one could, the precedent of 1614? . . . The Parlement of Paris had decided the case otherwise. A recent analysis of the eighteenth-century robe nobility suggests why it was "natural" for this body to do so.[15] But the Committee of Thirty seems to have originated in robe circles. Members of the Paris Parlement: Adrien du Port, Hérault de Séchelles, Le Pelletier de Saint Fargeau, and the unnamed "nationals" who obtained a reversal on December 5, 1788, worked hard and successfully to create a clamor against the ruling of the very body to which they belonged. It is this sort of purposeful action by active minorities, working both inside and outside duly constituted bodies, that one may unambiguously call "revolutionary." Since it could not be anticipated by contemporaries, authorities could not take measures to forestall it. Since it did not fit familiar formulas derived from prolonged experience with assassination plots and seditions during earlier "times of troubles" and since it could be traced to no court or cabinet, no foreign agents, no one class or group or region, new kinds of conspiratorial hypotheses would be woven to explain it (including those which involved impersonal agents set in motion by an invisible hand).

Instead of being isolated and studied, in *The Coming of the French Revolution,* the behavior of these active minorities, composed of like-minded individuals drawn from all three estates, is treated as marginal or inconsequential. Evidence pertaining to this behavior is invariably subordinated to the clear scheme of each large class acting independently in its own interests. . . .

> Should the Third Estate have contented itself, respectfully and submissively, with what the great majority of the aristocracy were willing to offer it? In any case it did not think so, and loudly demanded equality before the law. At this point, strictly speaking, the Revolution of 1789 began (36–37).

This kind of rhetorical question about what the Third Estate *should* have done does not help us much in our effort to understand how the Revolution came. Instead one might ask what the heterogeneous, scattered, and politically unconstituted members of the Third Estate *would* have done had they not been presented with a most appealing and very clear alternative to respectful submission. It seems likely that whatever they might have thought and done and however widespread was

[15] Franklin Ford, *Robe and Sword: The Regrouping of the French Aristocracy after Louis XIV* (Cambridge, Mass., 1953).

a latent resentment of aristocratic privilege, had they not been provided with many identical petitions to get signed and many similar pamphlets to read, local responses of a very limited shortwave resonance would have resulted. There are, even today, many different ways of demanding equality before the law. There were many more in the vast realm of France during the *ancien régime* where justice before the law was dispensed differently in different regions and for different social groups, where there was no uniform law before which any kind of equality could be demanded.

If in the winter of 1788 a single demand sounded "loudly," it was because a sufficient number of similar petitions, singling out for protest the Parlement's ruling and singling out from among all the issues relating to composition, election, convocation, and procedure this ruling might raise, that of double representation for the Third Estate, were forced through scattered municipalities throughout the realm. Since local initiative was required to force through the petitions and since this occurred in many scattered areas, one may agree, roughly speaking, that a considerable number of commoners throughout the country were not content to submit respectfully to what the constituted bodies offered. But when one remembers the long list of earlier insurrections and seditions, it seems evident that a failure to submit to established authorities was not what distinguished the protest movement of 1788 from earlier "times of troubles." Such insubordination had hitherto been spread out over much longer intervals resulting in "sporadic" episodes, or, when occurring in shorter intervals, had involved so many bewilderingly various localized issues and incidents that historians, even in retrospect, have difficulty patterning and polarizing them.[16] In the winter of 1788 protests came within a remarkably short interval and produced a remarkably uniform appearance. A considerable measure of central organization is suggested by the simultaneity of this action. The unprecedented use made of the duplicative powers of print largely accounts for the uniform character of the clamor.

This clamor, which rose from one end of the nation to the other, was made in the name of the Third Estate and appeared to come from that residual order of the realm. In some regions, we are told, "peasants and workingmen streamed into the halls and the whole Third Estate signed [*or marked?*] the petition" (56). Although they composed most of the nonprivileged, "the base and pillar of society," and although it was, as yet, by no means clear how the Third Estate was to be represented,[17] the participation of peasants and workingmen in this action is generally not regarded as evidence of revolutionary initiative. Whereas similar participation by a smaller residual category of literate commoners, who did not work with their hands and are diversely defined as "the bourgeoisie," is so regarded. Located in all the provinces of France, however, and presenting "an extreme diversity of condition" (46), this latter group were scarcely better situated than were their unlettered compatriots to ensure the uniformity and simultaneity that made

[16] On the debate over "vertical" alignments versus horizontal "fronts" resulting from the "thorny problem" of the involvement of social sectors in seventeenth-century seditions, see Leon Bernard, "French Society and Popular Uprisings under Louis XIV," *French Historical Studies*, III (Fall 1964), 454–74.
[17] It was proposed, as well as suggested in grievance lists, that the government should create a separate order of peasants or provide for the separate election of town deputies and rural ones (65).

the demands of the Third Estate sound loudly. They had yet to meet together, find some basis for a common accord, or discover how they differed.[18]

On the other hand, the leaders of the resistance to the crown had already gathered in Assemblies of Notables and had already discovered how they differed. The activities of the Committee of Thirty appear inexplicable if we assume, as the author seems to, that the "aristocratic revolution" was made by men who fought royal despotism only with old feudal war cries or the more up-to-date "thèse nobiliaire" in mind. His evidence shows that it had also been made by men who had more "liberal" views about how a modern state should be governed; who had, in addition to their public concern, private personal ambitions. From this evidence, we also infer that these liberal notables moved in social circles that included talented commoners, preferred the latter's company, respected their judgment and competence rather more than that of many of their peers. Such men, it turned out, comprised a minority of the aristocracy. But they were not, for that reason, paralyzed, silenced, or rendered inactive. They were a sizable and powerful minority who had already combined in a loose coalition with a sizable minority of talented commoners who were particularly skilled with their pens. They had already created an organization for political action and correspondence throughout the provinces, had already laid the basis for a shadowy "national" or "patriot" party. They did not lose their initiative when thwarted. To the contrary, they initiated action as leaders of an independent coalition party. . . .

In concluding his account of "the first victory" achieved by the "Bourgeois Revolution," the author conveys, always by indirection, that initiative remained in the same hands during the electoral campaign that followed the successful protest movement. The successful electioneering of the patriot party is contrasted with the failure of Necker and other royal ministers to draw up a list of candidates committed to a program of desired reforms. It is contrasted also with the clumsy, uncoordinated attempts at personal influence made, here and there, by the chairmen of bailiwick assemblies (66). "Since 1789 there have been political parties with much stronger organization than the patriots of that time but none has met with so little resistance on the part of the government" (67). Until 1789, however, the government had been engaged in mobilizing its forces against seditious elites: namely, the parlements, provincial assemblies, municipal corporations (not to mention a variety of religious orders, the long arm of Rome, and of foreign courts as well). It had no experience with an independent domestic opposition party led by a loose coalition of aristocrats, ecclesiastics, men of letters and of the liberal professions mobilizing opinion against these elites and utilizing for this purpose the full power of the printing press, earlier turned against the crown by the parlements, now, for the first time in France, released from the clandestine channels into which it had been forced.[19]

What is surprising is that even a rudimentary political party could be organized,

---

[18] The delegates to the Third Estate who arrived in Versailles in May 1789 "were unknown to each other and it was impossible to tell how far they would go" (78).

[19] The King in his traditional invitation to his subjects to express their views when promising to call an Estates-General on July 5, 1788, "had not intended thereby to grant freedom of the press," but pamphleteers disregarded his intentions, releasing a flood that "astonished contemporaries" (54).

lists of candidates drawn up, platforms of reforms proposed in less than a year before the Estates had convened—not that subsequent parties would be more strongly organized or that the government failed to forestall this one. With respect to this problem, the author tells us, "The Committee of Thirty . . . assumed a lead whose extent it is impossible to determine" (66–67). On the other hand, he has no doubts,

> It is hardly doubtful that enterprising bourgeois everywhere took concerted action[20] to steer the town and bailiwick assemblies, with as many parish assemblies as possible in addition, by suggesting candidates and circulating models for petitions of grievances. The models were either received from Paris, or, more often, drafted locally (67).

These "enterprising bourgeois" who suggested candidates and drafted local models, independently of those sent from Paris, are necessarily nameless. Two social groups are singled out as playing a predominant role: lawyers who "were very influential" and the village priests who "gave much aid." This is not the only instance, but it is the most transparent, where the vital distinction between being literate (as these village priests apparently were) and being "enterprising bourgeois" (as they surely were not)[21] is overlooked.

This distinction is so vital to all theories pertaining to the coming of the French Revolution, or to the "rise of bourgeoisie to political power," that it seems worth pausing over. Because the electoral assemblies were also deliberative, we are told,

> the most influential bourgeois, or those best informed on public affairs or most accustomed to speaking in public, namely the lawyers . . . [dominated] throughout the debates. In the bailiwick assemblies, the peasants lacking education and unable to express themselves, let themselves be docilely led. The result was that the representation of the Third Estate was made up uniquely of bourgeois (65).

In light of the vital distinction, we would argue that it was made up, almost uniquely (aside from three priests and a dozen noblemen [67]) of a nonprivileged literate laity. The acquisition of literacy, by whatever means and in whatever era since the sixteenth century, was the most important single determinant as far as the social composition of the Third Estate delegation went. As a group, literate commoners *had* no social structure or nomenclature—medieval institutions had not been designed to take them into account. But in countless villages and even in some small towns, they were nonetheless a very distinctive group. The village schoolmaster was yet to become as ubiquitous as the parish priest. The latter was out of the running

---

[20] However enterprising they may be, men who are located "everywhere" simply cannot take "concerted action" to steer an electorate toward a given slate of candidates. One group located in one place is required to see that all the others do not "steer" in all directions.

[21] Many bourgeois families sent one son into the priesthood as they sent another into law. But the former were more apt to be attached to cathedral chapters in towns than to village parishes. They were also apt to be the less enterprising among bourgeois offspring. Finally, to apply the term "bourgeois" to village priests as well as to "the upper level of the nobility . . . whose conditions of life drew them to the bourgeoisie" (14) is to stretch this much-abused term beyond its already frayed limits. There is something wildly askew about a structural model that includes the top layer of nobles and the bottom layer of the clergy within the middle ranks of "the middle class."

as a delegate of the Third Estate. Lawyers "who lived in the villages or often visited them for manorial pleadings" (67) represented in some cases the only possible alternative.

One reason for so many varying definitions of "the bourgeoisie" is the impossibility of making this group, however regarded in terms of status, occupation, economic class, style of life, and so forth, congruent with the much more amorphous body of men who had, ever since the printing press, been rising from the ranks of a preliterate population by mastering the written word. To whom else could this population turn but to such men when all the traditional literate elites—teachers, preachers, officers, bureaucrats—were out of the running? One may only guess how many more priests, aristocrats, or high magistrates might have been elected instead of the lawyers and other literate commoners who were, had not the former been eliminated from the running. Evidence is offered that the leaders of the patriot party feared the number might have been significantly large:

> Seeming to fear the prestige of the privileged persons and to think them capable of imposing on commoners to the point of being elected to represent them, the patriot party often demanded, even later on, that each order be required to choose its representatives from its own members (55).

This is presented to show, not how elections were partly rigged by rigorously enforcing the separation of orders, but rather as evidence of "the moderation of the Third" despite the atypical "trenchant tone" of Sieyès' pamphlet. "The patriot party, in fact, by no means asked that the Estates-General be elected without regard to the three orders" (55). Of course it did not ask this. To obtain an overwhelming majority composed of the doubled Third, parish priests, and liberal nobles, working under the leaders of the patriot party, the electorate had to be insulated until after the elections. The abrupt accession to political power of the Third Estate depended very precisely on how demands for "equality before the law" were formulated and phased. The sudden appearance of a commanding majority composed of hitherto politically quiescent, unknown literate commoners (often described as the political accession of the "revolutionary bourgeoisie") paradoxically depended just as much on preserving the medieval tradition of separate and qualitatively differentiated orders as it did on pressing the issue of doubling the Third, while holding in reserve—until after the scene of action had shifted from the provinces to the capital—insistence on merging the orders and voting by head. . . .

> Divide the human race into twenty parts and there will be nineteen composed of those who work with their hands and who will never know that there was a Locke in the world; in the twentieth part remaining, how few men are there who can read? and among those who can, there will be twenty who read romances to one who studies science. The number of those who think is excessively small and they do not think about troubling the world.[22]

---

[22] Voltaire, "Lettres Philosophiques: XIII—sur M. Locke," cited by J. H. Randall, *The Making of the Modern Mind: A Survey of the Intellectual Background of the Present Age* (Cambridge, Mass., 1926), 363; see also a longer, differently translated version in *id., The Career of Philosophy, From the Middle Ages to the Enlightenment* (New York, 1962), 870.

If we substitute eighteenth-century Frenchmen for "the human race," Voltaire's observation, ironic or not, appears to be well founded. The excessively small number of eighteenth-century Frenchmen who could read, who had heard of Locke, preferred science to romance, and could "think" were, most of them, surely not consciously thinking about troubling the world. They had never participated in noble seditions or popular *émeutes* before Voltaire's day; nor did they do so for a decade after his death. Their inner composure was possibly disturbed by silent dialogues with favorite authors whose messages tended to slip past inner censors much as they did, via clandestine channels, past outer ones. But whatever their fantasies—and no one can read the minds of book readers—they remained politically passive, probably the most orderly subjects of an occasionally disordered realm. Engaged, on the whole profitably, pursuing their diverse trades, occupations, and professions, they had, in fact, much to lose and little to gain from the disruption of domestic peace. Even after delegates drawn exclusively from this "excessively small number" of literate townsmen who "were for the most part mature men in comfortable circumstances . . . educated . . . proficient in some specialized calling . . ." (68) arrived at Versailles, six-hundred strong, the leaders of the patriot party had every reason to expect, if not peasantlike docility, at least solid support from these political unknowns. They had no reason to anticipate that future historians would regard their own role as subordinate to that of the deputies they dominated. At least another year would pass before their expectations would appear unwarranted. As the author notes, in discussing the National Assembly: "It is also characteristic that, at least at first, the most prominent leaders were men from the privileged classes" (69). . . .

On "the debated question of who 'started the Revolution,' " then, the author's evidence suggests that initiative came, beginning with the first Assembly of Notables called by Calonne in 1786 through the stormy year of 1789 and beyond, from a loose coalition of like-minded men drawn from all three estates. No conventional social nomenclature appears applicable to this group whose collective biography remains to be written. Judging by the frequency with which the same names turn up, in conjunction with the Committee of Thirty and the leaders of the patriot party, this group was not very large—roughly the same number as might appear in a composite portrait of our own "founding fathers" seems to be involved. Some sort of collective biography of these men appears to be indispensable to any understanding of how the Revolution of 1789 came. . . . Instead we are told that neither La Fayette, Mirabeau, nor Sieyès dominated "the scene to the point of personifying the Revolution of 1789, which remained the collective achievement of the Third Estate" (71). What has been described, however, was the collective achievement of more than one marquis, one *abbé*, and one count—the collective achievement of Sieyès, Mirabeau, La Fayette *and* Talleyrand, Condorcet, Adrien du Port, Hérault de Séchelles, Le Pelletier de Saint Fargeau, the Duc d'Aiguillon, La Rochefoucauld-Liancourt, Laborde, Target, Volney, Mounier, and so forth. In so far as a revolution such as that of 1789 may be personified or incarnated, this group of men did so. In so far as concerted collective action was involved, these men conducted it. As constant leaders of the patriot party who steered the protest movement of 1788 and the electoral campaign of 1789, who pushed through the transformation of the Estates-General into a National Assembly, who proposed and drafted the Declaration of the Rights of Man, who abolished all privilege on the night of August 4, they provided the basis for whatever unity or continuity may be perceived in the early phases of the French Revolution. . . .

To discuss how initiative passed into other hands thereafter would carry us far beyond the limits of this paper. Suffice it to say that unanticipated consequences more often than not result from a given course of action that is not grounded on precedent or prolonged experience. Here, at least, the revolutionary action initiated in 1788 proved unexceptional . . . and the leaders of the patriot party could scarcely have anticipated the subsequent roles they would enact in the drama. But they nonetheless did, by wielding all the considerable power and influence at their disposal, help determine the conditions under which the drama would be played out. Purposeful action directed toward desired goals is one thing; unanticipated consequences resulting from this action are another. This obvious distinction has to be stressed, in order to avoid entanglement in the empty and endless debate over whether the Revolution was "spontaneous" or "planned," the product of "circumstances" or "plot." The debate is empty because it is invariably held over a grand design, incorporating the full sequence of events which only began to unfold in 1789. This design is visible only in retrospect. It could not be foreseen by any contemporaries. Hence it could not have been planned or devised by any of them. The debate is endless because the sequence of events has no stopping point. It is still spinning itself out and will always be differently concluded for and by each successive generation. It is worth noting that those who weave conspiratorial legends or employ the "thèse de complots" [conspiracy thesis] are just as prone to ignore the real men who formed and led the patriot party as are those who insist on spontaneous mass or class action. In both cases, efforts to fathom a grand design result in perpetually unsatisfactory answers to the more limited range of questions which anyone curious about the coming of the French Revolution might be expected to ask: Who intervened in the conflict between crown and nobles in 1788–1789? How did they do so and why? To learn, for example, that many leaders of the patriot party were Masons or that their correspondents in the provinces belonged to "reading societies" does not get us very far. Or, rather, it leads us much too far with hints that we must look beyond a loose political coalition based on informal groupings of like-minded notables, in search of an invisible network controlled by a hidden hand (the Duc d'Orléans?) or manipulated by Protestants, aliens, libertine aristocrats, and would-be philosopher-kings. On the other hand, to be told that these leaders must have been, if not members of the bourgeoisie, then its agents, symbols, or incarnations and to examine the social structure of this ascending class in order to understand the behavior of these leaders does not get us very far either—or takes us much too far also in search of statistics pertaining to capitalist enterprise, industrial development, and landownership patterns. In both instances we are asked to look around, over, beyond, above, or below rather than at the assorted individuals whose group action we are curious about. What we have tried to suggest in the foregoing discussion is that evidence relating to this group action, undertaken by known individuals, using known means, to exert continuous pressure toward known ends is contained in *The Coming of the French Revolution.*

But a static framework derived from a structural analysis is incapable of containing this sort of dynamic group action. Instead it keeps apart, as socially stratified, the very cluster of men who gravitated together, mutually attracted by political goals that appeared to be within their reach.

The Uprising of July 14: Who Participated?

JACQUES GODECHOT

Jacques Godechot (1907–   ) is one of France's most distinguished historians. The son of a businessman from Lorraine, he studied history at the University of Nancy and at the Sorbonne in Paris. While teaching at the École navale in Brest, he published his important doctoral thesis, *Les Commissaires aux armées sous le Directoire* (1937). Since 1945 he has been a professor at the University of Toulouse. Among his many books on the revolutionary period, three are available in English translation: *The Counter-Revolution, France and the Atlantic Revolution of the Eighteenth Century, 1770-1799,* and *The Taking of the Bastille: July 14th, 1789.*

Professor Godechot is an authority on the reforms carried out during the French Revolution. He is noted also for his comparative studies of revolutionary outbreaks in France and elsewhere during the late eighteenth century.

On the morning of the 14th, while a huge crowd was marching towards the Invalides, another almost equally dense crowd was making its way towards the Bastille, to demand arms, powder and bullets from the Governor. But this was a more anxious crowd than that surrounding the Hôtel des Invalides. The latter building was a sort of great barracks, with a few cannon protecting it, indeed, but which presented no great threat to the population of the neighbourhood. The Bastille, on the other hand, was a fortress, and for the past week its Governor, de Launey, seemed to have been strengthening its defences. His garrison of 82 *invalides* [war veterans]—easy-going fellows, well-known figures in the faubourg

From Jacques Godechot, *The Taking of the Bastille: July 14th, 1789,* trans. Jean Stewart (New York: Charles Scribner's Sons, 1970), pp. 218–222, 225–226, 267–273. Reprinted by permission of Faber and Faber Ltd. and reprinted by permission of Charles Scribner's Sons from *The Taking of the Bastille: July 14th, 1789* by Jacques Godechot. Copyright © 1970 Faber and Faber Ltd. English translation.

Saint-Antoine—had been reinforced on July 7th by a detachment of 32 Swiss soldiers from the Salis-Samade regiment, commanded by a sergeant and by Lieutenant Deflue (who had in fact been promoted Captain a few weeks previously, although he had not yet been given a company). Now the Bastille was equipped with efficient artillery, fifteen eight-pounder cannon (firing eight-pound cannon balls) standing on the towers and inside at the foot of the walls, but mounted on naval gun-carriages which were difficult to manœuvre, three eight-pounder field cannon ready for action in the large inner courtyard, pointing towards the entrance gate, and twelve rampart guns each firing balls weighing a pound and a half. The Governor had reinforced the defences, built a second wall behind the garden wall (which was not very high and might have allowed attackers to find their way in), widened the embrasures to give the cannon more range, repaired the drawbridge to make it harder to force, and removed its parapet so that attackers could be more readily flung into the moats. A load of six cartloads of paving-stones and old iron had been taken up into the towers on July 9th and 10th so that, as in the Middle Ages, they could be hurled at the assailants. Tongs had also been taken up there, which could be used to break down the chimneys and make additional missiles out of the débris. Loopholes and windows which served no useful defensive purpose had been blocked up with solid pieces of wood, and new slits had been opened on the sides which were not threatened.

True, de Launey had not stocked up with provisions; he had only one day's supply of meat and two days' supply of bread, and moreover there was no drinking water inside the fortress. But, bearing in mind the experience of the Réveillon riots of April 28th, de Launey may legitimately have thought that if he were attacked by an unarmed or ill-armed crowd the assault would not last longer than one day and that at nightfall the rioters would disperse; or that if they attempted a siege the Bastille would soon get help from the many troops which had been assembled around Paris since the beginning of July.

It would thus have been easy for a determined leader to resist an attack. But Governor de Launey was no such thing. Lieutenant Deflue describes him thus:[1] "The Governor of this fortress, the comte de Launey, was a man without much knowledge of military matters, without experience and of little valour. As soon as the disturbances began, he appealed to the generals in command of the army and asked them to reinforce the garrison, which consisted only of eighty-four veterans. His request was refused, because the authorities did not believe that the rebellion would become so violent or that anyone would think of trying to seize the Bastille. He renewed his request. Finally I was detailed off with thirty men and sent to the Bastille on July 7th. The very day after my arrival I got to know the man, through all the preparations he was making for the defence of his post, in which there was neither rhyme nor reason, and I could clearly see, from his perpetual uneasiness and irresolution, that if we were attacked we should be very badly led. He was so terrified that at night he mistook the shadows of trees and other objects around him

[1] Letter from Deflue to his brothers, published by J. Flammermont, *La Journée de 14 juillet, fragment des mémoires inédits de L.-G. Pitra, électeur de Paris en 1789*, Paris, Société de l'Histoire de la Révolution, 1892, pp. lxvii–lxviii.

for enemies, and on this account we had to be on the alert all night. The staff officers, the *lieutenant du roi,* the regimental adjutant and I myself often argued with him, on the one hand to reassure him about the weakness of the garrison, of which he complained constantly, and on the other to induce him not to bother about insignificant details while neglecting important matters. He would listen to us, and seem to agree with our advice; then he would do just the reverse, then a minute later he would change his mind; in a word, his whole behaviour gave proof of the utmost irresolution. Although he had decided with his general staff and the officers of the garrison to defend the outer buildings as long as possible if they should be attacked, on the evening of July 12th he ordered us to withdraw within the fortress and to abandon the outer buildings, where the entire garrison had been stationed until then, and from which considerable resistance could be put up. We were forced to obey. We then found ourselves behind walls eighty foot high and fifteen foot thick, which inspired us with greater confidence than did the talents of the Governor."

What Deflue does not mention is the attitude of the pensioners [war veterans] and even of the Swiss soldiers [in the pay of the king]. The pensioners were most reluctant to fire on the people, and . . . on July 15th there [would be] 75 deserters from the Salis-Samade [Swiss] regiment. It needed a resolute leader to restore the morale of the soldiers, rather than this timorous governor.

As soon as the news of the disturbances of July 12th reached him, de Launey was seized with terror. His assistant, the *lieutenant du roi* du Puget, who was also commander of the nearby Arsenal, then asked for the powder in the Arsenal to be transferred to the Bastille. The 250 barrels, containing 30,000 pounds of powder, were taken thither during the night of July 12th–13th by Swiss soldiers, and placed under inadequate covering in the rear courtyard. Then, when the customs posts were seen to be ablaze on July 13th and on the morning of the 14th, the Swiss soldiers carried the heavy barrels down into the cellars; the Governor gave them each two louis by way of bonus for the job. However, "these soldiers were very tired by the morning of the 14th. They had not slept all the previous night. The crowd had begun to gather under the walls of the Bastille on the evening of the 13th; during the night several shots—seven, according to one report—were fired in the direction of the fortress. The alarm was sounded repeatedly, and on each occasion the garrison took up their posts on the towers and curtains [fortress walls]."

During the morning of the 14th, while the militia were demanding arms at the Hôtel de Ville, the inhabitants of the quartier Saint-Antoine conveyed to the Assembly of Electors their anxiety about the warlike preparations being made by the Governor of the Bastille. The guns that were pointing at them through the embrasures seemed to have an aggressive as well as a defensive significance. The electors, on whose behalf Ethis de Corny had gone to the Invalides (he had apparently not yet returned), decided to send a delegation to the Bastille. The delegates got there at about ten o'clock. De Launey received them in friendly fashion at his residence, the "Gouvernement," and as it was lunch time (for in France in those days *déjeuner* was eaten about half past ten, a tradition which was maintained until quite recently in barracks and monastic houses) he invited them to share his meal. There was apparently no question of distributing to the population the firearms and munitions stored in the Bastille, but the chief point at issue was the withdrawal of the guns that seemed levelled at the faubourg. The object of the demonstration began to change, and was to alter still further, for already people might be heard in the crowd talking about taking the Bastille. As [the politician and man of letters] Dusaulx wrote in his account: "The purpose of marching on the Bastille was solely to secure arms and munitions there. Little by little, more was ventured. The people . . . soon came and demanded from us the capture of this fortress . . ." [2] But the delegation did not go so far; it merely asked the governor to take such measures as might allay the people's fears. De Launey assured the delegates that he would do no harm to the quartier Saint-Antoine, and gave orders for the guns standing on the towers to be withdrawn and for the embrasures to be blocked with planks of wood.

During the time that this luncheon, and these talks, were going on—an hour to an hour and a half—the crowd had increased considerably and was thronging in the cour du Passage, in front of the porte de l'Avancée which, it will be remembered, gave access to the Governor's courtyard (cour du Gouverneur or du Gouvernement).

What did this crowd consist of? We can form some idea from the social structure of the group of 954 persons who, in June 1790, were awarded the title of *vainqueur de la Bastille*—the men who took the Bastille.[3] The professions of 661 of these are known. By far the greater number were artisans; in the first place, workers in the furniture industry from the faubourg Saint-Antoine, 49 joiners, 48 cabinet-makers, 41 locksmiths, 9 *tabletiers* (workers in ivory, inlay, etc.), 11 engravers, 28 odd-job men, more or less casually employed (though only four admitted to being *chômeurs,* out of work). Then we find 28 cobblers, 27 "carvers", 23 workers in gauze, 14 wine merchants, 9 jewellers, 9 hatters, 9 nailsmiths, 9 monumental masons, 9 tailors, 9 dyers; a total of 332. But there were also some bourgeois: 4 tradesmen, 3 industrialists, one brewer—the famous Santerre—35 various "merchants", 4 "bourgeois", that is to say *rentiers,* of independent means; 80 soldiers or officers; and the rest belonging to widely varying professions. Their ages range from 72 for the oldest—citizen Crétaine, a Parisian bourgeois—to 8 for the youngest, the boy Lavallée, who was one of the first up the towers. The index of professions is not enough to give an idea of the socio-economic group to which any one individual belongs. We should have to know his financial position. Such research, which is quite possible, would take a long time and has hitherto not been attempted. The 332 artisans include masters and journeymen, between whom it is impossible to distinguish. It may be said, however, if we add to the 332 artisans the 202 citizens of various professions, that five-sixths of the "conquerors"—and presumably of the crowd thronging beneath the walls of the Bastille—were artisans, masters or journeymen; the remaining sixth consisted of bourgeois.[4]

These demonstrators were undoubtedly all Parisians, the great majority of them (425 out of 602) from the faubourg Saint-Antoine, another fifty from the faubourg Saint-Marcel, and some more from the Halles. None of the "conquerors of the Bastille" lived further than two kilometres from the fortress. But most of them had

[2] Dusaulx, *De l'insurrection parisienne et de la prise de la Bastille*, Paris, 1790.

[3] G. Durieux, *Les Vainqueurs de la Bastille*, Paris, 1911.

[4] G. Rudé, "La composition sociale des insurrections parisiennes de 1789 à 1791", in the *Annales historiques de la Révolution française*, 1952, pp. 256–288.

only recently become Parisians; if we study the references to their birthplaces, we find that 345 of them came originally from the provinces. . . . The region of the Seine [suburbs of Paris] leads, naturally, with 244. But it is interesting to note that two other regions of France provided a quite considerable proportion of "conquerors"; the region between Paris and the northern frontier, where six departments (Seine-et-Oise, Nord, Oise, Aisne, Somme, Ardennes) provided more than ten each, and the eastern region, where the same is true of five departments (Côte-d'Or, Haute-Saône, Haute-Marne, Bas-Rhin, Moselle). This is easy to explain, the northern departments being affected by the proximity of Paris, the eastern ones by the relatively large number of soldiers and ex-soldiers who took part in the assault on the Bastille. Five other regions provided a somewhat smaller quota of insurgents (between 5 and 10 per department): the north-eastern region (Eure, Eure-et-Loir, Calvados, Orne and Sarthe), the east of the Parisian basin (Meuse, Marne, Aube and Yonne), the Jura (Doubs and Jura), the Lyonnais region (Rhône, Isère), the central and eastern parts of the Massif Central (Allier, Puy-de-Dôme, Cantal and Haute-Loire). Thus it is not really accurate to say, as does Albert Mathiez,[5] that the Fourteenth of July was a Parisian *journée* [insurrectionary day], while August 10th, 1792 involved the whole of France. True, on the latter occasion the *"fédérés"* [revolutionary volunteers] from Marseilles and Brest played an important part, but on July 14th at least half of the demonstrators were provincials who had only recently come to Paris. Moreover foreigners also took part in this *journée* and helped to give it an international character. Among the "conquerors of the Bastille" we find 13 Italians (six of them, however, being from Savoy, which was then subject to the King of Sardinia), 12 Germans, 12 Belgians, one Dutchman and one Swiss. Some of the men who captured the Bastille were already revolutionary veterans, having taken part either in the American Revolution or in that of Geneva. Citizen Crétaine had lost two sons in the American War of Independence, Pierre Delauzière had been through the campaigns of 1780–1783 in America, Second Lieutenant Elie . . . had served in Savannah as a sergeant under Admiral d'Estaing, François Folitot had fought in the same war as a corporal in the Cap regiment, Jean Founitillat as a sailor in d'Estaing's squadron, Abraham Pélerin as cabin-boy on a privateer which was captured by the English, and Jean-Georges Richard as marine gunner. Louis La Reynie, who played a notable part on the 12th, 13th, and 14th of July, had even been aide-de-camp to the American General Schuyler. Two "conquerors" had taken part in the Genevan revolution; the watchmaker Humbert, who was the first insurgent to climb up on to the towers of the Bastille, had had to leave Geneva after the defeat of the democrats in 1782; and the famous Hulin . . . had performed the functions of *adjudant-major de la place* in Geneva after its revolution. He had then had occasion to witness the results of the aristocratic reaction of which he had been an involuntary agent. He had subsequently, but in vain, tried to enlist in the Belgian army raised in revolt against Joseph II.

Of the men who were later to play a political role during the Revolution, very few were present. Stanislas Fréron, one of the most prominent members of the

---

[5] A. Mathiez, *Le dix août*, Paris, 1931, p. 43.

Convention during Thermidor, declared that he was one of the first to enter the Bastille, but no witness confirms his claim. When Camille Desmoulins and Danton arrived at the Bastille, the fortress had already fallen; Danton, who was captain of the militia in the Cordeliers district, was even appointed provisional commander of the Bastille after its fall. The marquis de la Salle, who had been appointed head of the citizens' militia by the electors on July 13th, was present at the siege and protected the prisoners.

Such was the social structure of the body of men who took the Bastille, and it probably reflects fairly closely the structure of the crowd that gathered towards noon under the towers of the fortress. We must doubtless assume the presence of a number of vagrants, homeless persons and former jailbirds, who would not be anxious to claim the title of "conqueror" because it might have brought them into contact with the police. . . .

What is the real meaning of the events that took place in Paris during that memorable week, July 11th to 17th, 1789? Those who, at the time, took an over-simple view of things—and there were many such, as there are today, in every social class and in every political party—interpreted these events as the result of a plot. The partisans of the monarchy denounced a conspiracy of freemasons or *philosophes,* or else of supporters of the duc d'Orléans. This idea found expression as early as 1789 and was later developed, particularly by the abbé Barruel.[6] The theory attracted many people, and still finds its adherents today. It is based on arguments which seem well-founded. Did not the Parisian uprising begin, on July 12th, in the Palais-Royal, property of the duc d'Orléans, Grand Master of French freemasons? Did it not conclude, on July 17th, with Louis XVI's forced passage up the staircase of the Hôtel de Ville, under the "Masonic" arch of steel [an arch of crossed swords, a Masonic symbol]? Everything would seem to have been contrived by the Freemasons, carrying out the ideas of the *philosophes.* But this theory ignores the fact that French masonic lodges at the end of the eighteenth century were composed of nobles, members of the clergy and of the upper bourgeoisie, and included none of those working class people who formed the overwhelming majority of the Parisian insurgents in July.[7]

Recognizing the truth of this objection, certain authors, at the end of the eighteenth century and later, reduced or eliminated the role of freemasonry and interpreted the rising of July 14th as a riot instigated by the duc d'Orléans. Strange stories were told, mysterious remarks reported which implied an invisible leader behind the Parisian insurrection. The Venetian envoy, Antonio Capello, wrote of the duc d'Orléans on July 6th: "His intentions are suspect, and his tolerance towards what takes place in his residence [*the Palais-Royal*] is condemned by all persons of good sense." He added that the orators who harangued the people in the

---

[6] Abbé Barruel, *Mémoires pour servir à l'histoire du Jacobinisme,* Hamburg, 1798, 5 vols., 8vo. But Barruel had expounded his thesis as early as 1789 in *Le Patriote véridique ou Discours sur les vraies causes de la Révolution actuelle.* See J. Godechot, *La Contre-révolution,* Paris, 1961, pp. 46–53.

[7] Alain Le Bihan, *Francs-maçons parisiens du Grand-Orient de France,* Commission d'Histoire économique et sociale de la Révolution française, *Mémoires et documents,* vol. XIX, Paris, 1966.

gardens of the Palais were "certainly in the pay of this unworthy man." Similarly the *bailli* de Virieu, Minister of Parma, asserted on July 13th: "It has been conjectured, not without good reason, that the disturbances have been provoked by a person of the highest rank. We blush to name him. He is a disgrace to the Nation and to the blood that flows in his veins. The vile creatures that serve as his tools were at first paid thirty sous a day, now they can be got for twenty." Later, in connection with the enquiry into the origin of the events of October 5th and 6th, when the King and Queen were brought back to Paris by force, three deputies to the National Assembly, Tailhardat de la Maisonneuve, Dufraisse (both from Riom) and Guilherny, of Castelnaudary, repeated a conversation they claimed to have heard between Malouet [deputy for Riom] and Coroller, deputy for Hennebont: "You would have achieved nothing," Malouet is supposed to have said, "without the defection of the *gardes-françaises* and the troops." "We were sure of the troops," Coroller replied, "we had had contacts in every regiment for a long time past." "Nonetheless you would certainly have failed, if the Court had not made the mistake of dismissing M. Necker." "That event only speeded up our achievement. We were assured of arming Paris, and to that end the Palais-Bourbon was to be set on fire." While according to another statement made during this enquiry, Mirabeau declared: "His [*the duc d'Orléans'*] timidity made him miss great opportunities; he was to have been made Lieutenant-general of the kingdom; it was entirely up to him, he had been told what to say." Mounier, who had emigrated to Geneva, declared in July 1790 that a "faction" existed which sought to give the throne to the duc d'Orléans. All these comments, which in fact refer to the events of October rather than to those of July, are unimportant.[8] Nevertheless there are still some people who are convinced of the considerable, and even essential, role played by the duc d'Orléans and his circle.[9] In actual fact the great objection to be made to the thesis of a Masonic or Orleanist plot is that the Parisian revolution was not an isolated phenomenon. It was only a link, although an important one, in the chain of revolutionary events that had been taking place in France since 1787 and that were to go on after July 14th. But for the revolt in the French provinces, from 1787 onwards, there would surely have been no Fourteenth of July, and but for the capture of the Bastille the peasant rising of July–August 1789 would probably not have taken place.

But supporters of the plot theory are not to be found only among the adversaries of the Revolution. Certain historians who are sympathetic towards it also seek to account for the Parisian rising by a conspiracy: the "nobles' plot," which was aimed at preventing the Revolution. The Parisian insurrection, according to this view, was an answer to this conspiracy. The idea of a "nobles' plot" had . . . been spreading throughout France since the middle of May, when the Estates-General had seemed smitten with paralysis. The closing of the salle des Menus-Plaisirs on June 20th, the Royal Session of June 23rd, the mustering of troops, particularly foreign troops, around Paris at the beginning of July, and finally the dismissal of Necker, had all given further plausibility to the theory. But can we believe that the Court, Marshal de Broglie, Besenval and the *intendant* of Paris, Bertier de

[8] They are quoted by J. Mistler, *Le 14 Juillet*, Paris, 1963, pp. 31–36.
[9] See particularly B. Faÿ, *La Grande Révolution*, Paris, 1959.

Sauvigny, had formed a plot to attack Paris and gain possession of the city by force? This was asserted by the Committee set up in August by the *commune* of Paris to investigate the "conspiracy of the preceding months of May, June and July." Their report even asserts that "at Versailles, people had seen the gridirons for heating the cannon-balls" which were to set the capital ablaze. In fact there never was a nobles' "plot" in the usual sense of the word. Louis XVI, the Queen, the princes and their entourage wanted to close down the Estates-General, by virtue of their traditional right, when they saw that this purely consultative assembly could no longer continue its sessions owing to disagreement between the three orders. But what had seemed legal in 1614 [the royal dissolution of the Estates-General] no longer appeared so in 1789. The Estates-General was by now considered not as a body representing "orders" but as an assembly of the deputies of the whole nation. Any attempt to interfere with its meetings seemed a plot against the Nation. But public opinion, which readily accepted this interpretation, could scarcely imagine that the King, the Princes and even the nobility would do so too. So that the victory of July 14th not only did not invalidate the idea of a plot, it even strengthened it. Since the King and the nobility had not been powerful enough to oppose the popular rising in July, they were assumed to have sought foreign allies to defeat the Revolution. The examples of the Genevan patricians in 1782, and of the stadholder of the Netherlands in 1787, justified this belief. We read in the *Mémoire des faits authentiques*:[10] "How did it happen that the finest monarchy in the world . . . was suddenly shaken and overthrown even to its foundations? . . . For . . . Louis XVI is now merely his people's plaything, a mere stage king . . . How is it that Spain and the other branches of the House of Bourbon, which in spite of their professed renunciation have an interest in preventing the dissolution of the French monarchy, and the Emperor [Joseph II], who must wish to avenge his sister's [Marie Antoinette] injuries, and the King of Sardinia, to protect the honour of his son-in-law [Comte d'Artois, brother of Louis XVI], have not all combined in a common cause and sent formidable armies against the rebels?" This was what many Frenchmen thought, and dreaded. The idea of an aristocratic plot, reinforced by a foreign plot, was to provoke many other popular movements in France during the revolutionary period, and to generate many risings. But there was in fact no plot, either aristocratic or Masonic, either foreign or Orleanist. The explanation of events by a conspiracy has always appealed to the masses because it seems a simple one. But things are always infinitely more complicated—particularly revolutions, which involve so many people and such diverse interests.

If the uprising of July 14th was not the result of a plot, if it was not the reaction to a plot, neither was it a violent riot by the Parisian population alone. . . . It takes its place in the context of an infinitely wider revolutionary movement. Under these conditions, can one wonder, as P. Chauvet has done,[11] if the Parisian proletariat, which provided the bulk of the rioters, failed to take advantage of the rising to seize power? Let us first point out that the term *proletariat* is ambiguous with reference to

---

[10] *Histoire authentique et suivie de la Révolution de France ou Correspondance avec un étranger*, 'Mémoire des faits authentiques concernant la Bastille', letter 1, September 29th, 1789.
[11] P. Chauvet, *L'Insurrection parisienne et la prise de la Bastille*, Paris, 1946.

1789. It is quite true, as we have seen, that some five-sixths of the insurgents consisted of artisans, workers who were independent but poor, if we are to judge by the analysis of the social structure of the "conquerors of the Bastille." It is moreover certain that the Permanent Committee and the Assembly of Electors endeavoured without delay, after July 14th, to keep power out of the hands of this class. On the 15th, the Assembly of Electors gave strict orders for the re-establishment of entry duties, under supervision by the Parisian militia. Thus it nullified what the Parisian workers had sought to achieve when they burnt down the customs posts. The Assembly, furthermore, took steps to disarm these workers. It offered to buy up all available muskets, hoping that this financial bait would induce the many *gens sans aveu* (vagabonds) who had got hold of firearms to hand these over. Thus, on July 18th, it "invited workers to resume their tasks, and fixed the price to be paid them for the arms they brought back, provided they could show a certificate from the master for whom they had resumed work." It cannot be doubted that the bourgeoisie lost no time in trying to appropriate the victory won by the workers of Paris. But could the latter have seized power themselves? True, the Réveillon riots on April 28th had looked like a revolt of the poor against the rich. But the Parisian "poor" were not organized. At that period one cannot speak of classes, nor of the class struggle. In 1793 the *sans-culottes,* who were to be for a time masters of Paris, did not form a social class, but a group that included both proletarians and independent artisans owning their own business, and this group had taken shape after 1791, particularly as a result of the formation of "sectional assemblies" and popular clubs.[12] Now in 1789 the "poor" of Paris had no class consciousness, whereas the bourgeois and the well-off artisans possessed the nucleus of an organization, thanks to the electoral assemblies of each district, from which the poor . . . were excluded, and the assemblies of second-degree electors, which met at the Hôtel de Ville. Moreover it must not be forgotten that in nations which had already achieved a degree of solid unity, as was the case with France by the end of the eighteenth century, national solidarity took precedence, on certain important occasions, over solidarity [within] "classes", orders or other social groups. This was the case on July 14th, 1789, as it was to be on other occasions, such as August 2nd, 1914.

The rising of July 14th was in fact a truly national rising. It was prepared by a gradual and deep-rooted movement of international character, which by its very amplitude precludes any notion of conspiracy.

The revolutionary movement, throughout the Western world, was the result of demographic and economic upheavals, of the rise of the bourgeoisie and the spread of "philosophic" ideas. It had made itself felt in North America, in England, the Netherlands and Switzerland before any signs of it were perceptible in France. It acquired its impetus, in France itself, from the Assembly of Notables; but the Parisian rising could not have taken place without the *journée des Tuiles* [insurrectionary Day of Tiles] at Grenoble on June 7th, 1788, or the affray at Pau, nor above all without the manifold riots which took place throughout almost the whole of France from January 1789 onwards, some of them provoked by the

---

[12] See A. Soboul, *Les Sans-culottes parisiens en l'an II*, Paris, 1958.

economic crisis and others arising from the elections to the Estates-General. One can surely not imagine that the troops which were brought into Paris caught the "revolutionary" spirit and tended to fraternize with the rioters after only a few days' stay in the capital. They acquired this attitude of "sympathy with the *Tiers État*" after weeks and months of contact with the leaders of the Third Estate in the provinces. The countless minor local risings, and the consequent division of the army into small detachments sent to suppress or prevent these, played a fundamental role in the victory of the Parisian insurrection. The institutions created in Paris as a result of the rising were not themselves original. Citizens' militias or *gardes bourgeoises* had been set up, as we have seen, in several provincial towns, notably Marseilles, Gaillac, Limoux and Orléans, before being introduced in Paris, and revolutionary authorities had seized municipal power in certain towns, such as Agde, Autun, La Ferté-Bernard, before doing so in the capital. The Parisian insurrection thus represents, as it were, the peak of the national insurrection. It was with good reason, therefore, that the three colours adopted as their badge by the Parisian insurgents on July 14th became the national emblem,[13] and that the anniversary of this rising was chosen for the day of national celebration. It was the national character of the rising of July 14th, 1789, which conferred on the fall of the Bastille prison an importance incomparably greater than that of other events of the sort, such as the attack on the Old Bailey in London on June 5th, 1780.

But if the Parisian rising of July 14th represents the peak of the national rising, it also marks a stage in it. Until July 14th the handful of revolutionary institutions set up in the provinces were disparate and isolated. Henceforward most of the towns and many of the villages of France were to imitate Paris with extraordinary swiftness. During the weeks that followed the fall of the Bastille there arose everywhere revolutionary Town Councils of permanent committees,[14] and citizen militias which soon assumed the name of national guards. But the dread of an aristocratic plot, which had been felt in Paris and which was already latent in many regions of France, soon spread, and finally took the form of an immense *grande peur,* a panic which brought the majority of the French peasantry out in arms by the end of July.[15] Once armed, these peasants attacked their lords' châteaux just as the Parisians had attacked the Bastille. They seized and burned the old charters on which feudal rights were inscribed. The people of Paris, by taking the Bastille, had destroyed the symbol of the feudal régime; the peasants, by attacking the châteaux and burning the seignorial papers, sought to destroy the feudal régime itself. And they succeeded, for the National Assembly realized that only the official abolition of this detested régime could re-establish order and peace in France. That is why, on the night of August 4th, it solemnly proclaimed the abolition of feudalism. Two

---

[13] [The national emblem, the tricolor, combines the colors of the city of Paris—red and blue—with the white of the Bourbons.—Eds.]

[14] See on this subject D. Ligou, "À propos de la révolution municipale," in the *Revue d'histoire économique et sociale,* 1960, pp. 146–177.

[15] G. Lefebvre, *La Grande Peur,* Paris, 1932 [translated as *The Great Fear of 1789* (New York: Random House, 1973)].

weeks later, when on August 26th it voted the *Déclaration des droits de l'homme et du citoyen* [Declaration of the Rights of Man and the Citizen], it laid the foundations for the new régime.

Thus the Parisian rising of July 14th, resulting from the provincial insurrectional movements which had begun the previous January, provoked in its turn a great national revolutionary impulse which irrevocably overthrew the *ancien régime* and gave France a new aspect. The Fourteenth of July is indeed one of the great days that made France.

2

The Character of the Constituent Assembly (1789-1791)

FROM 1789 to 1791, the National or Constituent Assembly began overhauling French institutions. Very few legislatures have ever attempted such a transformation in so short a period of time. It is not surprising, therefore, that there has been disagreement about the political ability of the Constituents and the wisdom of their reforms. Did these men act sensibly and moderately or were they impractical and fanatical? Were they moved by a humanitarian urge for national regeneration or by personal and class interests? Were their policies mostly blunders or long postponed necessities?

A classic attack on the deputies appeared during the Revolution itself. Watching from London, Edmund Burke was appalled by the destruction the assembly wrought to French traditions. To replace provinces by departments, to make the legislature almost omnipotent, to abolish the parlements, to issue new currency, and to seize Church lands—these were to Burke the most extravagant follies. Men are civilized by their religions, traditions, and prejudices; and to deride these or to seek to change them quickly for the sake of abstract ideals is to cause want and theft, anarchy and brutality. The Constituents were neophytes—incompetent and dangerous neophytes.

There could hardly be a greater contrast than that between Burke's inflammatory excoriation and Jacques Godechot's sober and carefully organized description of the most important reforms of the Constituent Assembly. Godechot judges many of them admirable; still he does not praise the deputies to the extent that Burke condemns them, for he thinks narrow bourgeois class interests too often determined their policies.

James M. Thompson also finds the bourgeoisie working for their own ends, but he stresses that we must lift our vision above this and see how the assembly benefited France as a whole: sometimes the deputies' bourgeois interests were identical with the needs of the great mass of the population; and sometimes they acted from motives having little to do with class.

Of the assembly's many reforms, perhaps no other caused more upheaval or had such far-reaching consequences than its attempt to reorganize the Gallican (French Catholic) Church. For this reason, we have included two contrasting views of the Civil Constitution of the Clergy. In his description of the conflict between the revolutionaries and the Church, the Catholic historian André Latreille believes that both sides erred, the Church perhaps less than the State. But he prefers to explain rather than to blame, and his account is quite moderate. It indicates how Church-State relations in mid-twentieth-century France have become much less acrimonious than at any time since 1789. The selection from Jean Jaurès also suggests the atmosphere in which it was written: the beginning of the twentieth century, when Jaurès and others were striving to weaken the political influence of the Catholic Church in France and to separate it from the State. Here one meets a vehement anticlerical defense of the assembly's religious policies—the deputies salvaged as much as possible from an inevitable conflict with a powerful, conservative, and outdated institution. They preserved the Revolution while weakening the Church, and they enlarged the people's intellectual freedom while diminishing their reliance on supernatural powers.

One may ask whether the assembly did have the moral or legal right to reform the Gallican Church. Did the Constituents blunder by not consulting Pope Pius VI and by requiring loyalty oaths from clergymen? On the other hand, was the pope so dilatory, inflexible, and unaware of French conditions that he himself precipitated the break? Was the Gallican Church so disunited and unsure of its way that it stumbled into a schism?

A word of caution must end this introduction. The points of view taken in the following five selections are closely entwined with their authors' political and religious beliefs. Is it possible to make an impartial and dispassionate historical judgment on the accomplishments and failures of the Constituent Assembly? Or is this one of those questions where a historian must inescapably be more advocate than social scientist?

Impractical Zealots

EDMUND BURKE

Edmund Burke (1729–1797), often styled the founder of modern conservatism, was born in Dublin. His father was a Protestant lawyer; his mother was a Catholic; and the boy was brought up as a Protestant. He trained for the law, but found his calling in English politics, where he became a spokesman for the aristocratic Whig magnates in the House of Commons. Unlike most politicians, Burke espoused a consistent political philosophy: the rule of an enlightened aristocracy against challenges from absolute monarchy and democracy. He was also a man of letters. His impassioned *Reflections on the Revolution in France,* published in November 1790 in the form of a letter to a Frenchman, was the most influential contemporary indictment of the Revolution.

You [Frenchmen] might, if you pleased, have profited of our example, and have given to your recovered freedom a correspondent dignity. Your privileges, though discontinued, were not lost to memory. Your [ancient] Constitution, it is true, whilst you were out of possession, suffered waste and dilapidation; but you possessed in some parts the walls, and in all the foundations, of a noble and venerable castle. You might have repaired those walls; you might have built on those old foundations. Your Constitution was suspended before it was perfected; but you had the elements of a Constitution very nearly as good as could be wished. In your old states you possessed that variety of parts corresponding with the various descriptions of which your community was happily composed; you had all that combination and all that opposition of interests, you had that action and counteraction, which, in the natural and in the political world, from the reciprocal struggle of discordant powers draws out the harmony of the universe. These opposed and conflicting interests, which

From Edmund Burke, *Reflections on the Revolution in France, Works* (4th ed.; Boston: Little, Brown, & Co., 1871), III, 276–278, 280, 282–284, 299–301, 331–332, 344–348, 524–525, 560–561.

you considered as so great a blemish in your old and in our present Constitution, interpose a salutary check to all precipitate resolutions. . . .

You had all these advantages in your ancient states; but you chose to act as if you had never been molded into civil society, and had everything to begin anew. You began ill, because you began by despising everything that belonged to you. You set up your trade without a capital. If the last generations of your country appeared without much luster in your eyes, you might have passed them by, and derived your claims from a more early race of ancestors. Under a pious predilection for those ancestors, your imaginations would have realized in them a standard of virtue and wisdom beyond the vulgar practice of the hour; and you would have risen with the example to whose imitation you aspired. Respecting your forefathers, you would have been taught to respect yourselves. You would not have chosen to consider the French as a people of yesterday, as a nation of low-born, servile wretches until the emancipating year of 1789. . . .

Compute your gains; see what is got by those extravagant and presumptuous speculations which have taught your leaders to despise all their predecessors, and all their contemporaries, and even to despise themselves, until the moment in which they became truly despicable. By following those false lights, France has bought undisguised calamities at a higher price than any nation has purchased the most unequivocal blessings. . . .

Laws overturned; tribunals subverted; industry without vigor; commerce expiring; the revenue unpaid, yet the people impoverished; a church pillaged, and a state not relieved; civil and military anarchy made the constitution of the kingdom; everything human and divine sacrificed to the idol of public credit, and national bankruptcy the consequence; and, to crown all, the paper securities of new, precarious, tottering power, the discredited paper securities of impoverished fraud and beggared rapine, held out as a currency for the support of an empire, in lieu of the two great recognized species [gold and silver] that represent the lasting, conventional credit of mankind, which disappeared and hid themselves in the earth from whence they came, when the principle of property, whose creatures and representatives they are, was systematically subverted.

Were all these dreadful things necessary? Were they the inevitable results of the desperate struggle of determined patriots, compelled to wade through blood and tumult to the quiet shore of a tranquil and prosperous liberty? No! nothing like it. The fresh ruins of France, which shock our feelings wherever we can turn our eyes, are not the devastation of civil war: they are the sad, but instructive monuments of rash and ignorant counsel in time of profound peace. They are the display of inconsiderate and presumptuous, because unresisted and irresistible authority. . . .

This unforced choice, this fond election of evil, would appear perfectly unaccountable, if we did not consider the composition of the National Assembly: I do not mean its formal constitution, which, as it now stands, is exceptionable enough, but the materials of which in a great measure it is composed, which is of ten thousand times greater consequence than all the formalities in the world. If we were to know nothing of this assembly but by its title and function, no colors could paint to the imagination anything more venerable. In that light, the mind of an inquirer, subdued by such an awful image as that of the virtue and wisdom of a whole people collected into one focus, would pause and hesitate in condemning things even of the very worst aspect. Instead of blamable, they would appear only mysterious. But no name, no power, no function, no artificial institution whatsoever, can make the men, of whom any system of authority is composed, any other than God, and Nature, and education, and their habits of life have made them. Capacities beyond these the people have not to give. Virtue and wisdom may be the objects of their choice; but their choice confers neither the one nor the other on those upon whom they lay their ordaining hands. They have not the engagement of Nature, they have not the promise of Revelation for any such powers.

After I had read over the list of the persons and descriptions elected into the *Tiers État*, nothing which they afterwards did could appear astonishing. Among them, indeed, I saw some of known rank, some of shining talents; but of any practical experience in the state not one man was to be found. The best were only men of theory. But whatever the distinguished few may have been, it is the substance and mass of the body which constitutes its character, and must finally determine its direction. . . .

It is said that twenty-four millions ought to prevail over two hundred thousand. True; if the constitution of a kingdom be a problem of arithmetic. This sort of discourse does well enough with the lamp-post for its second: to men who *may* reason calmly it is ridiculous. The will of the many, and their interest, must very often differ; and great will be the difference when they make an evil choice. A government of five hundred country attorneys and obscure curates is not good for twenty-four millions of men, though it were chosen by eight-and-forty millions; nor is it the better for being guided by a dozen of persons of quality who have betrayed their trust in order to obtain that power. At present, you seem in everything to have strayed out of the high road of Nature. The property of France does not govern it. Of course property is destroyed, and rational liberty has no existence. All you have got for the present is a paper circulation, and a stock-jobbing constitution: and as to the future, do you seriously think that the territory of France, upon the republican system of eighty-three independent municipalities (to say nothing of the parts that compose them), can ever be governed as one body, or can ever be set in motion, by the impulse of one mind? When the National Assembly has completed its work, it will have accomplished its ruin. These commonwealths will not long bear a state of subjection to the republic of Paris. They will not bear that this one body should monopolize the captivity of the king, and the dominion over the assembly calling itself national. Each will keep its own portion of the spoil of the Church to itself; and it will not suffer either that spoil, or the more just fruits of their industry, or the natural produce of their soil, to be sent to swell the insolence or pamper the luxury of the mechanics of Paris. In this they will see none of the equality, under the pretence of which they have been tempted to throw off their allegiance to their sovereign, as well as the ancient constitution of their country. There can be no capital city in such a constitution as they have lately made. They have forgot, that, when they framed democratic governments, they had virtually dismembered their country. The person whom they persevere in calling king has not power left to him by the hundredth part sufficient to hold together this collection of republics. The republic of Paris will endeavor, indeed, to complete the debauchery of the army, and illegally to perpetuate the Assembly, without resort to its constituents, as the means of continuing its despotism. It will make efforts, by becoming the heart of a boundless paper circulation, to draw everything to itself: but in vain. All this policy in the end will appear as feeble as it is now violent. . . .

It is now sixteen or seventeen years since I saw the queen of France, then the Dauphiness, at Versailles; and surely never lighted on this orb, which she hardly seemed to touch, a more delightful vision. I saw her just above the horizon, decorating and cheering the elevated sphere she just began to move in—glittering like the morning-star, full of life and splendor and joy. Oh! what a revolution! and what a heart must I have, to contemplate without emotion that elevation and that fall! Little did I dream, when she added titles of veneration to those of enthusiastic, distant, respectful love, that she should ever be obliged to carry the sharp antidote against disgrace concealed in that bosom! Little did I dream that I should have lived to see such disasters fallen upon her in a nation of gallant men, in a nation of men of honor, and of cavaliers! I thought ten thousand swords must have leaped from their scabbards to avenge even a look that threatened her with insult. But the age of chivalry is gone. That of sophisters, economists, and calculators has succeeded; and the glory of Europe is extinguished forever. Never, never more, shall we behold that generous loyalty to rank and sex, that proud submission, that dignified obedience, that subordination of the heart, which kept alive, even in servitude itself, the spirit of an exalted freedom! The unbought grace of life, the cheap defense of nations, the nurse of manly sentiment and heroic enterprise, is gone! It is gone, that sensibility of principle, that chastity of honor, which felt a stain like a wound, which inspired courage whilst it mitigated ferocity, which ennobled whatever it touched, and under which vice itself lost half its evil by losing all its grossness! [1] . . .

Thanks to our sullen [English] resistance to innovation, thanks to the cold sluggishness of our national character, we still bear the stamp of our forefathers. We have not (as I conceive) lost the generosity and dignity of thinking of the fourteenth century; nor as yet have we subtilized ourselves into savages. We are not the converts of Rousseau; we are not the disciples of Voltaire; Helvétius has made no progress amongst us. Atheists are not our preachers; madmen are not our lawgivers. We know that *we* have made no discoveries, and we think that no discoveries are to be made, in morality—nor many in the great principles of government, nor in the ideas of liberty, which were understood long before we were born altogether as well as they will be after the grave has heaped its mold upon our presumption, and the silent tomb shall have imposed its law on our pert loquacity. In England we have not yet been completely emboweled of our natural entrails: we still feel within us, and we cherish and cultivate, those inbred sentiments which are the faithful guardians, the active monitors of our duty, the true supporters of all liberal and manly morals. We have not been drawn and trussed, in order that we may be filled, like stuffed birds in a museum, with chaff and rags, and paltry, blurred shreds of paper about the rights of man. We preserve the whole of our feelings still native and entire, unsophisticated by pedantry and infidelity. We have real hearts of flesh and

---

[1] [This particular paragraph of Burke's has been called a landmark in the beginning of English literary romanticism.—Eds.]

blood beating in our bosoms. We fear God; we look up with awe to kings, with affection to Parliaments, with duty to magistrates, with reverence to priests, and with respect to nobility. Why? Because, when such ideas are brought before our minds, it is *natural* to be so affected; because all other feelings are false and spurious, and tend to corrupt our minds, to vitiate our primary morals, to render us unfit for rational liberty, and, by teaching us a servile, licentious, and abandoned insolence, to be our low sport for a few holidays, to make us perfectly fit for and justly deserving of slavery through the whole course of our lives.

You see, Sir, that in this enlightened age I am bold enough to confess that we are generally men of untaught feelings: that, instead of casting away all our old prejudices, we cherish them to a very considerable degree; and, to take more shame to ourselves, we cherish them because they are prejudices; and the longer they have lasted, and the more generally they have prevailed, the more we cherish them. We are afraid to put men to live and trade each on his own private stock of reason; because we suspect that the stock in each man is small, and that the individuals would do better to avail themselves of the general bank and capital of nations and of ages. Many of our men of speculation, instead of exploding general prejudices, employ their sagacity to discover the latent wisdom which prevails in them. If they find what they seek (and they seldom fail), they think it more wise to continue the prejudice, with the reason involved, than to cast away the coat of prejudice, and to leave nothing but the naked reason; because prejudice, with its reason, has a motive to give action to that reason, and an affection which will give it permanence. Prejudice is of ready application in the emergency; it previously engages the mind in a steady course of wisdom and virtue, and does not leave the man hesitating in the moment of decision, skeptical, puzzled, and unresolved. Prejudice renders a man's virtue his habit, and not a series of unconnected acts. Through just prejudice, his duty becomes a part of his nature.

Your literary men, and your politicians, and so do the whole clan of the enlightened among us [the English supporters of the French Revolution], essentially differ in these points. They have no respect for the wisdom of others; but they pay it off by a very full measure of confidence in their own. With them it is a sufficient motive to destroy an old scheme of things, because it is an old one. As to the new, they are in no sort of fear with regard to the duration of a building run up in haste; because duration is no object to those who think little or nothing has been done before their time, and who place all their hopes in discovery. They conceive, very systematically, that all things which give perpetuity are mischievous, and therefore they are at inexpiable war with all establishments. They think that government may vary like modes of dress, and with as little ill effect; that there needs no principle of attachment, except a sense of present conveniency, to any constitution of the state. They always speak as if they were of opinion that there is a singular species of compact between them and their magistrates [government officials], which binds the magistrate, but which has nothing reciprocal in it, but that the majesty of the people has a right to dissolve it without any reason but its will. Their attachment to their country itself is only so far as it agrees with some of their fleeting projects: it begins and ends with that scheme of polity which falls in with their momentary opinion.

These doctrines, or rather sentiments, seem prevalent with your new statesmen. . . .

It is besides to be considered, whether an Assembly like yours . . . is fit for promoting the obedience and discipline of an army. It is known that armies have hitherto yielded a very precarious and uncertain obedience to any senate or popular authority: and they will least of all yield it to an Assembly which is to have only a continuance of two years. The officers must totally lose the characteristic disposition of military men, if they see with perfect submission and due admiration the dominion of pleaders—especially when they find that they have a new court to pay to an endless succession of those pleaders, whose military policy, and the genius of whose command (if they should have any), must be as uncertain as their duration is transient. In the weakness of one kind of authority, and in the fluctuation of all, the officers of an army will remain for some time mutinous and full of faction, until some popular general, who understands the art of conciliating the soldiery, and who possesses the true spirit of command, shall draw the eyes of all men upon himself. Armies will obey him on his personal account. There is no other way of securing military obedience in this state of things. But the moment in which that event shall happen, the person who really commands the army is your master—the master (that is little) of your king, the master of your Assembly, the master of your whole republic. . . .

But am I so unreasonable as to see nothing at all that deserves commendation in the indefatigable labors of this Assembly? I do not deny, that, among an infinite number of acts of violence and folly, some good may have been done. They who destroy everything certainly will remove some grievance. They who make everything new have a chance that they may establish something beneficial. To give them credit for what they have done in virtue of the authority they have usurped, or to excuse them in the crimes by which that authority has been acquired, it must appear that the same things could not have been accomplished without producing such a revolution. Most assuredly they might; because almost every one of the regulations made by them, which is not very equivocal, was either in the cession of the king, voluntarily made at the meeting of the Estates-General, or in the concurrent instructions to the orders. Some usages have been abolished on just grounds; but they were such, that, if they had stood as they were to all eternity, they would little detract from the happiness and prosperity of any state. The improvements of the National Assembly are superficial, their errors fundamental.

Bourgeois Reformers

JACQUES GODECHOT

For biographical information on Jacques Godechot, see Chapter 1, "The Outbreak of the Revolution (1787–1789)."

The essential goal of the National Constituent Assembly was to construct a new regime which would guarantee to the bourgeoisie the peaceful exercise of power and eliminate the possibility of either a return to absolute monarchy, or rule of the aristocracy, or rule of the mass of the people. They envisioned this regime as a constitutional monarchy established upon the rational basis proclaimed in the Declaration of the Rights of Man and the Citizen.

The assembly proceeded to destroy the institutions of the old regime as soon as new institutions had been created to take their place. But not all of the old institutions were destroyed; some were continued either in their old forms or somewhat modified. The Constituent Assembly therefore did not build the new France from scratch; yet the Constituents never felt the least compunction about preserving the past and never hesitated to destroy inherited institutions.

The achievement of the Constituent Assembly has many aspects. Its political work, which its members unquestionably considered to be their most important accomplishment, was the least enduring, for it collapsed after two years. Its social, economic, and administrative achievements, on the other hand, left much deeper traces, which still persist in the structure of present-day France. We shall begin our analysis by examining these essential aspects of the work of the Constituent Assembly.

Social Achievements

The society of the old regime was built upon hierarchy and privilege, which is to say upon inequality. Contrariwise, in its first article the Declaration of the Rights of

From Jacques Godechot, *France and the Atlantic Revolution of the Eighteenth Century, 1770–1799*, trans. Herbert H. Rowen (New York: The Free Press, 1965), pp. 101–117. Reprinted with permission of Macmillan Publishing Co., Inc. from *France and the Atlantic Revolution of the Eighteenth Century, 1770–1799* by Jacques Godechot. Copyright © by The Free Press, a Division of The Macmillan Company.

Man proclaimed equality before law. The Constituent Assembly attempted to create institutions to put this principle of equality into practice. Because it attempted to reserve the reality of power for the bourgeoisie, the assembly met major difficulties in this endeavor and was not wholly successful.

Although on August 4, 1789, the Constituent Assembly abolished personal servitude (there were still 1.5 million serfs in France) and the three orders into which Frenchmen had been divided, although it granted civil rights to foreigners and actors, a proposal to give equality to Jews aroused very sharp debate and was only enacted by the assembly on September 27, 1791, three days before its final adjournment. Equality also presupposed the removal of all discrimination between Negroes and whites as well as the abolition of slavery. This was the logical consequence of the first article of the Declaration of Rights. But the French colonists, represented in the assembly by such influential deputies as the Lameths and Barnave, did not even accept civil equality between whites and free "colored men." After some hesitation the assembly finally accepted the position of the colonists. They did so in order to avoid the revolt which was forecast, it was explained. In fact the assembly thereby prepared a later explosion in the colonies which brought far greater harm to the planters than honest application of the principles of 1789 would have done.

The most important immediate consequence of the principle of equal rights was the opportunity for all Frenchmen to be appointed to any position in the state. The nobility thereby lost their monopoly of the higher offices. Actually only the bourgeoisie benefited from this change, for only they possessed the education necessary to hold these posts or the wealth necessary to acquire such education. In the army, however, where courage could still take the place of learning and sons of peasants and artisans could rise to the summit of the revolutionary hierarchy as a result of circumstances (the emigration of noble officers and the long wars of the revolutionary period), it could now be truly said that "every soldier carried a marshal's baton in his knapsack." All in all, upward social mobility became more rapid and more frequent than before the revolution.

Even more important in its consequences, however, was the abolition of the feudal system, adopted amid enthusiasm by the National Assembly during the night of August 4, although under the pressure of the peasant uprising. During the days that followed, the owners of manors strove to limit their concessions as much as possible. The decrees applying the decisions of principle taken on August 4 were only adopted on March 15, 1790, and the peasants found them unsatisfactory. The new decrees drew a distinction between the rights of feudal (manorial) overlordship, which the assembly presumed to have been usurped, and rights of "feudal contract," which it assumed derived from contracts made between the landlords and the peasant tenants. The rights of overlordship included honorific and personal obligations, which were abolished without payment. The tithe, which had been a very heavy burden for the peasants, was also abolished without compensation; but the landowners were the principal beneficiaries of this measure, for they ceased to transmit the tithes to the church although they continued to collect them from their tenants and sharecroppers.

On the other hand, most of the manorial dues, or "real rights," were not actually abolished outright but had to be bought back by the peasants at prices they found difficult to pay. Repurchases were to be made by individuals, not the state or communities, and no system of credit was provided to make the repayments easier to meet. Until the dues were completely repurchased, they still had to be paid, together with the arrears for thirty years. It was obvious that if this law were enforced the feudal system would last for many long years. The discontented peasants rose in rebellion again in many regions. It was only later, in 1792 and 1793, after the fall of the monarchy, that the Legislative Assembly and the Convention which followed it gave satisfaction to the peasants by abolishing all dues of "feudal character" without any compensation. Thereafter no servitudes on either person or land existed within the continental territory of France. The right of property became absolute, in the Roman sense of the term, and the transfer of land was vastly facilitated.

Economic Achievements

Circumstances rather than theories led the Constituent Assembly to make important reforms in the field of economics and finances. The Estates General had been summoned essentially in order to solve the financial crisis. Even before May 1789 many financiers considered that the best way of meeting the governmental deficit would be to sell the property of the clergy for the benefit of the state, which in return would be responsible for payment of the salaries of churchmen and the costs of religious activity.

Abolition of the tithes on August 4 proved that the assembly would not hesitate to follow this path. On August 6 the first proposal to put the property of the clergy at the disposal of the nation was presented from the rostrum. Discussion was long and sharp. Mirabeau and Talleyrand clearly posed the terms of the problem: The wealth of the clergy would be placed at the disposal of the nation in order to pay off the debt of the state; in return the government would provide for the costs of religious worship and pay the salaries of clergymen, although without maintaining the scandalous gap between the incomes of parish priests and bishops. Some deputies argued that it was necessary to take the clergy's wealth in order to remove its status as an estate. At last the wealth of the clergy was nationalized on November 2. The properties appropriated from the churchmen were to be employed to back the assignats, a form of paper money, with which the state would pay its indebtedness. Assignats could be used for the purchase of "national property," as the former ecclesiastical holdings were designated. Assignats so used were to be returned to the treasury and burned.

This decision had a considerable influence upon the history of the French revolution. It resulted in inflation and the devaluation of the assignat, and hence in a rise in prices and a higher cost of living; another consequence was a massive transfer of property, which passed from the hands of the clergy to the ownership of the bourgeoisie and prosperous peasantry.

The sale of "national properties" began in May 1790. Credit facilities were granted to purchasers; they had to pay only 12 to 30 percent of the purchase price in cash, depending on the kind of property; the balance could be paid over twelve years at 5 percent interest. The assembly hoped to assist the peasants by these arrangements. Only a small sum was necessary as a down payment for purchase of "national property," but the landless day laborers had used what little money they had to buy bread at very high prices during the spring of 1789, and many small landowners reserved their savings for the repurchase of feudal dues. Furthermore, although some lots were small and inexpensive, many were vast and the minimum acceptable price was very high. Sales were held at auction and bids on part lots were permitted only if their combined figure was higher than the highest bid offered for the same land as a single lot. The sales were very successful at first, but as we have said, it was especially the bourgeois and the prosperous peasants who profited. Nobles and parish priests were also among the buyers. Poor peasants could make purchases only by forming groups. The distribution of landed property in France was profoundly changed, but to the profit of the prosperous classes. The number of landless day laborers did not decline significantly.

The assignats were put to use at once to pay the government's debt. But the obligations inherited from the old regime were soon swollen by new indebtedness when the Constituent Assembly decided to abolish the former "venal" offices with compensation to the owners. New issues of assignats appeared in rapid succession. But Frenchmen did not accept them without suspicion; they had unhappy memories of the collapse of the paper money issued by Law's bank between 1716 and 1720. By 1791 devaluation of the assignats began. Devaluation would probably have been limited, and to some extent even beneficial (for it was at first a stimulant to the economy), if the financial situation had not forced the treasury to have recourse to new and bigger issues. The fact was that taxes were no longer being collected and the treasury was empty. Instead of being used for reimbursement of the state debt—the purpose for which they had been established—assignats began to be used for payment of current expenses. Inflation and devaluation continued at an accelerating rate. In 1792 the assignat dropped a third in value; when the decline became even more rapid, a grave monetary crisis resulted which did not terminate until 1797, with withdrawal of the assignats and a partial bankruptcy.

The Constituent Assembly did not foresee these difficulties and methodically pursued its economic activities. However, its members were divided on economic policy, and their divisions reflected the actual economic life of the nation. In one camp were the big merchants, the big industrialists, and all who advocated complete freedom of industry and trade, which assured the omnipotence of the employer over his workers and staff; in the other camp were those who were attached to the traditional forms of handicraft production and desired to preserve guild organizations and production regulations, most of which were not in accordance with the principle of economic freedom.

Abolition of feudalism contributed greatly to the emancipation of the land, as we have seen. But there also existed servitudes on the soil—rights of usage, the stubble right, collective communal property—which were not of feudal origin and were not immediately abolished. After long debate the supporters of economic freedom won a partial victory. The freedom for any man to enclose his lands and to till them as he pleased was proclaimed, but the stubble right was abolished only in artificial meadows;[1] a law introducing division of communal lands, to which the assembly was favorable, was drawn up but no decision was taken on it. In practice, landowning farmers found these reforms to their advantage, but day laborers were very strongly opposed to abolition of the common lands and the stubble right, which enabled them to keep a few goats or sheep. Furthermore, the right of enclosure could be exercised only with great difficulty, for in many parts of France the multiplicity of small holdings in the "open fields" made enclosure a practical impossibility. Despite these difficulties, the agrarian reforms of the Constituent Assembly were continued by the Legislative Assembly and the Convention. These reforms resulted in reduction of the average size of holdings and an increase in the number of landowners, and greatly strengthened the individualism of the peasantry.

In the areas of trade and industrial production, the Constituent Assembly was even more deeply divided. It did not even begin discussion of these matters until February 1791. Opponents endeavored to prove that the guilds enjoyed exclusive privileges and therefore should be abolished on the basis of the decisions of August 4. Abolition of the guilds was finally voted, but the Constituent Assembly also adopted the proposal of deputy Le Chapelier to maintain in force the old police ordinances which forbade workers to associate in journeymen's leagues (*compagnon-nages*), to form "coalitions" (unions), or to strike. The Le Chapelier law was voted under the pretext of maintaining freedom of labor, but it was in accordance with the ideas of the economists and the interests of the capitalist bourgeoisie. It passed almost without debate; not only was there no representative of the workers in the Constituent Assembly, but it must be added that the problem of labor did not arise in 1791 in the same terms as it did fifty years later, for the Industrial Revolution had hardly begun in France. Still it is true that in the Le Chapelier law the interests of employers won out under the pretext of economic liberalism. It was only repealed in the second half of the nineteenth century, by the law of 1864 which permitted strikes and the law of 1884 which legalized trade unions.

It was also on the basis of the principles of freedom and freehold property that the Constituent Assembly repealed the law on mines of 1744, which had required prior authorization from the government to use the subsoil for mining and thus limited the rights of the owner of the land. The Constituent Assembly returned full ownership of the subsoil to the owner of the land, but thereby disorganized operation of the mines and generated interminable lawsuits.

As for trade, the Constituent Assembly applied the principle of the economists [physiocrats], *laissez faire, laissez passer*,[2] at least as far as trade within the territory of continental France was concerned. All tolls and customs dues on imports and exports collected at the frontiers, within the country, and at city gates—and in general the majority of indirect taxes—were abolished. Government revenues were to come essentially from three direct "contributions"—the land contribution [tax], the personal property tax, and licenses on businesses and trades. Jurisdiction over

---

[1] [Stubble right is the right of peasants to graze livestock on crop land after the harvest; artificial meadows are meadows that are cultivated rather than allowed to grow wild.—Eds.]

[2] Loosely, "do not interfere or penalize" or "hands off."—*Trans.*

fairs and markets was reduced to the most elementary police regulations; all price-fixing was abolished. This measure encouraged an increase in prices and caused discontent among the poor, who feared famine. New disorders caused by the free movement of grain occurred in different parts of France.

Complete freedom of trade was to be favored by a system of uniform weights and measures, which was approved in principle. Freedom of trade led to development of banks, financial companies, and in general all forms of credit. Trade in securities was made nearly free. The profession of bond and mercantile brokerage was opened to all without restriction.

The Constituent Assembly showed itself to be less liberal with regard to foreign trade. In this area the interests of the big merchants no longer coincided with the principle of free trade. To be sure, the assembly abolished the privileges and exemptions which some ports such as Lorient and Marseilles enjoyed, and it suppressed the monopolist trading companies like the India Company. But it maintained a protectionist tariff and indicated its opposition to the trade treaties with the United States (1778) and England (1786), which had lowered tariff rates.

Colonial trade remained strictly regulated. Despite the violent protests of the deputies from the colonies, who desired freedom to trade as they pleased, the system of "Exclusion," permitting the colonies to trade only with the mother country, was maintained. On the other hand, perhaps in compensation, the Constituent Assembly established colonial assemblies with sole authority to legislate regarding persons and property in the colonies; these assemblies maintained the inequality between whites and "colored people," the slave trade, and slavery.

Most of the economic reforms of the Constituent Assembly endured. They continued to be in force long into the nineteenth century, some surviving even to our own day.

Administrative Achievements

The administrative achievements of the Constituent Assembly were also very enduring. They were indispensable reforms demanded by a majority of Frenchmen, for the complexity and incoherence of the monarchical administration scandalized eighteenth-century men infatuated with rationalism. A large number of the cahiers demanded a thorough administrative reform, such as had been in preparation for some years. The monarchical administration itself had desired to substitute a sensible organization of the national territory for the hodgepodge of "provinces," "bailiwicks" and "seneschalsies," civil and ecclesiastical "dioceses," "estate lands" and "election lands," "military governments" and "commanderships-in-chief," and unequal and illogical judicial districts.

In 1787, in connection with the establishment of provincial assemblies, the royal government had also conceived a plan for special districts for the allocation (in old French, *département*) of taxes. In 1789 the geographer Letrosne proposed an administrative division of France suggested by the federal system of the new United States of America; his plan called for 25 generalities, 250 districts, 4,500 wards, all approximately equal in shape. In approving the design of the project as a whole,

Condorcet felt that it would be necessary to "reconcile changes with local convenience." Mirabeau declared: "I should want a division based upon geography and facts and adapted to the localities and circumstances, not at all a mathematical division, which is almost perfect in theory but in my opinion, would be almost impossible to put into practice. I should want a division intended not only to establish proportional representation but also to bring the administration of men and things closer together and to permit greater participation of the citizenry in the work of government. Last, I propose a division which will not seem—shall we say?—too novel; a division which will permit—if I may be so bold as to use the terms—a compromise with prejudices and even with errors, and will be desired equally by all provinces and be founded upon familiar relationships." The Constituent Assembly accepted Mirabeau's ideas.

Reorganization was facilitated by the abolition of provincial and communal privileges during the night of August 4. The Constituent Assembly divided France into eighty-three "departments," but decided that the "former boundaries of provinces should be respected whenever there is neither real advantage nor absolute necessity for discarding them." Britanny was given five departments, Provence three, but the two small provinces of Aunis and Saintonge were combined to form a single department. The departments were given the names of their most characteristic geographical features, which they still retain. An effort was made to set the boundaries so that the capital of each department would be no more than a day's travel from its most distant point.

The departments were divided into up to nine districts. It was intended that residents would be able to make the round trip from their homes to the capital of the district in a single day. Each district comprised a number of cantons. The primary unit remained the parish, which dated from the early Middle Ages; it was now called the "commune."

Each of these divisions was to be administered by representatives of taxpayers, chosen directly in the commune and by two-stage elections in the district and the department. Councils at the head of the commune, the district, and the department were divided into two sections; one—a directory in the department and the district, a mayor and municipal officers in the commune—was given the executive power, and the other—a general council in the department, the district, and the commune—was deliberative. The king was represented by a procurator syndic, who was elected, not appointed. This was the most complete administrative decentralization which France has ever known. Each department was like a little autonomous republic. If the departments fell into the hands of opponents, the revolution would be in jeopardy. Not surprisingly, centralization had to be reestablished in 1793.

These new divisions had to be provided with courts, all alike and with perfectly defined jurisdictions. The capital of the canton received a "justice of the peace," in imitation of Holland and England. He was more an arbitrator than a judge; his task was to avoid trials rather than to suggest them. Assisted by two other citizens, he presided over the police court of the canton, which had the duty of punishing minor crimes. In each district capital there was a civil court, and in the departmental capital a criminal court. All judges were elected from the ranks of graduate lawyers and were paid by the state. In criminal cases it was the citizens themselves who decided upon indictments and guilt. A jury for accusations was composed of eight citizens drawn by lot from one list, and a trial jury of twelve citizens was likewise chosen by lot but from a different list. The judges, brought in from the district tribunals, merely fixed sentences. All courts were to judge according to uniform codes. The Constituent Assembly began drafting these codes but was able to complete only the penal code. Inspired by the humane ideas of Beccaria,[3] it abolished torture and barbarous punishments and increased safeguards for the accused. Nonetheless, despite a speech by Robespierre, the death penalty was maintained. Appeals in civil cases went from one district tribunal to another; the Constituent Assembly, not wishing to revive the former parlements, did not create appellate courts. It did establish national tribunals: the Court of Invalidation (*tribunal de cassation*), composed of one elected judge from each department, which had the duty of examining not the substance of cases but only their form; and a High Court which would meet in exceptional cases to try crimes by ministers and high officials as well as crimes against the security of the state. This judicial system was logical, coherent, and humane. It made justice totally independent of the king but, as a consequence of the system of property qualifications for the ballot, it placed justice in the hands of the bourgeoisie. Incontestably one of the most successful reforms, it was the work of an assembly more than half of whose members were lawyers.

In military matters the Constituent Assembly was much more hesitant. The assembly legalized the militia bands which had been formed spontaneously in July and August 1789 by making them a "National Guard." In the minds of the members of the Constituent Assembly as well as of the guardsmen themselves, they were not an army but a force whose sole function was to maintain order within the country and to safeguard the "conquests of the revolution." Despite the appeal of Deputy Dubois-Crancé in favor of universal military service, obligatory and equal for all, the Constituent Assembly retained the professional army, although promotion to even the highest ranks was opened to all soldiers. Nonetheless, the royal army soon began to disintegrate when its aristocratic officers went abroad in emigration. Often the soldiers rebelled against commanders who were hostile to the revolution. The Constituent Assembly became more and more inclined to call upon the National Guard to defend the country and the revolution. After June 1791 it ordered the formation of battalions of volunteers selected from the National Guard; an army of citizen-soldiers wearing blue uniforms, with white jackets and red braid, took shape at the side of the old royal army, which wore white uniforms. The navy was also reorganized, and all naval ranks were opened to every citizen, especially merchant marine officers.

Political Achievements

The fundamental objective of the members of the Constituent Assembly, as we have seen, was to establish a constitutional monarchy, which they hoped would last as

---

[3] [Cesare Beccaria, a jurist from Milan, was the author of *On Crimes and Punishments* (1764).—Eds.]

long as the ten-centuries-old absolute monarchy. In this endeavor they met almost total failure. The constitutional monarchy organized by the National Constituent Assembly lasted less than a year. Its fragility was a result of the fears of a majority of the deputies, who dreaded both giving the king too much power and entrusting the people with too much authority. The regime which they created therefore lacked strength and soon collapsed.

The Constituent Assembly began by transgressing one of the fundamental principles which it had proclaimed in the Declaration of Rights—equality. At Sieyès's suggestion, it introduced a subtle distinction among French citizens. Only the more prosperous, the "active citizens" (about two-thirds of the total), participated in political life. The remainder, called "passive citizens," enjoyed only civil rights. To be an active citizen one had to pay direct taxes equal to three days' wages. Because of the unequal distribution of taxes, the percentage of active citizens varied very widely; and they were proportionally much more numerous in the countryside than in the towns. The large majority of peasants who owned at least their cottages was included among the active citizens, while artisan journeymen who lived in rented rooms remained passive citizens. It must be noted, however, that the active citizens directly elected only the municipal councils. The Legislative Assembly, the general councils of the departments and the districts, and the judges were named at the second stage by electors who had to be chosen from among the 50,000 wealthiest Frenchmen, who owned or enjoyed the income from property worth from 150 to 400 days' work, depending on the locality.[4]

The Legislative Assembly was elected for two years. It received important powers: the initiative and the passage of laws, the voting of a budget which was not subject to the royal veto, the decision on war and peace, the right to address the people by proclamations. Still the king retained many elements of strength. Although he was no longer "king of France by the grace of God" but merely "king of the French," his person remained "inviolable and sacred." The succession to the throne was still governed by the Salic Law, that is, it was hereditary in the male line by order of primogeniture. The king named and dismissed the six ministers who were responsible only to him and had to be selected outside the membership of the assembly. The king continued to lead the army and the navy, since he named the majority of their officers. He was the director of France's diplomacy and proposed the declaration of war or conclusion of peace to the assembly, which had the power of decision. His principal prerogative was the right of suspensive veto. If he refused to approve a law it could become effective only if two successive legislative assemblies confirmed the vote of the first assembly. Thus the king could delay enforcement of a law for a period varying from two to six years. On the other hand, the king could not dissolve the assembly.

This constitution, which presents many analogies to the Constitution of the United States, required profound agreement between the executive and the legislature in order to function successfully. It was not possible to create such agreement because the two branches were deeply distrustful of each other and each

---

[4] [For a differing account of the franchise requirements for electors, see R. R. Palmer, *The Age of the Democratic Revolution* (Princeton: Princeton University Press, 1959), I, 524–527.—Eds.]

desired to utilize to the full, and more, the prerogatives granted it by the constitution. Furthermore, the religious problem, rising unexpectedly, caused significant worsening in the relations between the king on the one hand and the assembly and new authorities of the nation on the other. The religious question deepened the crisis in France. Some historians see in it one of the essential causes of the partial failure of the French revolution.

Liberal and Humane Reformers

JAMES M. THOMPSON

James M. Thompson (1878–1956), a great English historian of the French Revolution, was the son of a cleric. He attended the fashionable Winchester School and Christ Church College, Oxford University. For most of his professional life until he retired in 1938, he held various positions at Oxford. An Anglican clergyman whose first published works were on the New Testament, he lost his faith and turned to the teaching and writing of European history. His best-known books on the French Revolution are the popular *Leaders of the French Revolution* (1929), the standard biography *Robespierre* (1935), and the encyclopedic and perceptive *French Revolution* (1943).

On Sunday, September 18th [1791], the king's acceptance of the constitution was proclaimed from the Town Hall, and Parisians gave themselves up to public rejoicings. The *Te Deum* was sung at Notre Dame, and there was a balloon ascent in the Champs Élysées. On the 30th the National Assembly met for the last time, and Louis reaffirmed his loyalty to the constitution, amid cries of *Vive le roi! Vive la nation!* and *Vive la liberté!* But it could not be ignored that, of all the thousand deputies, only two were chaired and crowned by the waiting citizens—Pétion of Chartres and Robespierre of Arras, the most stubborn champions of popular rights, and the most persistent opponents of middle-class privilege.

Writing to Robespierre after her return home from Paris (September 21st), Madame Roland drew pessimistic conclusions from the reactionary conduct of the deputies. It proved, she said, that "the least aberration from the orbit of perfect equality and complete liberty necessarily tends to degrade human nature."

It was not unnatural that politicians who had lived in close touch with Paris opinion should sympathize with the point of view of the man in the street, and condemn much of the work of the assembly. They could not easily forget the red

From J. M. Thompson, *The French Revolution* (Oxford: Basil Blackwell, 1943), pp. 225–227. Reprinted by permission of Basil Blackwell, Ltd., and Oxford University Press, Inc.

flag of July 17th, or the undemocratic revision of the franchise, or the restoration of a traitor king.[1] They could not easily forgive the betrayal of the people's interests by representatives whom the people had saved from disaster at every crisis of the revolution. What was the working man's reward for July 14th and October 6th? What boon had the active citizen received from the lawyers and journalists whom his overwhelming vote had placed in power? A franchise which became less effective as it became more important: a ban upon the only available means of improving the conditions of the worker [that is, strikes]: a land-purchase scheme whose chief aim seemed to be to save the interests of the landlord: and a bureaucracy which provided thousands of well-paid posts for the sons of middle-class parents.

Men so disillusioned might easily overlook the real and general advantages won since '89—the destruction of an obsolete and arbitrary regime; the enthronement of the nation in place of the king; a new social equality and self-respect; a new responsibility in local government; a new hope of justice; and a new interest in living.

For what was obviously defective in the constitution of 1791 two circumstances were more to blame than the selfishness of the middle class. One was the speed with which the political revolution had been carried through. The other was the completeness of its break with the past.

Mirabeau, writing to a friend in August, '88, had anticipated a gradual revolution. "The first States-general," he said, "will be disorderly, and will perhaps go too far. The second will establish its right of way (assureront leur marche). The third will achieve the constitution." Mirabeau's three sessions had been compressed into one. Work that might well have been spread over ten years had been completed in two. Before one reform was launched, another was on the slipway.

But this was not all. It is as true of revolutions as it is of wars that those who have won the victory in the field are not the most fit to sit round the table at the peace conference. The bitter memories of the old regime which the deputies brought with them to Versailles, and the just resentment with which they regarded the conduct of the king during the summer of '89, made it difficult for them to view the situation realistically. Mallet du Pan was saying both too much and too little when he declared that France needed thirty years of preliminary training before it would be fit to support political liberty—too much, if thinking of the leaders; too little, if thinking of the rank and file. But almost every divergence between the revolutions of 1688 and 1789, so often too complacently contrasted by English historians, may be attributed to the different political antecedents and education of two great peoples.

It has become fashionable to condemn "a bourgeois revolution." There is a sense, and one creditable to the intelligence and energy of the middle class, in which every revolution is a bourgeois revolution. The French nation at the end of the eighteenth century was not exceptional in having to rely on its professional and propertied minority for liberalism and leadership. It was unusually fortunate in that

---

[1] [References to the massacre at the Champ de Mars; to the restriction of the franchise in August 1791, which raised the property qualifications for electors of the second degree; and to the fact that Louis XVI was not deposed despite his flight to Varennes.—Eds.]

this minority was too weak to establish its rule without the help of the majority, and too patriotic to exploit its private interests until it had carried through a programme of national reform.

No narrowing of the franchise, no obstacles to the revision of the constitution, could deprive the mass of the people, the sixteen millions who were the families of "active" citizens, of the power to call their representatives to account, or to settle the national affairs in a national way. They had overthrown the old privilege of class: they could overthrow the new privilege of cash—if only by another revolution. Meanwhile a bourgeois constitution was infinitely better than none. It protected their lives, their labour, and their land. It prevented the return of the royalist refugees, and of the ecclesiastical monopolists. It saved the country from a foreign invasion designed by its own royal and aristocratic families. It provided for the first time the possibility of an ordered and peaceful existence.

True, these benefits were not given in full measure to the "passive" citizens, the disfranchised third part of the people. But what other state in Europe would have enfranchised them? Or in what country, having no vote, would they have received so much consideration? If they were excluded from political responsibility, it was not by the propertied and professional minority only, but by their own comrades of the *petite bourgeoisie*—the tradesmen and artisans who were the bulk of the "active" citizens. If they were benefited, it was not by their own violence, but by the legislative action of deputies drawn from the whole hierarchy of the middle classes, who for a while forgot their class interests and enmities in a genuine zeal for national regeneration. The alliance of the middle and lower classes against tyranny and privilege may have been a *mariage de convenance* rather than a love-match. It did not long outlast their common victory. But its offspring was the liberal-thinking and liberal-living France of 1875–1939.

II THE CIVIL CONSTITUTION OF THE CLERGY

Tragic Errors

ANDRÉ LATREILLE

André Latreille (1901–   ) is a professional historian, as was his father before him. He studied at the University of Lyon and then taught at various French secondary schools and universities until his retirement from the University of Lyon in 1971. He also served in Charles de Gaulle's Provisional Government as director of religious affairs in the Ministry of Interior from 1944 to 1945 and as a regular reviewer of historical works for the eminent Paris newspaper *Le Monde*. A specialist in French religious history, he has published *Napoléon et le Saint-Siège (1935)*, *L'Église catholique et la Révolution française* (1946–1950), and, in collaboration with others, the *Histoire du Catholicisme en France* (1957–1962). He has also written *La Seconde guerre mondiale* (1966) and *L'Ère napoléonienne* (1974).

The Civil Constitution of the Clergy

On July 12, 1790, the National Assembly approved the measures that formed the *Civil Constitution of the Clergy*. It was called a constitution because it was intended as an essential part of a national regeneration and it was called civil because the assembly wanted to make clear that it dealt only with temporal issues. The idea was

From André Latreille and René Rémond, *La Période contemporaine*, Vol. III of *Histoire du Catholicisme en France* (3 vols.; Paris: Éditions Spes, 1957–1962), pp. 83–94, 96. These pages, written by M. Latreille, are printed by permission of the publisher. Editors' translation.

not to change the national religion, but to cleanse the ecclesiastical body of those abuses universally censured by the national will.

By-passing the Concordat of 1516,[1] which was the oldest of our treaties and actually represented a bilateral agreement with the Holy See, the assembly decided, by its own authority, to regulate the appointment, functions, and salary of the higher clergy.

The boundaries of the dioceses were altered so that henceforth there would be one diocese for each department. Instead of 135 there would be only 85; their size would be much less unequal than in the past; and they would be grouped in ten metropolitan provinces. In drawing up parish boundaries, the assembly ruled that each one had to contain at least 6,000 souls. A considerable reduction in the number of religious positions resulted from these two principles. In addition, all claims to ecclesiastical incomes other than those for bishops and parish priests were abolished. Consequently, clergymen with administrative functions, but who did not care directly for the souls of the faithful, lost their positions.

In the future all the Church's clergy would be elected. Bishops and priests would be elected exactly in the same manner as deputies and government officials—by the *active* citizens (those who paid the required amount of taxes) in the departmental or the district electoral assemblies. When elected, a bishop would request canonical institution from the metropolitan bishop of his province. As evidence of the unity of faith and communion, he would then notify the pope of his appointment; but he did not have to obtain Rome's confirmation of his powers. In the administration of all diocesan affairs, the bishop would be assisted by episcopal vicars, who would form a council and would have to be consulted before he could take any action based on his jurisdiction.

The clergy's salaries would be the responsibility of the state, which would every year (quarterly) pay in cash 20,000 livres to bishops, 1,200 to parish priests, and 700 to country vicars. In return, religious ceremonies would be performed without charge; special fees would disappear.

Such spokesmen for the assembly's Ecclesiastical Committee as the Abbés Goutte and Expilly (one might note that Protestant deputies refrained from commenting) insisted that they had only obeyed the needs of society without ever going beyond the incontestable rights of state authority. Boisgelin, archbishop of Aix-en-Provence, and the Abbé Maury replied skillfully for the right-wing in the assembly. They carefully pointed out the inevitable dangers: the claim that the cooperation of the spiritual power could be dispensed with when revising ecclesiastical districts; the establishment of a system of popular election of bishops, which would result in allowing non-Catholics to vote for clergymen; and the separation introduced between the bishops and the head of the Church, which "would harm that unity so essential to religion." Despite the conciliatory attitude of Boisgelin, they received nothing from the assembly, but instead aroused some alarming replies. Armand-Gaston Camus [a lawyer specializing in Church matters]

---

[1] [The Concordat of 1516 between Francis I of France and Pope Leo X served as the basis of relations between the French Crown and the papacy until 1789. Among other things, it recognized the right of the king to choose bishops and other officials of the Church, who would then receive canonical institution from the pope.—Eds.]

declared that the time had come for the French Church to be freed from "its servitude" to the bishop of Rome; and Mirabeau declared that "all the members of the clergy are public officials" and that "performing religious services . . . is a government function."

Controversy Over the Civil Constitution

Ever since the countless investigations and studies which flourished in 1790 and 1791, the birth and significance of the Civil Constitution of the Clergy have been examined frequently. The amount of influence particular groups had in the Ecclesiastical Committee will always be arguable. We agree with Edmond Préclin[2] that the measures were the result of "the not always harmonious efforts of several sponsors": we see first of all the Gallican and Caesarian legists;[3] also the Richerists (that is, the champions of the movement for the autonomy of the lower clergy) rather than the Jansenists (although these two movements had largely merged); and finally the *philosophes*. In any case, Canon Pisani is right to say that the Civil Constitution did not represent an unnatural conception "springing from the brains of some Jansenists and then violently imposed on a declining France by Machiavellian tactics." It was the inevitable outcome of a religious situation for which no one could find a solution in time, as well as the result of some rather confused and contradictory forces that did not consciously aim at schism. Does this mean (as is still said by modern historians writing since the appearance of Albert Mathiez's work) that it was not unacceptable to Catholics, that the Gallicans recognized this, and that it was Pope Pius VI's malevolence toward the French Revolution that made it unacceptable? Certainly not. What pervades the whole Civil Constitution is the statist postulate that the secular authority alone has the right to make changes which it deems wise not only in ecclesiastical organization but also concerning religious worship. Although there were in the Gallican Church some theologians and canon lawyers quite willing to make any effort to reach a compromise, willing to accept, for example, the changes in the ecclesiastical districts or the election of bishops, they continually warned the assembly that it was necessary to consult with the spiritual authority, according to the prescriptions of canon law, "or else religion would be fundamentally harmed."

Earlier, the first chairman of the Ecclesiastical Committee, Bishop de Bonal, had commented about the monastic reform of 1790: "What I believe to be

---

[2] [Some of the works by the historians mentioned in this selection are as follows: Edmond Préclin, *Les Jansénistes du XVIIIᵉ siècle et la constitution civile du clergé* (Paris: Gamber, 1929); Canon Paul Pisani, *L'Église de Paris et la Révolution* (4 vols.; Paris: Picard, 1908–1911); Albert Mathiez, *Rome et le clergé français sous la Constituante* (Paris: Colin, 1911); Dom Henri Leclerq, *L'Église constitutionnelle* (Paris: Letouzey, Ané, 1934); Frédéric Masson, *Le Cardinal de Bernis* (Paris: Plon, Nourrit, 1884); Abbé Fernand Mourret, *Histoire générale de l'Église*, Vol. VII: *L'Église et la Révolution (1775–1823)* (Paris: Bloud, Gay, 1913).—Eds.]

[3] [A Gallican favored the almost total freedom of the French Church from the ecclesiastical authority of the pope; and a Caesarist espoused the supremacy of the state in ecclesiastical matters.—Eds.]

illegitimate in the exercise of this authority is that the assembly alone tears down obstacles that it has not erected . . . before we hear a pronouncement from the only power in the spiritual realm that has the authority to tie and untie on this earth."

All the bishops who were deputies took the same position regarding the Civil Constitution of the Clergy. Three months after the vote, in a notable pamphlet entitled an *Exposition of Principles Concerning the Civil Constitution of the Clergy*, the thirty bishops who still sat in the Constituent Assembly (except for Talleyrand and Gobel, who had kept apart from the others) made the following declaration:

> If the civil authorities want to make changes in religious matters without the cooperation of the Church, they contradict the principles of the Church, but they do not destroy them; they contradict the principles and destroy the means that could help them carry out their opinions.
>
> We want to know the desires of the Church so as to reestablish a necessary agreement between the civil and religious authorities and by their concord put consciences at rest and maintain public tranquillity. . . .

Where did this religious authority rest? The Gallican bishops could not go astray. Since the high Middle Ages the papacy had never admitted that the secular authority could determine the choice of bishops without its consent. More and more since the Council of Trent [1545–1563], it had required bishops to recognize their subordination to the successor of Saint Peter; and it had established and organized dioceses, sometimes with the approval of secular princes and sometimes on its own. To be sure, Boisgelin urged that the Gallican Church be consulted in a national council, but only because the Gallican bishops considered it a point of honor to state their views before informing the pope of them. The two archbishops who sat in the king's Cabinet advised him to ratify the Civil Constitution, but only because they judged open resistance to be impossible and because they still clung to the hope of a compromise *with* the Holy See. So, before knowing the opinion of either the French episcopate or the pope, Louis XVI ratified the Civil Constitution on August 24, 1790. However, neither the precepts, nor the traditions of the Roman Curia, nor the attitudes of the reigning pope made it likely that the Holy See would acquiesce.

By the end of October 1790 the Gallican bishops had accepted their responsibilities. To the *Exposition of Principles*, which had been the work of the bishops who were deputies, almost all the other bishops (ninety-three to be exact) associated themselves—they explicitly referred the determination of the dispute about the Civil Constitution to the successor of Saint Peter. Placed in the center of Catholic unity and communion, he had to be the interpreter and spokesman of the universal Church's wishes. They had to wait eight months before Pius VI announced his decision on March 10, 1791. Eight interminable months, at a time when his silence left the faithful in France uncertain, at a time when the assembly multiplied the decrees designed to speed up the implementation of the Civil Constitution, eight months of irretrievable delays!

The Constitutional Oath

Fortified by its first victory over the king, the Constituent Assembly quite naturally felt in no way inclined to reduce its claims to legislate independently on religious problems. To rush matters, on November 27, 1790, it decided to require, under the threat of dismissal, that "all bishops, former archbishops, parish priests, and other public officials" take an oath that they would "be loyal to the nation, to the law, and to the king, and would uphold with all their power the Constitution decreed by the National Assembly and accepted by the king." This was the historically famous constitutional oath that unleashed dissension within Church and State and brought about the breakdown of a harmony between the two powers so often extolled as indispensable to the success of the Revolution.

Of 160 prelates, only 7 decided to take the oath; 4 of these—Brienne, Jarente, Savine, and Talleyrand—were heads of dioceses, but because of their disbelief and their morals they were completely discredited. All the other bishops refused to take the oath after a majority of the deputies had killed every proposal that would have definitely allowed the clergy to exclude anything dependent on the spiritual authority from the oath.

But to what extent would the lower clergy and the faithful follow the example of the bishops? The path to take was less clear than it would be for us today. Rome's silence was not the difficulty: the good country priest ordinarily did not look so far, and the voice of the First Shepherd did not reach him easily. Often he was estranged from his own bishop by many legitimate resentments and by a very different manner of understanding the political situation. He looked for "enlightenment from those whose way of life he shared and whose learning he admired, without seeking his doctrines outside the diocese" (Dom Leclerq). He would ask some canon lawyer or some canon from a neighboring city, but very contradictory views were expressed. Even if he ignored the material and spiritual advantages that the ecclesiastical reorganization promised him and even if he ignored the threat of being treated as "a disturber of the peace" and an enemy of national regeneration should he refuse to take the oath, he still hesitated to cut himself off from his flock, to abandon his post, his parish, and his rectory, to which he was bound by so many ties. This was especially true when the local officials, desirous of keeping him, were willing to ignore the reservations that he added to the oath. As well as can be determined from innumerable local studies and general statistical accounts, we can estimate that half of the parish clergy or even a little more than that—in other words, a third of the entire clergy—accepted the Civil Constitution immediately. A high average, but like all averages the result of extreme divergencies on both sides: in the Vendée or Bas-Rhin departments 90 per cent refused to take the oath; in Var 96 per cent accepted it. And the average conceals many inexplicable "cases": in the Haute-Saône department, 4 refused to take the oath and 178 surely took it; but it has been determined that 352 priests in Haute-Saône, two-thirds of the total, took it with reservations or later retracted their pledge.

The adherence of this rather large number of clergymen and laymen thereby allowed the "Constitutional Church" to organize. Every Sunday from the end of

January to the end of March 1791, in the capitals of the new departments, there were meetings of the active citizens responsible for electing the new bishops who were to replace the "refractory" ones. As no requirement of religious faith was stipulated, unbelievers took part in the elections, while those who were scrupulously faithful abstained. At Le Puy in the Haute-Loire department, 150 active citizens who were Catholics failed to attend the electoral assembly, while Protestants came from Yssingeaux [thirteen miles away]. With some exceptions these electoral activities took place in a calm atmosphere. The voice of the people chose as bishops eighteen of the priests who were members of the Constituent Assembly. When the final stage was reached everything almost came to nought, for someone had to consecrate these newly elected bishops so as to confer the apostolic succession on them, and even the bishops who had taken the oath shunned that task. Talleyrand finally agreed to assume this role: on February 24, 1791, the former bishop of Autun (just fifteen days earlier he had given up his authority there) took up the crosier again to consecrate Expilly as bishop of Finistère and Marolles as bishop of Aisne. Observers noticed that the liturgical ritual was followed exactly except that the reading of papal bulls was omitted, as was the oath of loyalty to the pope. Thereafter consecrations occurred in rapid succession, since by April 25 some sixty bishops were at their places in the new dioceses.

Precisely at this point the news began to spread in France that Pius VI had just condemned the Civil Constitution of the Clergy.

The Papal Condemnation

Historians have thoroughly investigated the motives for Pius VI's surprising delay in announcing his decision on the Civil Constitution. Frédéric Masson stresses the forbearance that he showed toward King Louis XVI, whose embarrassing position was explained to him by the French ambassador at Rome, Cardinal de Bernis. The Abbés Mourret and Richard insist on the pope's uncertainty about the intentions of the Gallican bishops. Mathiez and Canon Leclerq emphasize the political considerations behind his delay and in particular his concern with saving [the papal territories of] Avignon and the Comtat Venaissin from the covetousness of the revolutionaries. More attention must certainly be directed toward the customary slowness of the Roman Curia. The cardinals who surrounded Pius VI were highly indignant at the actions of the Constituent Assembly. Its measures exceeded in scope and boldness anything so far attempted by the most radical reformers and enlightened despots—like Joseph II for example. But, for one thing, we must consider the clumsy machinery of the papal government and the traditional prudence of its advisers, elderly men anxious not to commit the "Throne of Truth" rashly. Then, too, there was the feeling that in a European situation where papal authority found enemies everywhere, it had to refrain from providing any pretext for a Gallican schism, something always dreaded by the ultramontanes [those favoring papal supremacy within the Church]. Together, these factors had led and almost always would lead the popes to act slowly and to come to a decision on the fearful problems raised by the Revolution only after great care. From 1789 to 1815, throughout the twenty-five years of almost uninterrupted crisis between Paris and Rome, again and again we gain the impression that the Holy See was falling behind. In reaction to the hasty moves of a young and dynamic political group, it took its positions only belatedly.

The pontifical decision finally appeared, on March 10, 1791, in an important document, the papal brief *Quot Aliquantum*, which was sent to Cardinal de La Rochefoucauld and to the bishops who had signed the *Exposition of Principles*. Pius VI declared that the Civil Constitution had "as its goal and consequence the destruction of the Catholic religion." By its provisions concerning the consecration of bishops, the election of priests, and the operation of diocesan councils, it mortally wounded the divine constitution of the Church. Although it was an article of faith that the Roman Pontiff had the highest authority over the whole Church, the Civil Constitution claimed to upset this fundamental concept. While scrutinizing the doctrinal and disciplinary matters that had been decided illegitimately by the assembly, the Supreme Pontiff took the occasion to pronounce a severe judgment on the principles that this legislature had proclaimed earlier. And so he publicly condemned the Declaration of the Rights of Man. (He had already done the same thing a year earlier in an unpublished consistorial address.) He said that the Declaration was wrong to have granted to the citizen "that unconditional liberty which guarantees not only the right of being left undisturbed for one's religious opinions, but which also grants the right to think, to write, and even to publish with impunity anything on religious matters that may be the product of the most disordered imagination—a shocking right, which the assembly, however, seems to believe is the result of everyone's natural equality and liberty." But what could be more senseless than to establish among men this unbridled equality and liberty which seem to destroy reason? . . . What can be more opposed to the rights of God the Creator—who limits man's liberty by forbidding him to commit evil—than "this liberty of thought and action that the National Assembly grants to man in society as an imprescriptible natural right?" Thus, with a terrible solemnity, the theses of the Roman Church and the principles of modern liberalism confronted each other. We shall see them clash very often after 1789.

Responding to the brief, the Gallican bishops, with much dignity and moderation, tried to explain their conduct; they distinguished between the area of natural law and that of political action. Using the same words as the Holy Father, they condemned a liberty and an equality contrary to the truths of reason and dogma; but as citizens desirous of not opposing popular aspirations in the civil sphere, they had believed it possible to set up the true dominion of public liberty in a hereditary monarchy: ". . . And we recognized without any difficulty that there is a natural equality whereby no citizen is excluded from the positions to which Providence calls him because of his talents and his virtues. Political equality can be extended or limited by different forms of government; and we believed that we were free to express ourselves, as was any other citizen, concerning those more or less extensive areas that God himself declares as given over for men to dispute." Having preceded the pope in denouncing the Civil Constitution, the Gallican bishops had no difficulty in following the line of conduct he prescribed for them.

On April 13, 1791, Pius VI declared those consecrations of bishops already carried out to be criminal and sacrilegious, forbade all religious functions to the consecrators and those consecrated, threatened to suspend all priests who had taken the oath and did not retract it, and exhorted the misguided to repent and the faithful to a resolute firmness. It is and always will be impossible to judge the effects of these disciplinary measures. We know that the publicity given to the papal briefs by the loyal bishops brought about in certain dioceses a relatively large number of retractions of the oath, but of course many of these remained secret. The Constitutional bishops, however, were rather persuasive, whether in challenging the authenticity of the papal documents whose circulation was forbidden by the assembly, or in taking shelter behind the Gallican liberties in order to claim that the pope, having no direct jurisdiction over the French people, could pronounce no canonical punishment in this matter.

Soon diplomatic relations between Paris and Rome were broken. When the French government ended Cardinal de Bernis' mission as ambassador, the pope refused to receive a new ambassador. Turbulent demonstrations in Paris (during which the mob burned an effigy of "the Ogre of the Tiber" at the Palais Royal) led to the departure of Dugnani, the papal nuncio. At a time in France when it was especially important for an authorized representative of the Holy See to keep in touch with the loyal clergy, only a semiofficial chargé d'affaires stayed behind, and his position was unclear and indefinite.

The Two Churches

Henceforth there were two churches in the kingdom face to face. There were even frequent instances of two bishops or two priests in the same locality hurling anathemas at each other in front of a divided population which had its own way of interpreting the opposing issues. In fact the public did not understand much about the distinctions concerning ecclesiastical discipline: so long as the Mass was said as usual in the parish church and the sacraments were administered, it hardly cared whether the priest who officiated had legal jurisdiction or whether the taking of a political oath had made him a schismatic. The public was rather inclined to rate priests according to its own personal likes or dislikes and according to its support of the Constituent Assembly and the revolutionary cause. On one side were those clergymen who took the oath [*assermentés*], on the other were those who refused [*insermentés*]—contemptuously called *jurors* or *refractories*, approvingly called *civic priests* or *good priests*. Under such conditions, the antagonists had to fight for the favor of the public authorities and compete, with heated polemics, for the support of the faithful. . . .

Looking at the religious issue from a modern standpoint, it is rather hard to understand why the Constituent Assembly did not stand by its principles on the freedom of religious belief and quite simply adopt total freedom of religion, as it almost did during the last months of its existence. But one must clearly understand that this was impossible to do. All the Constituent Assembly's work had been based on the idea of a national religion serving the new political and social system. It had placed all its prestige behind the formation of the Constitutional Church, which it could not abandon, defenseless, to the relentless attacks of counterrevolutionaries. If the Constituent Assembly at the end of its term forbade refractory priests from preaching or opening new churches, at least it did have the merit of not banishing them.

Necessary and Admirable Decisions

JEAN JAURÈS

Jean Jaurès (1859–1914) was one of the most eloquent and influential political figures of his day. A méridional, or southern Frenchman, he came from a middle-class family. At the École normale supérieure he studied philosophy and gave promise of a brilliant academic career. But in the early 1890s he left teaching to enter politics full time and for the rest of his life he devoted himself to the cause of democratic socialism. He served as a leader of the Socialists in the Chamber of Deputies and in 1904 founded the French Socialist Party's newspaper, *L'Humanité*. He also edited the thirteen-volume *Histoire socialiste* (1901–1908), for which he wrote the four volumes on the French Revolution up to the fall of Robespierre. On the eve of World War I a demented nationalist assassinated him.

The French Revolution was bolstered by a great increase in wealth. And though the vigor of mind and soul, the passion for liberty and knowledge, the spirit of audacity and inventiveness which great crises produce all contributed a good deal to this growth of national wealth, it had its first and principal source in the revolutionary expropriation of Church property.

But the National Assembly could not restrict itself to seizing and distributing the Church's landed property. It had to regulate all the relations between the Church and the new society created by the Revolution, and we are going to witness the tragic encounter of Christianity and the Revolution.

The assembly could not ignore the ecclesiastical organization. In the first place, the temporal power of the Old Regime, the king, played a role in the proceedings of the spiritual power. The pope confirmed bishops, but it was the king who nominated them. To a great extent the Revolution substituted the power of the nation for the power of the king. It therefore had to decide what it was to do with that aspect of royal power. In the second place, a very large number of monks and

From Jean Jaurès, *La Constituante (1789-1791)*, Vol. I of *Histoire socialiste (1789-1900)*, ed. Jean Jaurès (13 vols.; Paris: Rouff, 1901–1908), pp. 521–522, 532–533, 535, 539, 541, 543–544, 546–548. Editors' translation.

nuns, who were bound to the cloister by perpetual vows upheld by civil law, petitioned the assembly requesting it to strike off their chains. Finally, by seizing the Church's landed property, the assembly, in order to give a legal pretext for that magnificent revolutionary expropriation, had taken on the responsibility of providing for the administration of the cult and the support of its clergy. The assembly was therefore completely involved in ecclesiastical problems. . . .

A great many details of the Civil Constitution of the Clergy seem bizarre to us, and a great many historians have said that it failed miserably. False. In the first place, it lasted in its original form until February 21, 1795, that is to say four years, and it was, at least for three years, really in operation. The electors charged with choosing parish priests and bishops took their duties seriously. The religious ceremonies which were a part of the electoral procedure were attended without any ill will, even by the freest thinkers among them; and very far from believing that by so doing they compromised themselves with the Church, the electors believed instead that they were acting as good revolutionaries.

But the Civil Constitution survived especially in the Concordat of 1801, although bastardized and debased. There are two great differences between the Concordat and the Civil Constitution: in the first place, the Concordat reestablished the papal right of intervention [in the life of the French Church]. Whereas the Revolution had nothing to do with the pope and confidently affirmed the sovereignty of popular suffrage in the appointment of Church officials as well as other national officials, the Concordat was the result of negotiations with the pope and it restored his supreme right of canonical institution. The other difference is that, according to the Concordat, bishops and parish priests were to be selected by the executive branch of the French government and not by popular vote.

From the Civil Constitution to the Concordat there is, therefore, a diminution of the revolutionary spirit. The Civil Constitution is much more laic, national, and democratic than the Concordat. The Civil Constitution recognizes no foreign power, and, in the last analysis, no theocratic power: it is the nation, in its absolute sovereignty and by means of popular suffrage, that chooses and installs the officers of the Church.

But what is retained of the Civil Constitution in the Concordat is the right of a sovereign with a revolutionary and laic origin to appoint bishops and priests even though it receives its legitimacy not from the Church but from the people. In the Civil Constitution, those electoral assemblies in which everyone—even Protestants, even Jews, even nonbelievers—took part in naming the bishop and the priest seem a little bizarre to us; but in fact the situation is much the same under the Concordat, where the minister of religion in the Cabinet, who might be a Protestant, a deist, or an atheist, chooses the bishops and priests. The essential thing is that a power that does not emanate from the Church and that represents the rights of man—a conception absolutely opposed to that of the Church—takes part in the functioning and recruitment of the Church. This is what survives of the Civil Constitution in the Concordat and this principle is, despite everything, a grave defeat for theocracy.

Those, like us, who desire not only the complete separation of Church and State, but even the disappearance of the Church and Christianity, those who impatiently await the day when the authority of the state will be freed from all contact with the Church and when individual consciences will be freed from all contact with dogma, may believe that the Civil Constitution of the Clergy was an inferior product and a bastardized mixture. Nevertheless, for its time it was basically an act of revolutionary boldness and not, as some have said, an uncertain gesture. In fact, when subjected to the pressure of reactionary and clerical forces, it suffered, as did most revolutionary institutions, a terrible diminution in value; but there still remained in it an intangible part of the Revolution, which survives to this very day. . . .

But why didn't the Constituent Assembly immediately proclaim the separation of Church and State? Why didn't it say that religion was a purely private matter and that the nation should not pay the salaries of the clergy nor persecute, support, or regulate any sect? Why didn't it, according to the famous formula of the positivists, bring about then and there the separation of the spiritual and temporal powers? In his very substantial studies of the religious movement in Paris during the Revolution, [Jean-François-Eugène] Robinet vehemently reproaches the assembly for this. . . .

But, actually, taking into account the forces of the year 1790, could the assembly, at that instant, have declared the separation of Church and State? *At that time, the question was not even raised;* it did not exist. None of the legislators, none of the journalists, none of the thinkers or *philosophes* suggested this idea to the assembly. . . .

It was not . . . from the philosophy of the eighteenth century that the politics of separation or of a systematic and immediate dechristianization could reach the Constituents. And the assembly (where Jansenists and legists were much more numerous than *philosophes*) was infinitely more concerned with freeing the French Church from the domination of Rome and with applying the public law of the Revolution to ecclesiastical organization than with intentionally precipitating the dissolution of Christian belief or breaking all legal bonds between Church and State.

Besides, for the state to cut all ties with the Church and proclaim that religion was simply a private matter would not have been tolerated by the overwhelming majority of the people in 1789 and 1790. In religious matters there is a world of difference between the working class today [1901], a part of which is resolutely nonbelieving, and the people of 1789. Not to recognize this vast difference and to be severely critical of the religious achievements of the assembly is to ignore the real significance of the Revolution itself.

The traditions of many centuries had accustomed the people of 1789 to consider public life impossible without the monarchy or religion. It cannot have been expected that the assembly could undo in a moment the results of centuries of servitude and passivity. It took innumerable shocks—the flight to Varennes, the repeated treasons of their leaders, the invasion by foreign hordes requested and aided by the court—to separate the people (I mean the revolutionary people) from the monarchy and the king.

It would take frightful ordeals—the underhanded and violent battle of the clergy against the Revolution, its obvious complicity with the enemies of liberty and the nation, its crimes in the Vendée, its fanatical appeals for civil war—to separate the revolutionary people first from the clergy and then even from Christianity. And still the breach was only superficial. Whoever does not take this into account is incapable of understanding history, incapable also of judging the real stature of those great bourgeois revolutionaries who in four years not only enacted the Civil Constitution, but began the dechristianization of that France so unquestioningly religious for centuries. . . .

One must admire the assembly for its great audacity in bringing the Church within the administrative framework of the Revolution and in placing it under the jurisdiction of popular suffrage, where it became one of many civil institutions.

Furthermore, how would the assembly have been able to separate the Church from the State and refuse all public subsidy to religion at the very moment when it was moving toward the general expropriation of Church property? I do not in the least imply by this that the budget for religion was a debt the State owed to the expropriated Church. There is no debt that the State, the Revolution, owes to the Church. . . .

What most concerned the *philosophes* of the assembly was how to regulate the difficult relationships between the Church and the Revolution without too much commotion and at the least possible risk. They did not abdicate responsibility, they were not indifferent. They hoped that little by little Catholicism as an institution, once taken into the framework of the Revolution, would be permeated by the dissolvent influence of revolutionary thought. And when they pretended to believe that there was no contradiction between the principles of Christianity and those of the Revolution, *in practice* they did not deceive the country, for nations, like individuals, have the admirable faculty of not feeling immediately the contradiction between opposing principles that they sometimes hold.

It took several generations and the painful experience of numerous events before people came to feel that contradiction to the point where it became intolerable; for, thanks to the power of the illogical in life, mankind comes under the influence of a new principle without suffering immediately the anguish and sadness of a total and conscious repudiation of the past.

Thus the Constituents hoped that pure reason would little by little free itself from the unnatural compound of Christianity and the Revolution which formed the base of the national consciousness in 1789. At that time the essential thing for them (and they were right) was that the revolutionary stamp be imprinted on the organization of the Church, that the latter not be treated as a special institution, but subject to the same conditions as all civil institutions.

In that way the Church, at the same time as it found its property expropriated, also found its spiritual primacy expropriated. It was above all deprived of its mystery: how long would the people revere as the interpreters of a supernatural power those men whom they chose themselves, whom by their own votes they put into office like any local administrator? . . .

I do not say that this intellectual mixture of Christianity and rationalism is very attractive; furthermore, it is a very mediocre and very unstable philosophical compound. But the people had been kept in ignorance and in Christian dependency as much by the disdain of the *philosophes* as by the Church's will to dominate. And even though they were beginning a Revolution, they could not attain all at once the pure philosophy of knowledge and reason. In the religious sphere, therefore, this first revolutionary period was necessarily a period of compromise. The essential thing once again is that this compromise, while it imposed disagreeable rituals and unpleasant posturing on free thought, did not impair the essential power of reason; on the contrary, by diminishing the masses' spirit of passivity and dependency, it struck at the essence of the Church's power. The four million active citizens who yesterday greeted the bishop as a double incarnation of God and the king now elected that bishop. The Church was in the position of a candidate before the electors. In the last analysis, popular suffrage must decide, popular suffrage becomes pope, and, to a certain extent, by the transfer of sacerdotal power, popular suffrage becomes God.

Such an exalting of the people causes the abasement of the Church, and dogma loses the halo of power which made it truth. In any case, having lived under the Civil Constitution, the people would find it easier to look point-blank at the altar, where the priest stood thanks to them. I am convinced that the Civil Constitution, so disdained by some haughty spirits, contributed a good deal to the intellectual liberty of the people in religious matters today. It was a first step in the secular accommodation of religion and it accustomed the people to the wide-ranging audacities of free thought.

The Church felt the gravity of the blow; for under the pope's direction it immediately began a furious resistance to the Civil Constitution. It claimed that the new arrangement of dioceses was absolutely counter to canon law. It claimed that the Constituent Assembly could not rightfully avoid consulting the leader of the universal Church. We can dispense with these claims. . . .

In its long life the Church has accepted too many different constitutions, it has adapted itself to too many diverse political and social conditions for it to be able to oppose revolutionary innovations with the authority of an unchanging tradition. The problem is summed up in a word. The Church aspires to domination; therefore, it declares as contrary to principle anything which hampers its domination, but since it is not obstinate before the inevitable and since it prefers to evolve rather than to disappear, it ends up by resigning itself to what it cannot destroy and by readjusting its principles to what exists.

If the Revolution had triumphed completely, if political liberty and popular suffrage had not been submerged in the despotism of the Napoleonic Empire, if the electoral principle had continued to function everywhere, and if the triumph of the Revolution and democracy had given France a vigorous national purpose, the clergy and the pope himself would have been forced to accept the Civil Constitution. The pope certainly would not have cut off revolutionary France from the universal Church; he would have confined himself as much as possible to maintaining "the unity of the faith" between the elected bishops and the Holy See. Therefore, the controversy did not concern a question of canon law. It was a political question. The issue was whether the Revolution would have the power to prevail in all its works and in the Civil Constitution itself.

I sometimes hear "moderates" regret that the French Revolution created so many enormous difficulties for itself by bestowing a Civil Constitution on the clergy. But truly they reason as if it were possible for the Revolution to ignore the existence of a Church which had dominated and molded France for centuries. They reason as if it were possible for the Revolution, by feigning ignorance, to abolish the profound conflict between the Catholic principle and revolutionary principles. There was not a single question on which the Revolution had to take a stand where it would not meet the Church in its path.

To raise only the question of the dioceses: at a time when the constitution abolished the old provincial boundaries and made France uniform, should it have allowed the dioceses to continue as a reminder of the old France superimposing itself on the lines of the new France and encouraging a universal hope of reaction? At a time when the nation took power from the king, surely it was necessary for it to decide what to do with that part of his authority which concerned the Church; or should it have left the Church for an indefinite period master of everything, of its recruitment, of its preaching, of schools, of the registers of vital statistics?

Again, the dramatic encounter of Christianity and the Revolution could not be postponed. The only task of the Constituent Assembly was to arrange that encounter in such a way that it would wound as slightly as possible the prejudices of the masses who would have turned against the Revolution and also arrange it in such a way that it would give the people new habits of freedom on religious matters. As much as possible, that is what the Civil Constitution provided. In fact the Revolution did find Constitutional priests for every parish, Constitutional bishops for every diocese. It could thus divide the Church against itself; it prevented a unanimous uprising of religious fanaticism in which it would have foundered; and it gave itself time to render the essential part of its work unassailable and irrevocable.

3
Who Was Responsible for the War of 1792?

T HE War of 1792 was one of the most momentous and tragic events of the French Revolution. It lasted for many years, resulted in the deaths of hundreds of thousands, and demanded such sacrifices from the French people that it helped provoke the Terror, counterrevolution, and military dictatorship.

Who was responsible for causing it? Some historians, such as Albert Goodwin, distribute the blame on both sides: in the French cabinet and legislature there were influential partisans of war; on the other hand, the *émigrés* and some European monarchs were determined to crush the Revolution by force of arms.

Other historians, such as Hippolyte Taine, blame the French assembly and especially the Girondins for using justified grievances against *émigrés* and foreign rulers as a pretext for war.

In analyzing this controversy, one may ask if we hold those who actually declared war responsible? Or those who had any part in causing the tension? Or those who uncompromisingly sought ends prejudicial to their neighbors? War "guilt" is difficult to assess, as anyone who has studied the events leading to World War I well knows.

The Outbreak: Revolutionaries and Counterrevolutionaries Both Responsible

ALBERT GOODWIN

Albert Goodwin (1906–   ) studied modern history at Oxford University and the Sorbonne and taught the subject at the University of Liverpool, Oxford University, and the University of Manchester. For more than thirty-five years he has been one of the outstanding British historians of the Old Regime and the French Revolution. He has edited *The European Nobility in the Eighteenth Century* (revised edition, 1967); *A Select List of Works on Europe and Europe Overseas, 1715-1815* (1956), with J. S. Bromley; and *The American and French Revolutions, 1763-1793* (1965), which is Volume VIII of *The New Cambridge Modern History*. He has also published many articles and a short survey, *The French Revolution* (revised edition, 1966), notable for its clarity and good sense.

The possibility of war with Europe had existed ever since the king's escape to Varennes, if only for the reason that the stricter confinement of the sovereigns in the capital confirmed Marie Antoinette in her views that the sole hope of salvation for the monarchy lay in foreign intervention. The king's acceptance of the constitution in September [1791] was a formal act, the effective results of which remained to be seen. For the moment, it merely stimulated further the reactionary fervour of the *émigrés*. By her continued intrigues the queen early aroused the suspicions of the Legislative Assembly and provoked a wave of anti-Austrian

From Albert Goodwin, *The French Revolution* (2nd ed. rev.; London: Hutchinson and Co., 1956), pp. 112–113, 114–120. Reprinted by permission of Hutchinson Publishing Group, Ltd.

feeling, which did much to impair good relations with the Emperor and to undermine the influence of the Feuillants.[1]

In contrast with the Feuillants' efforts to reconcile the refractory priests and to conciliate the Emperor, the Brissotins set out to repress the ecclesiastical counter-revolution and to intimidate the *émigrés*. Their first move in this direction was the passing of a decree on 31st October, summoning the count de Provence [one of the king's brothers] to return to France within three months, upon pain of forfeiting his rights to the succession. This, however, only produced a belated and evasive reply from the prince in December. The next step was taken on 9th November, when the Assembly decreed that all *émigrés* who had not repatriated themselves by 1st January, 1792, would be treated as traitors. Their goods would thus be subject to confiscation and, if caught, their lives would be forfeit. Though the *émigré* Court at Coblentz, now guided by Calonne, had undoubtedly been partly responsible for the Declaration of Pilnitz [August 27, 1791], and though the military forces of counter-revolution under the Prince de Condé at Worms were assuming greater coherence, it can hardly be considered that the threat represented by the *émigrés* was in itself a serious one. On the other hand, the effect of the emigration on the financial and commercial situation in France and on the discipline in the army could not be ignored. More disturbing were the administrative and political results of the religious schism. . . .

Though the decrees of 9th and 29th November[2] were vetoed by the king in December on the advice of the Feuillant leaders, the Brissotins continued with their policy of legislating against the agents of counter-revolution. Under pressure from this quarter and on the advice of [the Minister of War] Narbonne, the king announced in the Assembly on 14th December that he would summon the elector of Trèves to disband the armed gatherings of *émigrés* at Coblentz before 15th January, 1792, and that he would declare war on the elector if he refused to give satisfaction. To show that this was not an empty threat, Narbonne announced that three French armies would be formed under the command of Rochambeau, Lückner and Lafayette. The elector of Trèves, glad of the excuse of ridding himself of his unwelcome guests, and conscious of the Emperor's lukewarm support of the *émigrés*, replied without delay that he was willing to carry out Louis' wishes.

That these events did not bring about a relaxation of the tension between France and Austria may be attributed, on the one hand, to a sudden stiffening of the Emperor Leopold's attitude and, on the other, to the military and political schemes of Narbonne. Even before the French pressure on the elector of Trèves, Leopold had revived the question of the feudal rights of the imperial princes in Alsace. In accordance with the decrees of 4th–11th August, 1789, the feudal dues of the German princes with possessions in Alsace had either been abolished or made subject to redemption. In reply to this unilateral action taken by the Constituent

---

[1] [A loose-knit group of anti-Jacobin deputies and ministers who favored a peaceful foreign policy and constitutional monarchy in 1791. Its leading members included Lafayette, Sieyès, Adrien Duport, Barnave, and Alexandre de Lameth. Their club often met at a former convent of the Feuillants, hence their name.—Eds.]

[2] [These decrees provided for severe penalties against *émigrés* and those clergymen who refused to take an oath of loyalty to the nation.—Eds.]

Assembly, the German princes had refused to discuss the matter of compensation and had appealed to the Imperial Diet. After long hesitations, the Frankfort Diet had finally issued, on 21st July, 1791, a decree or *conclusum,* upholding the claims of the princes. On 3rd December the Emperor informed Louis XVI in a dispatch that he intended to ratify the decision of the Imperial Diet, which he did a week later. This issue, which had seemed likely to become extinct, was thus revived. More provocative was an imperial dispatch, dated 21st December, 1791, in which the Emperor, while approving the dispersal of the *émigrés* at Coblentz, announced that he had ordered Marshal Bender, commander-in-chief of the Imperial troops in the Netherlands, to protect the elector of Trèves, if the need arose, from any incursions on his territory by undisciplined French forces. This action was supported by the argument that the French government was no longer master of the situation on its own soil.

That there was some substance in these contentions is shown by the fact that, on 21st December, Narbonne had set out on a tour of the north-eastern frontier districts in order to tighten up the discipline of the troops. In three weeks, Narbonne practically put a stop to emigration in the army, raised its morale and returned to the Assembly with plans for raising 50,000 new recruits by fusing the National Guards with the regiments of the line. These plans, however, proved premature, and Narbonne soon concluded that the army could only be cured of the evils with which the revolution had afflicted it if it were tested in a limited war with the Rhineland electors. The protection offered by the Emperor to the elector of Trèves, however, threatened to transform the punitive expedition which Narbonne had in mind into a more general conflict. This situation forced Narbonne into an alliance of convenience with the Brissotins, with whom he had come to agree in thinking that France's real enemy was not the *émigrés* but Austria. It also induced him, at the suggestion of Madame de Staël, to set on foot negotiations with the idea of ensuring Prussian neutrality and an alliance with Great Britain. At the end of December 1791 the count de Ségur was dispatched on an official mission to Berlin with instructions to dissuade the King of Prussia from supporting the Emperor. Meanwhile, the son of Marshal Custine was commissioned to pay a secret visit to Frederick II's great captain, the duke of Brunswick, in order to offer him the post of generalissimo of the French armies. In January 1792 Talleyrand, a personal friend of Narbonne's, was sent on an unofficial mission to London to prepare the ground for a Franco-British understanding. All these overtures were rebuffed. Ségur's mission was wrecked by the agents of the *émigrés* and by Louis XVI's secret repudiation of his envoy, Custine's by the caution of the duke of Brunswick, and Talleyrand's by his intrigues with the parliamentary opposition and by the British Government's mistrust of his proposals.

The secret political design upon which these diplomatic manœuvres hinged was that the constitutional revision envisaged by the Feuillants should be effected by means of an army victorious in war, which could then be employed in the interest of the monarchy. Narbonne was thus the first to contemplate ending the revolution and restoring order by a military dictatorship. These plans, however, involved the minister in a situation which soon got out of control. His scheme for a limited war against the elector of Trèves alienated Barnave, who early in 1792 finally realized the hopelessness of his attempts to guide the queen and retired from the political scene. Narbonne's alliance with the Brissotins also had the effect of stimulating the rising demand in the country, not for a military promenade in the Rhineland, but for a fullscale war with Austria. Ever since October 1791 Brissot had been preaching an ideological war of peoples against sovereigns, and the war with Austria was envisaged as one in which France would be assisted by the subject races of the Habsburg dominions. In this illusion the Brissotins were encouraged by refugee patriots from Belgium, Liège, Holland and Switzerland. In January 1792 Robespierre, at the Jacobin club, did his best to expose the preparations for a military dictatorship made by Narbonne and to dissuade the war-mongers from becoming "armed missionaries," but he only succeeded in widening the breach between the Brissotins and his own followers. It is perhaps worth noting, in passing, that Robespierre, at this point, was neither an unqualified pacifist, nor a covert collaborationist. He was merely contending that counter-revolution should be defeated in France before its protectors abroad were assailed. Marat, too, argued in the same sense, but his influence was diminished by the fact that his popular newspaper, *L'Ami du Peuple*, had temporarily ceased to appear in the middle of December 1791.

A fresh stage in the events leading to war opened in the middle of January 1792 when Gensonné, in the name of the diplomatic committee of the Assembly, raised the question whether the Emperor's orders to Marshal Bender could be reconciled with the Franco-Austrian treaty of 1756. On 25th January, the Assembly decided to challenge the Emperor on this point. It invited Louis to ask Leopold whether he still regarded himself as an ally of the French nation and whether he renounced all engagements directed against French sovereign independence and the stability of the French constitution. If no answer were received to this inquiry before 1st March, France would feel compelled to declare war on Austria. From this point, all de Lessart's efforts, as Foreign Minister, to tone down the asperity of the notes which subsequently passed between Paris and Vienna only played into the hands of the Brissotins, who now determined to overthrow the Feuillant government by exposing the almost criminal weakness of its diplomacy. Meanwhile, on 7th February, the Emperor had succeeded in procuring the King of Prussia's signature to a treaty of defensive alliance, the preliminaries of which had been concluded in the previous July. In this treaty the two powers agreed to afford each other mutual aid and assistance and to promote a concert of other powers for the settlement of French affairs. Though the question of a possible further partition of Poland continued to divide the allies, and though the treaty did not protect the most vulnerable parts of Austrian and Prussian territory, it persuaded the Austrian chancellor, Kaunitz, that France could safely be hectored into submission. Hence it was that Franco-Austrian diplomacy in February and March of 1792 consisted merely of an exchange of mutual recrimination and abuse.

The final phase of these rapidly deteriorating relations opened on 10th March, when Louis XVI abruptly dismissed Narbonne and news was received in Paris of the death of the Emperor Leopold. Narbonne had virtually brought about his own fall by intriguing against the king's favourite minister, de Molleville, and by threatening Louis with the combined resignations of Rochambeau, Lückner and Lafayette. The king's action, however, provided the Brissotins with the excuse for impeaching de Lessart, and for denouncing the other members of the Feuillant administration. In this way, the ministry was overthrown and the Brissotins were left to construct one of their own. The Department of Foreign Affairs was given to Dumouriez, that of Finance to Clavière, a Swiss banker and former collaborator of Mirabeau, the Ministry of the Interior to Roland de la Platière, a civil servant, the Navy and Colonies to Lacoste, and the Ministry of Justice to Duranthon. Narbonne's place was taken by de Grave—a nonentity. The chief figure in the new government was Dumouriez, a fanatical opponent of Austria, ambitious and determined on war. The change of Austrian rulers also brought war nearer, for the successor of the cautious and pacific Leopold was Francis II, young, impetuous and with a taste for military adventure. His very youth threw him into the hands of the Imperial Chancellor Kaunitz, who was determined to humiliate France by threatening her with the newly concluded alliance with Prussia. It soon became clear, moreover, that Francis had made up his mind to champion the cause of the Alsatian princes and of the Pope, and to secure some guarantee of strong government in France.

In some respects, the policy of Dumouriez proved to be identical with that of his predecessor. He had the same conviction that Austria could be isolated by means of understandings with Prussia and Great Britain, and hoped that he might even be able to induce the German princes not to elect Francis as emperor. Like Narbonne, he secretly regarded war as an effective means of restoring the monarchical authority of Louis XVI. As a former agent of Louis XV's secret diplomacy, however, Dumouriez inherited from the *ancien régime* a bitter hatred of the Austrian alliance, and was convinced that the German powers intended to treat France as a second Poland. As soon as he became Foreign Minister, Dumouriez adopted a challenging and uncompromising attitude towards Vienna and pushed on with active preparations for war. Whereas, however, Narbonne had contemplated a French offensive on the Moselle and the Rhine, directed on Trèves and Mayence, Dumouriez laid plans for overrunning the Low Countries. His object there was not formal annexation, for that would have antagonized Great Britain, but the establishment of a Belgian federal republic. The attack was to be justified to the British ministers on the ground of military necessity, and it was intended that the French armies should live on the country and thus relieve the pressure on French finances. One of Dumouriez's first acts was to dispatch Maret—the future duke of Bassano—as an agent to incite the Belgians to revolt. Custine was once again charged with the duty of separating Prussia from Austria, and Talleyrand was entrusted with the task of preparing the way for a prospective alliance with England. The suggestions which were put to the British Government were bold and imaginative. As the basis of the alliance, Dumouriez offered to draw up a new commercial treaty, to surrender Tobago and to co-operate in the liberation of the Spanish American colonies. Great Britain, France and possibly the United States were together to share the opportunities for great commercial ventures, which would thus be opened up. The aggressive continental ambitions of Austria, Prussia and Russia could be checked, and the peace of Europe guaranteed by means of a balance between the liberal powers of the West and the autocratic monarchies of the

East. It was the same policy which Talleyrand was to champion with success after a quarter of a century of conflict at the Congress of Vienna in 1815.

These grandiose plans and calculations, however, soon came to grief. Custine's mission in Berlin was futile from the start, since the King of Prussia was obsessed with the danger from revolutionary France. Throughout Europe, Dumouriez's diplomacy was frustrated by the secret agents employed by the baron de Breteuil, who was now working in close association with Fersen and the count de Mercy-Argenteau.[3] The Austro-Prussian combination proved unbreakable, while the duke of Brunswick showed his real sympathies by accepting the post of commander-in-chief of the combined anti-French forces. As the interchange of notes between Paris and Vienna degenerated in the course of March into a series of ultimata, war became inevitable. On 20th April, 1792, war on the "King of Hungary and Bohemia" was declared on the proposition of Louis XVI in the Legislative Assembly, before Talleyrand had set out for London. Only seven votes were cast against the motion.

[3] [Breteuil, Louis XVI's unofficial adviser; Fersen, Marie Antoinette's Swedish admirer; and Mercy-Argenteau, the Austrian Ambassador to France, were all three avowed counterrevolutionary confidants of the royal family.—Eds.]

The Outbreak: The French Deputies Primarily Responsible

HIPPOLYTE TAINE

Hippolyte Taine (1828–1893) was one of France's best-known men of letters in the second half of the nineteenth century. This son of a Protestant lawyer from the Ardennes, after having attended the École normale supérieure in Paris, built his reputation with works of literary criticism and philosophy. Then, very distressed by the Franco-Prussian War and the Commune of 1871, he directed his powerful intellect to history and from 1876 to 1893 he published his multivolume *Origins of Contemporary France*. Although Taine has been criticized by historians for such faults as inadequate research and a biased presentation of evidence, his *Origins* nevertheless has had a broad and continuing influence in France and elsewhere, especially among those who deplore the Revolution.

War, like a black cloud, rises above the horizon, overspreads the sky, thunders and wraps France filled with explosive materials in a circle of lightning, and it is the Assembly which, through the greatest of its mistakes, draws down the bolt on the nation's head.

It might have been turned aside with a little prudence. Two principal grievances were alleged, one by France and the other by the Empire. On the one hand, and very justly, France complained of the gathering of *émigrés*, which the Emperor and Electors tolerated against it on the frontier. In the first place, however, a few thousands of gentlemen, without troops or stores, and nearly without money, need not excite much fear, and, besides this, long before the decisive hour came these troops were dispersed, at once by the Emperor in his own dominions, and, fifteen days afterwards, by the Elector of Trèves in his electorate. On the other hand,

From Hippolyte Taine, *The French Revolution*, trans. John Durand (2nd ed. rev.; New York: Henry Holt and Co., 1892), II, 96–102. Some of the footnotes have been omitted or clarified. This volume is part of Taine's *Origins of Contemporary France*.

according to treaties, the German princes, who owned estates in Alsace, made claims for the feudal rights abolished on their French possessions and the Diet forbade them to accept the offered indemnity. But, as far as the Diet is concerned, nothing was easier nor more customary than to let negotiations drag along, there being no risk or inconvenience attending the suit as, during the delay, the claimants remained empty-handed.

If, now, behind the ostensible motives, the real intentions are sought for, it is certain that, up to January, 1792, the intentions of Austria were pacific. The grants made to the Comte d'Artois, in the Declaration of Pilnitz, were merely a court-sprinkling of holy-water, the semblance of an illusory promise and subject to a European concert of action, that is to say, annulled beforehand by an indefinite postponement, while this pretended league of sovereigns is at once "placed by the politicians in the class of august comedies." [1] Far from taking up arms against new France in the name of old France, the Emperor Leopold and his prime minister Kaunitz, were glad to see the constitution completed and accepted by the King; it "got them out of trouble," [2] and Prussia likewise. In all state management political interest is the great mainspring and both powers needed all their forces in another direction, in Poland, one for retarding, and the other for accelerating its divisions, and both, when the partition took place, to get enough for themselves and prevent Russia from getting too much. The sovereigns of Prussia and Austria, accordingly, did not yet entertain any idea of delivering Louis XVI, nor of conducting the *émigrés* back, nor of conquering French provinces, and if anything was to be expected from them on account of personal ill-will, there was no fear of their armed intervention.

On the side of France it is not the King who urges a rupture; he knows too well what mortal danger there is to him and his in the chances of war. Secretly as well as publicly, in writing to the *émigrés,* his wishes are to bring them back or to restrain them. In his private correspondence he asks of the European powers not physical but moral aid, the external support of a congress which will permit moderate men, the partisans of order, all owners of property, to raise their heads and rally around the throne and the laws against anarchy. In his ministerial correspondence every precaution is taken not to apply the match or let it be applied to gunpowder. At the critical moment of the discussion[3] he entreats the deputies, through M. Delessart, his Minister of Foreign Affairs, to weigh their words and especially not to send forth a challenge on a "fixed term of delay." He resists to the very last as far as his

---

[1] Jacques Mallet du Pan, *Mémoires et correspondance . . . pour servir à l'histoire de la Révolution française* (Paris: Amyot, 1851), I, 254 (Feb. 1792). Mirabeau and the Comte de La Marck, *Correspondance . . . pendant les années 1789, 1790, 1791 . . .* (Paris: Vᵛᵉ Le Normant, 1851), III, 232 (note of M. de Bacourt). On the very day and at the moment of signing the treaty at Pilnitz, at eleven o'clock in the evening, the Emperor Leopold wrote to his prime minister, M. de Kaunitz, to this effect: "The agreement he had just signed does not really bind him to anything. The declarations it contains, extorted by the Count d'Artois, have no value whatever." He ends by assuring him that "neither himself nor his government is in any way bound by this instrument."

[2] Words of M. de Kaunitz, Sept. 4, 1791, as quoted in Alfred von Vivenot, *Recueil,* I, 242.

[3] *Réimpression de l'ancien Moniteur . . .* (Paris: Plon, 1847–1850), XI, 142 (session of Jan. 17, 1792). Speech by M. Delessart. Decree of accusation against him Mar. 10, 1792. Declaration of war, Apr. 20, 1792. . . .

passive will lets him. On being compelled to declare war he requires beforehand the advice of all his ministers, over their signatures, and, only at the last extremity, utters the fatal words "with tears in his eyes," dragged on by the Assembly which has just cited M. Delessart before the supreme court at Orléans, under a capital charge, and which qualifies all caution as treachery.

It is the Assembly then which launches the disabled ship on the roaring abysses of an unknown sea, without a rudder and leaking at every seam; it alone slips the cable which held it in port and which the foreign powers neither dared nor desired to sever. The Girondists are the leaders and hold the axe; since the last of October they have grasped it and struck repeated blows. As an exception, the extreme Jacobins, Couthon, Collot d'Herbois, Danton, Robespierre, do not side with them. Robespierre, who at first proposed to confine the Emperor "within the circle of Popilius," [4] [that is, to give him an ultimatum] fears the placing of too great power in the King's hands, and, growing mistrustful, preaches distrust. But the great mass of the party, led by clamorous public opinion, impels on the timid marching in front. Of the many things of which knowledge is necessary to conduct successfully such a complex and delicate affair, they know nothing; they are ignorant about cabinets, courts, populations, treaties, precedents, timely forms and requisite style.

Their guide and counsellor in foreign relations is Brissot, whose pre-eminence is based on their ignorance and who, exalted into a statesman, becomes for a few months the most conspicuous figure in Europe.[5] To whatever extent a European calamity may be attributed to any one man, this one is to be attributed to him. It is this wretch, born in a pastry-cook's shop, brought up in an attorney's office, formerly a police agent at 150 francs per month, once in league with scandal-mongers and black-mailers,[6] a penny-a-liner, busybody, and intermeddler, who, with the half-information of a nomad, scraps of newspaper ideas and reading-room lore, added to his scribblings as a writer and his club declamation, directs the destinies of France and starts a war in Europe which is to destroy six millions of lives. From the garret in which his wife washes his shirts, he enjoys the snubbing of potentates and, on the 20th of October [1791], in the tribune,[7] he begins by insulting thirty foreign sovereigns. This keen, intense enjoyment on which the new fanaticism daily feeds

[4] B.-J. Buchez et P.-C. Roux, *Histoire parlementaire de la Révolution française* . . . (Paris: Paulin, 1834–1838), XII, 402 (session of the Jacobin Club, Nov. 28, 1791).

[5] Gustavus III, King of Sweden, assassinated by Ankarström, says: "I should like to know what Brissot will say."

[6] On Brissot's antecedents, cf. Edmond Biré, *La Légende des Girondins* (Paris: V. Palmé, 1881). Personally Brissot was honest, and remained poor. But he had passed through a good deal of filth, and bore the marks of it. He had lent himself to the diffusion of an obscene book, *Le Diable dans un bénitier*, and, in 1783, having received 13,355 francs to found a Lyceum in London, not only did not found it, but was unable to return the money.

[7] *Moniteur*, X, 174. "This Venetian government, which is nothing but a farce. . . . Those petty German princes, whose insolence in the last century despotism crushed out. . . . Geneva, that atom of a republic. . . . That bishop of Liège, whose yoke bows down a people that ought to be free. . . . I disdain to speak of other princes. . . . That King of Sweden, who has only twenty-five millions income, and who spends two-thirds of it in poor pay for an army of generals and a small number of discontented soldiers. . . . As to that princess (Catherine II), whose dislike of the French constitution is well known, and who is about as good looking as Elizabeth, she cannot expect greater success than Elizabeth in the Dutch revolution." (Brissot, in this last passage, tries to appear at once witty and well read.)

itself, Madame Roland herself delights in, with evident complacency, the two famous letters in which, with a supercilious tone, she first instructs the King and next the Pope.[8] Brissot, at bottom, regards himself as a Louis XIV, and expressly invites the Jacobins to imitate the haughty ways of the Great Monarch.[9]

To the mismanagement of the interloper, and the sensitiveness of the upstart, must be added the rigidity of the sectary. The Jacobins, in the name of abstract right, deny historic right; they impose from above, and by force, that truth of which they are the apostles, and allow themselves every provocation which they prohibit to others. "Europe must know," exclaims Isnard,[10] "that ten millions of Frenchmen, armed with the sword, with the pen, with reason, with eloquence, might, if provoked, change the face of the world and make tyrants tremble on their thrones of clay." "Wherever a throne exists," says Hérault de Séchelles, "there is an enemy." [11] "Honest capitulation between tyranny and liberty," says Brissot, "is impossible. Your Constitution is an eternal anathema against absolute monarchs. . . . It places them on trial, it pronounces judgment on them; it seems to say to each—to-morrow thou shalt pass away or shalt be king only through the people. War is now a national benefit, and not to have war is the only calamity to be dreaded." [12] "Tell the King," says Gensonné, "that war is necessary, that public opinion demands it, that the safety of the empire [France] makes it a law." [13] "The state we are in," concludes Vergniaud, "is a veritable state of destruction that may lead us to disgrace and death. To arms! to arms! Citizens, freemen, defend your liberty, confirm the hopes of that of the human race. . . . Lose not the advantage of your position. Attack now that there is every sign of complete success. . . . The manes of past generations seem to me crowding into this temple to conjure you, in the name of the evils which slavery has compelled them to endure, to preserve future generations from similar evils, the generations whose destinies are in your hands! Let this prayer be granted! Be for the future a new Providence! Ally yourselves with eternal justice!" [14]

There is no longer any room for serious discussion with those Marseilles orators. Brissot, in response to the claim made by the Emperor in behalf of the

---

[8] Letter of Roland to the King, June 10, 1792, and letter of the executive council to the Pope, Nov. 25, 1792. Letter of Madame Roland to Brissot, Jan. 7, 1791. "Briefly, adieu. Cato's wife need not gratify herself by complimenting Brutus."

[9] Buchez et Roux, XII, 410 (meeting of the Jacobin Club, Dec. 10, 1791). "A Louis XIV declares war against Spain, because his ambassador had been insulted by the Spanish ambassador. And we, who are free, we give a moment's hesitation to it!" [Until late 1792 Brissot and many of his followers were members of the Jacobin clubs. That is why Taine can speak of them as Jacobins.—Eds.]

[10] *Moniteur*, X, 503 (session of Nov. 29 [1791]). The Assembly orders this speech to be printed and distributed in the departments.

[11] *Moniteur*, X, 762 (session of Dec. 28 [1791]).

[12] *Moniteur*, XI, 147, 149 (session of Jan. 17 [1792]); X, 759 (session of Dec. 28 [1791]). Already, on the 16th of Dec., he had declared at the Jacobin Club: "A people that has conquered its freedom, after ten centuries of slavery, needs war. War is essential to it for its consolidation." (Buchez et Roux, XII, 410). On the 17th of Jan. [1792], in the tribune, he again repeats: "I have only one fear, and that is, that we may not have war."

[13] *Moniteur*, XI, 119 (session of Jan. 13 [1792]). Speech by Gensonné, in the name of the diplomatic committee, of which he is the spokesman.

[14] *Moniteur*, XI, 158 (session of Jan. 18 [1792]). The Assembly orders the printing of this speech.

princes' property in Alsace, replies that "the sovereignty of the people is not bound by the treaties of tyrants." [15] As to the gatherings of the *émigrés*, the Emperor having yielded on this point, he will yield on the others.[16] Let him formally renounce all combinations against France. "I want war on the 10th of February [1792]," says Brissot, "if we do not receive advices of this renunciation." No explanations are to be listened to; we want satisfaction; "to require satisfaction is to put the Emperor at our mercy." [17] The Assembly, so eager to start the quarrel, usurps the King's right to take the first step and formally declares war, fixing the date.[18]

The die is now cast. "They want war," says the Emperor, "and they shall have it." Austria immediately forms an alliance with Prussia, threatened, like herself, with revolutionary propaganda.[19] By sounding the tocsin the Jacobins, masters of the Assembly, have succeeded in bringing about that "monstrous alliance," and, from day to day, this tocsin sounds the louder. One year more, thanks to this policy, and France will have all Europe for an enemy and for an only friend, the Regency of Algiers, whose internal system of government is about the same as her own.

Behind their *carmagnoles* we can detect a design which they will avow later on. "We were always opposed by the Constitution," Brissot is to say, "and nothing but war could put the Constitution down." Diplomatic wrongs, consequently, of which they make parade, are simply pretexts; if they urge war it is for the purpose of overthrowing the legal order of things which annoys them; their real object is the conquest of power, a second internal revolution, the application of their system and a final state of equality.

[15] *Moniteur*, X, 760 (session of Dec. 28 [1791]).

[16] *Moniteur*, XI, 149 (session of Jan. 17 [1792]). Speech by Brissot.

[17] *Moniteur*, XI, 178 (session of Jan. 20 [1792]). Fauchet proposes the following decree: "All partial treaties actually existent are declared void. The National Assembly substitutes in their place alliances with the English, the Anglo-American, the Helvetic, Polish, and Dutch nations, as long as they remain free. . . . When other nations want our alliance, they have only to conquer their freedom to have it. Meanwhile, this will not prevent us from having relations with them, as with *good-natured savages*. . . . Let us occupy the towns in the neighborhood which bring our adversaries too near us. . . . Mayence, Coblentz, and Worms are sufficient." *Ibid.*, p. 215 (session of Jan. 25). One of the members, supporting himself with the authority of Gelon, King of Syracuse, proposes an additional article: "We declare that we will not lay down our arms until we shall have established the freedom of all peoples." These stupidities show the mental condition of the Jacobin party.

[18] The decree is passed Jan. 25 [1792]. The alliance between Prussia and Austria takes place Feb. 7. (François de Bourgoing, *Histoire diplomatique de l'Europe pendant la Révolution française* [Paris: Lévy, 1865–1885], I, 457.)

[19] Albert Sorel, "La Mission du Comte de Ségur à Berlin" (published in the *Temps*, Oct. 15, 1878). Dispatch of M. de Ségur to M. Delessart, Feb. 24, 1792. "Count Schulenburg [the Prussian cabinet minister] repeated to me that they had no desire whatever to meddle with our constitution. But, said he with singular animation, we must guard against gangrene. Prussia is, perhaps, the country which should fear it least; nevertheless, however remote a gangrened member may be, it is better to cut it off than risk one's life. How can you expect to secure tranquillity, when thousands of writers every day . . . mayors, office-holders, insult kings, and publish that the Christian religion has always supported despotism, and that we shall be free only by destroying it, and that all princes must be exterminated because they are all tyrants?"

4

The Causes
of the Vendée Revolt
# of 1793

T

HE fascinating and tragic Vendée uprising in western France was a civil war in the midst of a revolution, a struggle that began on a large scale in 1793 and continued sporadically until Napoleon's early years in power. Historians, as well as such novelists as Honoré de Balzac, Victor Hugo, and Alexandre Dumas, have been attracted to this dramatic episode. They have asked, and one may still ask, what brought tens of thousands of men to fight against the Revolution.

Jacques Godechot considers that the geography of the region, religious passion, and social differences all helped to cause the revolt, and he also points to that *bête noire* of republican historians, the aristocratic conspiracy. Émile Gabory denies the importance of aristocratic and clerical plots and instead argues that religious feeling among the peasants was the main underlying cause of a revolt triggered by other provocations. Finally, John McManners reviews different points of view and concludes that abject poverty, social tension, and religious fervor all played a significant role.

How do we decide why people embark on civil war? Should we rely on what the rebels say are the reasons for their actions? Do we search for unexpressed or subconscious motivations? Which of the many forces—social, economic, political, or ideological—do we stress?

$\mathcal{A}$ Republican Interpretation

JACQUES GODECHOT

For biographical information on Jacques Godechot, see Chapter 1, "The Outbreak of the Revolution (1787–1789)."

The peasant insurrections in western France were but the first of their kind among the numerous counterrevolutionary insurrections. In the course of the period with which we are concerned [1789–1804], there were many other peasant insurrections directed against revolutionary leaders or institutions. For example, the Vendée insurrection revived after 1795, then reappeared in 1799, and again even as late as 1830. The peasants of Normandy, Brittany, and of the western fringes of the Paris basin took up arms against the Revolution from 1793 to 1799. This movement was called the *Chouannerie*. In southwestern France peasants rose up in the name of the king in 1799. Several peasant insurrections took place in Italy from 1796 to 1799, especially in Calabria [the "toe" of the Italian boot], in the Papal States, and in Tuscany. In Belgium there was a "peasant war" in 1798, which was also a counterrevolutionary insurrection. German and Swiss peasants took up arms against the Revolution on several occasions between 1796 and 1799. After 1800 numerous peasant insurrections of a counterrevolutionary nature broke out in different areas of Europe. The most famous such uprising, and the one which had the most important consequences, was that of the Spanish peasantry, known as the Spanish War of Independence. The German wars of "liberation" in 1813 and 1814 also were, in part, peasant insurrections.

All these insurrections belonged to the same family, and we can ask if they sprang from similar causes. Historians disagree considerably about the causes of the insurrections in western France. There are a great many books dealing with the subject, but most are apologetic and hagiographic works written by royalists who eulogize the Vendeans or *Chouans*.

In their studies of the causes of the insurrections in western France, historians are divided between two points of view, depending on their political sympathies. Those hostile to the Revolution favor the thesis of a spontaneous uprising: the Constitution of 1791 and the institutions of the Revolution contradicted the natural

From Jacques Godechot, *La Contre-Révolution: Doctrine et action, 1789-1804* (Paris: Presses Universitaires de France, 1961), pp. 216–229. Printed by permission of the publisher. Editors' translation.

order of things; and so the peasants, shocked by the aberration, revolted spontaneously. They also rebelled against atheism, against all religious innovations, and against unjustified reforms. On the other hand, historians favorable to the Revolution support the thesis of an insurrection incited either by the actions of the clergy and the nobility, or by the agents of the *émigrés*, or by the countries at war with France.

Because of insufficient research, we do not know enough about the economic or social structure of the insurgent areas in either western France or the other regions where peasant uprisings occurred. Only two works have sketched the social structure of the insurgent regions—for France, Léon Dubreuil's book, *Histoire des insurrections de l'Ouest*, and for Italy, that of Gaetano Cingari.[1] Other works are more anecdotal, describing the course of events without really analyzing their causes. Moreover, Dubreuil's study of the social structure of the insurgent regions is quite brief. But at the present moment, new research is attempting to add to our knowledge of this question.

General Characteristics of Counterrevolutionary Peasant Insurrections

We may ask if the peasant insurrections can be explained by geographical determinism. Upon examining the insurrections in western France, we see that they occurred in the *bocage* areas, where small fields were surrounded by hedgerows through which winding roads ran and where it was easy to hide. The peasants' fields were scattered, and they lived in isolated hamlets. But, an analysis of other peasant insurrections reveals that they took place in regions of a different character. In southern Italy, Calabria was an area of rather wild scrub land where the peasants lived in very large villages, actually rural cities which sometimes contained more than twenty thousand inhabitants. Yet, communications were as difficult as in western France. In Spain the 1809 insurrection occurred on the Castilian plateau as well as in the *huerta* [irrigated fruit lands] of Valencia and in the Aragonese plains. Communications were difficult in the Spain of the Old Regime too. Therefore, it is hard to identify a geographical determinism underlying the peasant revolts.

Can we speak of a sociological determinism, of a certain social structure which predisposed people to revolt? We must mention that in all insurgent areas during the revolutionary era, in France, Italy, Spain, and elsewhere, insurrections occurred most often in regions where the peasants were very submissive to their lords and landowners. Even today in the Vendée the peasants speak of the landowner as "our master," perhaps a vestige of their former submissiveness. In these areas the peasants either respect the landowner, the lord, and submit to him, or they hate him. The landlord exercises his authority in the secular sphere by collecting the rents due him, and in the religious sphere by requiring his peasants to attend mass, receive the sacraments, and send their children to Catholic school.

---

[1] *Giacobini e sanfedisti in Calabria nel 1799* (Messina, 1957). [Marcel Faucheux's *L'Insurrection vendéenne de 1793: Aspects économiques et sociaux* (Paris: Commission d'Histoire économique et sociale de la Révolution, 1964) and Charles Tilly's *The Vendée* (Cambridge, Mass.: Harvard University Press, 1964) have appeared since the present selection was originally published.—Eds.]

It has been pointed out that in these areas, the authority of the clergy, especially that of the local priests, was very great. In the Vendée as well as in Calabria, when the priest was a partisan of the new regime the local population followed him; when, on the contrary, he opposed it, so did the population. The influence of the clergy appears to predominate in all the areas where peasant insurrections have been observed, whether in western France, southern or eastern Italy, Spain, Belgium, or Switzerland.

Are we dealing here with a matter of religious faith or of custom? It is difficult to say. In these regions where communication was difficult and where formal education was rare and hardly developed, superstition was widespread. It appears that the clergy incited the peasants to resist changes in religious ritual rather than arousing them to fight for basic tenets of faith. We also can wonder about the role played in the preparation and development of the insurrections by a secret religious organization, the Aa, a group still very little understood. This association, growing out of the Congregation of the Holy Sacrament, which in turn was linked with the Society of Jesus, grouped together refractory priests, especially in southwestern France. It is possible that it also promoted the Vendée rebellion.[2] Signor Cingari states that in Calabria there were believers and nonbelievers in both the revolutionary and the opposing camps.

It appears, therefore, that the peasant insurrections were caused to some degree by geography—the difficulty of communication that hindered new ideas from spreading. Peasant insurrections were also a consequence of the social structure. They developed in regions where the peasants—sharecroppers or tenants—were very dependent on the landlords, as well as frequently in areas where the peasant was hostile to the bourgeois. The peasant was best acquainted with the bourgeois in his capacity as a tax collector, either for the state or the lord, or as a merchant exploiting the countryside and often lending money at usurious rates of interest. In addition, the effect of religion, of religious practice, is undeniable; the influence of the clergy is certain.

Turning to the particular conditions that affected the insurrections in western France, we must first point out the attitude of the peasants toward the Revolution. At the beginning of the Revolution the regions that were to rebel so extensively and violently were not hostile to reforms. The peasants, on the contrary, favored them. In 1789 they greeted the abolition of tithes and feudal dues enthusiastically—they already had requested such actions in their cahiers of grievances. In the Old Regime the salt tax had aroused much discontent among the peasants and they were happy that it was abolished. They also had been very hostile to the drawing by lot for *militia service*, even though this did not weigh very heavily on them.

There were some peasants, however, whose demands were not satisfied by the reforms of the revolutionary era. In western France there were tenant farmers in a special category—tenants on cancellable leases or *colons partiaires* [a type of sharecropper]. These particular kinds of land tenure existed only in this region.

---

[2] On the Aa, see B. Faÿ, *La Grande Révolution* (Paris, 1959), as well as P. Droulers, *Action pastorale et problèmes sociaux sous la Monarchie de Juillet chez Mgr d'Astros, archevêque de Toulouse* (Paris, 1954). Consult also the article on the Aa in the *Dictionnaire de spiritualité*. More probing studies of the Aa are in progress.

Peasants who were fettered by these especially onerous types of land tenure generally were loyal to the Revolution; in spite of everything, they hoped for changes in their land tenure.

Therefore, the peasant did not, a priori, oppose the revolutionary regime. On the other hand, he was frequently hostile to the bourgeois. He knew the bourgeois only as an employee of the lord, an agent of the noble. It was the bourgeois who collected feudal dues for the lord. It was the bourgeois who sold essential goods to the peasant, and the peasant believed that he was being exploited. Among the peasants, the bourgeois had a reputation for being miserly, grasping, and selfish. Peasants generally were hostile to him. The same attitude can be seen in Italy, Belgium, and Spain. The alliance between the bourgeoisie and the peasantry allowed the Revolution to succeed, but in France, as elsewhere, in those regions where this alliance could not be achieved, the Revolution miscarried.

The religious attitudes of the peasantry of western France have not yet been examined by recently developed methods of sociological analysis. But, in general, the peasant of the West was very attached to religious practices, if not to religion itself. He was very loyal to the forms, rituals, and ceremonies, to which he tended to attach a magical value. The closing of churches and the interruption of normal religious practices certainly caused discontent. He would not tolerate such innovations. In Calabria and Spain there were similar reactions.

The peasantry in western France was subject to the clergy's leadership. Before the Revolution, the clergy was divided into two categories. The lower clergy, poorly educated and very close to the common people, were obliging, charitable, and loved by their flocks. The upper clergy were usually very haughty. In sharp contrast to the poor parish priests, they were recruited from the nobility, often belonged to Masonic lodges, and were wealthy. The richest bishop was that of Bayeux. He had an income of 90,000 livres per year. The poorest bishop, that of Saint-Brieuc, had an income of 12,000. The lower clergy in western France warmly welcomed the meeting of the Estates-General. In the elections very few bishops were chosen. Only two out of seven bishops were elected from the archdiocese of Rouen; from that of Tours, only two out of twelve; and Brittany sent no bishops to the Estates-General. But from Bordeaux, seven out of ten were elected (the Bordeaux archdiocese was the one least troubled by revolutionary insurrections).

We see, then, that the clergy welcomed the Revolution enthusiastically. But, after the very first measures, they grew dissatisfied. Although pleased with the abolition of the old method of paying priests, they opposed the abolition of tithes, which was decided during the night of August 4, 1789, and they opposed even more the nationalization of Church property, which was voted November 2, 1789. Religious liberty, as set forth first in the Declaration of the Rights of Man and later even more clearly by various laws, also offended this region that was almost entirely Catholic (there were only a few Protestants). The clergy was irritated above all because the revolutionary reforms placed religion and its ministers in a subordinate position instead of keeping them in the top rank, as was true before 1789. On September 12, 1789, Bishop Le Mintier of Tréguier, Brittany, published a statement very hostile to the Revolution. It attacked the thought of the Enlightenment, condemned freedom of the press, warned the faithful against dangerous innovations which put "the essence of royal authority in the hands of the multitude." He deplored "the weakened military discipline and the fact that citizens were taking up arms against each other. . . ." "The Church," he said, "is falling into degradation and servility; its ministers are threatened with being reduced to the status of appointed clerks. Also, the highest courts are ignored and humiliated." Le Mintier went on to protest against the substitution of state welfare for charity and against the abolition of certain very wise old laws. Finally, he warned the peasant against buying nationalized Church lands, even though they had not yet been put on sale. Le Mintier's statement had a very great impact. All the nobles of the region approved of it, and it marked the beginning of the break between the people of the western area and the Revolution.

The publication of the Civil Constitution of the Clergy heightened the discontent, especially because it reduced the number of dioceses. Seven dioceses were abolished in the western region, and in an area of such poor communications this could have resulted in very serious inconveniences. Many priests, perhaps encouraged by the Aa, refused to take the oath required by the Civil Constitution. In the diocese of Angers over 50 per cent of the priests were refractory; in the Vendée and in Brittany more than 80 per cent. Nevertheless, this was not the major reason for the outbreak of the insurrection; for there was an equal or even a greater proportion of refractory priests in other areas of France where insurgency did not develop. For example, around the Massif Central over 80 per cent of the priests were refractory and in the departments of Moselle and Bas-Rhin, 92 per cent.

The replacement of refractory priests by those who took the oath and who were alleged to be bad priests began to arouse some opposition. Arrests of refractory priests made matters worse. Refractory priests then held clandestine services, and religious processions marched at night. Such nocturnal ceremonies awakened the mystical spirit characteristic of the people of western France. The Bretons, who believed in goblins prowling the moors at night, were attached to their legends. Their fears and superstitions were aroused, and this created an attitude hostile to the Revolution. Hatreds were inflamed.

The bourgeoisie's attitude, on the other hand, was generally favorable to the Revolution. The bourgeoisie in western France, as everywhere else, was a composite class—it included merchants, lawyers, and lower government officials. But added altogether, the bourgeoisie was less numerous in the West than elsewhere. In 1789 it actually was large only in Nantes.

From the beginning of 1789 the bourgeoisie gained entry into the municipal councils of the large cities. When Church property went on sale, most of the purchasers were bourgeois. We should not believe, however, that all the bourgeois had the same point of view. Though many of them supported the Revolution, others were quite hostile. An entire group of the bourgeoisie had connections with the nobility by family ties and aspired to noble rank. Nobles and bourgeois mingled in the "literary societies" and Masonic lodges. For example, the lodges of Le Mans included nobles, merchants, and government officials.[3] Yet, in general, the

---

[3] A. Bouton, *Les Francs-maçons manceaux et la Révolution française* (Le Mans, 1958).

bourgeoisie went along with the revolutionary movement. The majority of the western peasantry, on the contrary, grew more and more hostile to the reforms.

The Origins of the Insurrection

Certainly, the general conditions just analyzed played a very important part in the origin of the western insurrections, but a catalyst was necessary. The thesis of republican historians—that the insurrection originated in plots organized either by refractory priests or by the nobility—cannot be dismissed out of hand. Clearly, the actions of the nobility and the clergy played a decisive part in the preparation of the insurrection. In this regard, it appears that a plot organized by a noble, the Marquis de La Rouairie, had a great impact.[4]

The Marquis de La Rouairie was born at Fougères, Brittany, in 1750. He had a wild adolescence, with numerous duels and remarkable love affairs, and gained notoriety by an attempt at suicide. He took part in the American War for Independence: under the name of Colonel Armand he led a band of irregulars, which made him a celebrity. He came back from America very enthusiastic for liberty, but he had neither the intelligence nor the social rank of Lafayette; on his return to France, he was received rather coldly. It appears that the comparison between his reception and that given to Lafayette displeased and embittered him.

In 1788, during the agitation which preceded the calling of the Estates-General, he passionately favored the Parlement of Brittany and he was chosen to transmit to Paris the grievances of the Breton nobility, who were hostile to the recent decisions of the king. La Rouairie was arrested and thrown into the Bastille. Released at the fall of the Brienne ministry, he returned in triumph to his birthplace, Fougères. He protested against the ordinance regulating the methods of election for the Estates-General because it disregarded the laws and customs of Brittany. He was particularly hostile to the doubling of the Third Estate; and when the Constituent Assembly was created, he opposed the first reform measures. It appears that by the beginning of 1790 he was thinking of organizing a counterrevolutionary movement: he gathered a number of his aristocratic friends in his château near Saint-Brieuc; and at this time some of them already suggested appealing to England for aid in supporting a counterrevolutionary movement.

La Rouairie left France in May 1791. Furnished with an ordinary passport, he reached Coblenz. There he claimed to represent the Breton Association, which was composed of *émigrés* from this region. The Association had as its aim a restoration of a monarchy "checked" by the ancient constitution of France, a monarchy respectful of the traditional Breton liberties and of "the religion of our forefathers." As a striking force, La Rouairie hoped to provide the Association with guerrilla bands similar to those he had led in the United States. The Breton Association soon

[4] See on this subject A. Goodwin, "Counter-Revolution in Brittany: The Royalist Conspiracy of the Marquis de La Rouërie, 1791–1793," *Bulletin of the John Rylands Library*, 1957, pp. 326–355. The name can be spelled either La Rouairie or La Rouërie.

established branches in all the provinces of the West—Brittany, Normandy, Anjou, and Poitou. It was based on a whole series of committees organized in every city that had been an official seat of a diocese before the Revolution. Each committee was composed of six members and a secretary. There were less important committees in other cities. The committees received orders from their leader, the Marquis de La Rouairie himself. Article 6 of the manifesto distributed to the committees defined the Association's object: to contribute with "the least possible violence" to the restoration of absolute monarchy and to the recognition of "the prerogatives of provinces, landowners, and Breton honor." Association members were urged to do their best to win over National Guardsmen. Article 11 stated, "The military organization will be established later." Clearly, the Association was preparing to create a true counterrevolutionary militia.

In June 1791, the Comte d'Artois [the *émigré* brother of Louis XVI] recognized La Rouairie as the head of the Breton Association. For financing he went to see Calonne,[5] but received only a small subsidy in the devaluated paper currency of the Paris Discount Bank and in counterfeit assignats. Later, the Comte de Provence confirmed La Rouairie's powers. La Rouairie had many supporters in Brittany, among them his mistress Thérèse de Moëlien, his brother Gervais de La Rouairie, and other nobles, including Boisguy, the soon-to-be-notorious Pictot de Limoëlan, as well as the Chevalier de Tinténiac, a cashiered naval officer. It appears that the Breton Association also included Jean Cottereau, who would soon take the pseudonym Jean Chouan, from which the word *Chouannerie* seems to be derived.

The rank and file was made up of former salt-smugglers who had lost their livelihood now that the salt tax had been abolished; Breton *émigrés* who had gone to England, the island of Jersey, or Germany; those who had lost their jobs as a result of revolutionary reforms; and some members of the officer corps of the National Guard.

Large cities, such as Nantes and Brest, lent little support to the Association, but it had some success in the small ones. The Association charged the members of the conspiracy dues equal to a year's income, but many members did not pay them. It was never financially well-off. Nevertheless, at the beginning of 1792 the Association possessed over six thousand guns, some powder, and four cannon.

The plotters of the Breton Association hoped to seize Rennes at the same time as an *émigré* corps landed in Brittany and counterrevolutionaries aroused opposition in the Cévennes, Lozère, and Ardèche departments in south central France. But the coordination of all these movements could not be fully assured. In addition, the victory of the Revolution at the battle of Valmy disconcerted the plotters. They had expected to revolt at the moment when the Prussian and Austrian armies approached Paris. The defeat of the invaders completely changed their plans.

As early as May 1792 the revolutionary authorities learned of the plot. On the night of May 31–June 1, 1792, one of La Rouairie's secretaries, as well as several other plotters, were arrested and their papers seized. Others talked, especially a man named Chévetel. Still, before the fall of the monarchy, the authorities dared not act

[5] [The former Controller-General of Finances from 1783 to 1787 became a leader of the *émigrés* early in the Revolution.—Eds.]

against the conspirators. Only after August 10, 1792, did the new Minister of Justice, Danton, order an urgent investigation of the plot. The order to arrest the leading members of the conspiracy was issued. La Rouairie managed to escape the police, but he fell seriously ill and on January 30, 1793, he died in a château in the Côtes-du-Nord department.

Some of the plotters were arrested. Twelve were tried, convicted, and on June 18, 1793, guillotined. So the conspiracy failed. Yet it appears to have played an important role in preparing the insurrection of the West. It trained leaders and organized counterrevolutionary committees; it established contacts among those who were or might become the principal leaders of the counterrevolutionary movement.

The Breton Association sought, it appears, an insurrection not only in Brittany, as its name suggests, but also throughout the West between the estuary of the Gironde and the estuary of the Seine. The conversations of the Vendean leader d'Elbée with General Turreau on Noirmoutier Island shortly before d'Elbée's execution seem to reveal the aim of the Breton Association. In fact, d'Elbée said to Turreau, "Since the Vendée insurrection had broken out ahead of the time set for a general uprising, I did all I could to restrain and prevent any premature action because the whole organization was not completely set up and I foresaw the danger of a piecemeal movement."

In addition, among the documents about the *émigrés* in the Archives of the Ministry of Foreign Affairs in Paris, there is a paper containing the following question written by an agent of the Comte de Provence: "Who decided the moment for the Vendeans to revolt?" and the response, "Jeopardized by the death of M. de La Rouairie and the seizure of his papers, the coalition of counterrevolutionaries was forced to take action and its first move was to gather 150 men and disarm the National Guard of a small village." These documents prove that there were indisputable connections between La Rouairie's plot and the Vendée insurrection, which in turn marked the beginning of the general insurrections in the West. In fact, it even appears that the seizure of the papers of the Breton Association at the time of its leaders' arrest brought on the Vendée insurrection. The Vendean leaders, already compromised by their part in the Breton Association, feared arrest; and to forestall it, they decided to revolt in early March 1793.

Such was the immediate origin of the Vendée insurrection. But it profited from a whole series of earlier armed uprisings. Some small riots and insurrections already had occurred in the region. In the tiny village of La Croix de la Viollière, in the Vendée department, the peasants took up arms during a village fête in September 1790, but this riot was easily quelled. A government official wrote in October 1790, "The aristocrats have bent all their efforts . . . to bring on a civil war and they have hired men to take up arms against the friends of the people." Near Les Sables-d'Olonne a peasant riot broke out in February 1791, and local officials were roughly handled. On March 1, 1791, armed peasants attacked gendarmes at Saint-Christophe-de-Ligneron. Dumouriez, commander of the military district, was charged with reestablishing order. Again in 1791 another lord, the Marquis de La Lézardière, joined with other notables of his area to organize a plot. The authorities were informed. Before the uprising could break out, it was stopped. The plotters, meeting at La Lézardière's château, were imprisoned; while the peasants, on their way to assemble at the château, were dispersed. Thirty-six persons were prosecuted in the court at Les Sables-d'Olonne and were convicted. But since these actions were soon followed by the amnesty of September 15, 1791 (declared after the king had accepted the new constitution), this plot was not so severely repressed as that of the Marquis de La Rouairie. Nevertheless, the plot of the Marquis de La Lézardière played a part in unleashing the Vendée insurrection.

In 1792 there was another uprising in the Vendée. On August 20, a few days after the fall of the monarchy, the former mayor of Bressuire, Delouche, organized some peasants and occupied the small city of Châtillon. These peasants came from eighty different villages and were led by such nobles as La Béraudière and de Béjarry, who later headed the Vendeans. The National Guard of Bressuire managed to arrest the armed peasants and their leaders. If the Vendeans had been able to take Bressuire at this time, their insurrection might have begun in August 1792 rather than in March 1793. After their march on Bressuire, most of the nobles and peasants were arrested, but then released. No one was punished.

Such were the plots and riots that preceded the Vendée revolt. They seem to have been fostered by the social structure of the region, by the poor communications, by the influence of landowners, nobles, and clergy, by the discontent resulting from the Civil Constitution of the Clergy, and by the actions of refractory priests.

But one more factor played a decisive part. At the end of February 1793, the Convention decided on a levy of 300,000 men in order to resist the military coalition which now included nearly all the countries of Europe. But the peasants of western France always had been very hostile to military service. In the Old Regime volunteers filled the regular army, but it was supplemented by a militia comprised of peasants chosen by lot. This was not a heavy burden for them; only a small number were drawn, and they were subject to just a few training periods a year. Still, the militia was very unpopular throughout France and especially in the West. The peasants always made great efforts to escape being drawn for militia service.

The volunteers raised by the Constituent and Legislative Assemblies in 1791 and 1792 had really joined the colors spontaneously, but by 1793 the number willing to volunteer had been exhausted. The Convention was forced to decide that if there were not enough volunteers to fill the quota of 300,000 men, additional soldiers would be chosen by local authorities or by any other means. In practice, local officials could either designate those whom they wished or choose them by lot. So, the militia reappeared under another form. There can be no doubt that the 300,000-man levy considerably aggravated the discontent in the western region.

The insurrection's chronology is quite clear. The decree ordering the levy of 300,000 men was dated February 24, 1793. It was known at Angers on March 2 and published in the communes of the western region on March 10. On March 11, to the cries of "No conscription!" and "Down with the militia!" insurrection broke out along the left bank of the Loire. On March 12, peasants shouting these slogans seized Saint-Florent-le-Vieil, an especially important town on the left bank of the Loire, a crossing point that allowed one to go from the Vendée to Normandy and Brittany.

What tends to prove, however, that the insurrection was not spontaneous and not caused by conscription alone, was that nobles assumed leadership and organized the peasants from the very beginning. For example, d'Elbée led a band of peasants and occupied Beaupréau. Lescure and La Rochejacquelein took the leadership of peasant bands. However, peasant leaders also appeared, for such men as Cathelineau and Stofflet emerged during the Vendée War. But, at the beginning, on March 12, 13, and 14, noblemen were the most effective leaders.

Actually, the Vendée War presented two distinct features from the start. On the one hand, it was a peasant insurrection. Caring little about forms of government, the peasants wanted to keep their religion and their "kindly priests"; and they especially disliked the militia, the draft. On the other hand, it was a counterrevolutionary movement. The nobles wanted to profit from the peasant revolt; to use a contemporary phrase, they wanted "to restore the throne and altar."

$\mathcal{A}$ Religious Explanation

ÉMILE GABORY

Émile Gabory (1872–1954) was born in the Vendée. Trained at the École nationale des chartes in Paris, he served as a professional archivist in his native region and devoted much time to writing about its colorful and exciting history. His major works include *Napoléon et la Vendée* (1914), *Les Bourbons et la Vendée* (1923), *La Révolution et la Vendée* (1925–1928), and *L'Angleterre et la Vendée* (1930).

The Uprising

The civil war in the Vendée broke out when the Convention called up 300,000 men to protect the *patrie en danger*. The death of Louis XVI [January 21, 1793] had brought about a general coalition. After Austria and Prussia, the English, Russians, Spanish, and Dutch had struck at the frontiers with waves of soldiers. In three decrees issued between February 20 and 24, 1793, all single Frenchmen from the age of eighteen to forty were declared eligible for military service, and then 300,000 were called to the colors. Eighty members of the Convention were ordered to oversee these operations in the provinces. For the patriotic republicans this provided a new opportunity for emotional demonstrations. But among embittered souls, whose highest aims in life were far beyond personal and mundane goals, there arose a unanimous feeling of protest. However, the draft quota fixed for each department of western France was very small: for the department of the Vendée, 4,197 men out of a population of 305,610; in Maine-et-Loire, 6,202 men, of which 752 were to come from the Cholet district and 701 from that of Saint-Florent; and in Loire-Inférieure, 7,327 from a population of 430,000.

If there had been time to prepare the public and to explain the decrees, opposition certainly would have been less vehement; but the orders had to be carried out immediately. . . .

From Émile Gabory, *La Révolution et la Vendée* (Paris: Librairie académique Perrin, 1925), I, 146–148, 195–199, 201–206, 214–217. Printed by permission of the publisher. Editors' translation. Wherever possible, the author's citations of sources in footnotes have been clarified.

One detail of the draft procedure was especially exasperating. Article 20 of a decree dated March 4 exempted most public officials from military service. To be sure, the militia of the Old Regime had also exempted royal officials, as well as most manorial officials. Moreover, those peasants who were at all well-to-do had known how to slip through the net. But in the new regime, where that glorious word equality rang out in every sentence, why, exclaimed the peasants, were these old distinctions kept for the benefit of the privileged class? When all this was added with electrifying rapidity to the underlying causes, one of the most awful political tempests in human memory was unleashed throughout a part of the West. It was like a sudden growth of every bad seed, like the unexpected sprouting of gigantic plants under a tropical sun. . . .

The Circumstances of the Uprising Clarify Its Causes

In the crackling of volleys, the thunder of cannon, the incitements to massacre, and the imploring wails, one can recognize the signs of all the remote and immediate causes that provoked and then launched the uprising. The rebels shouted their various rancors and individual resentments; they insistently proclaimed their motives. One cannot misread them.

What does not appear is "the plot," the celebrated and legendary plot that several writers have seen as the origin of the movement. No doubt, it would take a bold man to deny any significance to the instigations of the nobility and especially the clergy. To deny the existence of agitation by these suspected persons would be to misunderstand the situation. After having desired a new order or at least acquiesced in it, they had come to loathe a regime of which they had much to complain; and they did not hide their opinions. But no tie among all these dissatisfied people can be found, nor can any expressed or secret intention to overthrow the government by force of arms be found. Although some blood had flowed since 1791, there was no general pattern. In many other departments, the installation of Constitutional priests had also been carried out by gunfire; yet no plot or concerted plan is suggested.

In an oppressive atmosphere the storm could be felt building up: "We are having disturbances in our district, and we are afraid of seeing the germs of a general insurrection develop here," said a report from the town of Montaigu in the Vendée department. A dispatch dated March 10, 1793, from Chapelle-Heulin in Loire-Inférieure, noted the arrival "of men known to be disloyal; they have influenced the citizens to such a point that most of the commissioners of the sections [elected officials of small administrative units] have resigned." But these individual agitators obeyed no single watchword—they were moved to action by their own passions. The officials of the Maine-et-Loire department wrote to the Convention, "The servants of clergymen and of former nobles were the first agitators and many of them are leading crowds." [1] Could it have been otherwise?

[1] François Grille, *Lettres, mémoires et documents . . . sur . . . l'esprit du I⁽ᵉʳ⁾ bataillon des volontaires de Maine-et-Loire . . .* (Paris: Amyot, 1850), IV, 215, 218, concerning March 17, 1793; F.-A. Aulard

Was it not natural that the leaders of the movement would be those whose masters had suffered the most, those who had listened to their masters utter the most violent recriminations? These servants were the best prepared and often were former noncommissioned officers. The plot? It was denied even by those supporters of the revolutionary government who were intimately acquainted with the disorders. One of them wrote, "I realized that these events could not be considered the result of a concerted plan." [2] Later, the republican General Travot, always so acute and fair in his judgments, asserted that although the peasants had to be forced and coerced to march in the year VIII [Fall 1799], the movement of March 1793 was spontaneous.

Some authors have tried to connect the pseudo-plot to the real one of Armand, Marquis de La Rouairie, in Brittany,[3] but the facts shout out against such an assertion. No one has been able to uncover the mysterious network which was supposed to have joined Brittany to the other provinces of the West. If some nobles in Anjou or Poitou were acquainted with the schemes of La Rouairie, which is possible, none were caught having any direct or indirect relation with him. No letter gives proof of such an association, no revelation to a friend, no admission before a court of law. Not one emissary of the Bourbon princes was arrested at this time while making his way toward the Vendée. There is total agreement in the statements of Vendean nobles carried along, despite themselves, by the popular flood and in the statements of peasants whose tongues were undoubtedly loosened by being so near the scaffold. All denied any prior agreement and insisted on the spontaneity of the movement's outbreak.

It has been asserted that d'Elbée[4] knew of the Breton plans, but neither at meetings nor among close friends did he ever mention them. "If the Vendeans had taken part in La Rouairie's plot," Madame de La Bouëre has wisely pointed out, "they would have obtained weapons and ammunition; they did not do so; instead they had to fight with sticks." [5]

The insignificant part played by those Vendeans who, according to the scheme of the Breton plotter La Rouairie, were to lead his artificial uprising, is quite revealing. The region had been split up and assigned to various leaders. If we can trust the historian Alphonse de Beauchamp[6] (who, as an employee of the Ministry of Police under the Napoleonic Empire, had access to documents that have since

---

(ed.), *Recueil des actes du comité de salut public avec la correspondance officielle des représentants en mission* . . . (26 vols.; Paris: Imprimerie nationale, 1889–1923), III, 432; the plot is mentioned in *Mémoires d'un ancien administrateur*, p. 10; on the causes cf. Dom François Chamard, *Les Origines et les responsabilités de l'insurrection vendéenne* (Paris: Savaète, 1898); and Henry Jagot, *Les Origines des guerres de Vendée* (Paris: Champion, 1914).

[2] Célestin Port, *La Vendée angevine* (Paris: Hachette, 1888), II, 202; Desmazières, *Précis des évènements dans le district de Cholet.*

[3] Charles-Louis Chassin, *La Préparation de la guerre de Vendée, 1789–1793* (Paris: Dupont, 1892), III, 285. [For biographical information on La Rouairie, see the selection on the Vendée revolt by Jacques Godechot.—Eds.]

[4] [Maurice Gigost d'Elbée, a former army officer, emigrated in 1791, returned to France in 1792, became a leader of the Vendeans in 1793, and was executed in 1794.—Eds.]

[5] Comtesse de La Bouëre, *Souvenirs* (Paris: Plon, Nourrit, 1890), pp. 30–31; also see M.-J.-N. Boutillier de Saint-André, *Mémoires* (Paris: Plon, Nourrit, 1896), p. 51.

[6] Author of *Histoire de la guerre de Vendée* . . . (Paris: Giguet and Michaud, 1806).

disappeared), the principal agents of La Rouairie in the Nantes region were Palierne and Gaudin-Bérillais. Palierne, however, appeared on the scene only after the uprising had occurred—he asked for a military post under General Bonchamps. Gaudin-Bérillais showed himself to be mainly interested in calming the fervor of the insurgents. In Poitou Prince de Talmont was supposed to be the head of the uprising. But Talmont had emigrated to Germany. He joined the rebel army at Saumur only after the tumult of the Vendean hurricane attracted him. Paris was not fooled: on May 30, 1793, the Provisional Executive Council, which the deputies accused of not having foreseen the revolt, drew up a brief account of the measures taken to deal with the disturbances in the Vendée. It flatly declared that the La Rouairie affair had no connection with them. . . .

The peasants, and not the agents of La Rouairie, succeeded in igniting the general conflagration. The Breton agitator thought the nobles would begin and the peasants would follow, but in fact it was the peasants who led and the nobles who obeyed. This was the reverse of the plan. As soon as the first shots were fired, the rustics recognized the seriousness of their action. If they gave up, it meant the gallows. Fighting was their safest bet, but they lacked leaders. The republicans were commanded by career officers; they had to have some also. Logic clearly pointed to the manor houses. "If we had some nobles to lead us," one of them cried out, "we could march on Paris." [7] The nobles had served in the army; they had learned strategy and tactics. Because of their social standing, they had gained an authority which they would know how to exercise and which could quiet the rivalries among the commoners who were vying for leadership. Finally, the rebels had the very natural thought—almost instinctive among peasants who had fallen into an unfavorable situation—that of appealing to those more powerful than themselves, to those whose châteaux had stood for centuries amidst their cottages, protecting or menacing them. . . .

Nor did the black robes of the clergy appear in front of the red glare of the early fighting. Can one seriously believe that they contrived a plot, but discreetly left it to the peasants to carry out? The clergy had suffered even more than the nobles. Outlawed in 1792 for refusing to take a schismatic oath, individual priests stirred up their faithful and fought back at the thresholds of their churches. But it is a long step from this kind of resistance to a general conspiracy. The day that the uprising broke out, the priests were not to be found amidst the crash and thunder leading the insurgents. No hidden thread bound the rectory to the parishioners. Studying the investigations made of those dramatic days, one can find no instance of a group led by clergymen. The priest of Saint-Martin de Beaupréau, tears in his eyes, rushed in front of his parishioners and begged them to return to their homes. It was too late, for they had already manhandled the government's recruiting agents. The bridges were burned between them and repentance. . . .

The older, underlying cause of the Vendée revolt, that of religion, was soon evident. Though rebels in the districts of Challans, Savenay, and Ancenis

---

[7] Port, III, 271, the words of Julien Chauvat; C.-L. Chassin, La Vendée patriote, 1793–1800 (Paris: Dupont, 1893–1895), I, 209, where Guerry du Cloudy wrote to Boulard, "Soon . . . the people felt that they had to organize; willy-nilly, they chose peaceful men and forced on them the difficult and paramount duty of command."

mentioned the call up of the 300,000 men in their manifestoes of March 14, 15, and 19, they especially emphasized their desire for the old religious arrangements and their vision of liberty. They complained of the many kinds of oppression. They boasted of bringing back "the good priests." They forced republicans to shout "Long live the pope, down with the nation." "God will end up being stronger than the devil," asserted the young women of the village of La Chèze. On March 24 Joly's insurgent army issued a declaration of justification while en route to Les Sables-d'Olonne. It sought to reestablish, so the army said, the throne and religion, order and peace. In this declaration the military draft was no longer an issue.

"Yes, we are defending the religion of our forefathers," declared the leaders of the Vendean army a little later, "and we shall defend it to the last drop of our blood, as did our divine Master, who did not fear to give His own life to establish it among us." And General Bonchamps, in the peroration of a speech, vehemently criticized republican officials for religious persecution, for hunting down priests, and for profaning churches. He did not refer to military service. Still later, replying to requests contained in M. de Gilliers' dispatch, sent by the Bourbon princes, the leaders of the revolt said the same thing: "The peasants took up arms mainly to reestablish the Catholic and Roman religion." Nothing about military service. Some rebels are even supposed to have said—and we learn this from the republican General Kléber: "Give us back our good priests and we will let you have the king." They were supposed to have added, "And we will let you have our nobles too." But that was not the way a Vendean thought.[8]

All the peasants who were arrested insisted on their Catholicism before their judges. Their enemies called this attitude a delirium: "They are really fanatical, as in the fourth century. Every day they are executed and every day they die while singing hymns and professing their faith. The use of capital punishment . . . only has the effect of rendering odious the power that employs it." This comes from a statement by the deputy Volney, on mission from the Convention in Loire-Inférieure. The republican General Berruyer wrote, "Death is the beginning of happiness for them." Turreau [on mission from the Convention] compared them to crusaders.[9]

No doubt, some nobles did say that they wanted to restore the king. The Vendean leader Sapinaud died crying out, "I die happy, for I am dying for my king." When the Vendean General Beauvollier was asked by his judges, "What was your aim?" he replied, "My aim was to have a king." On August 18, 1793, the Vendean generals wrote to the Comte d'Artois, "We have revolted in the defense of Louis XVII, a child so worthy and so unfortunate." But all these people had forgotten the truth. They were plunged into the struggle by the sinewy arms of the peasants and only later did they recognize the interests of the monarchy.

[8] *Kléber en Vendée (1793–1794). Documents publiés . . . par Henri Baguenier Desormeaux* (Paris: Picard, 1907), p. 29.

[9] Port, II, 330, statement of Pierre Davy and similar accounts, pp. 232 *et seq.,* and p. 260; Vicomte B. d'Agours (ed.), *Documents inédits pour servir à l'histoire des soulèvements de mars 1793 . . .* (Saint-Nazaire, 1883), p. 123; Chassin, *La Vendée patriote,* I, 358, a report to Minister Lebrun dated May 20; Jean Savary, *Les Guerres de Vendéens . . .* (Paris: Baudouin, 1824–1827), I, 170, dated April 28; Louis Turreau, *Mémoires pour servir à l'histoire de la guerre de la Vendée . . .* (Paris: Baudouin, 1824).

Not all of them so misrepresented the real cause of the revolt. While dying, d'Elbée confessed, "I swear on my honor that although I sincerely and truly wanted a monarchical government, I had no specific plan in mind, and I would have lived as a peaceful citizen under any regime as long as it assured my tranquillity and the free exercise of the religious beliefs that I have always practiced." On the republican side, Choudieu [a deputy on mission in the Vendée] asserted that the monarchical cause had no effect on the revolt. An Angevin, Joseph Clemenceau, insists in his *History of the Vendée War* (1909) that the military draft simply provided an opportune excuse. The views of the deputy Turreau do not differ from this.

The ridiculous has even been claimed—that the Vendeans wanted to revive the feudal dues. Why should they? In their cahiers they had requested abolition of these payments. Immediately after the abolition of these dues, why would they feel regret? What they really wanted was the restoration of property to its former owners—to churches, to monasteries, and to individuals; but they were not so stubborn as to want it returned still covered with the feudal moss that these properties had accumulated over centuries.

Such interpretations of the causes are errors made by republicans. Now to deal with a royalist error that can be quickly refuted in the light of events: some writers, more interested in edifying their readers than in instructing them, have characterized all the insurgent peasants as men of angelic sweetness. But this was a war, a religious war, not a war of religion—a religious war upholds liberties, a war of religion tries to impose beliefs. This was a war, and no war, even if made by the best of Christians, can be won by the cross alone without other weapons. The crusaders also used swords, and the old chronicles tell us how terribly they used them on entering Jerusalem. In the fire of battle the ethereal zephyrs of Christianity are not always enough to temper hatreds—icy breaths which rise from the inner depths of men. This is even more true in civil wars, so open to the interplay of resentment and hatred. The uprising was a peasant revolt, as were previous uprisings against the nobles in other provinces. The insurgents wore their rosaries around their necks, but they carried their scythes with them. Woe to the one who refused to join their ranks! The popular flood uprooted by brute strength anyone who hesitated.

Insurgent parishes forced their neighbors to march with them. Peasants placed convinced republicans at their head when they recognized their abilities. Menaced by grape pickers' knives, Citizen Gelligné, a well-known patriot of Saint-Aignan, was forced to command the rioters. They needed not only leaders but also rank and file. This caused recruitment to be extremely brutal. The rebels "scoured the countryside, forcing all the inhabitants to join them—everyone marched, even ten- to twelve-year-old boys." [10] Unless the peasant could furnish proof of a severe wound making it impossible for him to march, he was liable to be recalled. If he could not fight, but was able to do such work for the army as kneading dough, then he was forced to do so. If he could perform no service, he had to give money. Often curiosity led the peasant to follow the crowd. Once committed, he rallied to succeeding musters without difficulty. Woe to those who were known to oppose this conscription against conscription! . . .

[10] Henri Gibert, *Précis historique de la guerre de Vendée, publié par Baguenier Desormeaux;* see also Boutillier de Saint-André, p. 48; and the *Documents inédits* of Vicomte d'Agours.

It should not be imagined that the two sides in the war corresponded without exception to particular social classes: all peasants did not become insurgents; all nobles were not carried away by the uprising; nor were all bourgeois favorable to republican ideas. In the most patriotic cities, such as Cholet and Segré, there were strong movements against national conscription. On the other hand, one has only to glance through the lists of refugee patriots (to be found in the Archives in Nantes) to be struck by the preponderance of peasants. While many petty bourgeois from rural areas marched at the heads of rebel groups, nobles could be found in the front ranks of the republican forces in the Vendée or on the national frontiers. . . .

From the same peasant family some went to the Right, others to the Left. The two Bernard brothers from Vézins turned up in opposing camps: one was a city official who saw his workshop burned by rioters; the other joined the Vendean army and was shot after the battle of Savenay. Charles Davy des Nauroy, a surgeon at Saint-Étienne du-Bois, took part in the insurrection and became a major in General Charette's army; his brother stoutly proclaimed his republican sentiments. One bloody example of family hatreds deserves special notice. At the taking of Legé, Joly, commander of one of Charette's divisions, learned that one of his sons had just received a mortal wound. He ran to him; just then he was told that his other son, who was fighting on the republican side, had been captured. "What shall we do with him?" he was asked. "Shoot him," spat out the inexorable father. The two sons died at the same moment.

[The nineteenth-century republican historian] Edgar Quinet posed this question: if the land of the nobles and priests had been divided among the peasants, would they have revolted? He did not think so. But this is still an open question. For one thing, human self-interest seemed to be minimal in the uprising—rewards in the next world predominated over material desires. Some well-to-do peasants and some rich bourgeois, who would have been able to draw up chairs at the huge banquet of national property taken from the Church and the émigrés, refused to increase their fortunes by acquiring these confiscated properties. We do not hear from the mouths of rebels any regrets that they did not receive the government's manna in return for a little handful of depreciated assignats. But another point has to be made: those who are acquainted with the greediness of the farmer and his frantic desire for land would naturally think that a free gift, a total partitioning of the land, as was to be carried out in Russia, would have won over enough peasants to hinder the others, the great majority, from acting.

There are other unanswerable questions. Would the uprising have broken out without the draft of 300,000 men, that drop of water in a pitcher filled to overflowing, that spark in a building crammed with combustible materials? We do not know. Perhaps another cursed event would have occurred to unite all the discontented in one unanimous act. Or if religion had not been a factor, would the Vendée have obeyed the draft call? All we can say is that when complete religious liberty was granted under the Consulate, the conscription issue lost its sharp edge. A valuable piece of evidence, but in this kind of speculation, analysis loses its power and any attempt to see through the shadows is only vanity.

A Synthesis

JOHN McMANNERS

John McManners (1916–   ), a clergyman's son, was educated at Oxford and Durham universities before entering military service during World War II. After the war he became an Anglican priest and a teacher of history. At present he is canon of Christ Church College and Regius Professor of Ecclesiastical History at Oxford. His writings on French history include *French Ecclesiastical Society under the Ancien Régime: A Study of Angers in the 18th Century* (1960) and *The French Revolution and the Church* (1969). Both of these books combine sound scholarship with a sympathetic understanding of the Catholic Church and its clergy.

What part did religion play in the atrocious civil war that was waged in the Vendée? We must distinguish here between the motives of the rising as contemporaries saw them and as they appear today in the light of analyses of the social structure of the insurrectionary areas, and between the causes of the original outbreak and the forces which kept rebellion going once it had started, like draughts fanning a blazing torch. To their republican opponents the Vendéans were a cruel peasant rabble wearing pious images in their hats and chaplets round their necks, obeying the orders of royalist agents and fanatical churchmen. It was true enough that the rising, once started, was taken over by supporters of the *ancien régime*—nobles, or ecclesiastics like Bernier, ex-*curé* of Saint-Laud of Angers. But this was not how the insurrection had begun. About its origins there is a legend with a dual bias, for clerical historians have depicted pious peasants marching to defend their good *curés*, while anti-clerical historians have improved upon the same theme with a fable of a plot of priests who, in [the nineteenth-century historian] Michelet's words, "devised a work of art, singular and strange, a revolution against the Revolution, a republic against the Republic."

There is something (within limits) to be said for the clerical version and nothing at all for the anti-clerical one. The revolt began on the fringes of no less than five ecclesiastical dioceses—Luçon, La Rochelle, Angers, Nantes, Poitiers—and not a single bishop or ecclesiastical official made any attempt to organize resistance to the

From John McManners, *The French Revolution and the Church* (London: The Society for Promoting Christian Knowledge, 1969), pp. 81–84. Reprinted by permission of the publisher.

Revolution. The earliest leaders of the rioters were not priests or nobles, but an itinerant vendor of fruit and fish and a ruined *perruquier* [wigmaker]. True, the clergy of the heartland of the rebellion were overwhelmingly on the refractory side (though the proportion varied oddly from one locality to another: almost all refractories in the "Mauges" area of southern Anjou, but no less than ninety-six *curés* and five *vicaires* among the constitutionals, as against 134 *curés* and seventy-two *vicaires* remaining orthodox, in the insurrectionary area of the actual department of the Vendée). Many of the clergy dispossessed by the Civil Constitution were popular with their flocks—we know that some of them were remarkably generous with their alms in hard times—while those who were not popular were at least influential, for in such an isolated rural *milieu* they were indispensable in all local business. It is clear too that the reorganization of parishes by the District authorities under the Civil Constitution legislation was bitterly resented. There were riots to preserve [church] bells from confiscation and petitions to keep well-loved churches open. Envious clamour was raised against the intriguing "patriots" who stood well with the revolutionary officials and pulled strings to ensure that their own parishes were preserved while others were suppressed. Yet, all this could be said about many areas of Brittany, and Brittany remained comparatively quiet, passively accepting the revolutionary settlement of the Church. Why was the Vendée so different?

If an answer in one word is required that word is "poverty." Ever since the beginning of 1789 the peasants of the rough, infertile country of the rising had been on the verge of starvation. They had been unfairly taxed under the *ancien régime* in comparison with other areas. Their *cahiers* had made simple requests—lower taxation, the repair of their miserable roads, and help for the infirm and indigent, who abounded. What, in fact, they received from the Revolution was a new consolidated land tax based on the same unjust assessment, and so arranged that the cultivator had to pay it all directly, instead of some falling on the proprietor, as in the days before the reform. "In the special case of the Vendée," writes Faucheux, "there was a demoralizing impression that they were paying more out of a diminished revenue—as indeed they were." So the revolutionary government was hated. When it introduced a conscription law (Sunday 10 March was the date of enrolment) the rising began. In proportion to the population few conscripts were being called up. This made no difference. The point had been reached at which starving and disillusioned men would obey no longer. The broken nature of the country, the lack of urban rallying points for republican forces, the fact that troops were not available for quick suppressive action meant that isolated riots could combine into a full scale, wide-spread rebellion, and once it had begun those who had committed themselves were doomed if they surrendered.

But the Vendéan rising was more than an attack upon a hated government: it was also an attack upon a specific social class which was identified with the revolutionary régime—the bourgeoisie of the country towns, the officials, and the richer farmers. These were the men with capital who had bought the lion's share of ecclesiastical property when it came onto the market. Earlier historians had noticed the division between town and country and the peasants' envious hatred of the acquirers of the *biens nationaux* [expropriated Church and *émigré* lands], but the study of these social tensions upon a detailed statistical and geographical basis is a recent development, inspired by Paul Bois' *Paysans de l'Ouest* (1960). Bois' problem was to explain the motives of the *chouans*, the catholic-royalist brigands of the Sarthe, to the north of the main Vendéan war zone. In 1789 the peasants of the west of the Sarthe had been more hostile to nobles and clergy than their fellows in the rest of the department, yet from 1793 they furnished the recruits for a sinister guerrilla feud against the revolutionary bourgeoisie. The paradox is explained once the destination of the *biens nationaux* is analysed. In most of the department there was little ecclesiastical property for sale, and the peasants were too poor to buy it; in the west, there was more property for sale and the peasants were prosperous enough to have obtained it—had not the bourgeoisie outbid them at the auctions. A similar analysis, more straightforward in this case, has been made of the areas of the Vendéan rising by Charles Tilly and later by Marcel Faucheux. In the District of Sables d'Olonne, for example, out of 217 buyers of *biens nationaux*, only fifty-seven were small peasants or artisans; in the District of Cholet only 156 out of a total of 640. Those who were able to buy ecclesiastical property, one might conclude, became enthusiasts for the Revolution, which was their guarantee that they could keep it: those who were defeated at the auctions became acutely conscious of the religious loyalties which reinforced their hatred of their richer and victorious rivals.

That there is a sociological explanation for the role played by religion in the Vendéan rising does not mean that the religious motivation has been explained away. Collectively and statistically these obscure, grim fighters can be added together in groups acting in patterns which explain, in retrospect, why they were the ones to rebel, while other peasants with similar religious convictions did not carry their dissatisfaction to the point of civil war. But, taken individually, there is little doubt what their inspiration in battle will be, for the forefront of men's minds is filled by their most avowable motives. In their own eyes the "Whites" [Vendeans] who lay in ambush for the "Blues" [Revolutionaries] along the sunken lanes and dense hedgerows of the Bocage, and who were shot and guillotined in droves by republican military commissioners, were fighting for their families, for the Virgin and the saints, for their own local ideal of "liberty"—liberty to contract out of the nation's unjust wars and taxation, and to stay at home and hear mass said by their old familiar priests.

5
Why Terror in
1793-1794?

"MAKE terror the order of the day!" "Deliver a last blow against the aristocracy of merchants!" "Punish not only traitors, but even the indifferent!" These slogans were proclaimed in 1793 by Barère, Collot d'Herbois, and Saint-Just, members of the most powerful executive body in France.[1] It was clear that France had now entered the period called "The Terror."

The Committee of Public Safety had been created in April 1793. At first it guided the National Convention by issuing provisional regulations and by overseeing ministers. But during the next seven or eight months, it acquired new and vast powers: to make arrests, to staff parts of the bureaucracy, to name and remove generals, and to control the government's emissaries to the troops and the provinces. The legislators of the Convention, jealous of their powers and prerogatives, only reluctantly delegated this authority. But could the unwieldy assembly itself direct the armies combatting most of the countries of Europe? Could it quash the many revolts in the French provinces? In Paris, could it hold prices down, feed the starving, and restrain, if not satisfy, the disaffected?

There can be little doubt that, at least from September 1793 to July 1794, the Committee with its emissaries and supporters resorted to a

[1] The nine other members of the Committee of Public Safety from September 1793 to July 1794 were Billaud-Varenne, Carnot, Couthon, Hérault de Séchelles, Lindet, Prieur of the Côte-d'Or, Prieur of the Marne, Robespierre, and Saint-André.

policy of intimidation and political executions. Why it did so, however, is a matter of much controversy.

Some historians defending the Revolution stress that terrorism was the product of conditions—especially civil and foreign wars—and that most terrorists were neither bloodthirsty brutes nor impractical theorists. Albert Mathiez is concerned with how events affected the revolutionary leaders, and Richard Cobb describes the impact of circumstance on the rank and file.

Other historians are less favorably disposed to the revolutionaries of the year II. Crane Brinton finds that the leaders of the Terror, the Jacobins, were misguided humanitarian idealists. They attempted, under trying circumstances, to create a kind of heaven on earth; rigid and puritanical in their faith and zeal, they often imprisoned or killed those whom they could not convert. Pierre Gaxotte believes that a more important reason for the violence was that the Revolution was captured by a clique seeking to equalize wealth by means of force.

There have also been several notable attempts to suggest a combination of motives—some reasonable and some base—for the actions of the terrorists. The selection by Georges Lefebvre is an example of such a synthesis.

Living in the twentieth century, we have grown accustomed to violence and bloodshed, to foreign and civil wars. It should be possible for us to read dispassionately what leading historians say about the psychology of the terrorists and the circumstances of the Terror. Perhaps we can then decide whether the Terror was largely justifiable or reprehensible. Or perhaps we can only marvel at the complexity of events and see how gifted men and women interpret them in different ways.

The Desire to Communize

PIERRE GAXOTTE

Pierre Gaxotte (1895–   ) has been a member of the French Academy since 1953. From a small town in Lorraine, he went to Paris to attend two of his country's finest schools, the Lycée Henri IV and the École normale supérieure. After a brief teaching career, he devoted himself to right-wing politics, journalism, and historical writing. He has written much on French and German history, and the following selection is taken from his first book, *La Révolution française* (1928), which is still very popular among French conservatives.

The more firmly the Revolutionary Government was established, the more sanguinary it became, and the more actively the guillotine was kept at work. Those historians who are anxious at all costs to represent the hecatombs slaughtered by the Montagnards as regrettable excesses in what were perfectly legitimate reprisals find themselves in considerable embarrassment when they come to deal with the year 1794. Moreover, in their blind desire to exonerate the system, they find themselves forced to lay the blame for all the crimes which they cannot otherwise explain at the door of one man, Robespierre. Robespierre's ambition, Robespierre's hypocrisy, Robespierre's cruelty . . . these words appear on every page. Such excuses are as puerile as they are false. The Terror was of the very essence of the Revolution, because the Revolution was not merely a change in the system of government, but a social revolution, an attempt at expropriation and extermination. . . .

The Mountain was manœuvred by its extreme Left, known as the party of the *Enragés*. It is hard to say where this party began or ended, or to assign it any definite limits. There was mutual hatred and much squabbling among its members, and excommunications were prompt. But, with these reservations, it may be said that the movement sprang from the communistic preaching of Jacques Roux and his rivals, Varlet and Leclercq. It was they who launched the idea that the political revolution ought to be completed by a social revolution, and that equality of civil rights would be useless without equality of fortunes. Snubbed by the revolutionary

Reprinted with the permission of Charles Scribner's Sons from pp. 288–289, 291–292, 298–303, of *The French Revolution* (New York, 1932) by Pierre Gaxotte, translated by Walter Alison Phillips.

leaders, they found a hearing among the poorer classes in the towns, whom the inflation of the currency had plunged into the most appalling distress. By May [1793] they were so strong that Marat and Robespierre had to buy their assistance against the Girondins, and up to September their influence was constantly on the increase. . . .

The first decree fixing the price of wheat was passed . . . on the 4th of May, 1793, in return for the alliance of the *Enragés* against the Girondins. It was, however, very badly applied. The departmental authorities charged with the duty of applying it purposely dragged out the preliminary operations and used the obscurities and omissions in the law as a pretext for allowing it to be evaded in nine cases out of ten.

In July there was a drastic change; for Communist pressure was becoming more and more violent. On the 27th, after listening to the report presented by Collot-d'Herbois, the Convention passed, almost without debate, a law on the hoarding or forestalling of supplies which, according to [the French historian] M. Marion, "amounted to no less than treating as a public enemy anyone who should still have the courage to trade in those things the dearth of which caused the greatest complaint." Forestalling *(accaparement)* was defined as the fact of holding stored up in any place, without publicly exposing them for sale day by day, food-stuffs and articles of prime necessity, to wit: flour, bread, meat, wine, vegetables, fruit, butter, cider, vinegar, brandy, honey, fats, tallow, fish, wood, coal, oil, soda, soap, salt, sugar, hemp, wool, paper, hides, iron, copper, lead, steel, cloth, linen and stuffs generally. Those who were holding back these commodities were directed to declare them within eight days to the municipalities, which would nominate commissaries to verify the declarations, and, in case of need, to proceed to the sale of the goods. Those who should make false returns were to be punished with death, and those who denounced such frauds were to be rewarded with a third of the property confiscated.

The law did not affect the producer, nor did it interfere with prices. A great step had, however, been taken towards general confiscation. There were no longer any trade secrets. The *commissaires aux accaparements* were empowered to enter all premises, examine account-books and invoices, dispose of stocks, and visit barns and granaries. When once this road is started upon there is no stopping. It was not long before the idea took shape that the law of the 27th of July was only a preliminary, and that the State had the power to exert pressure on prices and lower them. From time to time a few tentative experiments were made in fixing the prices of some commodities. Finally, on the 29th of September, the Convention passed a decree fixing a maximum price for all commodities of prime necessity. This was known as the Law of the Maximum.

In addition to the things enumerated in the decree of the 27th of July, the sale of which was already under control, the new law mentioned grain, forage, tobacco, boots and wooden shoes *(sabots)*. In the case of some articles the maximum price fixed was the same for all France; in the case of others it varied in different communes. Those engaged in agriculture were obliged more especially to send in returns of the yield of their harvest, and were forbidden to sell their wheat anywhere save in the public market or at any except the official price. If they refused, the authorities were to supply the markets by force, requisition the standing [wheat], and have it reaped and threshed by labourers mobilized for this purpose. The transport of [wheat] was made subject to an official permit, while the millers and their equipment were requisitioned, their function being regarded as a public service. Finally, [although] the currency had already fallen to half its face value and the process of devaluation was becoming accelerated every day, *the maximum was fixed at only one-third above the prices current in 1790*. The law, in short, was not only tyrannous, but a measure of expropriation. Those who contravened it were threatened with the severest penalties: a year's rigorous imprisonment for bakers who should cease work, ten years in irons for millers who bargained over the sale of grain or flour, ten years in irons for farmers who sent in false returns, and death for those who tried to obstruct the requisitioning.

Having assumed control of internal trade, it now only remained to the State to assume that of foreign trade. This was the object of the decree of the 30th of May, 1794, which placed at its disposal all commodities, raw materials or goods imported either by land or sea. Agencies were established at the ports and on the frontiers for requisitioning what they saw fit, leaving to the owners nothing but the surplus, so that to all intents and purposes the State became the sole importer. As for export trade, this was forbidden so far as a large number of articles were concerned, and in the case of the others could only be carried on under strict control. Finally, the whole of the mercantile marine was requisitioned.

Goods having been requisitioned, it was next the turn of the men. The decree, passed on the 23rd of August, 1793, which ordered the *levée en masse*, had sent to the front only young men from eighteen to twenty-five years of age, but placed the whole population of France, women included, at the service of the State. It was a logical consequence that the State, being now the only master and the only shopkeeper, should also become the only employer. The law of the 29th of September, which prescribed a maximum price for commodities, also prescribed maximum wages. It was, however, a little more generous to the workmen than to the tradesmen, for, instead of only a third, it allowed them to be paid half as much again as in 1790.

The requisitioning of workpeople, in 1793 and 1794, was carried out by categories, according to the needs of the moment. First came the journeyman bakers, followed by printers for the manufacture of *assignats*, of cartwrights, metal-founders, turners, tailors, tanners, etc., for war supplies, and of carters and raft-men for the transport of fuel and grain. The whole of France was transformed into a vast barracks; and since a law [of June 14, 1791], passed on the motion of Le Chapelier, had deprived proletarians of the right to combine and strike, the burden of the Communist policy weighed as heavily on the working classes as on any other. Then, on the 4th of April, 1794, the Convention proclaimed a general requisition of all who could serve the State, whether with hand or brain, and threatened to hale before the Revolutionary Tribunal those who should try to evade this duty.

And now arose the real difficulty, namely, how to apply laws which were impossible to execute. The moment the maximum was promulgated the shops were emptied, for everyone hurried to buy at an artificially low price what had cost two or three times as much the day before; and when the stocks were exhausted no one was willing to renew them. In a single day there would be no sugar, oil or candles in Paris. Wine was still to be had, but it was doctored and undrinkable. In the provinces the country people rushed to the towns to exchange their notes for clothes, boots, pieces of stuff or groceries, which the law forced the tradesmen to sell at a ruinous price, and then hurried back to bestow their [wheat] in hiding-places which none could discover. In fact everyone wanted the maximum for his neighbour and liberty for himself. "Brothers and friends," said Frécine, a member of the Convention, to some workmen who had revolted against the maximum wage, "I learn with sorrow that there are individuals among you who are obstinately bent on obtaining an increase of wages which would be a charge on the Republic. What, citizens? Can it be that the detestable spirit of greed which the national justice has just destroyed in the case of the forestallers has insinuated itself into the pure soul of the *sans-culottes*? . . . You ask that the law shall be rigorously enforced in respect of what you buy, yet you refuse to obey it in respect of everything you sell to others! . . ."

The resistance of the peasants soon assumed formidable proportions. It was clear that they would use every possible means of making the legislation which despoiled them a dead letter. Wherever they were in a position to evade search they understated the yield of their crops and only sold them clandestinely, at the price that suited them. When they could not safely do this, they let the crops rot on the ground on pretext that they had not enough labour to gather them. In other places, since the maximum price for wheat had been imposed before that for oats, they consented to sell the oats, but fed their horses on the wheat. When the retail price of meat was fixed, they refused to supply the butchers. When the price of cattle on the hoof was fixed, they let their beasts perish.

Smuggling assumed enormous proportions on the frontiers. A quintal (200 lbs.) of wheat fetched 40 *francs* in gold at Geneva, while in France it had to be sold for 14 *francs* in paper money. However strict a watch might be kept, it would have been impossible to prevent so lucrative a trade.

In the Department of Haute-Saône, about which [the historian] M. Mathiez has given us so much valuable information, the immediate effect of the promulgation of the maximum was to aggravate the crisis in the supply of food. The farmers stopped threshing; the bakers ceased to bake; the innkeepers refused to serve guests; the workmen who had no work in the towns refused to undertake work in the country where it was needed. A young volunteer, whose correspondence is in the possession of M. Marion, wrote to his family from Pfalzburg: "The fixed prices of commodities have been promulgated here, but since then it is almost impossible to get anything to eat." From Toulouse the Committee of Public Safety received the following report: "The city seems as though it had been cut off by a hostile army; food-stuffs have ceased to reach it, and the inhabitants of the countryside only visit it in order to clear out the shops." And from Bergues came a note which sums up all the rest: In this part of the country "the Law of the Maximum has had the effect of a liberticide plot hatched by Pitt."

Communism was inconceivable without an unexampled display of coercion and force, and it was this which was the real significance of the Terror, and explained its development and duration. The terrorist dictatorship was connected with the social laws, and not with military events. Debated in the Convention on the 5th of September [1793], after the great Hébertist demonstration, the Terror was organized at the very time when the danger from abroad was diminishing. It was reduced to a code when the frontiers had been cleared of the enemy, and it reached its high-water mark when the French arms were victorious and Belgium had been reconquered.

A Realistic Necessity

ALBERT MATHIEZ

Albert Mathiez (1874–1932) came from a peasant family in eastern France. He combined great ability with energy and aggressiveness to gain entrance to the École normale supérieure and eventually to become one of the leading authorities on the French Revolution. A student of Alphonse Aulard, who was one of the first great professional historians of the French Revolution, Mathiez was also strongly influenced by the historical works of the socialist Jean Jaurès. Mathiez first began writing about the religious history of the Revolution. Eventually he went on to study its political and, to a limited extent, its economic and social aspects. His attempt to rehabilitate the character and policies of Robespierre and to denigrate those of Danton launched a famous quarrel with his former teacher, Aulard. In addition to writing many monographs and a survey of the Revolution, Mathiez started editing the journal *Annales révolutionnaires* in 1908. The journal's name was changed to *Annales historiques de la Révolution française* in 1924, and he continued as its editor until his death.

The Montagnards, a minority in the National Convention, based their power on the big city governments and on the Jacobin clubs from which they quickly expelled their rivals. Since the Montagnards had opposed the War of 1792, the common people could not blame them for the frightful economic crisis the war caused; and they kept in contact with the masses by their social welfare program. The military defeats in the spring of 1793, General Dumouriez's treason, and the revolt of the Vendée finally allowed them to take power. This was done by force of arms during the three days from May 31 to June 2, 1793. They purged their adversaries from the Convention and very soon organized a dictatorship, a collective dictatorship by two committees—the Committee of Public Safety and the Committee of General

From Albert Mathiez, "La Révolution française," *Annales historiques de la Révolution française*, X (1933), 13–18. Printed by permission of the editor of the *Annales historiques de la Révolution française*. Editors' translation.

Security—both supported by a Convention temporarily in the hands of the Mountain. These events constituted a new revolution. . . . The dictatorship by the committees was really a dictatorship by the Montagnard party and to some degree by the sans-culottes.

This dictatorship, which lasted a little more than a year, was much less the result of a well-thought-out ideology than of inescapable pressures brought on by civil and foreign war. The enemy had to be repulsed, the royalist and Girondin revolts crushed. The cities and the armies, starving because of the English blockade, had to be fed, while the million soldiers going to the frontier needed supplies and arms. Terror became the order of the day, and the regime set up the guillotine to deal with its enemies. It suspended elections and sent emissaries with full powers to crush resistance in the provinces. The watchword went out to the generals—victory or death! The statue of liberty was veiled, and authority replaced it in ascendancy. The revolution of the Mountain rested on premises opposed to the individualistic revolution of 1789. In the name of public safety, as formerly in the name of the king, conformity was enforced and property rights were limited when circumstances required. To further the defense of the nation and the Revolution, all provisions were pooled and all kinds of merchandise and food requisitioned. The regime established price ceilings on the most important commodities and opened municipal bakeries and butcher shops. In short, a sort of forced experiment in collectivism was set up. I say a forced experiment, since even those who attempted it considered it only temporary and hoped that it would soon disappear without leaving a trace.

The new dictatorship differed greatly from that of the Constituent Assembly of 1789–1791. The people had accepted and had even desired the earlier one; they merely submitted to this one and even detested it. Public opinion, while supporting the deputies of the Constituent Assembly, pushed them into taking more and more severe actions against the enemies of the Revolution. The assembly's committees were obeyed docilely by elected officials who accepted their authority. But now there was a marked shift, with a civil war to match a foreign war. The Vendée and federalist revolts, the execution of the king, the military defeats, the requisitions, the impoverishment caused by inflation, as well as the dechristianization campaign and the closing of the churches, the arrest of suspects, and the continuing use of the guillotine—all these formidable manifestations of crisis discouraged a large number of Frenchmen and created an opposition that desired peace at any price, even at the cost of restoring the Old Regime.

It was no longer possible to justify this new dictatorship, as the Abbé Sieyès had the earlier one, simply by referring to the theory of constitutional authority. It was only too noticeable that the new dictatorship was no longer an application of the sovereignty of the people but rather its opposite. Therefore, responding to an attack by the Dantonists, Robespierre justified the dictatorship by making the significant distinction between a state of war and a state of peace, a revolutionary government and a constitutional government. His two speeches, of 5 Nivôse [December 25, 1793] and 17 Pluviôse [February 5, 1794], based on this theme, express the theory of revolutionary government that foreshadows the future Marxian Dictatorship of the Proletariat. Constitutional government can function, he said, only in peacetime. It has to be suspended in wartime—otherwise it would cause liberty to perish. "The aim of constitutional government is to preserve the Republic, that of revolutionary government is to establish it. The Revolution is liberty at war against its enemies; the Constitution is the regime of a victorious and peaceful liberty." The Revolution is essentially a civil war; and therefore "its government has to be extraordinarily active precisely because it is at war, . . . because it is forced to employ unremittingly new and speedy measures so as to meet new and pressing dangers."

Whereas the theory of constitutional authority established dictatorship solely on the basis of the will of the people, the theory of the revolutionary regime based dictatorship on political and patriotic necessities stemming from the war!

Besides, Robespierre himself had seen and admitted the dangers of such a regime. What would become of the state if the dictators used their omnipotence to gain their own ends? A single remedy, a moral one, suggested itself—the dictators must be virtuous.

The French revolutionaries had believed that seizing political power would be enough to resolve the economic and social problems. Rather quickly they perceived their error. Their work crumbled under the weight of the wealthy. The rich, united against the revolutionary laws, made them inoperative. However, the revolutionaries did not think of modifying their principles. It did not cross their minds to found society on a consistent and permanent limitation of property rights, and they continued to regard individual property as untouchable. Their only intent was to correct momentary abuses, and they considered the revolutionary dictatorship merely a temporary expedient. They imagined that all they had to do to resolve the social problem—which in their eyes remained a political issue, a moral issue—was to frighten the aristocrats, imprison them, or exile them. This attitude can be understood if one bears in mind that a large number of the revolutionaries were landowners, well-to-do bourgeois, merchants, or professional men with some landed property. The terrorist dictatorship was meant to answer the needs of the people, but it was run by bourgeois.

Only a small minority of the bourgeoisie learned from experience and understood that the continuation of the sans-culottes in power would be possible and durable only at the cost of a gradual and permanent limitation of individual property rights. Robespierre, Saint-Just, and Couthon sought in the Ventôse Laws to expropriate the property of suspects and to distribute it to the poor. But their colleagues secretly resisted these efforts. The Committee of Public Safety had already been unwilling to nationalize civilian food distribution. Carnot had opposed government operation of factories, even those created by the representatives on mission. The Committee of General Security, with the concurrence of some members of the Committee of Public Safety, blocked the operation of the Ventôse Laws, and their sponsors were overthrown on 9 Thermidor.

The great majority of the deputies to the Convention were individualists, very hostile to anything resembling communism. The true communists, those who believed that the Fourth Estate [the common people] could reign only by the suppression of private property, were isolated and without influence; in any case, most of these men thought only of a collectivization of food and consequently of collectivizing only the land which produced the food. When Babeuf, after Thermidor, sought to unite them into a strong party, it was too late. The dictatorship had collapsed, and Babeuf was powerless to reestablish it. His attempt, which cost him his life, was both behind and ahead of its time. Behind its time because it occurred after the Montagnard party had been thrown out of power and had been already decimated by the proscriptions of Thermidor; ahead of its time because society was not yet prepared for communist ideas.

The revolution of July 1789, which had brought the bourgeoisie to power, was the offspring of the philosophy of the eighteenth century, a philosophy fundamentally liberal and individualistic. The revolution of June 1793, which raised the Montagnards to dictatorial power, was the product of circumstance and necessity. It was not the result of either intellectual training, systematic thought applied to the principles of government or society, or a profound investigation of economic development. And how could it be otherwise when machine production was only coming into being, when industrial concentration (which is the inevitable consequence of it) was not yet apparent? The boldest of the revolutionary thinkers, Babeuf himself, conceived only of agricultural communism. Most of the communists of the time made a careful distinction between industrial property, which, having been the product of work, was worthy of respect, and agricultural land, the only property that they wanted to collectivize.

One must keep this situation in mind to understand how the Jacobin dictatorship fundamentally differs from more recent dictatorships and to comprehend the underlying reasons for its failure.

If the Bolshevik dictatorship, like the Jacobin dictatorship, sought to justify its conduct by the necessities of war, it was, unlike the Jacobin, at least based on a coherent doctrine, Marxism, which it tried to put into practice. The Bolsheviks were quick to abolish not only private ownership but even the very structure of the state which they had seized. The Jacobins, on the other hand, touched only with trepidation and reluctance the regime established by the Constituent Assembly. They superimposed their economic dictatorship on the individualistic legislation without destroying the legislation. Their requisitions and their price controls did not abolish private property rights, but only hindered their exercise. Their communism, temporary and incomplete, was only an expedient for which they felt they had to apologize.

In the political domain, the same differences appear. The Russian Communists, faithful to Marx's thought, sought from their first days to give all power to the proletariat. The government they formed is basically a government of one class. On the contrary, the Jacobin Montagnards, although they had to rely on the sans-culottes, to govern in their name, and to benefit them, never arrived at the concept of class. They pursued the royalists, the Feuillants, and the Girondins not because they thought them class enemies but because they were considered to be political adversaries and accomplices of the enemy. The reason for this is clear. The leaders of the Mountain sitting in the committees and in the Convention were not proletarians but only the friends and allies of the proletarians. They had not rejected the philosophy of the eighteenth century. Its political aspect, which continued to inspire them, is the negation of the existence of classes—it ignores social groupings and stresses the individual.

That is why, unlike the Bolshevik dictatorship (which is based on class antagonism), the dictatorship of the Mountain (which remained fundamentally individualistic) was never a total or full-scale dictatorship. Lenin and his associates understood that in order to establish a dictatorship of the proletariat and to make it permanent, the separation and division of the State's powers would act as an impediment. The Council of People's Commissars legislates and administers at the same time. Such was not the case during the Terror in France, for unity was never entirely achieved within the revolutionary government. No doubt the Convention was purged and in theory it combined legislative and executive power. But actually the Committee of Public Safety took charge of the war effort, diplomacy, and administration, while the Committee of General Security took charge of the repression of plots and the secret police. Thus in France the legislative and executive powers were separated—the Convention retaining the one and the Committees the other. And there was even a separation within the executive branch, since two distinct committees shared its powers. The revolutionary machine of the Montagnards was infinitely more complicated and therefore its operation more delicate than the revolutionary machine of Soviet Russia.

A Kind of
Religious Faith

CRANE BRINTON

Crane Brinton (1898–1968) was one of America's most distinguished historians. He studied at Harvard and Oxford universities and then taught at Harvard from 1923 to 1968. His numerous studies of intellectual and political history delight many readers with their spritely and sophisticated style. On the French Revolution he wrote, among other things, *A Decade of Revolution* (1934), an admirable survey; *The Jacobins: An Essay in the New History* (1930), an original attempt at sociological history; and *The Anatomy of Revolution* (revised edition, 1952), a provocative comparison of the French, English, American, and Russian revolutions.

The Jacobins unquestionably held their political philosophy as a matter of faith. It is possible to sketch from the proceedings of the clubs the outlines of a polity held together by concepts primarily theological. Grace, sin, heresy, repentance, regeneration have their place in these records. Of course, no one individual is assumed to go through this cycle. The theological parallel is not a literal one; but it is not a forced nor an imaginary one.

That Robespierre and his more sincere followers conceived themselves to be the small band of the elect is of course a truism. The conception of election, however, like so much else in the Terror, goes back surprisingly far in the Revolution. Desmoulins speaks at the Jacobin club in Paris in 1791 of "the very small number of those *to whom only the witness of their conscience is necessary,* the small number of men of character, incorruptible citizens." [1] This insistence on an inner, emotional conviction or righteousness rather than on external rules—the very old opposition of faith and works—comes out again in the proceedings of the Paris club. "One must distrust," says the speaker, "liberty unaccompanied by virtue"; and by virtue he understands "not the mere practice of moral duties, but also an exclusive

From Crane Brinton, *The Jacobins: An Essay in the New History* (New York: Macmillan Co., 1930), pp. 218–222, 231–242. Reprinted by permission of the author.

[1] A. Aulard, *La Société des Jacobins* (Paris, 1889–1897), II, 103.

attachment to the unalterable principles of our constitution." [2] The club at Limoges was told: "It is not enough, in order to belong to a truly republican society, to call oneself republican, to have done guard duty, to have paid one's taxes; one must have given sure indications of hatred for kings and nobles, for fanaticism; one must have passed through the crucible of perilous circumstance." The idea of grace is actually complemented, in this same club, by the addition of a new Jerusalem, the city of the elect. Paris, for its work in the revolution, is to be "that holy city." [3]

There are also the damned. The Jacobins did not feel of their opponents merely that they were wrong, or inconvenient; but that they had sinned. A member at Rodez recalled to the society that just a year before, a deputation from the Tarn had "soiled the precincts of the society with the venom of federalism." The society therefore decided "as *expiation* for that scandalous session, to consecrate a portion of the present session to patriotic songs." [4] At Bergerac the society burned the papal bull condemning the civil constitution of the clergy, in order to purify the paper from "the outrageous blasphemies which insult our sublime Constitution." [5] The club of Toulouse delegated six members, and asked the "peuples des tribunes" [the spectators in the public gallery] (always that distinction, so out of place in an ideal republic!) to delegate six more, to help burn and lacerate certain evil journals.[6] At Beauvais, the club was delighted with a circular from the Committee of Public Safety asking for lists of Jacobins eligible for government places, and especially at the words, "Keep from these lists all these cold, selfish, or indifferent men. . . . The law of Athens would have inflicted death upon them. National opinion among us inflicts upon them political death." [7] The club of Le Havre was told by that of Harfleur "not to receive in its bosom a certain Duclos, priest of the protestant religion. He tried to compromise this society with that of Gaineville, and to ruin the reputation of several patriots." [8]

Some aristocrats at Vesoul having kissed the tree of liberty in mockery, the local club decided to purify it. So, with the president at its head, and with four members carrying vases of pure water and braziers of incense, the club marched in procession to the tree, where, after everyone had sworn to preserve it forever after from all contamination, "the tree was purified with the lustral water, and the president threw on the heated tripods generous handfuls of the most exquisite perfumes." [9] The club at Auch had so strong a conviction of sin that it adapted for its own use the attitude of the Church toward burial in consecrated ground. It proposed to have two town cemeteries, one for good citizens, the other for bad.[10]

Heresy is, of course, one of the easiest ways of falling into sin. The word itself was by no means shunned by the Jacobins. Even under the monarchy, Brissot is

[2] *Ibid.*, II, 235.

[3] A. Fray-Fournier, *Le Club des Jacobins* (Limoges, 1903), pp. 246, 169.

[4] B. Combes de Patris, *Procès-verbaux de la Société populaire de Rodez* (Rodez, 1912), p. 347.

[5] H. Labroue, *La Société populaire de Bergerac* (Paris, 1915), p. 118.

[6] Archives départementales, Haute-Garonne, L 746, April 19, 1793.

[7] Archives départementales, Oise, L IV, unclassified papers of the club of Beauvais.

[8] Archives départementales, Seine-Inférieure, L 5647, 24 Germinal, year II [April 13, 1794].

[9] *La Vedette, ou journal du département du Doubs,* No. 68 (June 29, 1792).

[10] F. Brégail, "La Société populaire d'Auch," *Bulletin du comité des travaux historiques* (1911), p. 152.

found at the Paris club objecting that an opinion of Barnave's is "a great heresy." [11] The rejections of members at the various *épurations* [weeding-out sessions] are, of course, usually for heresy of some sort. One man was excluded at Thann because, although at first he had been a good *patriote*, "the corrupting contact of his brother-in-law had completely perverted him"; another, though himself pure, because his maid was not.[12] At Carcassonne one of the questions put was: How long did you lack confidence in Marat and the Mountain? Several were excluded for honestly confessing that they had had a period of doubt on this subject.[13] The pressure of foreign and civil war made the Jacobins more than usually exacting towards their proselytes. One society at least penalized those converted after 1792 by not allowing them to hold office.[14] That of Moulins decided in the spring of 1794 never to admit a new member, except from other towns, and then only when such persons could prove membership in some club before September, 1793.[15] Heretics were apparently not even allowed to repent. Collot d'Herbois at Paris was seeking to get readmitted to the society some of those who had followed the *feuillants* in the schism. "Many of these," he said, "are exceedingly repentant, and would like to efface from their lives the days they spent at the *feuillants*." Yet at Robespierre's insistence they were rejected.[16] And, along with heresy, there is the concept of blasphemy. This is from a report of a session of a Paris club: "An officer, an exchanged prisoner, gives an account of the condition of the French and Austrian armies. But as he reports some violent words used by the enemy general, he is interrupted. Billaud-Varenne reminds the orator that he is repeating expressions which ought not to soil the mouth of a republican." [17]

A little club in Savoy took a milder, and perhaps more modern attitude towards those who disagreed with it. The majority of their fellow citizens they called "the sick ones we have to treat." [18] The club of Toulon, withdrawing its affiliation from the heretics of Pignans, wrote and warned other clubs of this *brebis galeuse* [black sheep].[19] But the best indication of the theological state of the Jacobin mind is to be found in a circular of the club of Montauban. The class of *émigrés* is to be composed, not merely of those who have gone off, *émigrés de fait*, but also of *émigrés d'opinion*.[20]

No less thoroughly religious a concept than that of regeneration is evident in these proceedings. The taking of the Bastille became the symbolic date, the moment when man was born anew, washed clean of the evils of the old régime. A little provincial society, accordingly, when it celebrates the "holy festival" of July 14, refers to it as the day "when man is resuscitated and born anew in his rights." [21]

[11] Aulard, II, 189.
[12] H. Poulet, "L'Esprit publique à Thann pendant la Révolution," *Revue historique de la Révolution française*, XIII (1918), 544.
[13] J. Mandoul, "Le Club des Jacobins de Carcassonne," *Révolution française*, XXV (1893), 326.
[14] A. Fray-Fournier, p. 243.
[15] Archives départementales, Allier, L 901.
[16] Aulard, III, 313.
[17] *Ibid.*, V, 618.
[18] A. Gros, *Le Club des Jacobins de St. Jean-de-Maurienne* (St. Jean-de-Maurienne, 1908), p. 70.
[19] H. Labroue, "Le Club jacobin de Toulon," *Annales de la Société d'Études provençales* (1907), p. 45.
[20] J. Bellanger, *Les Jacobins peints par eux-mêmes* (Paris, 1908), p. 123.
[21] H. Labroue, "La Société populaire de la Garde-Freinet," *Révolution française*, LIV (1908), 155.

The society of St. Jean-de-Luz held a festival to celebrate the "abolition of royalty and the *resurrection* of the republic." [22] It is hard to see how the word resurrection can here be taken in any but a theological sense, as the French Republic had never existed on this earth. Finally, the society at Saverne gave proof of the most extraordinary faith in the completeness of the rebirth brought about in 1789, for its secretary refers to "les ci-devant Juifs" [the former Jews].[23]

The Jacobins, then, were a band of the elect, thoroughly aware of their election, and determined to rule on earth as well as in heaven. The club of Ervy was told, "You must suffer but one caste of men, that of Republicans, Sans-culottes, Montagnards." [24] At Le Havre, the club voted that those of its members who belonged to any kind of corporation or brotherhood must choose between the Jacobin club and such other corporations.[25] The club of Besançon indignantly refused to open its doors to all, as "the wicked, mixed with the good, would predominate." [26] The club of Chablis hesitated before accepting affiliation with the club of the Ursulines at Tonnerre, and then turned it down on the grounds that there couldn't possibly be two clubs in a small town like Tonnerre.[27] The secretary at Gerberoy apologized to the club of Beauvais, because everybody passed the *épuration*. Three—their names are duly sent on to Beauvais—should have been expelled. But the mayor formed a party among the "little enlightened," packed the club, and notwithstanding their vices, these three were passed "by the multitude." The whole letter is filled with a consciousness of being right and being few.[28]

Finally, it was evident even to some of their number that the Jacobins were a sect. A member at Ars-en-Ré remarked that "the moral discourses delivered on *décadis* [every tenth day of the French republican calendar] are so many dogmas, and consequently, so much religion." He was, it is true, immediately suspended.[29] The Jacobins held firmly to their final superiority; theirs was no fanaticism. . . .

The fall of Jacobinism . . . can be quite plausibly accounted for; an explanation of its rise is a far more difficult matter. It is not that the actual triumph of the Jacobins over other groups during the Revolution is at all hard to understand. Given Jacobin organization and Jacobin faith, their triumph was almost inevitable. . . . Indeed, it is tempting to assert that the ultimate, if brief, victory of well-organized extremists can be accepted as a kind of sociological law applicable to all great revolutions. The really interesting and subtle problem is, how did the Jacobins themselves come to be what they were? . . . The Jacobins were not predominantly failures before 1789, frustrates, victims of maladjustment; nor were they members of a lower class struggling against oppression by their masters, and held together by economic solidarity. They were in the main ordinary, quite prosperous middle-class

[22] J. Annat, "La Société populaire de St. Jean-de-Luz," *Revue du Béarn* (1910), 170.

[23] D. Fischer, "La Société populaire de Saverne," *Revue d'Alsace*, XX (1869), 181.

[24] H. Destainville, "Les Sociétés populaires du district d'Ervy," *Annales historiques de la Révolution française*, I (1924), 446.

[25] Archives départementales, Seine-Inférieure, L 5644, September 19, 1793.

[26] *La Vedette*, No. 54 (May 11, 1792).

[27] Archives départementales, Yonne, L 1140, August 18, 1793.

[28] Archives départementales, Oise, L IV, unclassified papers of the club of Gerberoy.

[29] M. de Richemond, "Délibérations de la Société des Amis de la Liberté et de l'Égalité d'Ars-en-Ré," *Archives historiques de la Saintonge et de l'Aunis*, XXXIV (1904), 205.

people. And yet they behaved like fanatics. The Reign of Terror was marked by cruelties and absurdities which the greatest of misanthropes will hardly maintain are characteristic of ordinary human beings. The heart of our problem then, is this: how did the Jacobins come to produce, at least to accede to, the Terror?

Augustin Cochin saw with admirable clearness that all explanations of the Terror have fallen into two classes: that represented by Taine, which Cochin calls the *thèse du complot* [the conspiracy thesis], and that represented by Aulard, which he calls the *thèse des circonstances* [the circumstance thesis].[30] Taine in a famous metaphor asks what a spectator must think if he sees a man in apparently sound health take a drink, and suddenly fall down in a fit. The drink, obviously, contained a poison. The drinker was the Jacobin, and the poison was the philosophy of Rousseau. The Jacobins, then, were a group of madmen bent on realizing an impossible Utopia. The Revolution was plotted by these men, made irresponsible by fanatic devotion to their ideal. Their lack of principle made it easy for them, though in a minority, to overcome the good sense of the majority, and establish themselves in power. Once in power, they could maintain themselves only by the Terror. Cochin himself accepts a variant of this explanation. According to him, the Jacobins formed a "petite ville," a society of unpractical idealists, fanatics bent on imposing upon their fellows of the "grande ville" a rigid code governing all human actions, a code quite inconsistent with normal human conduct, as we know it from tradition and from observation.[31]

Now it is impossible not to accept much of this explanation. The Jacobins were certainly fanatics of the religion of humanity. It is tempting to maintain that the acceptance of certain tenets of eighteenth-century philosophy—the essential equality of men, the natural goodness of men—lead in action straight to the Terror. The trouble is that the acceptance of just these tenets by Thomas Jefferson, for instance, led to consequences so very different from those following their acceptance by Maximilien Robespierre. Moreover, granting to Cochin that the Jacobins formed a "petite ville," where are we to look for the "grande ville"? Cochin himself probably thought of decent, non-socialist Frenchmen of the Third Republic as the citizens of the "grande ville." But even in the fairly stable nation-state of the nineteenth century, the realist will discern numerous "villes," numerous groups of men with different aims and different ways of life struggling to maintain themselves, and achieving only a precarious equilibrium. And during the Revolution, when this equilibrium was completely destroyed, this "grande ville" did not exist in France. Surely it was not the royalists, nor the Catholics, nor the Feuillants, nor the Girondins. And if the citizen of the "grande ville" is simply the ordinary man who acts reasonably, and in accordance with traditional ways, then he hardly exists in the French Revolution. Any study of the various groups just mentioned should convince the impartial observer that their state of mind was almost as abnormal, as much inclined towards extremes of cruelty or absurdity as the Jacobins'. The White [counterrevolutionary] Terror was as real as the Red.

[30] A. Cochin, "La Crise de l'histoire révolutionnaire," in *Les Sociétés de pensée et la démocratie* (Paris, 1921).

[31] Jacobin virtue, for instance, is not attainable by ordinary human beings.

It is perhaps too easy here to make a synthesis of Taine and Aulard. The Jacobins were an organized minority bent on imposing their way of life on their fellow Frenchmen; so much for the *thèse du complot.* But circumstances—the inheritance of the *ancien régime,* the pressure of war from without, of civil disturbances and food scarcity from within—put such obstacles in their way that they were driven to extremes. In order to exist at all, they were obliged to be cruel and intolerant. Even in their factitious ritual, their republican catechisms and decalogues, the Jacobins appear beleaguered; the touch of Hebraic fury one finds from time to time in their records is not wholly artificial. The revolutionary government was a government of national defense. No fair-minded person need deny the value of Aulard's life-work. The war, at least as much the product of traditional European high politics as of anything Jacobin, made the Jacobin more righteous, and more bitter, and saved him from any chance of appearing ridiculous in his own eyes. Moreover, the introduction of circumstances at least disposes of the difficulty with Thomas Jefferson. But it gives little comfort to the sociologist seeking from history laws permitting human beings to adjust their actions to conditions in the present—little comfort, in short, to the new historian. For the circumstances of a great event like the French Revolution are unique—unique, if not to omniscience, at least in their extreme complexity unique to the historian. The fatal "ifs" of history in the conditional—if Mirabeau had not died, if the king had not fled to Varennes—enter in, and make scientific induction impossible. Men's beliefs are, for a given group, held in common and relatively easy to arrive at; so too a given group may have certain similar and perfectly describable characteristics in common—rank, occupation, social standing, wealth. Yet we have no right to assume that their actions can be predicted from these data.

For the whole point of our study is just this: when one considers the material facts about the Jacobins—their social environment, their occupations, their wealth—one finds sufficient evidence of their prosperity to justify predicting for them quiet, uneventful, conservative, thoroughly normal lives. When one studies the records of their proceedings, one finds them violent, cruel, intolerant, and not a little ridiculous. The antithesis, it must be insisted, is real. Where material evidence indicates normality, we find abnormality. Rightly enough, no doubt, this material evidence seems real and important. Therefore the Jacobins present a genuine paradox. Their *political* being seems quite inconsistent with their *real* being. Their words and their acts *qua* members of the clubs are not what we should expect from them *qua* members of civil society. Or to put it as crudely as possible, the Jacobins present for a brief time the extraordinary spectacle of men acting without apparent regard for their material interests.

This, of course, will never do. The economic interpretation of history would tell us that we are either mistaken in our facts (which is always possible) or that there is an explanation which will show men properly and decently following their material interests. Yet perhaps after all the economic interpretation of history is not the whole explanation of the Terror. We are in a realm of thought where the professional psychologist could no doubt add greatly to the precision of our argument. But to a layman it would appear that voluntary human action must have either a more or less directly physical, bodily source (desire, habit, desire partly intellectualized into interest) or a more or less immaterial and intellectual source (principle, idea, desire thoroughly intellectualized into ideal) or finally, must have its source in mere chance. Now if certain important Jacobin actions did not originate from interest, they must have originated from principle or from chance. The first alternative suggests the old-fashioned belief that men act on principle, and leads us back to the school of Taine. If it can be shown that Jacobin ideas logically produce Jacobin actions in 1794, then we need not worry because Jacobin interests and Jacobin habits would not produce such actions. There is just the possibility that the old-fashioned belief about the importance of ideas is justified, at least for certain historical crises, and for certain groups of men. It is not even necessary to refer to such examples of corporate madness as the Children's Crusade; one need only reflect on how much the *interests* of the average man were at stake in the late highly popular war [World War I]. But to accept this explanation would lead to the restoration of ideas to their active role in human life, and would put the history of ideas, at least during times of crucial change, on a level with the history of institutions, customs, commerce, and the rest of man's material environment. This will hardly content the new historian, for whom intellectual history is largely a reflection of social history, for whom ideas are most decidedly born of, and consistent with, material interests.

There is the final possibility of accepting chance as the determining factor in human conduct. This need not be as shocking as it seems. Chance may merely stand for a complexity unfathomable to human beings; or it may mean that historical events—that is, of course, human actions—are really unique and exempt from the play of cause and effect as nineteenth-century science understood it. That would still leave the play of cause and effect as the artist, and perhaps even the philosopher, have always understood it. It would still leave narrative history; it would merely destroy the new history.

Our enterprise in retrospective sociology has not perhaps been altogether satisfying. The kind of information about the Jacobins available to the social scientist has not provided us with any fashionable explanation of why men take part in revolutions. The Jacobins seem not to have been crudely at odds with their environment before the Revolution; they certainly were not starving; they were hardly a social or an economic class. They were certainly a collective body—a group—of more than ordinary cohesion, reasonably well disciplined, active, with a definite program, a ritual of their own, a faith charged with emotion, and a pertinacity, a vitality that has enabled the group to survive under changing forms into the Third Republic. Yet so disparate were the social and economic origins of these revolutionaries that we have been driven to the conclusion that large numbers of them, by espousing the Jacobin cause, acted against what they must have been aware were their true selfish interests. Before so surprising a conclusion sociology rightly recoils. The exploded intellectualist fallacy is obviously trying to creep in, and we had better not open the door any wider.

But if we have not got far with applications to the French Revolution of a science of social dynamics, can we not at least give a clearer definition of Jacobin at the end of this enquiry than at the beginning? Here, however, as with so much of modern history, the trouble is that we know too much. A fragment of the rules of one of the clubs would be illuminating to the historian at work in the dark; the records of hundreds of them are blinding. Where statistics fail—and they fail very soon—there is no way of arriving at what is common to the Jacobins. No classification of the complete records of these clubs can be so made that the members of each class can be counted. One might count the number of references to Rousseau; but would such a count serve to weigh the influence of Rousseau on the clubs? The historian must fall back on the normal functioning of his mind, which classifies loosely and pragmatically enough what he experiences in daily life, and which with urging can so classify the matter of his historical studies. But no matter how honest he is, into the making of this classification will come much of his own personal history. What one finds in the Jacobin clubs is what one finds important; and importance, when it is not mathematical, is as subjective as good and bad or sweet and sour.

And yet perhaps the true Jacobin is the rare and perfect Jacobin of the imagination—the Jacobins, let us say, of Anatole France's [novel] *Les Dieux ont soif*. One rarely meets an American like Uncle Sam or an Englishman like John Bull, and never a Frenchwoman like the cartoonist's Marianne. Indeed, just as a mass of unbarbered and untailored human animals, Englishmen, Frenchmen, and Americans are probably more alike than we are apt to think. Yet national types do exist, if only in our minds and aspirations. To define them is in a measure to create them; whether we create scarecrows or flesh-and-blood will perhaps not suffer ultimate determination.

This true Jacobin, who may be a scarecrow, but who we hope will be of flesh and blood, is then of no one occupation, of no one social class, of no determinable rank and wealth. He has no ordinary, daily, selfish human interests. He is a religious fanatic, a man inspired and possessed, a man bent on changing overnight this earth into his heaven. What his notion of heaven was we have tried to learn. It was not an uncommon notion of heaven, not one that many men of modern times, if they entertained at all the notion of heaven, would reject—a place where pain and strife could not exist, where the traditional Christian virtues had banished forever the traditional Christian vices, where men were free and equal, and contented with their freedom and equality. The Jacobin was not a revolutionary in that he believed in heaven, or even in that he believed in a special kind of heaven, but in that he attempted to realize his heaven here on earth. That attempt led to the Terror. You cannot have disagreement in heaven. When the Jacobin found he could not convert those who disagreed with him, he had to try to exterminate them. *La sainte guillotine* was not so christened in the spirit of Villon or of Rabelais, but in the spirit of Calvin.

Now common sense, to say nothing of the social sciences, would tell us that most of our five hundred thousand Jacobins were not of this heroic mold. Yet the Terror was a reality, a reality not to be diminished by statistical proof that even in 1794 violence was the exception, not the rule. The slightest document of the period—a theater program, a fashion plate—is no ordinary document, but a sign from another world. Most men in 1794 no doubt ate, drank, slept, and went about most of their business as they had in 1784; most men were no doubt as stupid, as selfish, as kindly, as good in 1794 as in 1784. But into the whole lives of some

Frenchmen, into some part of the lives of all Frenchmen, had come this indefinable, incredible pattern of action and feeling we have called Jacobinism. Very real, very earthly grievances had gone into making the pattern; wise, selfish, ordinary men had helped make the pattern to achieve wise, selfish, ordinary purposes. But a few foolish, unselfish (as the world uses the term) and extraordinary men—with circumstances aiding—had by 1794 turned the pattern into the madness of true Jacobinism. Yet still most Jacobins were normal men. They were still of respectable middle class origins. What had happened to them? Were 499,000 of them hypocrites, trembling before a thousand fanatics? Probably not. It seems more likely that, for a few short months, these ordinary men were possessed by a faith, a contagion, an unearthly aspiration. Jacques Dupont, the man in the street, the economic man, the sociological man, the psychological man, ceased for a brief while to behave in the orderly fashion laid out for him by these sciences, and took instead to the ways of Carlylean heroes or Emersonian representative men.

Jacobinism is, then, first of all a faith. Were they not believers, the Jacobins would be unintelligible to us. As it is, the Jacobin may be strong or weak, tall or short, rich or poor, gentleman or vagabond; what makes him a Jacobin is none of these varying and individual attributes, but a fixed faith. "Liberty, Equality, Fraternity," as words, may be subject to definition and contain the seeds of infinite dispute; as symbols, they were to the Jacobins a common property above logic. The emotions which they evoked allowed the Jacobins to form, for the moment, one body; they provided a common fund of pooled emotions, an inexhaustible and immaterial fund.

Now, in time, this very immateriality of the fund began to pall on many Jacobins. Tough-minded philosophers who, from the utilitarians to the economic interpretationists have perhaps thought a little too highly of their fellow men, would of course maintain that the fund must have been material, or held out the promise of materiality, ever to have held human beings at all. To them, there must somehow be a connection between the individual's standing, and the position he takes in politics. Perhaps they are right as a general rule, right in the long run and in normal times. Yet our study of the Jacobin clubs has failed to establish such a connection for the French Revolution. Neither the class struggle theory nor the maladjustment theory seems in itself to account for the extraordinary diversity of membership in the clubs, nor for the extraordinary variety of things the clubs endeavored to do.

What was meant sincerely as a study in the new history has come to a conclusion strangely like that of very old-fashioned history indeed. If the subject matter of the social sciences be natural man, then the Jacobin appears to have a touch of the supernatural. The French Revolution appears, as it did to Maistre, to Wordsworth, and to Carlyle, as utterly inexplicable in terms of daily life, of common sense, of scientific causation. Yet perhaps we need not call the Revolution a miracle. Only if man is wholly at the mercy of his simpler appetites need we have recourse to the miraculous to explain Jacobin aberrations. If the incredibly complex world which human thought has added to the world of our simpler appetites can at times give ordinary men motives for action even stronger than these simpler appetites, then the French Revolution is explicable. It seems too bad to have to conclude that sometimes some men—or even many men—believe for no more apparent reason than that they want to believe, that their beliefs have, at least in part, independent and immaterial lives. Yet, if only in his capacity for adjusting his conduct to illusion and not to fact, man is most obviously an animal apart. Surely there is nothing surprising if a study of the Jacobins forces us to the conclusion that man cannot live by bread alone?

A Mentality Shaped by Circumstance

RICHARD COBB

Richard Cobb (1917–   ) is Professor of Modern History at Oxford University. He has characterized his own family background and schooling as typical of the English upper middle class—his father was a colonial civil servant, and Cobb himself was educated at boarding schools and at Oxford. His first books were written in French. The best known of these is *Les Armées révolutionnaires* (1961–1963), a study of the paramilitary forces whose main task was to insure that the cities of France were adequately provisioned and whose reputation for bloodthirstiness and rapine he denies. Among his later publications are *A Second Identity: Essays on France and French History* (1969), *The Police and the People: French Popular Protest, 1789-1820* (1970), *Reactions to the French Revolution* (1972), and *Paris and Its Provinces: 1792–1802* (1975). As a historian he has attempted to break with the conventional history that he learned as a student. He writes vivid, impressionistic accounts, drawn largely from archival material, of ordinary people caught in the revolutionary whirlwind.

We have spoken elsewhere of the revolutionary sans-culotte during the period of his greatest activity, between April 1793 and Germinal year II [March–April 1794], and we have been especially interested in describing his personal attitudes and his emotional life.[1] These men were puritans for whom vice went hand in hand with counterrevolution. They therefore condemned celibacy, gastronomy, gambling, prostitution, obscenity, finery, and luxury; but on the other hand, they showed a marked indulgence for drunkenness. Such then was the essence of their private behavior. It now remains to describe some aspects of their collective behavior, their "public" life. . . .

From Richard Cobb, "Quelques aspects de la mentalité révolutionnaire," *Revue d'histoire moderne et contemporaine,* VI (April–June 1959), 86–87, 96–104, 116–120. Printed by permission of the author and the Secretary General of the Société d'histoire moderne. Editors' translation.

[1] Richard Cobb, "The Revolutionary Mentality in France," *History,* XLII (1957), 181–196.

The revolutionary was not an evil man, still less a professional informer or writer of anonymous letters. So if he occasionally did denounce someone, the main reason was his political credulity . . . caused by his belief in the dangers, the plots of all kinds, which he continuously saw about him. It must be said that the enemies of the regime certainly managed to strengthen his sense of always being "in danger of an assassin's sword"; for they were incredibly indiscreet, and this was certainly not because of drunkenness alone. The evidence is unmistakable: in spite of the Terror, in spite of the sight of the guillotine prominently displayed in the busiest places, in spite of the informers who might be anywhere, and especially in the cafés and the public squares, those Frenchmen who disliked the revolutionary regime had no qualms about expressing their dissatisfaction as loudly and publicly as possible, reproaching the Revolution and its works in the most vulgar language. They were the Pères Duchesne[2] in reverse, as noisy as street vendors. Even very young women in Lyon, waitresses in the cafés patronized by the troops of the garrison, did not hesitate to justify the [counterrevolutionary] events of May 29 [1793] right in front of the government soldiers; and they added that they were proud to have helped the federalist troops by bringing them food and ammunition and that if the insurrection were to resume, they would again aid "our brave lads of Lyon." [3] Common people and fashionable people alike were not satisfied with muttering to themselves, and if the men from Paris trusted only what they heard, they would not have had any difficulty in persuading themselves that they were in a completely royalist region. It was not in Lyon alone that people were so indiscreet in what they said; a similar garrulousness is to be noted among the enemies of the regime and the discontented at Nantes, Brest, Rouen, and especially in the countryside, where farmers did not hesitate to say what they thought about a Republic they viewed mainly in the forbidding light of price controls, requisitions, and the closing of churches. Avowed counterrevolution marched in the open; royalism was on display; and even at the height of the Terror, federalism still sought converts, especially in such areas as Lyon, where it could be identified with local patriotism.

A denouncer on occasion, a denouncer in spite of himself, the average revolutionary supported the great measures of repression; he had, besides, called for them insistently in the political clubs during the autumn of 1793. At least in his public statements and collective actions he was even harsher on domestic enemies than was the government itself. In particular, he demanded that it legalize the Terror. Repression in the year II followed the rules of "revolutionary legality"; but repression in the year III [the anti-Jacobin terror after the fall of Robespierre], even when carried out by criminal courts, was largely a matter of undisguised murder, individual violence, and class vengeance. The revolutionary of 1793 wanted to punish domestic enemies according to the rules of a justice that was summary to be sure and that was administered of course by the sans-culottes. This was therefore a political justice, but it was justice which nevertheless permitted certain rights to the

---

[2] [A reference to the inflammatory revolutionary newspaper edited by Jacques-René Hébert.—Eds.]

[3] Archives départementales, Rhône 42 L 149 (Commission temporaire, série alphabétique, dossier de Franchette Mayet, an eighteen-year-old girl whose fiancé had been killed during the siege of Lyon). She was denounced by the artillerymen of the Paris Revolutionary Army. See also 42 L 151 (concerning the woman Miou).

accused. In the year III there was a reversion to [acts like the massacres of] September 1792, the difference being that this time the terrorists were the victims; for even in the courts, justice revolved around class and social background. In 1795, in the Midi [southern France], people claimed that the "bloodthirsty sans-culottes" could be recognized by their dress; that is, they were clothed like artisans, like workers. The repressive justice of the year III was marked therefore by a class bias scarcely present in the revolutionary repression of the preceding year.[4] In the year III a goldsmith of Salon-de-Provence was accused "of having called for the death of citizens who powdered their hair and wore shirt cuffs with ruffles," [5] which is also a way of making justice a class matter; but we think this was mostly just talk. Certain frivolous dress had been much denounced by the sans-culottes, but bewigged members of society did not persecute them because of this.

These *buveurs de sang,* these *mathevons,*[6] were they therefore so fierce? Their language certainly was. Here, for example, is what they said and wrote about Lyon and the Lyonnais. Marcillat, a former parish priest of Jaligny in Allier and a member of the Temporary Commission [set up to pacify Lyon and punish the rebels there], wrote the following to his colleagues on the Revolutionary Committee of Moulins: ". . . Our Commission has sworn to revive public spirit; but what am I saying, comrades, there isn't any, it is gone. Ville-affranchie [the name the revolutionaries gave Lyon] is composed of aristocrats and the selfish: the former we will send to the guillotine; we will make the latter pay and we will make them recognize that poor unfortunates are their equals." We notice, in passing, this didactic aspect of the repression, a repression which people at the time also called a "regeneration." The former priest went on to say, "Blood must be shed in order to consolidate the Republic and to have it recognized in the city where we are living." And he concluded rather unexpectedly: "The people of this city (which had once been called Lyon) are fools. . . ." [7] A member of the Society of Valence [a revolutionary political club] even proposed that all federalists be expelled from Commune-affranchie [Lyon] and from Ville Sans Nom (Marseille), which would really mean the expulsion of nearly all the inhabitants, and that the two cities be repopulated with sans-culottes who would move into their homes. A statement to this effect was sent to the National Convention.[8] Rather often similar sentiments came from the pens of Parisian revolutionaries when referring to Lyon, whose population was accused of being both counterrevolutionary and "crassly merce-

---

[4] Arraigned before the tribunal of Aix, some terrorists from Marseille, accused of having participated in the riot of Vendémiaire year III [September–October 1794], challenged some of the jurors: "In behalf of his co-defendants, one declared that they did not want merchants, clerks, and property owners as jurors, but workers like themselves . . ." (Archives nationales de France, D III 31 (3) (405), Comité de Législation, Marseille; report made by the criminal tribunal of Bouches-du-Rhône, Ventôse year III [February–March 1795]).

[5] Archives nationales, D III 29 (2) (61), Comité de Législation, Aix; sentence handed down 3 Thermidor, year III [July 21, 1795], against twenty-four terrorists from Arles and Salon.

[6] [Two terms of disparagement directed against militant revolutionaries.—Eds.]

[7] Archives départementales, Allier, L 879, Comité de Moulins, correspondance (Marcillat to the Committee, 29 Brumaire, year II [November 19, 1793]).

[8] Archives départementales, Drôme, L 1086*, Société de Valence; meeting of 5 Pluviôse, year II [January 24, 1794].

nary." [9] In public and, more important, in private, they, like Marcillat, approved of rigorous repression that struck, with little regard for social distinctions, sometimes nobles, sometimes the upper middle class, and sometimes silkworkers. A proprietor of a gift shop on the Rue Saint-Denis in Paris, a loyal republican who was to be outlawed twice (after the affair at the Camp de Grenelle and again in the year IX),[10] wrote to his section: "In my last letter, I told you that the guillotine is taking care of some *dozens* of rebels every day, and that about the same number are shot. Now I want to inform you that several *hundreds* are to be shot every day so that we will soon be rid of those scoundrels who seem to defy the Republic even at the moment of their execution. . . ." [11] Officers from Montpellier, at the time also stationed at Lyon, revealed the same kind of unqualified approval; and since their sentiments were expressed in letters to their personal friends, they are all the more reliable as evidence of sincerity. One of them noted that "every day the Holy Guillotine cleanses the soil of liberty of all federalists in the department of the Rhône and Loire; so it goes, so it will continue. . . ." Another officer from Montpellier, in an almost jovial tone, wrote to someone back home that "everything continues to go well here, all rebels are being guillotined and shot. . . ." [12]

However, these men were neither professional executioners, nor naturally bloodthirsty. But they felt no pity for the people of Lyon, federalists who attacked the indivisibility of the Republic, an unpardonable crime deserving capital punishment. Their hatred for the population of Lyon, already strongly conditioned by a Parisian press that unanimously called for quick reprisals against federalists, was undoubtedly reinforced on the spot by the state of isolation imposed on them by a silent and hostile people. A tour of duty at Lyon in the year II was not a laughing matter, and the troops complained bitterly about the ill-will and the unfriendliness of the city. Whether Parisians or men of Nivernais and Allier, they were disliked even though *they* were the good sans-culottes, the real revolutionaries. This is therefore one more piece of evidence that "the stupid Lyonnais" lacked the republican spirit. It is true that a few soldiers, on seeing the extreme poverty of the inhabitants and on talking to some women of the lower classes, did feel compassion; and there was one revolutionary officer who even dared to denounce the repression by declaring that "in a Republic no one should be singled out for proscription." [13] But these examples are rare. Most soldiers did not mingle with a population they

[9] See, for example, Friedrich Christian Heinrich Laukhard, *Un Allemand en France sous la Terreur*, trans. Wilhelm Bauer (Paris, 1915), p. 267: ". . . They claim that almost all the people of these areas are crassly mercenary and shamelessly rob poor artisans, workers, and laborers of their pay. . . . Here the aristocracy of money rides high. . . ."

[10] [These two events concern abortive plots against the government, the first quelled by the Directors in 1796 and the second by Napoleon and his Minister of Police Fouché in 1800–1801.—Eds.]

[11] Archives nationales, F7 4767 d 2, Lassagne (Réaume to the president of the Revolutionary Committee of the Bonne-Nouvelle section).

[12] Archives départementales, Seine-et-Oise, IV Q 187 (confiscated material, papers of Mazuel) (Fayet à Mazuel, 2 Pluviôse, year II [January 21, 1794]; Penelle à Mazuel, 27 Frimaire, year II [December 17, 1793]).

[13] See my study *L'Armée révolutionnaire parisienne à Lyon et dans la région lyonnaise* (Lyon, 1952), p. 31. Also Archives départementales, Rhône 31 L 50, Société de Lyon; meeting of 16 Frimaire, year II [December 6, 1793].

distrusted—the bodies of soldiers were sometimes fished out of the Rhône River—and the local imitators of the *Père Duchesne*, Dorfeuille and Millet, made it their business to encourage the zeal for repression by sounding the trumpet for revolutionary vengeance.[14]

It is very easy to condemn the repression at Lyon straight off. Not only can it be considered a horrible crime, but also an incredible political blunder which succeeded only in turning all Lyon against a Republic that, in its eyes, seemed inseparable from the guillotine and the firing squad. Couthon saw this quite clearly. But we must also recapture the life of the year II; do not forget the great federalist revolts of the Summer and how they had almost swallowed up the Republic in a terrible civil war. No doubt little effort was made to understand the causes of these revolts, but what was remembered was the critical situation in which they had placed France by June and July 1793. That is why the revolutionary, whether he was a small shopkeeper, a professional soldier, a former priest, a physician, or an artisan, approved the use of force against the people of Lyon, Marseille, the Vendée, and Toulon. He favored it also when it struck at refractory priests and more generally when it struck at those whom he accused of being "fanatics," for he could not forgive the latter for having caused "small Vendées" in various regions. Moreover, the soldiers, who had everywhere helped develop a definite revolutionary mentality, were especially hostile to the Catholic people of the countryside, whom they regarded as allies of the *Chouans* and the other avowed enemies of the regime. In their hatred of the "fanatics," there was also something more personal; for many of the soldiers had witnessed atrocities committed against republicans by the peasants, both men and women, of the Vendée.

But the revolutionary demanded even harsher measures against the hoarder, the economic criminal, and the disobedient, "selfish" farmer and tried to show that these acts of repression had an economic basis. If the Parisians and the little people of Moulins and Nevers so favored the use of force in Lyon, it was primarily because they saw the city as that "big business capital" where even the workers were unworthy of liberty.[15] For similar reasons, Hébert and members of the Paris sections demanded that the machinery of terror and the temporary commissions of popular justice be sent to that other business capital, Rouen; for the revolutionaries also had a very low opinion of the population there.[16] Some people even wanted to extend repressive measures to every rural area and terrorize the farmers, but on this occasion government policy did not go so far as the one advocated by the urban sans-culottes.

[14] *Le Père Duchesne* [of Lyon] (Dorfeuille and Millet), No. XX (17 Pluviôse, year II [February 5, 1794]) and No. XXVIII (14 Ventôse, year II [March 4, 1794]). Referring to the "embroidery merchants," they said quite delicately: "We are going to send over our dragoons . . . to make them dance the carmagnole to the tune of the commander of the garrison, and he will, with all due respect, shoot their faces to bits."

[15] Dorfeuille and Millet, editors of the Lyon *Père Duchesne*, wrote on the 17 Pluviôse [February 5, 1794]: "The workers of Lyon seem to think they have lost everything because they have lost their rich merchants." Almost all the men from Paris were indignant about the "federalist" spirit of the entire population of Lyon (article "Grande colère," *Père Duchesne* of Lyon, No. XX).

[16] See my article, "La Campagne pour l'envoi de l'armée révolutionnaire dans la Seine-Inférieure," *Annales de Normandie*, August 1952.

This approval of force and the Terror was therefore the result of a combination of very diverse elements. With regard to the measures taken against the people of Lyon and Marseille, there were intermingled the economic prejudices of the small shopkeeper and the small merchant against the big merchants, the shipowners,[17] and the big firms; there was the condemnation of the "special interests" who had placed themselves between the citizen and the sovereign people and who had dared to strike a sacrilegious blow against the Convention; and of course there was the desire to conform to the customs of the time, as well as a vivid memory of what dangers the federalist crisis had inflicted on the Republic. Moreover, the press was ingenious in keeping public opinion at a fever pitch favorable to severe acts of repression; and the revolutionaries themselves, living as if in combat, as an occupation army, as strangers amidst hostile populations, were easily persuaded that only terror and repressive force saved them from the blows of their enemies. If they did not strike first, they would be "struck down by the assassin's sword." Such was the part fear and credulity played, and it was amply fed by the unbelievably imprudent remarks of the enemies of the regime, who did not hesitate to shout at Parisians their hatred for the Republic and the capital.

A taste for blood and vengeance does not seem to have played an important part; still it is very difficult to distinguish between what may have been a political and group attitude and what reveals a personal bent for violence and brutality. In the affair of the *noyades*,[18] some members of the Marat Company and of the Revolutionary Committee of Nantes were extremely cruel. They persecuted their prisoners, chased the wives of the *Chouans* while clubbing them with their musket butts, pulled girls by the hair, and shoved and cursed everyone. But according to witnesses, drunkenness could explain this especially odious example of brutality, just as it had fortified so many of the murderers at the Carmes prison in September 1792. To be sure, at the trial of Carrier, there was one witness, a young man of twenty, who not only admitted taking part in the "drownings," but who added that he had no regrets, and that if he had it to do over, he would again volunteer to carry out similar acts. But he was a young soldier of the first Nantes battalion and he had seen his comrades tortured by the wives and daughters of Breton peasants when the soldiers were captured by the *Chouans* in the countryside around Nantes; and he had himself escaped torture and mutilation thanks to a wound that was more horrible to look at than it was serious.[19] During the trial, most of the witnesses almost became sick while recalling the horrible scenes that had taken place on the small boats when the trap doors installed in the holds were opened. The men of the eighteenth century were somewhat accustomed to brutality, but this did not make them sadists. It is true that the revolutionary regime did allow some sadists to use their deplorable

---

[17] Thus at Le Havre the merchants and shopkeepers who composed the Committee of Surveillance pursued the shipowners with special vigor, so much so as to hinder their business dealings with the shipowners of Lübeck, Altona, and Copenhagen, even though these had been undertaken for the Food and Supply Commission.

[18] [The *noyades* of Nantes were mass executions by drowning conducted by the deputy on mission Jean-Baptiste Carrier, who had been sent to the city in October 1793 to suppress the revolt there.—Eds.]

[19] Archives de la Préfecture de Police, Paris, A A 269; notes of Topino-Lebrun on the trial of Carrier.

talents under exceptionally favorable circumstances, and everyone has heard of Mathieu Jouve Jourdan [called Jourdan the Decapitator] and other bloodthirsty brutes of his ilk, but these monsters were, we think, the exceptions. The revolutionaries were often violent, especially in speech; they were hot-tempered and fanatical; when they drank to excess they must have appeared at times terrifying and obscenely brutal in the manner of the *Père Duchesne*. Some civilian officials were hotheaded and violent, their fiery temperaments being most apparent in the years of proscription after the fall of Robespierre. No one would be so bold as to claim that a Collot-d'Herbois and a Javogues[20] were normal, sensible men, and many must have resembled them. But even this sort of violence was to be temporary; it was connected with the recent dangers brought on by the federalist crisis. The Revolution had its professional fiends, its murderers, its sadists; and in the cities of the Midi, some of the assassins of the years II and III were also to be the perpetrators of the bloody brutalities of 1814 and 1815. But the average revolutionary was neither a sadist nor a brute.

Finally, there was an educational aspect: the work of "regeneration" had to be undertaken, and the use of force was a part of a general program of civic education. A revolutionary in the Yonne department insisted that "all youths from seven to ten be brought together in order to watch all public punishments, including executions." [21] Now this *Émile* of repression was not a *buveur de sang;* and neither were the revolutionaries of the year II, despite all efforts of Thermidorian propaganda to identify them with the murderers. Actually, the epithet is much more appropriate for those young dandies of the year III who attacked individual terrorists or men of modest appearance and poor dress and who could not even claim that they acted from fear. It is just as wrong to label the revolutionary a killer as it is to call him a denouncer. Because of certain circumstances, to be sure, at times he had to be both, but the revolutionaries with whom we are familiar—shopkeepers, small merchants, physicians, former priests, lawyers—do not resemble in the slightest those "sanguinary brutes" of Thermidorian and royalist iconography.

It would be equally wrong, I believe, to try to explain the origins of the Terror and the revolutionaries' approval of the great repressive measures by stressing hidden psychological motives in the traditional mentality of the common people, a mentality in which the fear of plagues aroused a climate of panic and mutual fear in bourgeois and artisan alike.[22] The revolutionary of the year II did not have the

---

[20] [Claude Javogues, deputy of the Convention, was an ultrarevolutionary who accused the Committee of Public Safety of counterrevolution and when on mission used terror against the rich, the priests, and others. See also Colin Lucas, *The Structure of the Terror: The Example of Javogues and the Loire* (New York: Oxford University Press, 1973).—Eds.]

[21] Archives nationales, D III 306, Comité de Législation, Yonne; petition to the Convention by Héry, I Pluviôse, year III [January 20, 1795].

[22] René Baehrel, "Épidémie et terreur: histoire et sociologie," *Annales historiques de la Révolution française,* April–June 1951, pp. 113–146, and "La Haine de classe en temps d'épidémie," *Annales: Économies, sociétés, civilisations,* July–September 1952. The first of these studies provides very interesting information on the spread of the great plague of 1720 in Marseille and on the social and "terroristic" consequences of other plagues in French cities during the sixteenth, seventeenth, eighteenth, and nineteenth centuries. In particular, the author has analyzed the reactions of the

slightest need of very old historical memories in order to demand a pitiless outlawing of all those who, at the time, menaced the existence of the Republic. It was not a question of proscription based on class or even of a tradition of violence. The danger was there, it was obvious, and when the danger passed, it had to be prevented from recurring by "striking a mighty blow." From the year III on, all this seemed quite unreal even to the revolutionaries themselves when they recalled the crisis. This is so because the atmosphere had already changed, the time of extreme measures had passed. The justification for the Terror is that it was a response to circumstance, not a permanent state of mind or one act of a naturally violent temperament. It was just as transitory as the revolutionary man himself. . . .

Our "revolutionary man," if he existed at all, is only known to us by a kind of historical documentation unique to the revolutionary period, and it reveals at least the public attitudes of a whole social group, a complete cross section of the common people of the cities and even of the towns. All of this is entirely hidden from us in other periods of history. It is therefore difficult for us to distinguish clearly between the public and the private man, since we know him only at that one time, and then only for one year or eighteen months, a unique time in the life of the individual and in the history of France.

Let us try nevertheless to draw the essential features of our portrait. I believe we are concerned especially with a matter of temperament; and it seems to me that to rely solely on studies of social structure will not furnish us with the basis for a satisfactory answer. The revolutionary man seldom behaved the way he did because

---

common people to the measures taken by health officials and by "Boards of Health" to halt the spread of epidemics and to isolate the victims, measures which the poor especially—the probable sources of the infection—had to bear, while the well-off frequently went to their country homes. But doubtless Monsieur Baehrel is a little hasty when he identifies these measures and the very violent social conflicts they provoked with the executions and the Great Terror of the year II. Surely these two series of events had in common only the fear they aroused (fear of "conspiracies," fear of the spread of infection) and the rumors and panic they also aroused, especially among the common people of the cities and countryside. Fear, panic, and rumor are, however, evident throughout the history of the common people, but they do not always cause the same reaction. The people are often afraid, but only in 1792, 1793, and 1795 did fear set off a great outburst of anger and popular violence resulting in massacres, drownings, and mass shootings. And the great institutions of terror in the year II, the special commissions responsible for carrying out the repressive policies, were in no way instruments of any one class or any very distinct social group. The Terror was directed against almost every group that composed French society during the revolutionary period. To claim, as does Monsieur Baehrel, that "Frenchmen in 1792 inherited a long tradition of terrorism" and that the memory of the great plague of 1720, of the periodic famines during the eighteenth century, of the epidemics—the most recent occurring in 1775—helped create a climate of terror and helped inculcate among the French common people a class hatred, a use of terror against other social groups, is to argue abstractly and to advance some very speculative theories. We prefer to say that the Terror of the year II sprang from the special circumstances of that year—the civil war, the foreign war, the treasons, the victories of the coalition, the common people's suspicions of prison plots, the fear of prison breaks, federalism, etc. These seem to us to explain adequately why a terrorist mentality appeared that was as brief and fleeting as the revolutionary man himself. To suggest that there is no need to look for the origins of the terrorist mind in the memories of the plague of 1720 in no way detracts from the originality of Monsieur Baehrel's thesis. As for the rest, the author is certainly right to stress the importance of plagues and epidemics in the development of class hatred and sometimes in the outbreak of insurrectionary events. But such considerations are not relevant for 1793.

of social struggles, except to the extent that he typified the world of the small property owner, the small tradesman, and the artisan. His predominant characteristics were incontestable political and physical courage, strong beliefs, also of course a certain love for power, and finally an undeniable fondness for speech-making and display. Public life in the year II, we must remember, was an opportunity for many of these small tradesmen to play the role of men of importance, of "politicians," of Roman Senators, while at the same time meddling in their neighbor's affairs. The rewards? Well, they were not to be sneered at: first of all there was the presidency of a political club, or much more influential though less conspicuous, a position on its executive committee. Any prominent place in one of these clubs could sometimes provide excellent free publicity for one's business. Think for example of the club member at Vaison, a painter by trade, who when asked to paint the tree of liberty in three colors, declined the honor. (He was not to be paid for the job.) But after the society had asked another of the local painters, the first changed his mind and declared that he would be delighted by the club's confidence.[23] These posts and honors, furthermore, caused bitter personal strife and dispute often having nothing to do with republican propriety, but this proves that they were worth a lot of effort and ingenuity. We know little about the elections of officers and noncommissioned officers in the National Guard stationed in the cities, but we surely can guess that the competition was just as acrimonious.[24] The revolutionary was all the more avid for honors, sashes, and stripes, since they compensated for years of obscurity and insignificance.

But in the final analysis, in spite of these material incentives, the revolutionary temperament was mostly a product of faith, enthusiasm, and generosity. The poet Coleridge was not the only one who, recalling the enthusiasms of his youth, remarked how glorious it was to be alive at that time. How many mature men, settled in occupations as obscure as they were honorable, recalled in their old age the *Radiant Days of '93*! For the revolutionaries were mostly young men or men in the prime of life, and their enthusiasm must have been in part the enthusiasm of youth.[25]

In the birth of such a mentality of battle and crisis, the role of the war must also be stressed. The revolutionaries thought of themselves as always standing in the breach, and this was not merely a figment of the imagination. Those at Nantes knew that they were surrounded by almost universal hatred; those in Lyon, even more isolated, could never forget the head of Chalier, and most of the *mathevons* were to die in the terrible massacres of the year III.[26] Like the leaders of the great

23 Archives départementales, Vaucluse, L VI 12; Register of the Société populaire de Vaison.

24 My friend Rémi Gossez has told me that during the Revolution of 1848 there was fierce competition for promotions in the National Guard. Unfortunately we know little about the way such elections were conducted during the period of the French Revolution.

25 A general study of lower-echelon revolutionary personnel would certainly demonstrate that men between twenty-five and forty were in the majority. Regarding the famous Temporary Commission of Lyon, thirty was the average age among some forty members. Revolutionary France was a country offering innumerable opportunities to young men of talent.

26 Renée Fuoc, *La Réaction thermidorienne à Lyon (1795)* (Lyon, 1957). [Marie-Joseph Chalier was the leader of the Jacobins of Lyon. During the city's counterrevolution, he was arrested, tried, and on July 16, 1793, guillotined. After the revolt was quelled, he became a martyr; and a model of his decapitated head was publicly displayed, even carried to Paris, where it was presented to the Convention.—Eds.]

revolutionary committees, they were absolutely sure that Pitt had put their names on his death lists. It is true, in general, that nothing happened to them in the year II, but the Thermidorian proscription, owing to its blind vengeance against anyone, without exception, who had held power in the year II, certainly played a large part in causing this revolutionary temperament to survive somewhat, thanks to persecution. A political club in Vaucluse asked the following question when screening candidates for admission: *What have you done for which you would be hanged if the counterrevolution should triumph?*[27] This was not simply rhetoric. The revolutionaries had to face such an eventuality, especially in a region like the former Comtat Venaissin, where they constituted a very small minority isolated from the rest of the people.[28] They were, in every sense of the word, embattled.

Yet to maintain this spirit of combat, danger had to be constant. But beginning in Floréal year II [April–May 1794], it receded more and more from a France which until then had been besieged and invaded. The great victories of the Summer of 1794, which made the threat of invasion and the military triumph of the counterrevolution more remote, inevitably resulted in some relaxation of tension. The feeling of urgency waned. It was also at this very time that the Robespierrist government chose to attack the political institutions of the common people. And then with the coming of Summer, daily affairs demanded attention, and a great deal of it, since they had been neglected for so long. This was not only true for the country people, whose revolutionary temper did not usually survive the resumption of work in the fields. The urban sans-culotte also had to make a living, to think of his business. His wife kept reminding him of that. But the political clubs met almost every evening from five to ten o'clock, sometimes until midnight; and his life as an active revolutionary, which included guard duty and many other obligations, encroached not only on his leisure, but also resulted in long absences from his shop, which, however, still had to be kept open sixteen hours a day. Such obligations, of course, also took time from billiards. Thus gradually normal life, banal existence, regained the upper hand. We can see quite well what constituted the drama in these men's lives. One from Anduze said in protest, *The bow breaks if bent too far.*[29] In fact, for most of the club members, politicians only for the moment, the bow did break; revolutionary enthusiasm and activity ended. In general, their billiards and wives had the last say.

Furthermore, the Robespierrist Republic was far from amusing. It oozed boredom and virtue, just like the insipid and pedantic speeches of Robespierre the Incorruptible. Think of those vapid and interminable celebrations of the Supreme Being, after which one sat down to eat the "republican plate," a single course,

[27] Archives départementales, Vaucluse, L VI 12; Register of the Société populaire de Vaison, meeting of 28 Messidor, year II [July 16, 1794].

[28] Archives nationales, D III 292 (2) (4), Comité de Législation, Vaucluse, Avignon: ". . . The department of Vaucluse, which is largely inhabited by men who lived under the domination of the Roman priesthood, has a great number of those opportunists . . . who call themselves patriots so that they will be able to get rich with impunity at public expense . . ." (to the Committee of Public Safety from Barjavel, Public Prosecutor of the Revolutionary Tribunal of the department, 25 Frimaire, year II [December 15, 1793]).

[29] Archives nationales, F7 4609 d 2, Borie (letter of Cavalié from Anduze to the Committee of Public Safety, 25 Pluviôse, year II [February 13, 1794]).

sometimes served without wine! It was useless to say to these men, *Look out; don't slacken; above all, don't miss club meetings; we still need you; the hidden enemies have not been defeated; victory is not yet won.* It was a waste of words if all they were called upon to do was vote on congratulatory speeches delivered in a bombastic and trite style. One grew weary. This is proven by the sharp drop in attendance at meetings of provincial clubs beginning in Germinal year II [March–April 1794]. Long before the fall of Robespierre, the revolutionary man began to fade away, to resume his anonymity. The time "to make revolution" was already long past.

To summarize, the revolutionary man was only a temporary phenomenon. A product of exceptional circumstances, he did not resist time, wear and tear, fatigue, and boredom. He was not a professional in the art of revolution. Anyway, what is a professional revolutionary if not a bureaucrat like all the others, a bureaucrat solidly installed in a petrified Revolution; or else a half-baked conspirator, a romantic, a "cardboard revolutionary." Except in the imagination of the policemen and the informers reporting to the Ministry of Police, the followers of Babeuf had very little in common with the revolutionaries of the year II. Our men of 1793 were neither "cardboard revolutionaries," nor ideologists and professors of revolutionary theory. And the very moment they put on their slippers and relaxed, their role as politicians ended. Thus, after the great hopes and dangers had passed, they returned to their everyday banal existence. In the year III, when inequality became more marked and one's daily bread became the biggest problem, the matter was settled. The revolutionaries were less the victims of the *muscadins*, of those young assassins in fine shoes, than of an economic crisis and a food shortage which struck their families and which, in many cases, reduced them to wretchedness, to the anonymity of the beggar.

Something survived of the revolutionary mentality, of course, especially in the army, where it often took the form of violent anticlericalism. It also was to reappear in the political sphere beginning with the elections of the year IV [October 1795], which saw numerous attempts at regroupment among the former terrorist cadres. But these efforts were confined to a handful of leaders. As for the conspirators among the revolutionaries, they constituted a very small minority—the tough and pitiless, the totally convinced, perhaps also the *violent;* for the revolutionary temperament certainly included a dash of violence. Among the others, silence descended as before 1789. The revolutionaries vanished along with the extraordinary circumstances that had given them an intense but fleeting existence; so did those institutions whose extant records allow us to uncover a few months of the submerged history of the common people and thus to see the attitudes and prejudices of a world of stores and workshops. These voices would be heard again only through the very distorted screen of police reports.

$\mathcal{A}$ Synthesis

GEORGES LEFEBVRE

For biographical information on Georges Lefebvre, see
Chapter 1, "The Outbreak of the Revolution (1787–1789)."

In the revolutionary mentality, as has been noted,[1] the punitive will was associated
from the beginning with the defensive reaction against the "aristocratic plot." They
were inseparable elements, although one might predominate and the behaviour that
resulted might differ greatly as the result of circumstances and individual
temperaments. Repressive action arose as early as July, 1789. The permanent
committees confined themselves to surveillance and to investigations made on
suspicion, but in a few cases summary executions by the aroused mob occurred. The
deployment of the police force was not always enough to prevent these, and it was
necessary to check the agitation through the all-out pursuit of conspirators and by
prompt and severe penalties. The assemblies instituted committees of investigation
or of general security, and referred crimes against the nation *(lèse-nation)* to a special
jurisdiction, first Le Châtelet, then the High Court, and finally the tribunal of
August 17, 1792.

During this first period, however, repression was not made uniform. In times of
calm, with the danger fading and the bourgeoisie disliking hasty procedures that
threatened individual security, the penalties seemed absurd; but a local incident was
enough to cause renewed popular executions. With the war and invasion these
multiplied, and in Paris they culminated in the September Massacres. The response
of the Girondins, far from bringing about the reinforcement of governmental
action, was to suppress it. The High Court disappeared, then the tribunal of August
17, so that political trials returned to the jurisdiction of ordinary courts.

The crisis of 1793 posed the problem once again, for the punitive will was
joined with the defensive reaction to give birth to the revolutionary government. It
aroused its leaders as much as its partisans. The September Massacres had nearly
destroyed them, however, and resolving not to tolerate a repetition they undertook
to organize the Terror. By so doing they opened a second period. At the lowest
level, the watch committees, created on March 21, 1793, assumed the power to

From Georges Lefebvre, *The French Revolution from 1793 to 1799,* trans. John Hall Stewart and James
Friguglietti (New York: Columbia University Press, 1964), pp. 116–125. Copyright © 1964 Columbia
University Press. Reprinted by permission of Columbia University Press, Inc., and Routledge & Kegan
Paul, Ltd.

[1] [For Lefebvre's description of what he means by the revolutionary mentality, see pp. 21–22.—Eds.]

arrest suspected persons; and after the law of September 17 they were left full discretion, under the control of the Committee of General Security. If there were grounds for indictment, the Revolutionary Tribunal (instituted on March 10, reorganized on September 5, and appointed by the Convention) intervened. For some crimes the criminal court of each department, sitting "revolutionarily," followed the same methods. Finally, in the areas of civil war, military commissions became active. Procedure was simplified in all cases. The grand jury was replaced by judges, and recourse to appeals disappeared. Moreover, the Convention reduced trials to a simple verification of identity and pronouncement of the death penalty for individuals who had been outlawed, rebels, émigrés, and deported priests who returned to the territory of the Republic.

In reality the government lost some control over the repression. Like administration, it was decentralized by the emergency. Nothing could serve better than local committees, because of the information which their members had long since acquired. The centrifugal tendency was curbed in principle by the deputies on mission. For months concentration of powers was displayed chiefly at this regional level, but in many communes the revolutionary committees were established solely for appearances, or never existed. Having difficulty in recruiting competent and reliable administrations in the villages, the deputies often preferred to leave political policing either to the committee of the chief town of the district or canton, or to the committees of public safety created spontaneously by the revolutionaries of the locality. By virtue of their full powers, however, the deputies on mission claimed to direct the Terror as they pleased. At times they collaborated with the local terrorists; at times they opposed them. The result of this inconsistency was that the scope of repression was expanded, but its severity varied greatly.

Suspicion was directed not only towards probable authors of acts already committed, on grounds of definite circumstances susceptible of discussion and of proof, but also towards the possible perpetrators of eventual crimes, who were believed capable of them because of their opinions or even their real or simulated indifference. The margin for uncertainty and the risk of arbitrary action, which normal judicial procedure reduced only slightly (because of its attention to detail and its slowness), increased enormously. The dangers were multiplied in a singularly perilous fashion when it came to arraignment. In investigating the past of persons concerned, acts or declarations that were irreproachable in their time (such as the petitions of the "8,000" and the "20,000" [2]), or that were justified according to law (notably the protests against August 10, 1792, or June 2, 1793), were introduced. Although no subsequent opposition could be charged to these Feuillants or federalists, many of them were imprisoned and even guillotined.

Yet the "aristocratic plot" was not the sole factor involved. The economic situation and its social consequences now revealed other "enemies of the people"—the rich who hid their money or sent it abroad, the producers who evaded the Maximum, and those who refused assignats. The Terror thus became the prop

[2] [The first of these petitions (June 10, 1792) opposed the stationing near Paris of National Guardsmen from the provinces. The second (July 1, 1792) protested the indignities the king suffered during the demonstration of June 20, 1792.—Eds.]

of the controlled economy on which the sans-culottes depended for their own existence. Undoubtedly crimes of an economic nature did not all fall within the special jurisdiction. Still, they exposed their authors to detention as suspects; and if their opinions and circumstances tended to impute counter-revolutionary intentions to them, their lives were at stake.

Nevertheless nothing contributed as much to spreading the Terror as dechristianization. Former clergy, constitutional priests, and practising faithful were treated as dangerous or culpable. Thus conceived, the terrorist repression was unquestionably effective, because it intimidated, reduced to impotence, or suppressed many enemies. Yet it was no less responsible for injuring, or far more frequently, for disturbing and vexing a host of people who, although hostile to the revolutionary government for various reasons, were resigned to obeying it, and who, in any case, dreamed neither of conspiracy nor of revolt.

Even making great allowances for the opinions of those who applied the Terror, its harshness depended upon their character and upon circumstances. Personal hatreds, the desire for vengeance that had permeated the punitive will from the outset, and particularly the impulsive authoritarianism of certain individuals occasionally aggravated its severity or rekindled it after a period of calm. Conversely, forbearance, friendships, and political spirit often tempered it, and numerous deputies on mission confined themselves to setting a few examples or making a few imprisonments. Likewise, the commissioners of the committees varied in their behaviour: in the district of St.-Pol one arrested 141 persons in the canton of Frévent, while his colleagues elsewhere apprehended only one or two.

Yet circumstances exerted a more considerable influence. An estimate of the relative danger, and not temperament alone, prompted some deputies to assume responsibility for establishing revolutionary tribunals or popular commissions. These, ignoring the Paris tribunal, precipitated executions. In the matter of suspects, mass arrests coincided with specific events: those of August, 1793, period of the greatest peril and the levy *en masse;* those of the autumn, when terror had just been made the "order of the day"; and those of Ventôse [March 1794], at the opening of the [military] campaign. The role of circumstances is more clearly evident from the statistical analysis of death sentences made by Donald Greer.[3] Seventy-one per cent occurred in the two areas of civil war—19 per cent in the south-east and 52 per cent in the west—as against only 15 per cent in Paris. Moreover, this agrees with an examination of the motives for these condemnations: in more than 72 per cent of the cases they were due to rebellion. Six departments, on the other hand, had no executions, thirty-one had fewer than ten, and fourteen fewer than twenty-five.

Of course it is not percentages but the figures themselves that account for the impression made on public opinion. Greer's statistics are limited to death sentences, which he estimates at almost 17,000; but the number of deaths was far higher. Apart from rebels who fell in combat, it is necessary to add the executions without trial, whether by order, as at Nantes and Toulon, or by refusal to grant quarter on the battlefield, in pursuit, or in police roundups. Besides, conditions in the prisons

---

[3] [*The Incidence of the Terror* (Cambridge, Mass.: Harvard University Press, 1935).—Eds.]

caused a high mortality. Since an exact computation is impossible, Greer suggests an estimate of 35,000–40,000 dead. It is well to recall that the property of condemned persons, of émigrés, and of deported priests was confiscated, and that of relatives of émigrés was sequestered until the inheritance belonging to the fugitives was deducted. Finally, suspects should not be forgotten. The district of St.-Pol confined 1,460 of them, and the total number of 300,000, although hypothetical, is not improbable. The fright and rancour of contemporaries, and the indelible memory which they handed down to posterity, are quite understandable.

Greer's findings are important particularly because they confirm the nature of the Terror. It was in the two areas where counter-revolutionaries took up arms and committed open treason that it raged with the greatest fury. Despite the elements that spread it thoughtlessly or abused it, it remained until the triumph of the Revolution just what it had been at the outset—a punitive reaction indissolubly linked to the defensive spirit against the "aristocratic plot." Some will object that 85 per cent of the known dead—bourgeois, artisans, peasants—belonged to the Third Estate, while the clergy accounted for only 6.5 per cent, and the nobility 8.5 per cent; but in such a struggle, turncoats were treated more harshly than original enemies.

Yet to a large extent this is merely the outward aspect of the Terror. Another may be revealed within if it is observed that, associated with the revolutionary government, the Terror conferred upon the latter the "coercive power" that restored the authority of the state and allowed it to impose upon the nation the sacrifices indispensable to public safety. If the majority of Frenchmen clung to the Revolution and detested foreign intervention, their civic education was not enough to repress selfishness and make them all submit to discipline. The Terror forced it upon them and contributed greatly to developing the habit and feeling of national solidarity. The Montagnards undoubtedly shared the punitive will of the sans-culottes, but the fact remains that from this point of view the Terror became an instrument of government that regimented the nation, without making even occasional exception for the sans-culottes themselves. This was, so to speak, its internal aspect.

Henceforth, as the dictatorship of the Committee asserted itself, a third aspect was revealed. Some Montagnards condemned the harshness of the system, and some sans-culottes reproached it for not doing enough for them. This time the Terror was turned against those who had created it. The drama of Ventôse and Germinal [March–April 1794] thus marked a new stage in its history. It appeared destined to maintain in power the small group of men who, entrenched in the committees, embodied the revolutionary dictatorship.

Still, its earlier characteristics persisted during this third period. Centralization had progressed slowly. The Committee of General Security required justificatory reports on imprisonments, the Committee of Public Safety sent agents here and there to investigate (Jullien of Paris to Nantes and Bordeaux, and Demaillot to Orléans), and the most notable terrorists (Carrier, Barras, Fréron, Fouché, and Tallien) returned one after another. Now the decree of 27 Germinal, Year II (April 16, 1794), ordered the suppression of revolutionary tribunals in the provinces, and most of them were terminated on 19 Floréal (May 8).

Once more, circumstances produced exceptions. In the north the campaign took a turn for the worse: Landrecies surrendered on 11 Floréal, Year II (April 30, 1794), and Cambrai was threatened. Dispatched to the army, Saint-Just and Lebas appealed to Lebon,[4] who established a branch of his Arras tribunal, which was then allowed to remain until 22 Messidor (July 10). In Provence, when [the deputy on mission] Maignet declared it impossible to transfer thousands of prisoners to Paris, the Committee, on 21 Floréal (May 10), created the popular commission of Orange, which was still functioning on 9 Thermidor. On the other hand, with the Committee of Public Safety and that of General Security both directing the repression, centralization drove the former to dispossess the latter; and at the end of Floréal it established a Bureau of General Police. Its rival did not give way, and . . . this rift within the revolutionary government hastened its downfall.

As an instrument of government, the terrorist methods might have given the victorious committees cause for reflection. All authoritarian regimes, and others, too, resort to them in time of war or insurrection. But it is a rule among politicians to confine themselves to setting a few examples that assure the submission of the multitude without reducing it to desperation. There were signs that some members of the Committee perceived the danger. Robespierre had opposed the trial of the deputies arrested following their protest against the "day" of June 2 [1793, when the Convention arrested twenty-nine of its own members]; and thanks to Lindet, a general proscription of federalists was avoided. The vain efforts against dechristianization, and the recall of the worst terrorists, were steps in the same direction.

On 5 Nivôse, Year II (December 25, 1793), it was agreed to "perfect" the Revolutionary Tribunal. Did this mean that the crimes to be repressed would be precisely defined, that guarantees for the defendant would be increased, and that arrests would be reviewed? Such was not the case. Once more, circumstances were decisive. Until the end of June, victory remained doubtful and required an all-out effort. The moment did not seem ripe for any slackening of energy. On the contrary, the decree of 27 Germinal, Year II (April 16, 1794), expelled nobles and foreigners from Paris and the fortified towns. In proscribing Indulgents and extremists, however, the committees had no intention of sparing the counter-revolutionaries. They shared the sans-culottes' urge to punish, and had no desire to risk being accused of treason.

In Paris, in Floréal [April–May 1794], notable trials—those of the deputies compromised by their attitude in 1789, of the farmers-general (who included Lavoisier), and of Madame Elisabeth [Louis XVI's younger sister]—proved that the Terror, faithful to its origin, had not become simply an instrument of government. The widespread belief in the "aristocratic plot," extended to all those accused of hostility towards the regime, explains the increasing practice of the "amalgam." This, by denying all truly judicial procedure, threw together under the same sentence accused persons who did not know each other, and whose deeds or words had nothing in common other than their supposed solidarity in the "conspiracy against the French people." Finally, with this state of mind exaggerated because of

[4] [One of the Convention's deputies on mission who headed a Revolutionary Tribunal in Arras.—Eds.]

attacks threatening the personal safety of revolutionary leaders, terrorist procedure was altered, but only to be even more greatly simplified.

Late on 4 Prairial, Year II (May 23, 1794), a certain Admiral fired his pistol at Collot d'Herbois, but missed his target. On the evening of the 4th, Cécile Renault, who insisted upon seeing Robespierre, was arrested. She refused to reveal her intentions, but voiced her hopes of victory for the [antirevolutionary] Coalition. Earlier that day Barère had denounced Admiral as the agent of the plot, financed by Pitt, against the Republic. On the 7th (May 26), the Convention forbade the granting of quarter henceforth to British and Hanoverian soldiers. This was an unprecedented step, and the army could scarcely apply it; but it attested the emotion aroused by the memories of the assassination of Lepeletier and Marat. This feeling was again expressed in the appeal from the Committee of Public Safety to Saint-Just, on the 6th, in the midst of the campaign: "Liberty is exposed to new dangers. . . . The Committee needs to unite the knowledge and energy of all its members."

Obviously, in the eyes of the revolutionaries these assassination attempts, which they linked (without any convincing proof) to the intrigues of the elusive Baron de Batz,[5] foreshadowed some attempt to disorganize the national defence on the eve of decisive battles. Saint-Just arrived on the 10th, but discussions (of which we know nothing) and preparations for the Festival of the Supreme Being (set for the 20th) delayed the result. This took shape on 22 Prairial (June 10), when Couthon presented the famous law, the draft of which is in his handwriting. Robespierre, who was presiding, stepped down to the tribune to secure the approval of the Convention. Later, when threatened by the reactionaries, the members of the Committee of Public Safety ascribed the initiative for the law to their vanished colleagues, and declared that they themselves had not been consulted. But the Thermidorians did not believe them. It is at least certain that the Committee of General Security was not called upon to give its opinion, and that it did not forgive this oversight.

Suppressing all preliminary questioning, leaving the summoning of witnesses to the discretion of the court, and refusing the accused the aid of counsel, the law succeeded in destroying the judicial guarantees for the defence. Furthermore, the court was left with no choice but acquittal or death. Considered as an instrument of government in the service of revolutionary defence, the Terror did not require such reinforcement. Besides, Couthon had said, "It is not a matter of setting a few examples, but of exterminating the implacable henchmen of tyranny." This was scorning the point of view of a statesman, a yielding completely to the passion for repression, which the threat of assassination tinged with personal animosity.

In the Convention, on the other hand, the law brought a long-felt uneasiness to its height. The opponents of the Committee claimed, on the 23rd, that the law implicitly authorized it to arraign deputies without referring the matter to the Assembly. On the next day, not without difficulty, Robespierre secured the

[5] [Baron de Batz (1760–1822) was a royalist plotter involved in many counterrevolutionary conspiracies but never apprehended.—Eds.]

repudiation of such a charge; but doubts persisted. For this reason the conviction spread that the Committees were accelerating the Terror in order to maintain themselves in power. So the new trend, which had been foreseen on the day following the deaths of Hébert and Danton, now prevailed.

The Law of 22 Prairial, Year II (June 10, 1794), gave birth to the "Great Terror." As early as the 29th it was applied to a "batch" of 54 persons who had been implicated in the assassination attempts and the Batz conspiracy. Yet it was the anxious attention paid to the prisons which extended its scope. This was nothing new: it had been admitted in July, 1789, and September, 1792, that a prisoners' revolt was part of the "aristocratic plot." The great number of imprisoned suspects—now more than 8,000 in Paris—could only increase this fear. The prison system justified it. A report in Prairial acknowledged, in short, that the prisoners were virtually free to revolt. Such a plan had been charged to the Hébertists, and later to Dillon and Lucille Desmoulins.[6] In June, after a planned escape was denounced at the Bicêtre prison, three "batches" were brought before the Revolutionary Tribunal on these grounds.

Since the attacks of Prairial were linked to the counter-revolutionary conspiracy, it is not astonishing that the prisons were again made the order of the day. But the intention to "exterminate," expressed by Couthon, also explains why denunciations by informers were welcomed complacently. With the approval of the Committee of Public Safety, and under the direction of Herman, the head of the Commission on Civil and Judicial Affairs, seven "batches" were taken from the Luxembourg, Carmes, and St.-Lazare prisons between 19 Messidor, Year II (July 7, 1794), and 8 Thermidor (July 26). ([The poet] André Chénier was included in one of them.) In all, the "Great Terror" cost the lives of 1,376 persons, while only 1,251 had been executed in Paris from March, 1793, to 22 Prairial.

Public opinion was shaken, and the practices of the repression abetted the fear. The tumbrils slowly transported the condemned across the Faubourg St.-Antoine as far as the Trône-Renversé gate, the new emplacement for the scaffold. The executions were public, and the guillotine, cutting off heads and spattering blood, struck the imagination. But precisely because the victory of the Revolution no longer appeared in doubt, fear of the "aristocratic plot" faded, the punitive will was dulled, and the popular fever subsided.

---

[6] [Comte Arthur Dillon, a French general, and Lucille Desmoulins, the widow of the guillotined Camille Desmoulins, were convicted and executed on the basis of this accusation.—Eds.]

6

The Revolutionary
Common People of Paris

ANY present-day historians try to see events from the point of view of the common people rather than from the perspective of political, social, religious, or intellectual elites. Three of the best practitioners of "history from below" have written about the revolutionary common people of Paris. George Rudé has made a social analysis of those who took part in the great riots from 1787 to 1795, and he has found that a large majority of the participants were shopkeepers, craftsmen, and wage earners, usually protesting high food prices and shortages. Albert Soboul has concentrated on the Parisian sans-culottes fom 1793 to 1794—those political militants active in Paris during that period of mass radicalism; and he describes, among other things, their image of themselves, their political ideals, their violence, and their lack of social cohesiveness. Richard Cobb has preferred to depict vividly the lives of common people who became revolutionaries in Paris and the provinces.[1]

From the research of these and other historians, controversies about the revolutionary common people have arisen. One problem is whether they were admirable or detestable human beings. Were they in general plainspoken, unpretentious patriots defending popular sovereignty, as they often claimed themselves to be? Or ordinary people driven to acts of desperation? Or vengeful, violent sadists, including in their ranks

[1] See also the selection by Cobb in the chapter entitled "Why Terror in 1793–1794?"

shiftless beggars, vagrants, and criminals? Moreover, did they have a similar enough social background and lifestyle to be considered a social class? Soboul denies that they were a social class, but other historians suggest that they were.[2] Finally, did they cooperate with each other and act together so that one can speak of "the popular movement"? And if they were so united, was it a democratic mass movement or a movement of small, intolerant groups grasping for power?

[2] See, for example, Robert R. Palmer, "Popular Democracy in the French Revolution: Review Article," *French Historical Studies*, I (Fall 1960), 468–469.

The Rioters

GEORGE RUDÉ

George Rudé (1910–   ) is Professor of History at Sir George
Williams University, Montreal. A descendant of a governor of
Gibraltar and a graduate of Cambridge University, he first
taught French and German in secondary school. In his thirties
he switched fields and took a Ph.D. in history at the University
of London. He is an authority on eighteenth-century riots.
Among his many books are *The Crowd in the French Revolution*
(1959), *Wilkes and Liberty* (1962), *The Crowd in History,
1730–1848* (1964), and *Paris and London in the 18th Century*
(1970). Disagreeing with such popular works as Hippolyte
Taine's *The French Revolution* and Charles Dickens' *A Tale of
Two Cities*, both of which describe most rioters as vicious and
contemptible, Rudé presents a much more precise and sympathetic picture of them, as the following selection indicates.

One aspect of the French Revolution that has been largely neglected by historians is
the nature of the revolutionary crowd. It has, of course, long been recognized that
the Revolution was not only a political, but a profound social upheaval, to the course
and outcome of which masses of ordinary Frenchmen, both in the towns and
countryside, contributed. Not least in Paris; and, in the history of revolutionary
Paris, a particular importance has been justly ascribed to the great *journées*, or
popular insurrections and demonstrations, which, breaking out intermittently
between 1789 and 1795, profoundly affected the relations of political parties and
groups and drew many thousands of Parisians into activity.

So much is common knowledge and has long been commonly accepted. But
how were the crowds composed that stormed the Bastille in July 1789, marched to
Versailles to fetch the king and queen to the capital in October, that overthrew the
monarchy in August 1792, or silently witnessed the downfall of Robespierre on 9
Thermidor? Who led them or influenced them? What were the motives that
prompted them? What was the particular significance and outcome of their

From George Rudé, *The Crowd in the French Revolution* (Oxford: Clarendon Press, 1959), pp. 1–4,
184–190, 207–209, 232–233. Copyright © 1959 Oxford University Press. Reprinted by permission of
the Clarendon Press, Oxford. All footnotes are included except for those that refer to appendixes or are
cross-references. Quotations orginally in French have been translated by the editors.

intervention? It is not suggested that the great historians of the Revolution have had no answers to these questions: far from it; but, for lack of more precise inquiry, they have tended to answer them according to their own social ideals, political sympathies, or ideological preoccupations. In this respect we may distinguish between those writers who, like Burke and Taine, adopted a distinctly hostile attitude to the Revolution and everything that it stood for; Republican historians like Michelet and Aulard, for whom the Revolution marked a great regenerative upsurge of the French people; and, again, a Romantic like Carlyle who, while broadly sympathetic to the "Nether Sansculottic World," was torn between admiration for its "heroism" and fascinated horror at the "World-Bedlam" or "anarchy" that it appeared to unleash.

To Burke the revolutionary crowd was purely destructive and presumed to be composed of the most undesirable social elements: the crowds that invaded the *château* of Versailles in October 1789 are "a band of cruel ruffians and assassins, reeking with . . . blood"; and the royal family, on their return journey to Paris, are escorted by "all the unutterable abominations of the furies of hell, in the abased shape of the vilest of women." The National Assembly, having transferred to the capital, is compelled to deliberate "amidst the tumultuous cries of a mixed mob of ferocious men, and of women lost to shame." [1] Yet Burke's invective is far outmatched by Taine, the former Liberal of 1848, soured by his experiences of [the French defeat and the Commune of] 1871, whose vocabulary of expletives has served the conservative historians of the Revolution ever since. The provincial insurgents of the early summer of 1789 are presented as "smugglers, dealers in contraband salt, poachers, vagabonds, beggars, habitual criminals." The Paris revolutionaries and the captors of the Bastille are the lowest social scum:

> The dregs of society came to the top . . . the capital seems taken over by the lowest of the low and by bandits . . . Vagabonds, ragamuffins, several "almost naked," most armed like savages, with terrifying faces, they are "among those that one does not remember having met in broad daylight."

The market women and others who marched to Versailles in October are thus described:

> The prostitutes of the Palais Royal . . . add to their number laundresses, beggars, women without shoes, fishwives recruited several days before for pay . . . [T]he troop absorbs women it meets, janitresses, dressmakers, charwomen, and even some bourgeoises. To these join vagrants, street prowlers, bandits, thieves, all those dregs crammed into Paris and who surface at each disturbance . . . Here is the muck which, ahead and behind, moves with the flood of the masses.

The insurgents of 10 August 1792, who drove Louis XVI from the Tuileries, become:

> Almost all the lowest of the low or people supporting themselves by disreputable trades, bullies and hangers-on in evil haunts, bloodthirsty . . . fearless and ferocious

[1] E. Burke, *Reflections on the Revolution in France* (London, 1951), pp. 66–69.

adventurers of any origin, men of Marseille and foreigners, Savoyards, Italians, Spaniards, expelled from their country.[2]

Following Taine, such terms as "la canaille," "la dernière plèbe," "bandits," and "brigands" have been commonly applied to the participants in these and similar events up to the present day.[3]

On the other hand, Michelet and the upholders of the Republican tradition have presented the revolutionary crowd in entirely different terms. Whenever it advanced, or appeared to advance, the aims of the revolutionary *bourgeoisie,* it has been presented as the embodiment of all the popular and Republican virtues. To Michelet the Bastille ceased to be a fortress that had to be reduced by force of arms: it became the personification of evil, over which virtue (in the shape of the People) inevitably triumphs: "The Bastille was not captured . . . it surrendered. Its bad conscience troubled it, drove it crazy, and made it lose its courage." And who captured it? "The people, all the people." Similarly, on 5 October, while the revolutionary leaders are groping for a solution to the crisis: "The people alone find a remedy: they go to look for the King." The role of the women takes on a more than merely casual significance: "The women are, assuredly, the most people-like among the people, that is, the most instinctive, the most inspired."[4] Louis Blanc, though lacking Michelet's exaltation, follows him closely;[5] and Aulard, the Radical professor of the Sorbonne, for all his sobriety of language and wealth of documentary learning, is in the same tradition: "Paris, all of Paris, rose up, took arms, and seized the Bastille." [6]

Great as has been the influence of these two rival schools on the historiography and teaching of the Revolution in France, in this country [Great Britain] perhaps an even greater influence has been exerted on generations of students, teachers, and textbook writers by the striking imagery of Carlyle. The social forces unleashed by the Revolution and composing the active elements in each one of its decisive phases are variously described as an "enraged National Tiger"; "the World Chimera, bearing fire"; "Victorious Anarchy"; and "the funeral flame, enveloping all things . . . the Death-Bird of a World." With all this, it is perhaps not surprising that he should gravely warn his readers against attempting a more precise analysis: "But to gauge and measure this immeasurable Thing, and what is called account for it, and reduce it to a dead logic-formula, attempt not." [7]

Yet, widely different as these interpretations are and the influences they have

[2] H. Taine, *Les Origines de la France contemporaine. La Révolution* (3 vols., Paris, 1876), i. 18, 53–54, 130, 272.

[3] See, for example, L. Madelin, who freely uses the terms "bandits" and "brigands" in relation to the Paris insurgents of July 1789 (*La Révolution [Paris, 1914],* pp. 60, 66, 68); and P. Gaxotte, *La Révolution française* (Paris, 1948), *passim.*

[4] J. Michelet, *La Révolution française* (9 vols., Paris, 1868–1900), i. 248, 377–9. The original edition dates from 1847 to 1853.

[5] L. Blanc, *Histoire de la Révolution française* (12 vols., Paris, 1868–70), ii. 352–3; iii. 184. The first edition is dated 1847–62.

[6] A. Aulard, *Histoire politique de la Révolution française [1789–1804]* (Paris, 1905), p. 37.

[7] T. Carlyle, *The French Revolution* (3 vols., London, 1869), i. 226, 258, 264–6, 303. It is of some interest to note that Carlyle's first edition of 1837 bore the subtitle "A History of Sansculottism."

exerted, there is one common thread running through them all: whether the revolutionary crowd is represented as "la canaille" [rabble] or "vile multitude" by Taine and Burke; as "Victorious Anarchy" by Carlyle; or as "le peuple" or "tout Paris" by Michelet and Aulard—it has been treated by one and all as a disembodied abstraction and the personification of good or evil, according to the particular fancy or prejudice of the writer. . . .

We may note both the common feature and certain significant differences in the composition of the rioters and insurgents of this period. The common feature is, of course, the predominance of *sans-culottes*[8] in all but one of these *journées*. Yet other social elements played some part: overwhelmingly so in Vendémiaire of the Year IV; but there were also small groups of *bourgeois, rentiers* [property owners], merchants, civil servants, and professional men engaged in the destruction of the *barrières* [toll gates in the city walls] (possibly as direct agents of the Orleanist faction at the Palais Royal[9]), in the capture of the Bastille, the Champ de Mars affair, the assault on the Tuileries, and in the outbreak of Prairial [May 20–23, 1795]. Women, . . . were particularly in evidence in the march to Versailles, the food riots of 1792–3, and in Prairial. This is, of course, not altogether surprising, as in these episodes food prices and other bread and butter questions were well to the fore; we find women playing a less conspicuous part in such an essentially political movement as that culminating in the "massacre" of the Champ de Mars—less still, of course, in largely military operations like the assaults on the Bastille and the Tuileries and in the expulsion of the Girondin deputies from the Convention. Again, while wage-earners played a substantial part on all these occasions, the only important outbreak in which they appear to have clearly predominated was the Réveillon riots in the Faubourg Saint-Antoine. The reason for this is not hard to find: though it cannot be termed a strike or a wages movement (Réveillon's own workers do not appear to have been engaged), it was the only one of these actions in which there is the slightest trace of a direct conflict between workers and employers. It is also no doubt significant that craftsmen—whether masters, independent craftsmen, or journeymen—were more conspicuously in evidence in some of the *journées* than in others. This seems particularly to have been the case when a district of small crafts became substantially involved—like the [Île de la] Cité in the riots of 1787 and 1788 or the Faubourg Saint-Antoine on various other occasions; but it also appears to have been a feature of the more organized, political movements—such as the Champ de Mars affair and the armed attacks on the Bastille and the Tuileries—when the driving element was no doubt the small shopkeepers and workshop masters who, in many cases, brought their *garçons*

---

[8] [In the glossary of *The Crowd in the French Revolution*, Rudé says he has used the expression sans-culottes "in its purely social sense as an omnibus term to include the small property-owners and wage-earners of town and countryside: in its Parisian context, the small shopkeepers, petty traders, craftsmen, journeymen, labourers, vagrants, and city poor. Contemporaries tended to limit its application to the more politically active among these classes or to extend it to the 'popular' leaders, from whatever social class they might be drawn. Historians have frequently used the term in this political sense."—Eds.]

[9] [The Orleanist faction consisted of the political followers of the Duc d'Orléans, Louis XVI's cousin, who lived in the Palais Royal.—Eds.]

[helpers], journeymen, and apprentices along with them. In this connexion it is perhaps of interest to note the sustained militancy of members of certain trades such as furnishing, building, metal-work, and dress. Most conspicuous of all were the locksmiths, joiners and cabinet-makers, shoemakers, and tailors; others frequently in evidence were stone-masons, hairdressers, and engravers; and, of those engaged in less skilful occupations, wine-merchants, water-carriers, porters, cooks, and domestic servants. Workers employed in manufactories (textiles, glass, tobacco, tapestries, porcelain) played, with the exception of the gauze-workers, a relatively inconspicuous role in these movements.

A study of these records confirms the traditional view that the parts of Paris most frequently and wholeheartedly engaged in the riots and insurrections of the Revolution were the Faubourgs Saint-Antoine and Saint-Marcel. This is strikingly borne out in the case of Saint-Antoine, whose craftsmen and journeymen initiated and dominated the Réveillon riots, the capture of the Bastille, and the overthrow of the monarchy, and played an outstanding part in the revolution of May–June 1793 and the popular revolt of Prairial; the police reports suggest, in fact, that it was only in the events of 1787–8 and in the Champ de Mars affair that Saint-Antoine played little or no part. The Faubourg Saint-Marcel, on the other hand, while it contributed substantially to the commotions of September–October 1788 and was represented by a score of volunteers at the siege of the Bastille, only began to play a really conspicuous role in the spring and summer of 1791. After this the part it played was second only to that of Saint-Antoine in the revolutions of August 1792 and May–June 1793, and in the days of Prairial [May 20–23, 1795]. In Vendémiaire [October 4–6, 1795], of course, the pattern was quite different. Although property-owners and "moderates" had by now taken charge of even the popular Sections, it was not they but the traditional *bourgeois* Sections of Lepeletier (Bibliothèque) and Butte des Moulins (Palais Royal) that took the lead and held the initiative, while—characteristically—it was the [Section of] Quinze Vingts in the Faubourg Saint-Antoine which alone dispatched a contingent of armed volunteers to oppose the counter-revolutionary rebels.

But even if it can be demonstrated that the overwhelming majority of the participants in all but the last of the revolutionary *journées* were Parisian *sans-culottes*, how far can they be considered typical of the social groups from which they were drawn? Taine and his followers, while not denying the presence in revolutionary crowds of tradesmen, wage-earners, and city poor, insisted, nevertheless, that the dominant element among them were *vagabonds, criminels,* and *gens sans aveu* [persons without a fixed abode].[10] In view of the panic-fear engendered among large and small property-owners by vagrants, petty thieves, and unemployed at different stages of the Revolution, it is perhaps not surprising that such a charge should be made: it was certainly voiced on more than one occasion by hostile journalists, memorialists, and police authorities of the day. Yet, in its application to the capital at least, it has little foundation in fact. Among the sixty-eight persons arrested, wounded, and killed in the Réveillon riots for whom details are available, there were only three without fixed abode—a cobbler, a carter, and a navvy

[10] Taine, op. cit. i. 18, 41, 53–54, 81, 130, 135; P. Gaxotte, *La Révolution française*, pp. 122, 133–4, 146.

[ditchdigger].[11] Of nearly eighty scheduled for arrest after the burning of the *barrières* and four arrested for breaking the windows of the Barrière Saint-Denis, all were of fixed abode and occupation.[12] Of some sixty persons arrested at the time of the looting of the Saint-Lazare monastery in July 1789, nine were unemployed workers without fixed abode, who were caught up in the general drag-net directed against vagrants, *gens sans aveu*, and dwellers in lodging-houses at the time of the July revolution, and probably had no direct connexion with this affair at all.[13] Every one of the 662 *vainqueurs de la Bastille* [conquerors of the Bastille] and of those claiming compensation for themselves and their dependents in August 1792 was of fixed abode and settled occupation.[14] In the weeks preceding the Champ de Mars demonstration one beggar was arrested for abusing the king and queen, another for applauding their flight from Paris, and two more for causing a disturbance and insulting the National Guard; three other persons are described as being *sans état* [without livelihood]; the rest of the 250 arrested during this period appear to have been of settled abode.[15] Nor is there any mention in the records of vagrants or beggars among those arrested in Germinal and Prairial of the Year III; nor, even more surprisingly perhaps, among those implicated in the grocery riots of 1792 and 1793. Doubtless these elements mingled with the rioters and insurgents on such occasions, and we know that they caused concern to the Paris Electors during the revolution of July 1789;[16] but they appear to have played an altogether minor role in these movements.

This does not mean, of course, that unemployed workers or workers and craftsmen living in furnished rooms or lodging-houses (the often despised *non-domiciliés*) did not form a substantial element in revolutionary crowds. This was particularly the case in the early years of the Revolution, when, quite apart from the influx of workless countrymen, there was considerable unemployment in a large number of Parisian crafts; this, however, became a declining factor after the autumn of 1791. We find that eight of some fifty workers arrested or wounded in the Réveillon riots were unemployed and that the proportion was somewhat higher among those arrested in connexion with the Champ de Mars affair. In July 1789, too, there is circumstantial evidence to suggest that unemployed craftsmen, journeymen, and labourers (only a handful of whom were from *ateliers de charité* [public workshops]) were among those that took part in the assault on the Bastille: we know, for example, that substantial sums were raised after the fall of the fortress to relieve the distress of the *faubourg* [Saint-Antoine] and that, of 900 stone-cutters who later petitioned the Assembly for unemployment relief, several claimed to have been present at its capture.[17] . . . Unemployed workers from neighbouring *ateliers de charité* played a certain part in the destruction of the *barrières* and the raid on the

[11] Arch. Nat., Y 18795, fols. 444–62. [Arch. Nat. is the abbreviation used by the author to designate the French Archives nationales.—Eds.]

[12] Arch. Nat., Z¹ᵃ 886; Y 10649, fol. 18.

[13] Ibid., fols. 20–21.

[14] Arch. Nat., T 514¹; F¹⁵ 3269–74; F⁷ 4426.

[15] Archives de la Préfecture de la Police, Aa 167, fol. 51; 157, fol. 134; Ab 324, pp. 28–29, 32, 36, 37.

[16] *Procès-verbal des séances* . . . *de l'assemblée générale des Électeurs de Paris* (Paris, 1790), ii. 156 ff.

[17] Arch. Nat., C 134, doss. 6, fols. 14–15; S. Lacroix, *Actes de la Commune de Paris* (2nd series, 8 vols., Paris, 1900–14), v. 260.

Saint-Lazare monastery. The *non-domiciliés* formed a substantial proportion of the wage-earners, small craftsmen, and petty traders of the capital, by no means limited to the unemployed or casual labourers, though it was a fiction of the time that the *hôtel* or *maison garnie* [cheap boarding house] provided only for provincials, foreigners, cut-throats, thieves, and *gens sans aveu:* indeed, the *logeurs* or tenants [lodging-house keepers] of such premises were compelled by law to keep a daily check and to give a daily report to the police on all their lodgers.[18] In view of their numbers[19] it is hardly surprising to find them fairly well represented among those taking part in these disturbances—perhaps one in four of those arrested in the Réveillon affair, one in ten among the *vainqueurs de la Bastille,* one in five of those most actively concerned with the Champ de Mars movement, and one in six of those arrested and jailed in the grocery riots.[20] But this is, of course, a quite separate question from that of Taine's *gens sans aveu* and gives no further indication of the number of vagrants involved.

The further contention that criminals and bandits played a significant part in the revolutionary *journées* collapses no less readily when looked at more closely. The police in cross-examining their prisoners habitually inquired whether they had served previous terms of imprisonment and it was easy enough to verify whether, as in the case of more serious offences, they had been branded with the notorious V [for *voleur*] of the thief or G of the galley-convict. The eight commissioners examining the Réveillon prisoners were able to find only three who had incurred previous convictions of any kind—in two cases these had involved short terms of detention in the Hôtel de la Force on minor charges, whereas the port-worker Téteigne was found to be branded with a V.[21] Yet such a case is exceptional. Of those arrested for looting the Saint-Lazare monastery only one had served a prison sentence—the butcher's boy Quatrevaux, who had spent seventeen days in the Force on a previous conviction.[22] Not one of the twenty-one arrested for the murder of Châtel, lieutenant to the mayor, during a food riot at Saint-Denis in August 1789, appears to have had a criminal record; and only three of fifteen arrested in a similar disturbance at Versailles in September had served previous sentences—one for stealing four pieces of wood in 1788 and two for minor breaches of army discipline.[23] Of some 150 persons arrested in the Paris Sections for political

---

[18] H. Monin, *Paris en 1789* (Paris, 1889), pp. 21, n. 5; 419, n. 4.

[19] In the census of 1795—the only census of the period in which the *non-domiciliés* are accounted for—they number 9,792 for 25 Sections (P. Meuriot, *Un recensement de l'an II,* p. 32); but this was a period of mass exodus, which was draining the hotels and lodging-houses of a large part of their residents (J. de la Monneraye, *La Crise du logement à Paris pendant la Révolution* [*Paris, 1928*], pp. 12–13).

[20] To take a random sample from Maillard's list of the *vainqueurs de la Bastille:* J. A. Lamoureux, a tinsmith, lodged with one Boichamp, lodging-house keeper of the rue de Lappe; Marc-Antoine Saint-Paul, a master fisherman, lived in a lodging-house in the Faubourg Saint-Marcel; Jean Gabriel, a printer, lodged with a wine-merchant of the rue de Plâtre, off the Place Maubert; and Gambi and Semain, riverside workers, lodged at the Hôtel de Châlons in the rue du Figuier in the parish of Saint-Paul (Arch. Nat., T 514¹).

[21] Arch. Nat., Y 15101, 13454.

[22] Arch. Nat., Z² 4691.

[23] Arch. Nat., Y 10497; Archives départementales Seine-et-Oise, series B, Prévôte de l'Hôtel du Roi. Procédures, 1789, fols. 7–21.

offences during the months preceding and following the Champ de Mars affair, only four appear to have served previous sentences, and these, again, were of a trivial nature.[24] Not one of the thirty-nine tried in the Year IV for alleged complicity in the September massacres had appeared in court before.[25] Such information is, unfortunately, not available for the other great *journées* of the Revolution; yet this evidence, as far as it goes, is overwhelming and should prove conclusive. By and large it does not appear, in fact, that those taking part in revolutionary crowds were any more given to crime, or even to violence or disorder, than the ordinary run of Parisian citizens from whom they were recruited. . . .

We must avoid the temptation, to which some historians have succumbed, of presenting the popular insurrections of the Revolution as being almost exclusively dominated by short-term economic considerations—as though each of these movements were, in essence, an "émeute de la faim" [hunger riot]. This was, of course, far from being the case. Not only [did] the *sans-culottes* [identify] themselves fully with a wide and varying range of political ideas and calls to action as the Revolution advanced; but we noted in particular the essentially political nature of the Champ de Mars demonstration and the whole preparatory movement leading up to it, not to mention the active support of the *sans-culottes* for such exclusively military-political actions as the assault on the Bastille and the Tuileries and the expulsion of the Girondins from the Convention. In the case of the Champ de Mars affair at least, the threat of famine or of rising prices played no part whatsoever. On the other hand, we have noted the abstention of the *sans-culottes* from any direct political intervention in the events of Vendémiaire of the Year IV—in striking contrast with their active participation, a few months earlier, in the days of Germinal and Prairial, though popular concern with bread-shortage and inflation was as acute in the one case as in the other. The essential difference lay of course in the changed political conditions and in the very differing aims of the rebels of Vendémiaire from those of Prairial:[26] in spite of continuing inflation and near-famine conditions, the active *sans-culottes* were not prepared to carry their hostility to the Thermidorian Convention to the point of giving comfort to the declared enemies of the Republic. The point is of interest: for one thing, it serves to disprove the contention that the *menu peuple* [common people], for lack of political maturity, were prepared to follow the lead of any demagogue irrespective of their own interests or inclinations; for another, it shows that a satisfactory explanation of popular participation in, or abstention from, these movements cannot be given without proper account being taken of both political and economic factors and that concentration on the one to the exclusion of the other will only produce a distorted picture.

Yet, when all is said and done, the inescapable conclusion remains that the primary and most constant motive impelling revolutionary crowds during this period was the concern for the provision of cheap and plentiful food. This, more than any other factor, was the raw material out of which the popular Revolution was

[24] Archives de la Préfecture de la Police, Aa 137, fols. 177–8; 173, fols. 24, 25–26; 215, fols. 451–2.
[25] P. Caron, *Les Massacres de septembre* (Paris, 1935), p. 111.
[26] It is true that there were other factors involved, of which the most important was the purely technical difficulty of staging a concerted action after the crushing defeat of Prairial; but this does not invalidate the argument in any way.

forged. It alone accounts for the continuity of the social ferment that was such a marked feature of the capital in these years and out of which the great political *journées* themselves developed. Even more it accounts for the occasional outbreaks of independent activity by the *menu peuple,* going beyond or running counter to the interests of their *bourgeois* allies and castigated by them as "counter-revolutionary" —such outbreaks as the blind fury of the Réveillon rioters or the more constructive efforts of Parisians to impose a form of popular price-control in the grocery riots of 1792 and 1793. Yet without the impact of political ideas, mainly derived from the *bourgeois* leaders, such movements would have remained strangely purposeless and barren of result; and had the *sans-culottes* not been able to absorb these ideas, as claimed by some writers, their influence on the course and outcome of the Revolution would have been far less substantial than in fact it was. . . .

We return to our central question—the nature of the crowds that took part in the great events of the Revolution in Paris. From our analysis these crowds have emerged as active agents in the revolutionary process, composed of social elements with their own distinctive identities, interests, and aspirations. Yet these were not at variance with, or isolated from, those of other social groups. In fact . . . the Revolution was only able to advance—and, indeed, to break out—because the *sans-culottes,* from whom these elements were largely drawn, were able to assimilate and to identify themselves with the new political ideas promoted by the liberal aristocracy and *bourgeoisie.* But, even when revolutionary crowds were impregnated with and stimulated by such ideas, they cannot for that reason be dismissed as mere passive instruments of middle-class leaders and interests; still less can they be presented as inchoate "mobs" without any social identity or, at best, as drawn from criminal elements or the dregs of the city population. While these played a part, it was an altogether minor one and on no occasion corresponded to the unsympathetic picture of the all-prevailing *canaille* painted by Taine and other writers.

Michelet's use of *le peuple* corresponds, of course, far more closely to the facts: we have seen Barnave, for one, applying the term to those participants in revolutionary events who were neither of the aristocracy nor of the *bourgeoisie.* Yet it is too indefinite; for while the *menu peuple,* or *sans-culottes,* taken collectively, formed the main body of rioters and insurgents, the part played by their constituent elements—women, wage-earners, craftsmen, journeymen, petty traders, or work-shop masters—varied widely from one occasion to another. This, of course, merely emphasizes the point that revolutionary crowds, far from being social abstractions, were composed of ordinary men and women with varying social needs, who responded to a variety of impulses, in which economic crisis, political upheaval, and the urge to satisfy immediate and particular grievances all played their part.

The Sans-Culottes

ALBERT SOBOUL

Albert Soboul (1914–   ) came from a peasant family in the South of France. After his father had been killed in World War I, he was raised by an aunt, a schoolteacher. In the 1930s he attended the Lycée Henri IV and the Sorbonne in Paris. A student of Georges Lefebvre, he gained a reputation as the leading French Marxist historian of the French Revolution with the publication, in 1958, of *Les Sans-culottes parisiens en l'an II* (which has been abridged and translated into English). The result of years of careful archival research, the work is a very long, detailed political and sociological study of this group of wage earners, artisans, and shopkeepers; and it probes more deeply into their aims and lives than any earlier account. Among his many other books are *The French Revolution: 1787–1799* (1975, originally 1962), *Paysans, Sans-culottes et Jacobins* (1966), *La Ier République, 1792–1804* (1968), and *La Civilisation et la Révolution française, I: La Crise de l'ancien régime* (1970). At present he is Professor of the History of the French Revolution at the Sorbonne and edits the journal *Annales historiques de la Révolution française*.

From June 1793 to February 1794, the Parisian sans-culotte movement played a major role in the political struggle leading to the consolidation of the Revolutionary Government and the organization of the Committee of Public Safety. During the same period, it imposed economic measures upon a reluctant Assembly intended to improve the living standards of the masses. If we wish to study the motives which explain the attitude of the people at this time, some kind of social definition of the Parisian sans-culotterie, some assessment of its composition is required.

This is not an easy task, for the economic or fiscal documents which could provide us with detailed analyses are missing, and what little statistical evidence we have is both vague and misleading. It is mainly through the political documents that

From Albert Soboul, *The Parisian Sans-Culottes and the French Revolution, 1793–1794*, trans. Gwynne Lewis (Oxford: Clarendon Press, 1964), pp. 18–22, 23–24, 37–38, 99–100, 159–162, 254–260. Copyright © 1964 Oxford University Press. Reprinted by permission of the Clarendon Press, Oxford.

we can explore the social characteristics of the sans-culotterie, particularly the dossiers dealing with the anti-terrorist repression of the Year III [1794–1795]. The true image, the mentality and behaviour of the Parisian sans-culotte, only emerges by comparing the attitudes of two social groups. Not particularly conscious of class distinctions, the sans-culotte reveals himself most clearly in relation to his social enemies. This absence of class-consciousness is reflected in the social composition of the Parisian population—in so far as it is possible to analyse it—and even more strikingly in the social composition of the political personnel of the Sections.

If we attempt to delimit the social contours of the sans-culotterie, we should, first of all, discover how the sans-culotte defined himself. There are enough relevant documents available for us to make, at least, an approximate definition.

The sans-culotte was outwardly recognizable by his dress, which served to distinguish him from the more elevated classes of society. Trousers were the distinctive mark of the popular classes; breeches of the aristocracy and, generally speaking, of the higher ranks of the old Third Estate. Robespierre used to contrast the *culottes dorées* with the *sans-culottes*—those who wore fancy or embroidered breeches with those who simply wore trousers. The sans-culottes themselves made the same distinction. The police-agent Rousseville, listing the intrigues which had undermined the *comité de surveillance de Sceaux* in his report of 25 Messidor Year II [July 13, 1794], emphasized the hostility which existed between the *bas-de-soie* and the *sans-culottes*.[1] Dress also distinguished the latter from the *muscadins*. Fontaine, a gunner in the Section de la Réunion, was arrested on 5 Prairial [May 24, 1794] for repeating that he wished to revenge himself on the *muscadins*, defining the latter as "those (citizens) in the National Guard who appeared to be better dressed than himself."

With the dress went a certain social comportment. Here again, it is in his opposition to accepted social behaviour that the sans-culotte asserts himself. The manners of the *ancien régime* were no longer fashionable in the Year II; the sans-culottes no longer accepted a subordinate position in society. Jean-Baptiste Gentil, a building-contractor and timber-merchant, arrested on 5 Pluviôse Year II [January 24, 1794] for having failed to fulfil his obligations towards the Republic, was criticized by the *comité révolutionnaire* of the Section des Quinze-Vingts for his manners: "People had to take their hats off before they could approach him. The expression 'Monsieur' was still used in his house, and he always affected an air of importance." As a result, he had never been regarded as a good citizen.[2]

The sans-culottes readily judged a person's character from his appearance; his character then decided what his political opinions would be. Everyone who offended their sense of equality and fraternity was suspected of being an aristocrat. It was difficult for a former noble to find favour in their eyes, even when no definite accusation could be levelled against him, "because such men cannot rise to the

---

[1] *A.N.*, F⁷ 4708. Concerning the origin of the word *sans-culotte*, and how its usage spread, see Ferdinand Brunot, *Histoire de la langue française*, ix, 715. [*A.N.* is the abbreviation used by the author to designate the French Archives nationales. *Bas-de-soie*—literally, a silk stocking—was a term of disparagement used by the sans-culottes to describe their more genteel enemies.—Eds.]
[2] *A.N.*, F⁷ 4721.

heights of our Revolution. Their hearts are always full of pride, and we will never forget the air of superiority which they used to assume, nor the domination which they exercised over us." It was for these reasons that the *comité révolutionnaire* of the Section de la République arrested the duc de Brancas-Céreste on 16 October 1793, pointing out that he still enjoyed a yearly income of 89,980 *livres*.[3] The sans-culottes could not endure pride or disdain, since these feelings were thought to be typically aristocratic and contrary to the spirit of fraternity which should reign amongst citizens equal in rights: they obviously implied a political attitude hostile to the kind of democracy which the sans-culottes practised in their general assemblies and popular societies. For this reason, such personal defects are frequently mentioned in the reports justifying the arrest of suspects.

On 17 September 1793, the committee of the Section Révolutionnaire decided to arrest Étienne Gide, a wholesale merchant in watches and clocks, because he had given his allegiance to the Brissotin party, but also because he was of a "haughty and proud" disposition, and had often been heard to speak "ironically." On 28 Brumaire [November 18, 1793], the committee of the Section des Marchés arrested a music-dealer named Bayeux. It was alleged that he had said in a meeting of the general assembly that "it was disgusting to see a cobbler acting as president, particularly a cobbler who was so badly dressed." In the Section du Contrat-Social, the crime of the watchmaker Brasseur, who was arrested on 23 Floréal [May 12, 1794], was his remark "that it was very disagreeable for a man like himself to be in a guard-room with the sort of people whom, in the old days, one had nothing to do with." In extreme cases, a mere attitude of indifference towards a sans-culotte was enough for a person to be charged with harbouring "aristocratic feelings." Explaining the arrest of a former banker, Girardot-Marigny, on 12 Brumaire [November 2, 1793], the committee of the Section de Guillaume-Tell simply observed that it was a case of "one of these rich citizens who would not deign to fraternize with Republicans." [4]

Even more incriminating in the eyes of the sans-culottes than an attitude of pride, contempt, or plain indifference, was an insinuation of their social inferiority. In its report of 9 Frimaire [November 29, 1793] upon Louis-Claude Cezeron, arrested as a suspect, the committee of the Section Poissonnière referred in particular to some remarks he had made at a meeting of the general assembly in the preceding May, "that the poor depended upon the rich, and that the sans-culottes had never been anything but the lowest class of society." Bergeron, a dealer in skins from the Section des Lombards, "when he saw the sans-culottes fulfilling their obligations as citizens . . . said that it would be better if they got on with their own affairs instead of meddling in politics": he was arrested as a suspect on 18 Pluviôse [February 8, 1794]. The sans-culottes also had no time for the type of person who took advantage of his social position, wealth, or even his education, to impress or influence those beneath him. Truchon, a lawyer from the Section de Gravilliers, who had been denounced on several occasions by [the Enragé] Jacques Roux in his *Publiciste*, was finally arrested on 9 Prairial in the Year II [May 28, 1794]: the *comité révolutionnaire* accused him of having influenced citizens of "little discern-

[3] *A.N.,* F⁷ 4615, d. 3.
[4] *A.N.,* F⁷ 4584, pl. 5; 4615, pl. 4; 4726.

ment," and of expressing the opinion that "positions of authority should be filled by enlightened men with private means, since they alone had the time to spare." [5]

It is true that the sans-culottes had an egalitarian conception of social relationships. But beneath the general theory, there were more clearly defined factors which help to explain their behaviour, and it is interesting to consider to what extent they themselves were conscious of, and able to express, this deeper motivation.

Above all, the sans-culottes were conscious of the social antagonism which divided them from the aristocracy. The aristocracy had been the real enemy from 14 July 1789 to 10 August 1792, and it was against the aristocracy that they continued to struggle. The address of the *société des Sans-Culottes de Beaucaire* [in the department of the Gard] to the Convention on 8 September 1793 is significant in this respect: "We are sans-culottes . . . poor and virtuous, we have formed a society of manual workers and peasants . . . we know our friends—those who have delivered us from the clergy, the nobility, feudalism, the *dîme* [tithe], royalty and all the evils which accompany it. They are the same people who are called anarchists, trouble-makers and followers of Marat by the aristorats." [6] The idea of a class struggle emerges more clearly in the address of the *société populaire de Dijon* [in the department of the Côte d'Or] on 27 Nivôse Year II [January 16, 1794] which stated that "in future, we must be a united people, not two nations in opposition." To achieve this the society advocated the death penalty "for everyone, without exception, who is known to be an aristocrat." [7]

The aristocrat was such a figure of hatred to the sans-culotterie that it was not long before the expression was being used to describe all their enemies, irrespective of whether they belonged to the former nobility or to the higher ranks of what had been the Third Estate. This failure to distinguish between the real aristocrat and a member of the upper bourgeoisie—which was peculiarly sans-culotte—helps to underline the separate and distinct character of their contribution to the Revolution. . . .

The economic crisis helped to sharpen these social conflicts, and as the crisis developed and the *patriote* party of 1789 began to disintegrate, differences of opinion between the sans-culottes and the upper classes of the old Third Estate were added to the fundamental sans-culotte–aristocrat antagonism. A note intended for the Committee of General Security in Pluviôse Year II [January–February 1794] referred to the existence of two parties in the Section de Brutus: one representing the people—*sans-culottisme*—and the other composed of "bankers, stock-brokers and moneyed-people." An address to the Convention on 27 Ventôse [March 17, 1794] contrasts with the "brave sans-culottes," not only the clergy, the nobility and the sovereign heads of Europe, but also solicitors, barristers, notaries, and particularly "well-to-do farmers, selfish citizens and all these fat, wealthy merchants. They are fighting against us instead of our oppressors." [8] Is this simply

[5] *A.N.*, F[7] 4775[35].
[6] *A.N.*, C 271, pl. 666, p. 37.
[7] *A.N.*, C 289, pl. 394, p. 9.
[8] *A.N.*, C 295, pl. 994, p. 27.

a struggle between citizens who owned property, and those who did not, a struggle between *possédants* and *non-possédants?* One cannot really say that it is, for we find craftsmen and shopkeepers amongst the sans-culotterie who were themselves property-owners. It is rather a conflict between those who favoured the idea of restricted and limited ownership, and those who believed in the absolute right of property as proclaimed in 1789; and even more clearly, a conflict between the defenders of a system of controls and fixed prices, and those who preferred an economic policy of *laissez-faire*—in general terms, a struggle between consumers and producers.

The sources enable us to probe fairly deeply into the social antipathies and preoccupations of the sans-culotterie. They denounced *honnêtes gens*—those citizens who, if not rich, enjoyed at least a comfortable and cultured life, and also those who were conscious, if not necessarily proud, of being better dressed and better educated than themselves. They denounced *rentiers*—citizens who lived off unearned incomes. And finally they denounced "the rich"; not just property-owners or *possédants,* but the *gros* as opposed to the *petits*—the wealthy, big business-men as compared with those of their own kind who possessed but limited means. The sans-culottes were not hostile towards property so long as it was limited; they accepted property of the kind which artisans and shopkeepers already owned, and which many *compagnons* [journeymen] dreamed of owning themselves in the future. . . .

The sans-culotte . . . is defined by his political behaviour as much as by his place in society—the latter is more difficult to ascertain than the former.

A document dated May 1793 attempts to answer part of this difficulty, at least, in replying to "the impertinent question—what is a sans-culotte?" [9] The sans-culotte ". . . is someone who goes everywhere on foot . . . and who lives quite simply with his wife and children, if he has any, on the fourth or fifth floor." Jacques Roux also referred to the sans-culottes living in attics, and the *Père Duchesne* wrote, "If you wish to meet the cream of the sans-culotterie, then visit the garrets of the workers (ouvriers)." The sans-culotte is useful "because he knows how to plough a field, how to forge, to saw, to file, to cover a roof and how to make shoes. . . . And since he works, it is certain that you will not find him at the café de Chartres, nor in the dens where people gamble and plot, nor at the théâtre de la Nation where they are performing *l'Ami des lois* . . . [10] In the evening, he goes to his Section, not powdered and perfumed, not elegantly dressed in the hope of catching the eye of the citizens in the galleries, but to give his unreserved support to sound resolutions. . . . Besides this, the sans-culotte always has his sword with the edge sharpened to give a salutary lesson to all trouble-makers. Sometimes he carries his pike with him, and at the first beat of the drum, he will be seen leaving for the Vendée, for the *armée des Alpes* or the *armée du Nord.*"

The modest social condition of the sans-culotte is clearly of importance here;

[9] *A.N.*, F⁷ 4775⁴⁸.
[10] The café de Chartres was a favourite royalist meeting-place; *l'Ami des lois* was a comedy by Jean Laya performed in 1793.

but, as we can see from the above document, a definition of the sans-culotte would not be complete without a statement of his political conduct. . . .

Although the sans-culotte militants were unable to devise an original and effective social programme, the coherent pattern of political ideas which they adopted distinguishes them as the most progressive group to emerge during the Revolution. Their demands for the autonomy and permanence of the Sections, the right to approve legislation, the exercise of control over their elected representatives and the power of revoking their mandate, based upon a wide interpretation of the expression "popular sovereignty", moved the sans-culotterie nearer the exercise of direct government and popular democracy.[11] But could the bourgeois conception of democracy and the exigencies of the Revolutionary Government be reconciled with the political leanings of the sans-culotterie?

The political behaviour of the militant sans-culotte can only be explained by his unqualified acceptance of the principle that sovereignty resides in the people. For the sans-culotte, this was not an abstract idea, but a concrete reality of the people gathered together in the assemblies of the Sections exercising the totality of their rights.

Popular sovereignty was "imprescriptible and inalienable; a right which could be delegated to no one," and on 3 November 1792, the Section de la Cité announced that "anyone who claims that he is invested with this right will be regarded as a tyrant, a usurper of the people's freedom who deserves to be punished by death." On 13 March 1793, after a citizen in the general assembly of the Section du Panthéon-Français had stated that "people are threatening us with a dictator," the assembly rose to its feet and swore to kill "any director, protector, tribune, triumvire, or any other kind of ruler, whatever title he chooses for himself, who attacks the principle of the people's sovereignty." This anxiety to defend the sovereignty of the people clearly explains why so many proposals by Marat to nominate a tribune of the people, or a dictator, were so unsuccessful, as well as the importance of the accusation that Hébert and others were planning to create an office of *grand juge,* a charge designed to weaken their popularity in the eyes of the people. . . .

Violence was adopted as a last resort by the sans-culotterie against anyone who refused to unite with them in their struggle: it became one of the most characteristic features of their political behaviour. Popular violence had enabled the bourgeoisie to launch their first attacks against the *ancien régime,* and there was never any question of the aristocracy being completely crushed without it. In 1793 and in the Year II, the sans-culotte adopted violent tactics, not only against the aristocracy, but against the moderates who refused to accept the idea of an egalitarian republic.

To understand this violence, and the feeling of exaltation which accompanied it, we would doubtless have to look sometimes for biological reasons: temperament often explains many reactions which would otherwise remain obscure. The reports of Prairial Year III [May–June 1795] on the terrorists of the previous year often stress the quick-tempered or violent sides of their nature. As one informer stated, a

[11] The expression "popular republic" can be found in Étienne Barry's *Essai sur la dénonciation politique.*

man with such a temperament was subject to fits of passion "which might have led him to make exaggerated statements without foreseeing or even thinking about their consequences." Reactions were more immediate and more extreme because the sans-culottes were often rough and crude, lacking any real education, their lives inflamed by misery.

In the Year III, terrorists were indiscriminately described as *buveurs de sang* [bloodthirsty men], and although we must be careful not to generalize, or to take police reports and denunciations literally, it would be very difficult to deny that violence for some actually meant the spilling of blood. Arbulot, a cloth-shearer from the Section des Gardes-Françaises, arrested on 9 Prairial [May 28, 1795], was reputed to have been a very dangerous husband and neighbour, with a fierce and unyielding nature: it was said that he had taken great pleasure in the September massacres. Bunou from the Section des Champs-Elysées, arrested on 5 Prairial [May 24, 1795], was alleged to have asked for a guillotine for the Section in the Year II, "and that if they could not find an executioner, he would take the job on himself." Similar statements were supposed to have been made by Lesur from the Section du Luxembourg who was arrested on the following day. He was convinced "that the guillotine was not doing its work quickly enough; that there should be a bit more blood-letting in the prisons; and that if the executioner was tired, he would mount the scaffold himself, even if it meant soaking the two-pound loaf he had just bought with blood." In the Section des Gardes-Françaises, Jayet was arrested on 6 Prairial [May 25, 1795] because he had said in the Year II "that he wanted to see streams of blood flowing until they had reached ankle-height." Another citizen on leaving the general assembly of the Section de la République stated: "The guillotine is hungry; it has been fasting for too long." [12]

Temperament alone, however, does not explain why practically all the militant sans-culottes should have justified, if not exalted, a recourse to violence and the use of the guillotine. For many, brutal force appeared to be the only answer in times of acute crisis. Yet these same men, who did not hesitate to spill blood on these occasions, were quite peaceable citizens in the ordinary course of their daily lives; good sons, husbands, and fathers. Duval, a shoemaker from the Section de l'Arsenal, was condemned to death on 11 Prairial Year III [May 30, 1795] for his part in the rising of the first of the month. His neighbours described him as a good father, a good husband, and a good citizen—"a man of good morals." The awareness of the danger facing the nation, the belief in the aristocratic plot, the atmosphere of the great insurrections, the tocsin, the warning cannon-shot and the parade of arms all played their part in lifting these men outside themselves, completely altering their characters. According to the *comité civil* [the political or administrative committee] of the Section du Faubourg du Nord, Joseph Morlot, a house-painter arrested on 5 Prairial [May 24, 1795] had two distinct natures: "The one, when governed by his natural disposition, is gentle, honest, and kind; it presents a combination of all the social virtues which he practises discreetly in his everyday life. The other, awakened by momentary dangers, produces the worst

[12] *A.N.*, F⁷ 4581, pl. 1; 4627, d. 2; 4636, d. 2; 4749; 4774⁸⁶.

possible evils presented in their most lurid form which he parades in the most indiscreet manner." [13]

But violence was not adopted simply for its own sake: it had a political aim which was not devoid of a vague consciousness of class differences, forced upon the sans-culotterie by the continued resistance of the aristocracy. The *comité révolutionnaire* of the Section Poissonnière was alleged to have planned the arrest in Brumaire Year II [October–November, 1793] of a citizen named Charvin, well known for his moderation "which weakens the people's confidence in revolutionary acts and leads to a deterioration of public morale in the Section." Moussard, a teacher employed by the Executive Commission of Public Instruction, was arrested on 5 Prairial Year III [May 24, 1795]. "I was often over-enthusiastic," he wrote in his defence statement, "What person does not go a little beyond himself in a revolution? . . . I am too exalted in my opinions, they say. Yes, the passion for good burns inside me; I respond to the joys of freedom, and my blood will always boil when I hear of the enemies of my country." [14]

The guillotine was popular because the sans-culottes regarded it as the avenging arm of the nation, accounting for such expressions as "national hatchet," and "the people's axe"; the guillotine was also "the scythe of equality." Class hatred against the aristocracy was exacerbated by the widespread belief in the "aristocratic plot" which, since 1789, had represented one of the motivating elements of popular violence. Foreign and civil war helped to strengthen the conviction of the sans-culotterie that the only way of crushing the aristocracy completely was by terror, and that the guillotine was necessary if the Republic was not to be overthrown. Becq, a clerk in the Admiralty who, according to the *comité civil* of the Section de la Butte-des-Moulins, a good husband and father and generally well thought of but extraordinarily exalted in his attitude towards the Revolution, directed his fanaticism against priests and nobles for whom he prescribed, as a rule, assassination. Jean-Baptiste Mallais, a shoemaker and *commissaire révolutionnaire* from the Section du Temple, sympathized wholeheartedly with these views. When he began one of his many arguments, the subject would inevitably be his hatred of priests and nobles whom he considered to be enemies of the people; and when he spoke of arming the wives of patriots, it was "so that they, in their turn, could cut the throats of aristocrats' wives." Barrayer from the Section de la Réunion was alleged to have stated in the Year II "that they had to kill the young devil in the church" because if they did not, then "one day he would massacre the people." More significant still of the political significance which the sans-culottes attached to violence and the Terror were the remarks taken down by the police-agent Perrière on 6 Ventôse Year II [February 24, 1794]: "Are there any executions today? a small well-dressed moderate asked.—Without any doubt, replied an honest patriot, since we are still surrounded by treason." [15]

In the year III, the recourse to violence had an even greater significance for the

[13] *A.N.,* W 546; F⁷ 4774⁵³.
[14] *A.N.,* F⁷ 4776; 4774⁵⁴.
[15] *A.N.,* W 112.

sans-culotterie. The Terror had also had an economic aspect: it had enabled the General Maximum to be applied which had guaranteed the people their daily bread. Reaction coincided with the end of price-fixing and the most acute food-shortage. Some sans-culottes naturally identified the Terror with a well-stocked larder, as they associated popular government with the Terror. The shoemaker Clément from the Section de la République was denounced on 2 Prairial [May 21, 1795] for having said "that they could not build the Republic without blood." A citizen named Denis from the Section Brutus was arrested on 5 Prairial [May 24 1795] because in his opinion there were not so many "good republicans to be found as when they used to guillotine people." Chalandon, a wife from the Section de l'Homme-Armé, used to say "that things would never improve until they erect permanent guillotines on all the public thoroughfares of Paris." The remarks made by Richer on 1 Prairial [May 20, 1795], a carpenter from the Section de la République, were more precise. Richer was convinced "that the only way to get bread is to spill a little blood," adding "that during the Terror there was no shortage of it." . . .[16]

The contradictions peculiar to the Parisian sans-culotterie were equally as important in explaining the collapse of the system of the Year II as the conflicts which divided the Revolutionary Government and the popular movement.

There was a social contradiction between the Jacobins, drawn almost exclusively from the ranks of the lower, middle, and even the upper bourgeoisie, and the sans-culottes, if we accept [the revolutionary politician] Petion's description of the latter as day-labourers and *compagnons de métiers* [journeymen artisans]. But it would be wrong to identify the sans-culotte with the wage-earner, despite the fact that wage-earners formed the largest section of the sans-culotterie. The reality is far more complex. The sans-culotterie did not constitute a class, nor was the sans-culotte movement based on class differences. Craftsmen, shopkeepers and merchants, *compagnons* and day-labourers joined with a bourgeois minority to form a coalition but there was still an underlying conflict between craftsmen and merchants, enjoying a profit derived from the private ownership of the means of production, and *compagnons* and day-labourers, entirely dependent upon their wages.

The application of the maximum [price ceilings] brought this contradiction into the open. Craftsmen and shopkeepers agreed that it was a sound and reasonable policy to force the peasantry to feed the population of the towns; but they protested immediately [when] the provisions of the maximum began to affect their own interests. *Compagnons* reacted in much the same way. By creating a shortage of labour, the *levée en masse* and the civil war led to a rise in wages: if producers and "middlemen" refused to observe price-fixing, why should the workers offer themselves as victims? The demands of the revolutionary struggle had welded the unity of the Parisian sans-culotterie and momentarily pushed the conflict of interests into the background: there was no question, however, of suppressing them altogether.

Differences in social outlook complicated the problem even further. The contradictions within the ranks of the sans-culotterie were not simply those which

[16] *A.N.*, W 548.

separated the *possédants* and producers from the salaried workers. Amongst the latter we find, in particular, those who belonged to the clerical and teaching professions, who, because of their way of life, regarded themselves as bourgeois, not to be identified with the *bas-peuple* [common people], even if they embraced the same cause. On the other hand, many citizens recognized as being members of the bourgeoisie described themselves as "sans-culotte" and acted as such.

The sans-culottes, recruited from so many different levels of society, could not, therefore, have been really conscious of belonging to a certain class. Although they were generally hostile to the new methods of production, it was not always from the same motives—the craftsman was afraid of being reduced to the status of a wage-earner; the *compagnon* detested the monopolist because he held him responsible for the rising cost of living. As for the *compagnons* alone, it would be anachronistic to speak of them as being class-conscious, since their mentality was still conditioned by the world of the craftsman in which they lived and worked. The capitalist concentration of industry, by bringing them into daily contact through the factory, had not yet created the mentality which would awaken the feeling of class solidarity.

However, if class-consciousness cannot be attributed to the sans-culotterie as a body, it is possible to detect a certain awareness of class amongst the wage-earners. Entirely dependent upon their employers, they regarded themselves as a distinct social group, not only because of the manual nature of their work and their place in the system of production, but also on account of the clothes which they wore, the food they ate, their pastimes, social habits and, in particular, their living accommodation. The fact that they were mostly uneducated—education being reserved solely for citizens privileged by birth and wealth—also tended to distinguish them from their fellow citizens, creating a feeling of inferiority and, sometimes, of powerlessness amongst the lower classes. Militant sans-culottes frequently reveal their hostility towards *hommes-à-talent,* but, by raising themselves to the same level, longed to play a decisive part in controlling their destiny.

Composed of diverse elements, not constituting a class and, therefore, devoid of class-consciousness, the Parisian sans-culotterie, despite a few hesitant attempts to co-ordinate their activity, lacked a really effective weapon of political action—a strictly disciplined party which could only have been created by a drastic purge followed by recruitment on a class basis. This was equally true of the Revolutionary Government, since the Jacobins themselves were not representative of any one social class. The entire régime of the Year II rested upon an abstract conception of political democracy which largely explains its weakness. The consequences of this were particularly disastrous for the popular movement.

Although there were many militants who tried to discipline the general assemblies and popular societies, leading figures in a number of the Sections aggravated the situation by disputing power amongst themselves, occasionally by abusing it when they eventually succeeded in gaining control. As for the mass of the sans-culotterie, apart from hatred of the aristocracy and the summary methods envisaged for dealing with the problem—chiefly massacre—they do not appear to have been gifted with any degree of political insight: they were simply waiting to receive the benefits which the Revolution would inevitably bring. They campaigned for the maximum, not so much in order to defend the *assignat* and guarantee the production of war supplies, but because they believed that price-controls would help to maintain their standard of living. When they realized that, in many respects, a controlled economy did not meet this requirement, they abandoned it in favour of a new policy. Would the sans-culottes have agreed to drop their demand for higher wages if—an untenable hypothesis—*possédants* and producers had agreed to respect the provisions of the maximum by accepting a margin of profit which the Revolutionary Government considered to be reasonable. The possibility appears to be extremely remote. The war made certain sacrifices inevitable—one of them was that no section of the community should try and profit from the circumstances it created in order to further its own particular interests.

From this point of view, the 9 Thermidor was, indeed, a *journée de dupes* [day of deception] for the sans-culottes. Disillusioned by the effect of the maximum, discontented with the Revolutionary Government, they failed to realize that its collapse would also involve their own ruin. Ten months later, their resistance weakened by the effects of famine and the high cost of living, realizing at last what they had lost, they demanded a return to a controlled economy, rose in insurrection for the last time only to be completely crushed and swept from the stage of history.

The internal contradictions of the sans-culotterie, however, do not entirely explain the collapse of the popular movement: its gradual disintegration was inscribed in the dialectical march of history itself. The indirect attacks of the Committees and the consolidation of the Revolutionary Government, the drama of Germinal and the feeling of deception which followed, only partly explain its weakness. It was, in fact, inevitable that the popular movement should have lost momentum: its development, its very success, only strengthened those factors which finally contributed to its defeat.

There was, in the first place, a reason of a biological nature. Most of the militants had been actively engaged in the revolutionary struggle since 14 July 1789; they had participated in every insurrection. Since 10 August 1792, they had redoubled their activity. But the enthusiasm and excitement of the great *journées* involved a certain expenditure of nervous energy which, after the victory, increased the tension and strain involved in the daily life of the militant. Five years of revolution had drained the physical resources of the sectionary personnel who provided the cadres of the popular movement. It was only natural that this physical exhaustion which, at different times, forced many of the leading figures of the Revolution—Robespierre himself in Messidor [June–July 1794]—to retire momentarily from the political scene, should not also have affected the militants always in the thick of the battle. Robespierre had predicted that as the war dragged on, the people would begin to "show signs of apathy." This apathy communicated itself to the popular movement, depriving it of its vigour and initial enthusiasm.

There was also a psychological reason arising out of the events of the Year II. The end of the civil war, the halt to the invasion, and, finally, the realization of victory, led to an understandable relaxation of tension. This was true of the population as a whole, although the relief felt by the bourgeoisie cannot be explained by the end of the Terror alone—there was also the prospect of an end to the economic policy of controls and fixed prices, as well as the return of administrative and governmental authority into the hands of the *notables*. The people were anxious to reap the benefits of all their effort. The opening of a register in the Section de la Montagne for new adherents to the Constitution cannot be regarded simply as a political manœuvre: in the eyes of the militants, the *Acte constitutionnel* of June 1793 was the symbol of social democracy; they had continuously campaigned for the right to receive public relief and the right to instruction. But the majority of the people were primarily concerned with their right to subsist. Since victory was at last in sight, they expected, if not exactly abundance, then, at least, less difficulty in being provided with food as well as a guranteed daily supply of bread. In fact, victory led to the demobilization of the popular movement.

The Parisian sans-culotterie were also weakened from month to month by the dialectical effect of the war effort. The conscription of 300,000 men, the recruitment for the Vendée, then for the Eure, the *levée en masse* and the creation of the Revolutionary Army, deprived the Sections of a considerable number of the youngest, most active, often the most conscientious and enthusiastic patriots who regarded the defence of the nation as their first civic duty. In order to assess the vitality of the popular movement, an exact calculation of the number of men who enlisted for the various campaigns would clearly be of the greatest possible advantage. But, if we cannot attempt a general study, we can, at least, gain some idea of the significance of the loss of human energy suffered by the Parisian Sections in 1793. In the Section des Piques, which had 3,540 voters aged 21 and over in the Year II, 233 volunteers enrolled for the Vendée from 3 to 17 May 1793 alone—mainly sans-culottes in the prime of life. The lists of citizens capable of carrying arms drawn up by the Sections underlines this sapping of the armed strength of the Sections: men of over 50 and, occasionally, of 60 years of age represent a large proportion of the companies formed. Out of the 3,231 men in the Section de Quatre-Vingt-Douze, 767 (23.7 per cent) were over 50 years of age. In the Section des Arcis, the companies totalled 2,986 men "of whom, a quarter would have to be subtracted" of men aged over 60.[17] The popular movement grew old as a result of these successive enrolments: the inevitable effect on the revolutionary enthusiasm and combative keenness of the Parisian masses can readily be appreciated.

Finally, the dialectical effect of success led to a gradual disintegration of the framework of the popular movement. Many of the sectionary militants, even if they were not motivated by ambition alone, regarded an official position as the legitimate reward for their militant activity. The stability of the popular movement largely depended upon the satisfaction of these personal interests which happened to coincide with the need for purging the various committees. But, in such cases, success breeds a new conformity, as the example of the *commissaires révolutionnaires* illustrates. At first, their revolutionary ardour had distinguished them from the other members of the political organizations of the Sections. But since they had been recruited chiefly from the lowest social ranks of the sans-culotterie, it became necessary, even for the success of the Revolution, for them to be paid a salary. The fear of losing their position, just as much as the strengthening of the Revolutionary

---

[17] *A.N.*, AA 15, d. 783. Lists by Section of citizens capable of carrying arms.

Government, soon turned them into willing instruments of the central power. Throughout the Year II, many of the militants were transformed into salaried civil servants as a result of this process, which was not only a necessary outcome of the internal evolution of the sans-culotterie, but also of the intensification of the class struggle within France and on her frontiers. The really politically-minded elements of the sans-culotterie became part of the administrative machinery of the State; the sectionary organizations suffered a corresponding loss of political activity, allowance having been made for the accumulated demands of national defence. At the same time, the democratic ideal was being weakened in the Sections, the process of bureaucratization gradually paralysing the critical spirit and activity of the masses. The eventual outcome was a relaxation of the control exercised by the popular movement over the Revolutionary Government which became increasingly authoritarian in character. This bureaucratic encroachment deprived the sans-culottes of many of the channels through which the popular movement had operated.

These various considerations—which have a far wider application than to the events of the Year II—account for the weakening of the popular movement, and clearly precipitated its collapse.

It would be wrong, however, to draw up a purely negative balance sheet of the popular movement in the Year II. Doubtless it was impossible for it to attain its particular objective—the egalitarian and popular republic towards which the sans-culottes were moving without any clearly defined programme—prevailing circumstances as well as its own contradictions raised far too many obstacles. Nevertheless, the popular movement has still contributed towards historical progress by its decisive intervention in support of the bourgeois revolution.

Without the Parisian sans-culotterie, the bourgeoisie could not have triumphed in so radical a fashion. From 1789 to the Year II, the sans-culottes were used as an effective weapon of revolutionary combat and national defence. In 1793, the popular movement made possible the installation of the Revolutionary Government and, consequently, the defeat of the counter-revolution in France and the allied coalition in Europe. It was the Thermidoreans who really benefited from this victory; and if they failed to use their advantage to secure peace, it was because the decision to abandon a controlled economy, added to the demoralization of the troops totally deprived of supplies, paralysed the army and gave the enemy the necessary time to prepare new campaigns. This contrast helps us to appreciate the work of the Revolutionary Government as well as the importance of the popular movement of the Year II.

$\mathcal{A}$ Critique

RICHARD COBB

For biographical information on Richard Cobb, see Chapter 5, entitled "Why Terror in 1793–1794?"

Both contemporaries and several generations of liberal or reactionary historians were shocked by the spectacle of popular violence during the French Revolution. Contemporaries feared that these new, unexpected, and unpredictable forms of violence might be used against property-holders and respectable people, rather than against poachers and lawbreakers. In fact, what seems to have shocked contemporaries and historians alike is that the violence should have been popular (and, by implication, lawless, brutish, chaotic, undirected). [The writer Louis-Sébastien] Mercier, in 1797, frequently refers to the violent language of the common people, rich in incitation to murder, varied too in cannibalistic metaphor—"I would like to eat your liver," "I would like to open up your belly and eat your guts," "I would like to eat a bourgeois' head," "let's eat a good hunk from an aristocrat," and so on—and he describes the evolution of this popular violence in its verbal expressions: "The words *carnage, blood, death, vengeance,* that ABC of the Jacobin idiom [*vengeance, in fact, belongs by right to the Thermidorian period, even on the admission of the Thermidorian local authorities*] is repeated, shouted, roared . . . by the *Mob.* The *Mob* has ruled for nearly fifteen months, has tyrannized the city. . . ." Referring to the verb *lanterner,* he observes: "Previously that word had meant to waste time by doing nothing . . . at the beginning of the Revolution, it meant to hang a man from a lamppost. The words *guillotiner* and *guillotine* have become so popular in usage that these words have completely driven out the words *lanterne* and *lanterner.* . . ."

> I heard [*he claims to recollect*] screamed in my ear: "Let the French perish so long as liberty triumphs!" I heard someone else cry out in a section meeting: "Yes, I would grab my head by the hair and lop it off, and offering it to the despot, I would say to him: 'Tyrant, this is the action of a free man.' " This sublime degree of extravagance was created for the revolutionary common people, it was heard, it was a success. . . .

We may recall the women of the people, as depicted by *La Lanterne Magique,* eating the "naked and quivering bodies of their victims"; and this was the language

From Richard Cobb, *The Police and the People: French Popular Protest, 1789–1820* (London: Oxford University Press, 1970), pp. 87–90, 120–127. Copyright © 1970 Oxford University Press. Reprinted by permission of the Clarendon Press, Oxford. All footnotes included except for cross-references to notes in the appendix. Quotations originally in French have been translated by the editors.

which, in the year III [1794–1795], changed sides, to be used by former terrorists when describing the horrors of the White Terror; in Pluviôse of that year [January–February 1795], the survivors of the first wave of massacres at Nîmes—and the future victims of the next—describe the scene: "Each of these unfortunate people suffered a thousand deaths before finally expiring; they were mutilated, and the murderers, covered with blood, carried and raised as trophies the still throbbing limbs that they had just cut off. . . ." There is by then a standard vocabulary of massacre. A jeweller from the Lombards Section in Paris is accused, in a Thermidorian report, "of boasting that he had cut off eighteen heads" in September 1792, and, whatever we make of this popular boastfulness, there is no doubt as to the intentions of the man who made the report. They are as clear as those of Mercier and the lantern slide lecturer. All conveniently forgot the violence of others—of the old royal government, of the old royal army, and of la Royale [a prison off the coast of French Guiana], with its barbarous punishments; of the old penal system and the bagne [a forced-labor prison] with its ball and chain and similar refinements; of the old police ordinances and the language of the old administration, which, when addressed to the common people, could express itself only in threats and in the promise of retribution; of the treatment of Protestant children, especially in the Généralité de Rouen; of the old ruling class, and of their servants; of the Parlements, and of the basoche [law clerks]; of the cavalier of the maréchaussée [mounted police]; of the Garde française [a member of an army regiment stationed in Paris], so proud of his proficiency in killing quickly and hardly admissible into the inner sanctum of regimental solidarity until he had a corpse or two to his credit; of the hussar and the dragoon; of the sailor, and of the guet [the night police in Paris]—just as everyone often tends to ignore the violence of 1795 and the years following and to forget that Terror could be White as well as Blue. Nor do they ask themselves how else the people could exercise their will and get their grievances seen to.

Certainly an enraged crowd, a group of rioters in full cry, the repeated invitation of À mort! [Put him to death!] screamed like a litany, the bestiality of massacre and lynching, the near-cannibalism of some women and a very few male rioters, are repellent, dreadful, hideous, and above all depressing, just as the corpses that are strewn so copiously in every print, patriotic or counter-revolutionary, of the great revolutionary journées or of the great massacres are absolutely inadmissible, whatever their clothing, whichever their uniform, just as severed heads and headless bodies cry out endlessly against the Revolution and all its works.

Certainly, too, what is so often clothed over and "historicized" as something called the "popular movement" (how much is the historian's terminology dominated by thought of syllabus or by the search for a chapter heading?) was frequently cruel and cowardly, base and vengeful, barbaric and not at all pretty to watch. Professor Rudé's Crowd is somehow altogether too respectable; one hesitates to credit all these worthy shopkeepers and all these honest apprentices, family men too, with such horrors, and, in identifying the assailants, one is in danger of leaving the assailed out of the picture. Any honest historian of popular movements—and especially those of the French Revolution—must at times be seized with doubts. Is he not attempting to steer away from a violence that, on close inspection, becomes unbearable? Is he not trying to find excuses for brutality and murder? Is he not taking refuge in the convenient jargon of collective behaviourism to explain, to rationalize, massacre? Is there not something indecent, obscene, on his part, thus to pause, for so long, among yellowed sheets that describe, in the stilted language of French law, the details of a village lynching, or of a Christmas Day brawl ending in bloodshed? Is he not trying to get it both ways—the exhilaration of riot, experienced in the safety of a record office? Is he not making his *homme révolutionnaire* gentler, kinder, more tolerant, more whimsical, than he really was? Is he not trying to take the sting out of the *massacreur* by emphasizing the conceit, the *naïveté*, and the credulity of the *sans-culotte*, even if the one is not, in a particular instance, the other? Should not he, who, in fact, would never march behind the banner, would always stay at home, or who would be the first to run at the sound of firing, keep away from popular protest altogether and take refuge in the History of Parliament? Most historians of the French Revolution must have asked some of these questions, at one time or another, and especially in moments when they have been glutted with horror. And it would of course be both dishonest and misleading to represent the "popular movement" as a study in rumbustious good fellowship, enthusiasm, generosity, fraternity, and hope, or as an early groping towards various forms of socialism, while leaving out of account the violence.

Yet this violence is not so odious and inadmissible as that of war or of diplomacy; it was never gratuitous, nor was it ever exclusive to any one class—or any one party: all classes, all parties were enthusiastic advocates of violence when there was a good chance of using it against their immediate enemies, though they tended to discover the advantages of mercy when they looked like being on the losing side. . . .

Most historians are now familiar with Albert Soboul's rather formalized account of the relations between the classes—especially the urban classes—in the course of the revolutionary period, both from his *Précis*[1] and from his even shorter *Que sais-je?*[2] A *pas de deux* or sometimes a *pas de trois*, that might be set to music as a historical ballet. Opening scene: bourgeoisie and people, hand in hand, dancing on the prone figure of Privilege. Scene Two: (the people having done their stuff) bourgeoisie and monarchy, hand in hand, dancing on the prone figure of the people. Scene Three: bourgeoisie and people, hand in hand, dancing on the prone body of monarchy. Scene Four: an intermezzo between bourgeoisie and people, only occasionally hand in hand, more often hands vainly extended, both playing hard to get. Scene Five: bourgeoisie dancing alone, on the prone bodies of people and monarchy. One knew it would turn out like this all along, for that is the rule of a particularly rigorous choreography that will not allow a step to be taken out of place (and, if necessary, the *sans-culotte* may have to be nudged and reminded of his part: "Get back into line, you are part of the Popular Movement"; the bourgeois, too, forgetting that he is either a Girondin, or Jacobin, or Montagnard, or Thermidorian, may have to be recalled rather roughly to realities, and not be allowed to wander off on his own to look at the shops or enjoy a walk in the country). It is

[1] Albert Soboul, *Précis d'histoire de la Révolution française* (Paris, 1962).
[2] Albert Soboul, *La Révolution française (Que sais-je?)* (Paris, 1963).

admirably done, the actors know their parts, sink to the ground on the appropriate note, rise again when summoned. The prompter is very discreet and hardly at all in evidence.

Yet one has doubts; it all seems too well rehearsed. And the doubts are confirmed by the same author's definitive account of the *mouvement sectionnaire* in Paris and of its relations with the Revolutionary Government. For in this great work[3] the ballet steps are only briefly remembered, as a matter of form, at the opening and closing of chapters that in their massive middle disclose a much more confusing scene: uncertainties of contour, difficulties of definition, lack of clear objectives, shifting loyalties, internal contradictions, personal squabbles, the role of personalities and of militant minorities, preliminary committee work, the "fixing" of an agenda, passion, confusion, credulity, myth, anarchy, noise. It is not even certain whether the two tentative partners are, at all times, aware of each other's existence, and there is much more groping and shuffling and searching and back-turning than anything like an ordered movement. This, in its always complicated, detailed narrative, looks much more like the real thing. Soboul's great merit is to have explored that narrative, recreated it, and put it end to end, so that, in the long-drawn-out and complicated process of gradual divorce between a very varied, highly decentralized *mouvement sectionnaire* and a Revolutionary Government that contains a wide range of revolutionary fervour, one is guided by a day-to-day chronology. . . .

Albert Soboul is describing a mass movement that operated, for a limited period, through certain institutions. The movement did not create the institutions, but the institutions, which already existed, created the movement and imposed upon it certain inbred structural weaknesses. These weaknesses necessitated forms of organization that were tentative and strongly federalist, and that in turn involved a great deal of preliminary negotiation. It is often stated that the popular movement during the French Revolution tended towards extreme forms of decentralization, and Soboul's Paris *sectionnaire* is taken as the obvious example. But the *sectionnaire* is federalist because the Section is; thus the institutions model the movement, and the Section forms the *sectionnaire*. The Section was an urban village, the Quarter, a world to itself. Of course, when confronted with threats from outside, the Sections would seek to work together, and to impose a common programme. But the peril had to be very great; and much time and energy were taken up by quarrels between different Sections and by personal bids for power within the Section itself. The movement, all forty-eight Sections lumped together as a *mouvement sans-culotte*, may reasonably be described as a mass one comprising some two hundred thousand Parisians; but within each Section, effective power is exercised by small minorities of revolutionary militants—twelve or twenty men at the most,[4] who, thanks to their

---

[3] Albert Soboul, *Les Sans-culottes parisiens et le mouvement sectionnaire* (Paris, 1958).

[4] Mercereau, a policeman in the Panthéon Français Section, comments on the manner in which the Section committee was run: "I declare that the committee is the source of all kinds of hatred, it is composed of at most 60 men and the same number of women and with this small minority they would like to lead the Section which is composed of 8 to 9,000 men. I do not accuse all the members of the committee, but really 6 or 8 individuals . . ." (Archives Nationales, F7 4774 d 3 [*Mercereau*]).

skill, to the strength of their vocal organs, to their physique,[5] to the time they are prepared to devote to militancy, to their own prestige, to their own patronage (for a number were important employers of labour), are able to manipulate the proceedings of the larger assemblies *en petit comité* and push through their proposals well in advance. (Later their opponents made much of this, in their efforts to isolate the *dominateurs*, the *aboyeurs* [those who were domineering and noisy], from the general mass of *sectionnaires*, and suggested that the experiment in "direct democracy" disguised what was in fact the workings of a "secret committee" manipulated by a handful of men. This is a constant theme in Thermidorian *enquêtes* [investigations] and propaganda, and all the more convincing in that it corresponded to a certain degree with the reality, as recalled by people of many shades of opinion, a year later.)

Soboul's own account shows that a great deal of preliminary work went into preparing Sectionary business, that there was often a lot of lobbying, that matters were seldom left to the chance of a free vote, and that the *sans-culotte* movement could hardly be described as spontaneous or even as particularly democratic unless we admit that there existed a degree of super–*sans-culottisme* which placed some *sectionnaires* over their fellow citizens, in a category apart, élitist and unassailable. For there existed, at least in the *bureaux* [executive committees], an inner ring of self-taught militants who, though political amateurs, were soon learning how to manipulate an assembly and prepare business from within a *comité*. In time, they would have become professionals. Already, by the first months of the year III, when in *commune* after *commune* they were dislodged from their entrenched positions, generally by the outside intervention of a *Représentant en mission*—it would take nothing less to prise them out of their hold on a *comité* or a municipality—they had acquired a professional mentality, considering themselves indispensable to the forward march of the Revolution and to the particular interests of their own town or village. So much was this the case that, right up to the summer of 1795, their one thought was that they would soon get back, as their fellow citizens were bound to realize, sooner or later, that they could not do without their valuable services. But they were, of course, removable, even in the circumstances of the year II, and many of the bitter personal squabbles that take up so much space in Sectionary minutes—sometimes for weeks on end, to the exclusion of all else—arose out of attempts to dislodge the reigning clan that had, for one reason or another, made itself generally intolerable—and most of these *meneurs* were loud-mouthed, arrogant, intolerant, some of them were impossible little tyrants, constantly boasting of how they disposed of the power of life and death, gaily talking of the heads that would fall and taking an obvious enjoyment in sending shudders down the backs of those whom they were seeking to impress or to cow—and to replace it by people who were popular in the assemblies or in the *sociétés*, areas in which the virtues of the proverbial "good committee man" were likely to be less appreciated.

Even at this level, there were bound to be conflicts between the general mass of

---

[5] One *meneur* [ringleader], who is also an *inspecteur*, is accused, in the year III, of having terrorized his fellow *sectionnaires* by attending all the meetings of the *assemblée générale* and of the *société*, accompanied by an enormous and very fierce dog (Cobb and Rudé, "Le Dernier Mouvement populaire de la Révolution à Paris," *Revue historique*, October–December 1955).

sectionnaires, for whom politics could only be very much of a part-time evening occupation, and the small groups of committed men, who claimed to do their thinking for them. Sectionary politics are full of clans, and so are those of provincial *sociétés;* for these were mostly people who knew each other well—that is to say, who knew much that was damaging about one another—and posts in the *bureaux,* especially those which raised their holders to a prominent position, above most of their fellows, on a *tribune* or in the president's high chair, were objects of as much envy and back-biting as an officer or non-commissioned rank in the *Garde nationale.* The butcher, the grocer, the shoemaker of the Quarter or of the *bourg* are bound to live in conceit. Their wives lived even more so and it was because of the corroding influence of feminine jealousies that some popular assemblies sought to exclude women, even as onlookers. The greatest glory was that which was visible to the whole street, to the whole village. The soldier decorated for gallantry and the scholarship boy will hurry home to exhibit themselves. And, though women did not vote in the assemblies, they did much to blow on the furnaces of neighbourly discord if they felt that their husbands or companions were not getting the recognition that they deserved for their patriotism and long service to the Revolution. If the *patriotes de 93* were in control, then the whole syndicate of the *patriotes de 89*—and the *sans-culottes* could generally muster a few of these—would be grumbling in the wings about newcomers, demagogues, and so on, in sulky deprivation. Revolutionary patriotism, they suggested, should be calculated in terms of length of service to the Cause.

To this the newcomers might reply that the first in the field had fallen by the wayside, having compromised themselves on one of the many occasions between July 1789 and May–June 1793 when it was possible to plump for the wrong side. There was much to be said, in the conditions of the year II, for having been out of public life till 1793. It might, in fact, more often be a conflict between the April men and the September men, for not a great many *sans-culottes* could show service much before 1792, and the great internal revolutions within the Sections occurred between the spring and the late summer of 1793. Many *meneurs* (*aboyeurs* as the Thermidorians were to call them) made themselves intolerable by their insolent bearing, and, at the beginning of the year III, there was a genuine and very widespread revulsion against the former *dominateurs.* They had at best been meddlesome, "superior," and impatient of criticism, at worst tyrannical, heartless, brutal, and insufferable. Militancy is not likely to breed fraternal love; the militant had few friends and many toadies; and in the year III such people would have no friends at all, those whom they had once obliged or protected being the first to keep their distances. But already in the year II it is possible to distinguish between a minority of activists and the general mass of good, middling, or indifferent *sans-culottes.* As popular institutions everywhere declined, after Floréal [April–May 1794], this distinction would already have become more marked, with a vast increase in this last category, so that the militants would become members of a tiny *cénacle* [coterie], devoted to keeping going a "movement" that no longer existed—an act of revolutionary piety that was to be the principal concern of those who survived for the next twenty years.

Perhaps one of the greatest weaknesses of the popular movement of the year II was this reliance on very small groups of individuals, easily isolated and immediately identifiable, who through imprudence, conceit, or the foolish notion that their power would endure for ever, had made themselves and the movement with which they had become identified (and Thermidorian propaganda was devoted to "personalizing" *la sans-culotterie* in a handful of names and character sketches) thoroughly disliked by a wide section of the community that included many people of their own condition. The hatred so often shown to them in the conditions of the year III cannot only have been the result of intelligent vilification; in some cases at least, particularly in Lyon and the Midi, they were hated because they had been hateful. Nothing very terrible happened to the former terrorists of the Upper Norman Departments. The most surprising thing about these zealous servitors of Terror and Repression was that they should have taken so many risks and offered themselves up so completely as hostages to the future. For few of their victims, real or potential, ever made the mistake of calculating that the Terror and the "popular movement" would go on for ever, or that they could be anything other than temporary and accidental. Perhaps the enjoyment of power and genuine revolutionary patriotism were stronger inducements than common prudence. If one is to judge at all from Thermidorian reports—and these are, of course, heavily loaded—it is amazing how suicidal many of these militants had been, though more in speech than in action. Many of them were to pay with their lives for words uttered as boasts, to demonstrate that there was nothing that they could not, or would not, do.

In principle, Soboul is writing about a mass movement—this is his own approach—but in fact his celebrated thesis is mostly concerned with the role of élites and the methods employed by individual militants. He does name the militants, but he does not give any of them the benefit of a personality. The result is that we can see how they operated, but we gain virtually no impression of what they were like, whether they were sincere or were time-servers, whether they were out for publicity or for the fruits of office, whether they had sound sense or were crackpots. We just have to accept that they were militants and that something, whether ambition or sincerity, distinguished them from the general mass of their neighbours. He introduces us to *les sectionnaires*—that small core of six or seven hundred, sometimes even fewer, twenty or thirty in places like Le Havre or Dieppe, ten or fifteen in small towns like Salon or Martigues—upon whom was to fall the weight of future successive proscriptions; but we do not meet *le sectionnaire,* the man himself, swimming in the history of the Revolution, fighting to keep his head above tormented and fast-flowing waters.

This is partly the author's own choice, for he is dealing with so large a team that, in a study of this kind, there could hardly be room for portraits of individuals. It might be objected too that recourse to personal "case histories" puts too great a burden on the historian's imagination or on his powers of selection, that such a method is "unscientific," and even borders on the anecdotal.[6] Even so, the

---

[6] The present author has been criticized for having, in his *Armées révolutionnaires,* allowed certain of his characters too long an audience, simply because they had a lot to say for themselves, or because they were attractive, or amusing, or curious. See the review article by Hr. Kåre Tønnesson, in *Past & Present,* No. 27, 1964.

impression remains that there is an element missing: Soboul has lived with his *sans-culottes,* but, perhaps, not very intimately—they are there to serve a purpose, and can then be dismissed. He gives only a cursory glance at their domestic arrangements and makes little attempt to track them down into non-political leisure; and, after 1795, they enter the night of time—unless they are lucky enough to have attracted the approving attention of Babeuf and his Revolutionary Selection Board.

This is a pity. The *sans-culottes,* particularly the more extravagant figures who, especially in small towns far from Paris, emerged at the head of them for a few months, were often intense individualists. They regarded the revolutionary movement as their own personal property and were unwilling to take orders from any man, however high placed and however covered in sash and ribbon. It is quite possible to add that further dimension by extending the time limit of research, as far as the Paris *sans-culottes* are concerned—hence the interest of following the "popular movement" in Paris into the Slough of Despond from 1795 to 1816 or beyond, not so much to discover why the popular movement failed as to discover what happened to its leaders after the year III. The scope of research can also be extended by, for instance, investigating the "pauperization" of the former *sans-culotte* cadres in the years IV and V, through petitions to the *Commission des Secours* [Welfare Office], in order to justify indigence and so qualify for relief, at least in the form of free bread.

Another method is to choose a smaller canvas and to study the *sans-culotte* milieu and certain dominant traits of the "revolutionary temperament" in a provincial setting.[7] For the real terrain of "ultra-revolutionism"—a "movement," if the term can be used for anything so individualistic and anarchical, far more extreme and less calculating than that of the Paris *sectionnaires*—was not in the capital, for the Parisians had the Revolutionary Government on their doorsteps and could not make a move without provoking threatening rumblings from the Committee of General Security. The opportunity for the "ultra-revolutionary," a man who might be described, according to tastes, as *le révolutionnaire intégral,* as *un grand exaspéré,* or as *un grand naïf* [a complete revolutionary, an absolutely outraged person, a total innocent] and a fool of suicidal proportions, was in the Departments.

[7] [For an example, see the selection by Richard Cobb in the chapter entitled "Why Terror in 1793-1794?"—Eds.]

7

The Directory
(1795-1799)

After the fall of Robespierre, the Convention continued to rule for another fifteen months. Then it gave way to the government known as the Directory, which placed power in the hands of a five-man executive and a bicameral legislature.

The dramatic events and personalities before and after the Directory have tended to minimize its attractiveness and reputation. This is clearly shown in the selection from Albert Vandal. In an effort to justify the work of Napoleon Bonaparte as First Consul, he finds it necessary to unleash considerable passion in condemning the preceding regime. We are left to decide exactly which of Vandal's strictures come from an impartial analysis of fact.

Albert Goodwin and Denis Woronoff present a less one-sided view of the Directory. One of the first historians to advance a detailed defense of this regime, Goodwin sees the Directors as advocates of moderate republicanism. Their weaknesses and failures were, he thinks, largely attributable to the actions of misguided predecessors and to such contemporaries as Napoleon and Talleyrand. Moreover, the regime was on the way to solving many of its major problems and was a better government than the military dictatorship that followed. To Woronoff, the Directory was the creation of the republican bourgeoisie and deserves credit for some solid achievements, but fell victim to its own class biases and contradictions.

Who is right? Perhaps one can only say that more facts are needed before reaching a conclusion. Or one can argue that all the facts are never in, and that it is time to judge whether the Directory came close

to any satisfactory standard of what constitutes good, or even acceptable, government. Or one may ask what the realistic alternatives to the
Directory were and whether their triumph would have resulted in a
better regime.

A Shameless Regime

ALBERT VANDAL

Albert Vandal (1853–1910), whose father directed the French Post Office during the rule of Napoleon III, trained for the law and then entered public service. But the teaching and writing of history attracted him more; and he eventually became a professor at the École libre des Sciences politiques in Paris, one of the few institutions of higher education in the Third Republic that flourished under the aegis of neither the government nor the Church. His great book of diplomatic history, *Napoléon et Alexandre Iᵉʳ* (1891–1896), was followed by his *Avènement de Bonaparte* (1902–1907), which extolled the beneficent work of Napoleon as First Consul.

The old order had collapsed; the new order had not yet been established. On domestic matters the Directory had inherited all the faults of the Revolution. Beset by immense difficulties, it found a lasting solution for none. Its burden was heavy, but it was lamentably incapable of bearing it. It could neither restore nor establish anything. It gave to the French neither order nor liberty. . . .

In the Spring of 1799, when the direct causes of the coup d'état of 18 Brumaire appeared, the chief officials of the revolutionary group were the five Directors—Reubell, La Revellière-Lépeaux, Barras, Merlin, and Treilhard. The well-known corruption of this government has tended to overshadow the violent nature of its rule. After the purging of the great and upright Carnot and of Barthélemy—who had been expelled by their colleagues [in 1797]—the Directory appeared "unspeakably corrupt." [1] This was due to the squalid intrigues swarming around it and to the brazen peculation of its most notorious member [Barras]. Other Directors displayed the traits of dishonest servants rather than of outright robbers.

From Albert Vandal, *L'Avènement de Bonaparte* (Paris: Plon, Nourrit, 1902), I, iv, 9–13, 16–18, 21–22, 26–28, 33–34, 70–73, 77. Editors' translation. Wherever possible, the author's citations of sources in footnotes have been clarified.

[1] Eric Magnus Staël-Holstein and Baron Brinkman, *Correspondance diplomatique du Baron de Staël-Holstein et de son successeur . . . le Baron Brinkman . . .* (Paris: Hachette, 1881), p. 369, Brinkman to Sparre.

Some did not lack ability. Merlin (of Douai), a remarkable jurist and a very clever prosecutor, excelled in making crime legal; his enemies declared that he was most suited to be "a minister of justice under Louis XI." [2] Treilhard might have rendered valuable service to another regime. La Revellière, completely honest, a visionary bigot, was as weak in mind as he was deformed in body; but the Alsatian Reubell, hard, greedy, cunning, a glutton for work, seems to have been the aggressive leader of the crew.

Although decked out in theatrical costume and provided with a military guard, the Directors usually displayed little extravagance; neither "their mistresses" nor "their carriages" excited comment.[3] They lived side by side in the Luxembourg Palace, which had been divided into five apartments for their use and decorated with carpets, tapestries, and gilt furniture taken from royal palaces. In these sumptuous surroundings, the Directors lived like bourgeois. Carnot's habits were simple; he invited friends familiarly "to take pot-luck; we sit down between four-thirty and five and never eat out." [4] Evenings, La Revellière and his daughter would go to the home of friends, the Thouïns, "to spend a couple of hours in their simple kitchen." [5] Reubell had a reputation for stinginess and a taste for sordid pilfering.[6] Merlin's wife was a frightfully common housewife, as Bonaparte said, a *Madame Angot*.[7] At first the Directors, by an annual deduction from their salaries, set up a fund to be given to the one who had to retire from office each year—the "kitty" of the Directory. Later, they worked out less legal methods so as not to leave office with empty hands. They also claimed the right to take with them the bourgeois carriages provided for their official use and which would have been too painful to relinquish.

Only Barras showed himself to be ostentatious and magnificent; he was the peacock of the Directory. With flair, he wore the outfit designed by [the painter] David—a full red cloak with a lace collar, a Roman sword, and a hat overladen with plumes. When not at an official function, he usually wore a large blue frock coat and boots.[8] With his chest thrown out and his shoulders back, he resembled, as Bonaparte put it, a "handsome fencing master." [9] His voice was strong

[2] From a session of the Council of Five Hundred, 30 Prairial, year VII [June 18, 1799]. [Louis XI, King of France from 1461 to 1483, was noted for his Machiavellian methods in the pursuit of power.—Eds.]
[3] *Lettres de Charles de Constant*, p. 63.
[4] Letter to Le Coz, quoted in Alfred Roussel, *Un Évêque assermenté (1790–1802); Le Coz: Évêque d'Ille-et-Vilaine* (Paris: Lethielleux, 1898), p. 259.
[5] Louis-Marie de La Revellière-Lépeaux, *Mémoires* (Paris: Plon, Nourrit, 1895), II, 411.
[6] When Reubell retired from the Directory and when the press became free again, the newspapers wrote: "The former Director Reubell, on leaving office, took everything with him—furniture, effects, china belonging to the nation, including a service worth 12,000 francs." The following correction was later inserted: "Citizen Reubell has had those things returned which had been removed from the Luxembourg Palace upon his departure, things which did not belong to him, and of which he had only the temporary use. We are assured, furthermore, that the removal came about neither by his doing nor his orders, but by the action of his sons and the orders of his wife and his sister-in-law." See especially the *Gazette de France*, 5 and 6 Messidor, year VII [June 23 and 24, 1799].
[7] Gaspard Gourgaud, *Journal inédit, de 1815 à 1818* (Paris: Flammarion, 1899), I, 468. [A Madame Angot is a lower-class woman suddenly enriched who retains the coarse traits of her previous condition. From a comic opera by Ève popular during this period.—Eds.]
[8] Victorine de Chastenay, *Mémoires* (Paris: Plon, Nourrit, 1896–1897), I, 359.
[9] Gourgaud, I, 468.

and well modulated; in the tumult of the Convention it had rung out like a bell.

He knew how to entertain and to put on a good show. When he threw open his rooms at the Luxembourg Palace the rather mixed company that gathered, moving among "the large armchairs of red velvet trimmed in gold," [10] were surprised by the series of brilliantly lit gilt rooms. Once again they were happy to encounter luxury, as well as women dressed in filmy elegance and displaying delicate flesh. They believed themselves transported to an Olympus where Mme. Tallien[11] and her rivals played the roles of goddesses in suitable costumes. Barras also entertained in his château of Grosbois, his country house in Suresnes [near Paris]. When he went there in his carriage drawn by cream-colored horses[12] with silver-inlaid harnesses, Parisians remarked that he must have stolen a lot to be able to show off in such splendor. His usual circle included big financiers and speculators, promoters of all types, parasites, questionable people, well-born women with bad reputations, and nobles brought low by the Revolution. He strutted about amidst this corruption and deluded himself that this demi-monde was really high society. He was corrupt to the very core, rotten with vice, unbridled and consummate in his pleasures, a connoisseur of wine, women, and elegance. All the perfumed profits and the pleasures of power he kept for himself.

A rather easygoing temperament, a taste for munificence, some flexibility of mind, and a rather remarkable political flair distinguished him from his narrow-minded colleagues. But whenever his interests and his pleasures were disturbed, he became capable of anything. Ordinarily lazy and sluggish, he regained his native energy for the occasional violent acts which had made him the supporter and the strong man of that faction in the Councils composed of former deputies of the Convention. The shady game of intrigues pleased him even more. Fundamentally treacherous, selling himself to each and deceiving all, a man who enjoyed lying, he had the soul of a whore in the body of a handsome man. La Revellière considered him "ill-bred," [13] because one could surely see in him the speech and manner of a man who had always lived among bad company. Nevertheless, he retained a certain air, a certain demeanor, that he owed to his origin. No matter how deeply degraded he was, he never departed from "some of the manners customary among men of quality." [14] He gladly played the part of a soldier—it pleased him to be called *citizen general.* Posing as being on extremely friendly terms with the other Directors and eagerly using the intimate form of address with them, he really scorned their pettiness. This déclassé, this gentleman from the Midi [southern France] who had gone bad, disdained the upstarts that the accidents of annual elections gave him as colleagues.

The distinctive feature of all these men was their moral baseness. In them, there

---

[10] Chastenay, I, 360.

[11] [The leader of a social set during the Directory noted for its rejection of the prudishness of the earlier years of the revolutionary period.—Eds.]

[12] Edmond and Jules de Goncourt, *Histoire de la société française pendant le Directoire* (Paris: Charpentier [1880]), p. 300.

[13] La Revellière-Lépeaux, I, 337.

[14] MS Document by Cambacérès. The present Comte de Cambacérès has been so kind as to allow us to consult this valuable document.

was no elevated conception of their duties and rights, no generosity of heart or mind, no willingness to pacify or rally the nation, no compassion for an unhappy France which was enduring so many evils. They governed meanly, stupidly, crudely. Their policy consisted in slashing out sometimes at the Right, sometimes at the Left, and retaining power by these alternate blows. This was the famous seesaw system, which humbled one party only to raise the other. . . .

How did France live under this shameless regime? All the wounds made by the Revolution continued to bleed, and the violent actions of the Directory reopened those that had begun to heal. A France, no longer revolutionary, remained revolutionized, that is, in a state of complete subversion from which a great many evils followed. All of them can be attributed to certain general causes of suffering that were constant and endemic and that oppressed the various regions of France more or less severely.

First, there was the physical disorder. Actually, at the beginning of 1799, some months before the obscure beginnings of the Consulate, large-scale seditious movements were not evident. There had hardly been a time during the Revolution when the government had been held in such contempt and the whole of the country been so manageable. But it was apathy rather than calm, apathy still troubled by thousands of fears, unceasingly assailed by the vexations caused by those in power and by the violence of extremist groups. Although the Directory posed as a government defending the social order and the middle of the road, it could not stop the guerrillas, men of blood and pillage, from oppressing many areas and terrorizing their inhabitants. As late as 1798 there were cruelties in Tours reminiscent of the Terror.[15] And even when the left-wing anarchists, the sans-culottes or *bonnets rouges*, seemed for the moment under control, their presence could still be felt, and people trembled at the thought of a repeat attack. In the bowels of a great many cities and small towns, groups of malevolent men, human slime, secretly plotted a thoroughgoing revolution, a universal abolition of order, babouvism[16] in action. Panic-stricken landlords told each other that sooner or later the agrarian law [splitting up large rural holdings] would come.[17]

At the other extreme swarmed right-wing anarchists, genuine, active anarchists. For the moment, the royalists had given up large-scale armed uprisings, real insurrections. Civil war was splintered into individual actions. Its current form was political brigandage. If Jacobinism was one career for scoundrels and desperate men, highway robbery by royalists was another. . . .

Although this kind of rural terrorism was more or less the common fate of all France, political brigandage centered in certain areas. In the West, *Chouannerie* spread again through nine or ten departments. This large ulcer kept all the surrounding areas irritated and feverish. If we cut obliquely across central France to its southeastern limits, the Bouches-du-Rhône, Vaucluse, Var, and Basses-Alpes

---

[15] Jean-Nicolas Dufort, Comte de Cheverny, *Mémoires sur les règnes de Louis XV et Louis XVI et sur la Révolution* (Paris: Plon, Nourrit, 1886), II, 376.

[16] [A reference to the radical revolutionary Babeuf, a proponent of economic equality who was guillotined in 1797.—Eds.]

[17] Dufort, II, 365. Dufort de Cheverny lived in Blésois. His *Memoirs* are valuable. Written by a man free of strong passions, they are almost a day-by-day history of the Revolution in an average department.

departments, we find another *Chouannerie,* that of Provence, a *Chouannerie* whose history has still to be written. Along the entire lower and middle valley of the Rhône River, there were scattered acts of vengeance—Nemesis unchained hovered over this whole murderous region. The Pyrenees region remained in continuous ferment. Along the Cévennes mountains there were remnants of the royalist bands which had made religious war on the Convention and Directory. In most of the other departments brigandage occurred sporadically, appearing as scattered crimes. Even in the vicinity of the capital no road was entirely safe. More than a year after the establishment of the Consulate, a stagecoach was held up at Charenton [a suburb southeast of Paris].[18] Any place that was suitable for ambushes experienced a marked increase in insecurity; it seemed as though the Revolution had spread the Forest of Bondy [a legendary haunt of robbers] everywhere.

Aside from the West, the Midi, and some regions in central France, brigandage almost lost its aspect of counterrevolutionary guerrilla warfare to become simple forays by deserters, vagrants, or *chauffeurs* [robbers who would burn their victims' feet until they revealed where their money was hidden]. Nevertheless, these ruffians tried to give themselves a political coloration by destroying republican symbols and by preferring to attack government officials and buyers of land confiscated from the Church or *émigrés.* Even in Paris and its suburbs, some royalist commandos, precursors of Cadoudal and his companions, dreamed of abducting or assassinating the Directors.[19] No beneficiary of the Revolution felt completely secure from attack by these armed and vagrant bands.

Against this persistent disorder, from wherever it came, the public authorities were able to do little or nothing. Although innumerable communes were in a state of siege, their means of defense were often lacking; for the continuation of the war kept the largest part of the army out of the country. The rural constabulary was poorly organized and infected by the presence in its ranks of formerly active Jacobins. The units of the National Guard—from which were recruited the flying columns assigned to chase bands of thieves and to organize roundups—were weak and disheartened. The ever changing, unstable civil authorities nowhere constituted a meaningful protective force. . . .

Wherever government action played a part, the harshest and most thoroughgoing tyranny was added to revolutionary disorder. Whoever was not in armed revolt against the law or did not evade it by subterfuge had to endure its cruelty. The revolutionaries in power, although they spurned the Jacobin label and had not reopened that famous club, still remained infected by the Jacobin spirit—the urge to persecute. Liberty existed for the Jacobins alone; they refused it to others, while ordering everyone to worship it on his knees. They had made the word divine but forbade the real thing. This is why the French welcomed Bonaparte as a liberator and so easily exchanged the oppression of wretched despots for a lofty and impartial tyranny.

[18] MS Papers of General Mortier, Commander of the Seventeenth Division. Archives of Trévise. The Duc de Trévise kindly allowed us to consult these papers.
[19] See the documents cited by André Lebon, *L'Angleterre et l'émigration française de 1794 à 1801* (Paris: Plon, 1882), pp. 265–269. [Cadoudal was a Vendean leader who, in 1803–1804, plotted to assassinate Napoleon.—Eds.]

Among the accepted legends about 18 Brumaire, none is more erroneous than the supposition that it brought the death of liberty. For a long time it was a historical commonplace to present Bonaparte in the Council Hall of the Five Hundred at Saint-Cloud[20] destroying a genuine legality with one stroke of his sword and smothering, while his drums rolled, the last gasps of French liberty. Such solemn nonsense can no longer be repeated in the presence of some clearly recognized and understood facts. Bonaparte can be reproached for not having established liberty, he cannot be accused of having destroyed it; for the excellent reason that on his return from Egypt it was nowhere to be found in France. He could not end something that did not exist. In the early days of the Directory, amidst violent reactionary movements, tension had started to relax and a few liberties were recognized. But the death of liberty came not on 18 Brumaire but on 18 Fructidor [September 4, 1797], when the revolutionaries, to stop a resurgence of royalism, ruthlessly seized dictatorial power again. After this coup d'état against the nation, almost all the liberties constitutionally guaranteed to the French were forcefully snatched away or treacherously withdrawn.

The primary right of a free people is to elect representatives and through them control the management of public affairs. All persons authorized by the constitution to exercise the rights of citizenship should cooperate in this delegation of sovereignty. In the Fructidorian Directory, according to a series of special laws, a whole category of Frenchmen—relatives of *émigrés* as well as ex-nobles who had not given formal pledges of loyalty to the Revolution—were excluded from the right to vote and to hold office. In addition, the legislature, twice purged—in Fructidor [September 1797] and in Floréal [May 1798]—did not at all represent a true image of the electorate, which already had been arbitrarily reduced in number. The representation was in essence corrupt and fictitious, a mockery.

Public platforms were available only to those revolutionaries furnished with the government's stamp of approval. The press was servile. After the coup of Fructidor a decree of deportation had been issued against the owners and editors of thirty-five opposition newspapers, a radical method of destroying them. Thereafter, a law of the year V [September 5, 1797], which was renewed in the year VI, submitted all newspapers to supervision by the police, who suppressed them at their pleasure and at their discretion. Public opinion no longer had a channel of expression. Freedom of association and assembly appeared only in the text of the constitution. At any moment arrests arbitrarily carried out and arbitrarily upheld could outrage individual liberty.

Religious liberty existed only in words. After the Terror and the great sacrilegious madness of 1793, the Convention returned to fundamentals and proclaimed religious freedom. The law of 3 Ventôse, year III [February 21, 1795], declared, "The exercise of any religious cult shall not be disturbed, and the Republic will not subsidize any of them." In this way the separation of Church and State replaced the celebrated Civil Constitution of the Clergy, and the Schismatic [Constitutional] Church lost its privileged position. The law declared all cults free of control and placed them on an equal footing before the State. In actual fact this

[20] [The château near Paris where the last act of the coup d'état took place.—Eds.]

theoretical freedom was reduced by the Convention to a minimum by the way in which it was regulated. Toward the Christian cults the State called itself neutral and remained hostile.[21] . . .

Sometimes the revolutionaries had to accept strange anomalies. In this France dotted with monasteries falling into ruin and desecrated cloisters, some female religious orders were still permitted to continue—those devoted to helping the poor and caring for the sick. Nothing else could be done, for there was no one to replace them. At the famous Hospital of Beaune in Burgundy, the sisters doffed their four-century-old garb, but managed to keep the hospital a Catholic stronghold. In a rather large number of communes and even right in the middle of Paris—at the Hôtel-Dieu [a large city hospital]—the sisters, dressed as nurses, furtively continued to serve humanity.[22]

Elsewhere the antireligious mania exceeded all limits, reaching the height of absurdity and ridiculousness. The executive order of 14 Germinal, year IV [April 3, 1796], forbade the selling of fish on what formerly had been called Friday; war was declared on fasting; fish was prohibited as Catholic contraband—to the great distress of our fisheries; in Paris, the oratory was closed in the former Carmelite chapel because the feast of Epiphany had been celebrated there;[23] in Strasbourg a merchant was fined for displaying in his shop more fish than usual on a fast day; and 350 truck gardeners were prosecuted for hallowing Sunday by not bringing their vegetables to market on that day.[24] Such severe measures continued until after Brumaire with local officials acting as the clumsy instruments of the rationalist tyranny. O Reason, what stupidities are committed in thy name! . . .

The Fructidorian Directory kept itself in power by war and victory; it succumbed in a crisis brought on by defeat and aggravated by domestic scandal. After the death of General Hoche and Bonaparte's departure for Egypt, the Directory continued the policy of conquest, or rather of plunder—occupying territories for their money, holding governments for ransom, pillaging the people, making France an object of execration. Rome was invaded. Switzerland was literally sacked. After General Championnet conquered Naples, the Austrians, who had considered the peace of Campo-Formio only a truce, reopened hostilities; the Congress of Rastadt had its bloody epilogue;[25] all of Germany except Prussia seemed ready to fight once more; England supplied ships and subsidies; and finally a Russian army came down from the North. The Second Coalition was formed. Aided everywhere by insurrections, it threatened our conquests and soon our frontiers. Against us was this second kings' war and the first peoples' war.

The Directory ran dreadfully short of money. It had been unable to solve the

---

[21] While speaking of the revolutionaries of the year III, Antonin Debidour was quite right to say: "In general they saw that the separation of Church and State, recently put into effect, was simply a means of destroying the Church." *Histoire des rapports de l'Église et de l'État en France de 1789 à 1870* (Paris: Alcan, 1898), p. 158.

[22] See especially Léon Lallemand, *La Révolution et les pauvres* (Paris: Picard, 1898), pp. 137–146.

[23] Ludovic Sciout, *Le Directoire* (Paris: Didot, 1895–1897), III, 176.

[24] The documents are cited *ibid.*, III, 390.

[25] [Two of the three French delegates to the Congress, when returning to France in 1799, were murdered by Austrian soldiers.—Eds.]

problems arising from an unprecedented monetary crisis and from the ruin of public finance. No one questioned that there was a deficit, the only issue was its size. The executive listed the figure at 67 million francs, but the Councils tended to reduce the estimate so as to avoid voting new taxes.[26] When the ministers and department heads were questioned, it appeared that the abyss was bottomless. All expedients, all subterfuges, had been tried in turn. Abroad, the conquered territories yielded no more money. At home the taxpayers refused to pay any levies; and the government felt itself unable to force them, since it had not succeeded in establishing a regular method of collection. It fell more and more into the hands of a tremendous gang of exploiters, for whom it was less an accomplice than a victim.

A swarm of suppliers and contractors relentlessly set upon the Republic. Summoned to provide for the needs of the various departments and especially the War Ministry, they turned the regime into an object of cynical speculation. Having to deal with a government that paid irregularly and with light-fingered public employees, they thought only of insuring for themselves excessive guarantees and illegal profits. They billed the state for the graft given to its employees, forced ruinous contracts on it, drained off the little cash that remained in the Treasury's coffers, and delivered only worthless materials.[27] This was the era of gigantic plundering and vile swindles, of massive influence peddling, and of illegal commissions and rebates to lower officials. The era of all kinds of dishonor, the age of mud after the age of blood. This nearly universal plundering found its way into the mainspring of state power and submerged it in a heap of mire; but when the spring had to be used against foreigners, everything had become decayed and rotten.

Our soldiers were without provisions, without shoes, "without pots, kettles, and mess-tins," [28] without linen for the wounded, and without medicine for the sick. And they had to fight enemies much more redoubtable than those of 1792 and 1793: in Germany Archduke Charles and in Italy the strange Russian general Suvarov, a man who joined to the extravagances of an eccentric the talents of a great leader and the soul of a crusader. With us, politics often determined the assignment of generals. What is more, the excessive length of our line of

---

[26] According to the recent and learned work of René Stourm, *Les Finances du Consulat* (Paris: Guillaumin, 1902), pp. 270–271, the deficit was 300 million *at the very least.*

[27] A report written after Brumaire by a former minister, General de Beurnonville, gives an idea of the way things were done in the Department of War. "It is, I believe, mathematically provable that the government overpays by more than 50 per cent for all supplies that it receives. . . . Just imagine the path a supplier has to travel. Without the minister's knowledge, he pays an enormous bribe when his contract is signed. Often his contacts take, more or less, 5 or 10 per cent of the profits. In order to put the agreement into effect, the contractor hires his own minions who get rid of the former subcontractors and who, knowing full well that the job is temporary, think only of making a killing. In return for a share of the take, their supervisors become their accomplices. Step by step, all this mounting individual greed raises the costs by fake accounting until they are often double, or more, the value of the actual goods supplied. The State thus finds itself in debt for what it has not received; and it is only by such a system that the contractor is paid back for the sacrifices that he has made to get the contract, for the losses that he has suffered by the manner in which he is paid, and for the delays in the final payment settling the account." Archives of the Ministry of War, MS Correspondance générale, 1799.

[28] *Le Publiciste,* 6 Thermidor, year VIII [July 25, 1800].

operations—stretching from Texel [an island north of Amsterdam] to Naples—offered the enemy openings for attack. Together, these causes led to a series of disasters in Germinal, Floréal, and Prairial of the year VII (March to June 1799): Jourdan defeated at Stokach in southern Baden and forced back to the Rhine; Schérer and Moreau defeated in Italy; Lombardy lost; the Cisalpine Republic swept away; Piedmont entered by Suvarov; Naples evacuated; the overthrow of all the governments established by France in Italy. Within France, agitation in the West became more serious; and in the Midi a campaign of brigandage and assassination continued. In the light of these disastrous events, the inability of the Directory stood clearly revealed. The errors and shamefulness of this dictatorship by incompetents appeared in sharp relief. An outcry of disgust and criticism arose in the army. In Paris the muzzled press could say nothing, and the political agitation of the parties continued to operate on a level above the general apathy. Nevertheless, without the Directory noticing the formation of an organized, vocal, and open opposition, the regime collapsed by itself under the weight of its own misdeeds. . . .

In the minds of its civilian authors, the coup d'état of 1799 was to take place for precisely the same reason as had those of 18 Fructidor and 22 Floréal. It was inspired by a passionate desire for political survival. Differing from other coups carried out by men who had nothing to lose and everything to gain, this one was the act of those who had a terrible fear of losing everything. To this motive was added, among some, the honorable desire to purify and regenerate the Republic, to start it at last on a normal course. They wanted to create a true constitutional order in place of the one that Fructidor and Floréal had virtually abolished and they wanted to insure, by a final illegal step, the reign of law.

The Legend Combated

ALBERT GOODWIN

For biographical information on Albert Goodwin, see Chapter 3,
"Who Was Responsible for the War of 1792?"

The French Executive Directory which assumed office on 11 Brumaire year IV (2
November 1795), and was destroyed by Bonaparte's *coup d'état* of 18 Brumaire year
VIII (9 November 1799), has been traditionally regarded by historians as a byword
for corruption, governmental incompetence and political instability.[1] Its rule is
usually associated with the financial bankruptcy of 1797, defeats of French armies in
the field, administrative chaos at home and the Directors' policy of self-perpetuation
in office by means of a series of "purifications" of the elected Assemblies. In 1799
the Directory is supposed to have been ripe for dissolution and France ready for
Bonaparte. It is the purpose of this paper to suggest that such an interpretation does
not do full justice to the governmental record of the Directory between 1795 and
1799, and that it represents an over-simplification of the situation in France on the
eve of 18 Brumaire.

It is not difficult to see why, in the past, the Directors have been so harshly
treated. The assumption that the Directors were themselves not exempt from the
vices of corruption and immorality characteristic of French society at that date was
perhaps unavoidable, especially as the Directory came to be identified in the popular
mind with Barras. This impression of Barras as representative of the general
standards of the Directory, although entirely erroneous, was to some extent
intelligible. Of the thirteen individuals who at various times held office as Directors,
Barras alone succeeded in retaining his position throughout, and he was
undoubtedly the most colourful personality of them all. The danger of generalising
from the single case of Barras is, however, obvious. Another reason why injustice
has been done to the Directory is that French history between 1795 and 1799 has
tended to be studied by historians, very largely for the sake of convenience, as a

---

From Albert Goodwin, "The French Executive Directory—A Revaluation," *History*, n.s., XXII
(December 1937), 201–218. The entire article is reprinted by permission of the author and the editor of
History. Quotations originally in French have been translated by the editors.

[1] The chapter on "Brumaire" by H. A. L. Fisher in the *Cambridge Modern History*, VIII (1904),
665–88, in the main, follows rather closely the opinions of Vandal, but also expresses views which do
not altogether accord with them, so that the total effect does not seem altogether consistent.

period of *coups d'état*.[2] This approach has had two unfortunate results. On the one hand, it has gained general acceptance for the impression that the age was one of perpetual crisis, thus distracting attention from the more solid achievements of the Directory, and, on the other, it has led to the supposition that it was this series of illegal expedients alone which ensured their survival. It is true that an informed interpretation of the *coups d'état* is essential for the understanding of the period, but due attention should be paid to other factors. Lastly, the reputation of the Directors may have suffered because it has been blackened by the apologists of Robespierre and the admirers of Bonaparte. Between Mathiez,[3] who spent a lifetime in defending the Jacobin leader, and Madelin,[4] equally intent on eulogising Bonaparte, the Directors have come in for a good deal of unmerited abuse. Few French historical scholars have been able to free themselves from partisanship in their accounts of the revolution, and the way in which the work of the Directory has been consistently underrated as a means of heightening the contrasts with the immediately preceding or following period is a good illustration of the evils implicit in such zeal. In this way a popular failure to distinguish between Barras and the other Directors, an inadequate historical approach and unconcealed historical bias have combined to enhance the evil repute and minimise the achievements of the Directorate. Recently, however, the researches of French scholars, by making possible a juster appreciation of the record of the Directory, have demonstrated the necessity of re-examining the unfavourable judgments which have often been passed on its rule.

Shortly stated, the usual indictment may be said to be based on four main charges—that the personnel of the Directory was both corrupt and incapable; that its administration of the finances brought the country within measurable distance of ruin; that its foreign policy involved an indefinite postponement of the prospects of a general peace; and, finally, that the government could not even fulfil the first condition of effective rule by securing public order and individual freedom at home. What modifications must be made in these charges in the light of the fuller evidence which is now available?

On the score of venality there is ample authority for the view that the Directors themselves were, with perhaps a single exception, reasonably honest. The corruption of Barras was, of course, notorious and remains indefensible.[5] The evidence against the rest, however, is slight. Certain passages in Thibaudeau's *Memoirs* suggest that Reubell, who for some time virtually controlled Directorial finance, deserved censure,[6] and some suspicion was apparently directed against

---

[2] Recent examples of this treatment are A. Meynier, *Les coups d'état du Directoire*, 3 vols., and C. Brinton, *A Decade of Revolution 1789–1799*, chap. IX. Brinton, however, takes a much more favourable view of the Directory than most writers. See also Sorel, *L'Europe et la Révolution française*, vol. v, p. 11.

[3] At the time of his death in February 1932 Mathiez was engaged on a detailed study of the Directory the first volume of which, covering the period down to 18 Fructidor, was published in 1934.

[4] See particularly *La France du Directoire; La France de l'Empire; Le Consulat et l'Empire* and *Napoléon*.

[5] Gohier, President of the Directory on 18 Brumaire, was anxious to rid the government of Barras and thus to make its moral standing unassailable. A. Vandal, *L'Avènement de Bonaparte*, vol. i, p. 323.

[6] Thibaudeau, *Mémoires*, vol. ii, p. 37.

Merlin de Douai and La Revellière. It is true that Reubell's reputation for financial integrity was not unblemished, since he had suffered disgrace for peculation under the Terror,[7] and he was well known to be avaricious. On the other hand, there is no real evidence against him of corruption while a Director, and it should also be remembered that the Commissions of Inquiry specially appointed by the Councils to investigate his guilt in August 1799 completely exonerated him as well as Merlin and La Revellière.[8] When he retired from the Directory by lot on 16 May 1799, Reubell felt compelled to accept the allowance given by his colleagues as compensation,[9] and he died poor. The rest of the Directors seem never to have been the objects of contemporary criticism on the ground of their dishonesty.

How far is it true to say that the Directors were individually men without ability? For the present purpose it is only necessary to consider the members of the original Directory and three others—François de Neufchâteau, Merlin de Douai and Treilhard. Sieyès may properly be excepted, as his efforts, after he became a Director, were concentrated on the destruction of the constitution of the year III. The others may be disregarded because of the shortness of their period of office—Barthélemy was in power three and a half months, Gohier less than six months, Ducos and Moulin four and a half months. The usual opinion of the original Directory—"les Pentarques"—is that they were a group of mediocrities. If only the highest standards are applied, such a judgment would not be unfair. But if the ordinary criteria of capacity are accepted, then the Directors must be credited with more than average ability. Mature they were bound to be since article 134 of the constitution insisted that they should be at least forty years of age, and although the manner of their nomination left something to be desired,[10] they were all men of wide experience, most of them with special aptitudes and qualifications for the conduct of the departments of government they controlled. The least remarkable from the point of view of sheer ability were Le Tourneur and Barras. Le Tourneur was entirely devoid of political gifts, and in all matters of policy he followed without question the lead of his school-friend Carnot. He did, however, possess a good knowledge of the technical side of naval affairs. The Directory needed a naval expert, and Le Tourneur admirably filled the gap. Similarly, it would be hard to think of any revolutionary leader, apart from Fouché, better fitted to organise the police than Barras, whose whole life had been spent in intrigue. Nor is it accurate to regard Barras as a political cipher. Especially when resolute action was needed, Barras could be counted on, as he had already shown on 9 Thermidor and 13 Vendémiaire.[11] That he had an eye for talent as well as for beauty is proved by those

[7] A. Mathiez, Le Directoire, p. 44.

[8] Lefebvre, Guyot, Sagnac, La Révolution française, p. 457.

[9] Meynier, Les coups d'état du Directoire, vol. 11, pp. 168–9.

[10] They were the nominees of the former members of the Convention, two-thirds of whom had been re-elected to the new Councils. The procedure for their nomination was that the Council of Five Hundred submitted a list of fifty candidates from whom the Council of Ancients made the final choice. The list drawn up by the Five Hundred consisted of forty-five complete nonentities and the five persons whom they wished to be elected. This manœuvre was completely successful in forcing a group of "hand-picked" Directors on the Ancients. Mathiez, Le Directoire, p. 36.

[11] [On both occasions, Barras had organised troops to defend the Convention against armed popular demonstrations.—Eds.]

whose careers he helped to make—Bonaparte and Talleyrand, Saint-Simon and Ouvrard. Luck alone cannot account for his survival till 18 Brumaire.

La Revellière was in many ways a curious mixture, half crank, half fanatic, a botanist, student of Rousseau, high priest of the new revolutionary cult of Theophilanthropy and a believer in the *juste milieu* in politics. A sincere republican, he was consumed with a hatred of priests and aristocrats, and yet he had small liking for the rural or urban proletariat. In foreign policy he was an advocate of the war of propaganda and conquest—an attitude which he had consistently maintained ever since the day he had been the prime mover of the decree of 19 November 1792 by which the Convention had promised its aid and protection to all nations who wished to recover their liberty. His special sphere in Directorial policy was education, the *fêtes nationales* [patriotic holidays] and manufactures.

Carnot has been aptly described by Mathiez as "almost entirely a man of learning and a patriot." A former member of the Committee of Public Safety, and famous as the "Organiser of Victory," he had been nominated, in place of Sieyès, who had refused to serve as Director, in order to stem the run of French reverses on the Rhine. Carnot was a paragon of executive efficiency, and had real genius in the administration of war. He proved a failure as a Director, and for obvious reasons. He had a biting tongue and alienated his colleagues by his cynicisms. He was a convinced pacifist at a time when both Reubell and La Revellière, for different reasons, were keen supporters of foreign war. He disappointed the expectations of his Jacobin friends by evolving in the direction of the Right.[12] Lastly, although he had little or no talent for politics, he was never satisfied to confine himself to his departmental duties. Still, he can hardly be described as a mediocrity.

There is general agreement that Reubell was a man of great ability.[13] An Alsatian barrister of eminence, he had a good command of modern languages and an encyclopædic knowledge. He owed his ascendancy over his colleagues to his industry and his strength of will. Utterly devoid of scruple and severely practical, he may be described as the main driving force behind Directorial policy. At one time he maintained a close supervision over the three most important departments of government—justice, finance and foreign affairs. Subsequently, however, he was content to delegate responsibility to ministers of proved capacity, such as Merlin and Ramel, and concentrated his own attention on the conduct of diplomatic affairs. In this sphere he identified himself with the policy of conquest and expansion which he hoped would culminate in the acquisition of the natural frontiers. As Reubell was only eliminated from the Directory by lot in May 1799, his influence upon policy was exerted throughout, and gave it a much-needed continuity.

Of François de Neufchâteau, Merlin and Treilhard, it is only necessary to say that the former was a distinguished administrator whose work as Minister of the Interior conferred lasting benefits on the French state and anticipated many of the Napoleonic reforms, and that Merlin and Treilhard were the leading jurisconsults of

---

[12] He took an active part in the suppression of the conspiracy of Babeuf and the Jacobin plot of the year IV [September 1796] at the camp of Grenelle. He was evicted from the Directory along with Barthélemy on 18 Fructidor (4 September 1797), largely because of his moderate and royalist activities.

[13] R. Guyot, *Le Directoire et la Paix*, pp. 45–9.

the day. Any government which could count on their services might well have considered itself fortunate.

The subject of Directorial finance is both technical and controversial.[14] Here attention can only be directed towards one or two points which serve to modify the severe criticisms usually passed upon it. The two leading events upon which discussion has centred are the collapse of the Assignats in 1796 and the repudiation of two-thirds of the public debt in September 1797. Both these occurrences were, in some ways, regrettable, but, by themselves, do not entail an utter condemnation of the finance of the period. Their full significance does not lie on the surface, and can only be determined by a close study of the financial situation during the Terror and later under the Consulate. Each can, moreover, be interpreted in a way which considerably eases the burden of discredit to be borne by the Directory. The collapse of the Assignats prompted, it is true, an unsuccessful attempt to stabilise the paper currency by means of the *mandats territoriaux* in 1796, but this was followed by a return to a metallic currency without undue deflationary effects—a policy which may be said to have paved the way for that revival of confidence which is so often attributed to the Consulate. Similarly, the bankruptcy of 1797 should not be viewed in isolation, but be regarded as part and parcel of Ramel's economy campaign. Nor should it be overlooked that the bankruptcy itself was not only partial but conditional, and that the final blame for its becoming definite must rest with the Consulate. In fact, the suggested contrast between financial maladministration and chaos under the Directory and financial retrenchment and reform under the Consulate has no real relation to the facts, and should be abandoned. The foundation of the Bank of France in 1800 may have been symptomatic of a new regime, but it was only rendered possible by the financial reforms of the preceding period.

The immediate financial problem to be faced by the Directory was how to arrest the continued fall of the Assignats. One of the last acts of the Convention had been to establish by the law of 21 June 1795 a sliding scale of depreciation for contracts and other debts, the value of which was to be fixed according to the quantity of Assignats actually in circulation at the time of the signing of the contract. This experiment failed because it was not applied to all contracts and because the treasury had not a sufficient reserve.[15] The first important proposal made by the Directory was for a forced loan payable in specie, grain, or in Assignats taken at 1 per cent. of their face value (6 December 1795). The manufacture of Assignats was to be discontinued and the plates broken on 21 March following. As the Assignats were worth less than 1 per cent. of their nominal value, and as receipts for payments of the forced loan were to be accepted in payment of direct taxes, this plan really amounted to a timid attempt at deflation and an effort to increase the revenue from

---

[14] It is fair to say that M. Marion's standard work *Histoire financière de la France depuis 1715*, vols. III–IV, takes a highly unfavourable view of Directorial finance. Other authorities, however, such as Hawtrey, *Currency and Credit*, Chap. XV, and Pariset, *Études d'histoire révolutionnaire et contemporaine*, pp. 79–134, hold contrary opinions. See also R. Stourm, *Les Finances de l'Ancien Régime et de la Révolution*, vol. I, pp. 258–446, and the recent study *Les principes financiers de la Révolution* by J. Barthélemy in *Cahiers de la Révolution française*, vol. VI, pp. 7–44 (1937).

[15] Mathiez, *Le Directoire*, p. 91.

taxation.[16] The over-valuation of the Assignats and the lack of specie for their conversion, however, effectually ensured the failure of this scheme.

The next experiment—the issue on 18 March 1796 of *mandats territoriaux*—was devised by the Finance Minister, Ramel-Nogaret. These *mandats* were in effect a new form of paper money which it was hoped would gradually displace the Assignats and be immune from depreciation.[17] To render them attractive to the public they were to entitle the holders to obtain *biens nationaux* [expropriated Church and *émigré* lands] at the fixed valuation of twenty-two years' purchase of the annual value of 1790.[18] Unfortunately, however, a committee of the Council of Five Hundred made the Assignats convertible into *mandats territoriaux* at one-thirtieth of their nominal value. Thus, although the new facility provided for the acquisition of unsold national property prevented the *mandats* from depreciating immediately, they were bound to collapse eventually because of the over-valuation of the Assignats in terms of the new paper currency.[19] It had been thought that the capitalists would eagerly take up the *mandats* in order to acquire the estates of the Belgian monasteries, but the more cautious of them hesitated to buy property so near to the frontier before the conclusion of a general peace, while the speculators preferred to discredit the *mandats* in order to effect purchases at a later stage at less cost. An additional difficulty was that the new currency was not immediately available, since the government only issued *promesses de mandats*.[20] For these reasons the *mandats* failed to gain general acceptance, and despite the efforts of the government to force their currency, they quickly fell to a discount. In the course of July, August and September 1796 laws were passed whereby the *mandats* were to be accepted by the government in payment for taxes and in exchange for *biens nationaux* at their market price only. The *mandats* were finally withdrawn from circulation by a law of 4 February 1797. Thus failed the Directory's main effort at stabilisation. The failure was not, however, without its redeeming features, since it at all events prevented the inflation from getting completely out of hand, and it did in fact result in the resumption of a metallic standard.

In its essentials, the "repudiation" of 1797 was a comparatively simple operation. The law of 9 Vendémiaire year VI (30 September 1797) enacted that one-third only of the public debt should be consolidated and entered on the Grand Livre as a sacred charge,[21] and that the capital of the other two-thirds should be redeemed by the issue to stockholders of bearer bonds *(bons des deux tiers mobilisés)*. By way of compensation, the state guaranteed that interest payments should in the

[16] Lefebvre, Guyot, Sagnac, *La Révolution française*, p. 319.

[17] R. G. Hawtrey, *Currency and Credit*, p. 256.

[18] Although secured upon the *biens nationaux*, the Assignats had never given holders the right to any particular share of this security. Previously the national lands had been put up for auction and sold to the highest bidder.

[19] G. Pariset, *Études d'histoire révolutionnaire et contemporaine*, p. 84. The 100-livre Assignat was then worth 7 sous, so that 100 livres *mandats* equivalent to 3000 livres Assignats would have been worth only 10 francs.

[20] Hawtrey, *Currency and Credit*, p. 256; Marion, *Histoire financière*, vol. III, p. 471.

[21] The Great Book or Register of the public debt had been opened by Cambon on 24 May 1793 with the object of consolidating the debt which had been issued under various denominations before the revolution. See *Cahiers de la Révolution française*, vol. VI, pp. 39–40.

future be made subject to no deductions as they had been in the past,[22] and that the *bons des deux tiers* should be available for the purchase of national property.

It is clear that many of the contemporary arguments in support of the measure were either specious or merely absurd. Such, for example, was the suggestion that no injustice to fundholders would be involved, since their stock had already lost two-thirds of its value owing to the inflation.[23] Yet repudiation ignored the possibility of a recovery in the value of the public debt and made the former losses irretrievable. Another contention was that the bankruptcy would have a depressing psychological effect on France's enemies, who would be more anxious to sue for peace when they saw the financial burdens of the French state thus lightened. If this view had been correct, the question was, Why did the Directory stop short of complete repudiation? A much more probable result would have been that the consequent loss of public credit would have prevented France herself from continuing the war. Equally it must be admitted that the bankruptcy demolished the incomes of the rentier class. An example will suffice to show the extent of the injury and to elucidate the actual nature of the operation. A rentier with a capital of 3000 livres invested in the public debt which before September 1797 had given him, at 5 per cent., 150 livres interest, now received 50 livres as interest on one-third of his capital *(tiers consolidé)* and a nominal holding of 2000 livres in *bons des deux tiers mobilisés.* In the final liquidation of 30 Ventôse year IX (21 March 1801), when the two-thirds were converted into perpetual annuities at the rate of ¼ per cent. of their capital value, the 2000 livres would be exchanged for an annuity of 5 livres. The net result was that instead of receiving 150 livres interest, the fundholder received 55 livres, which meant that 63.34 per cent. of his capital had been destroyed.[24] In this way the state repudiated in all nearly 2,000,000,000 livres of public debt.[25] The consequent shock to public credit may be imagined. The spectre of national bankruptcy which had haunted Mirabeau in the early days of the revolution had at last materialised. In M. Barthélemy's words, "The Directory misunderstood the overriding importance of maintaining the government's credit. It thought it could evade economic laws that were inflexible, but in so doing it came to grief. The repudiation of two-thirds of the debt weighed heavily on France's credit for a long time." [26]

It is, however, necessary to say in defence of the consolidation that bankruptcy in France had really been made inevitable by the misguided financial policy of the Constituent Assembly. The issue of the Assignats and the failure to levy sufficient taxation to balance the budgets had compromised the efforts of all subsequent administrations to grapple with financial shortage.[27] The repudiation of 1797 was, in fact, only part of a larger scheme to effect reforms in the French budget. By reducing governmental expenditure from 1,000,000,000 to 616,000,000 livres,

---

[22] In March 1795 the perpetual annuities had been made liable to a stoppage of a tenth and the life annuities to a deduction of a twentieth.

[23] Marion, *Histoire financière*, vol. III, p. 64.

[24] R. Stourm, *Les Finances de l'Ancien Régime et de la Révolution*, vol. II, p. 342.

[25] G. Pariset, *Études d'histoire révolutionnaire*, p. 86.

[26] *Cahiers de la Révolution française*, vol. VI, p. 44.

[27] R. Stourm, *op. cit.,* vol. II, p. 341.

Ramel was able, for the first time in the history of revolutionary finance, to establish a balanced budget. Part of this economy was achieved by drastic reductions in the military estimates, but the main saving came from the consolidation of the public debt. The financial end in view was, therefore, sound enough in the circumstances, although the means were not. Finally, the responsibility for the final liquidation of 21 March 1801 must be borne by the Consulate. The real bankruptcy only came after the Directory had fallen.

One aspect of Directorial finance, also mainly due to Ramel, which deserves more general recognition, was the recasting of the whole system of direct and indirect taxation. Concentrated in the short interval of peace between the preliminaries of Leoben and the war of the Second Coalition [April 1797 to March 1799], these reforms present several points of interest. The new legislation relating to direct taxation was to be one of the most lasting achievements of the revolution, for it survived down to 1914. Some of it was fairly obviously a direct imitation of the younger Pitt's war finance, while the altered arrangements for the assessment and collection of revenue afford one more instance of a reorganisation, the credit for which has been wrongly attributed to the Consulate. Finally, the fresh recourse to indirect taxation, itself a result of inflation, marked a significant reversal of the taxation policy of the early years of the revolution.

The first direct tax to be reorganised was the tax on trade licences *(contribution des patentes)*. This had been re-established in 1795, not for fiscal purposes, but as a means of preventing unjustifiable trade practices. Some changes were introduced in the method of its assessment in 1796, and the final adjustments were made by the law of 22 October 1798. The land tax *(contribution foncière)* assumed definitive shape in the law of 23 November 1798, the new tax on doors and windows in that of 24 November. The latter duty, payable in the first case by the owner, but ultimately by the tenant, encountered considerable opposition, on the ground of its English origin. It may be regarded as a first approximation to an income tax, and the manner in which it was first doubled (1 March 1799) and then quadrupled (23 May 1799) as a means of meeting renewed war expenditure may be compared with Pitt's tripling of certain assessed taxes in 1797. Lastly, on 23 December 1798, the *contribution mobilière et personnelle* which was partly a poll tax and partly a tax on movable property was entirely reconstructed. These four direct taxes (subsequently known as *les quatre vieilles*) formed the essential structure of the French taxation system down to the outbreak of the [First] World War.[28] Equally important was the change instituted on 13 November 1798, whereby the assessment and collection of the direct taxes and the adjudications on appeals were removed from the hands of local elected bodies and entrusted to committees composed entirely of officials and working in the departments under the direct control of a commissioner of the central government. This fundamental reform was not inaugurated, but only continued by the Consulate. The only modification subsequently introduced was the change in the name of the officials.[29]

Some of the features of the legislation on direct taxation reappeared in the

---

[28] Pariset, *Études d'histoire révolutionnaire*, pp. 87–8.

[29] Lefebvre, Guyot, Sagnac, p. 442.

revival of the indirect taxes. The very adoption of indirect taxation marked a reaction against the financial policy of the Constituent Assembly which had relied almost exclusively on direct taxes. Some of the new duties, such as the highway tolls, imposed on 10 September 1797, were again adopted from England. And hardly less permanent than *les quatre vieilles* were the new mortgage, registration and stamp duties (November–December 1798).[30] Other indirect taxes which proved indispensable were those on powder and saltpetre (30 August 1797), on gold and silver ornaments (9 November 1797), playing-cards (30 September 1798) and tobacco (22 November 1798).

A tendency to exaggerate the financial straits of the government may have inclined historians to accept with greater willingness Sorel's thesis that continued European war became a necessity to the Directors.[31] The theory is at least plausible. On Sorel's view, war would ensure that the French armies would be occupied and prevented from interfering in politics at Paris, that the cost of clothing and feeding the troops would be borne by the foreigner, and that the empty coffers of the republic would be replenished by the confiscations and forced contributions levied on the conquered countries. Several unjustifiable assumptions have, however, to be made if this position is to be upheld. Sorel's assertion that France was "without industry, credit, or public confidence" is demonstrably false.[32] French industry might very well have absorbed the returned French armies—they need not necessarily have been put on half-pay. Nor should generalisations about the financial resources which the government drew from the activities of its armies abroad be accepted without caution. It requires to be proved that the war provided on balance a net income for the Directory. What figures we have point in the opposite direction.[33] Moreover, if the main danger to the executive government was felt to be the existence of a class of ambitious generals, the real solution would have been not to prolong but to curtail the war, and thus to put an end to the extravagant pretensions and illicit gains of the commanders.[34] There could be little doubt that the country as a whole wanted peace, and the Directors knew it. On *a priori* grounds, therefore, it is conceivable that the problems of peace confronting the Directory would not have been so insuperable as they have been made out.

Nor does the actual diplomacy of the period disprove the contention that the Directors were not averse from the conclusion of a satisfactory peace. The failure of the conference at Lille in July 1797, when [the British representative] Malmesbury had Pitt's instructions to spare no efforts for peace, was not entirely the result of the purge of the moderate party in the *coup d'état* of Fructidor[35] or of the overbearing attitude of the Triumvirate [Barras, Reubell, La Revellière]. The breakdown must be placed at the door of Barras and Talleyrand, whose secret intrigues both before

[30] Pariset, *ut sup.,* p. 90.

[31] *L'Europe et la Révolution française,* vol. v, p. 12.

[32] *Ibid.*

[33] In 1795 Cambon estimated the average cost of the war at 2,000,000,000 livres. The highest figure given for the total extraordinary revenues drawn from abroad is that of Sciout, who places it at between 1,000,000,000 and 1,500,000,000. Pariset, p. 91.

[34] Meynier, *Les coups d'état du Directoire,* vol. II, p. 185.

[35] This is the impression given by Dr. Holland Rose in his *Short Life of Pitt,* p. 143.

and after Fructidor did so much to prevent the English and French governments from reaching a frank understanding.[36] Malmesbury at the outset agreed to the preliminary conditions put forward by the French agents. Recognition was given to the Republic, the annexation of Belgium and the French treaties of alliance with Holland and Spain. At the same time, however, he excepted secret treaties and made no promise about a "general restoration" of conquered colonies. The French negotiators, Le Tourneur, former Director, Admiral Pléville Le Pelley and Maret, accepted Malmesbury's reservations, although these were quite inconsistent with the public articles of the Spanish treaty and the secret treaty with Holland. This initial ambiguity, with regard to the surrender of Dutch and Spanish colonies, was never explained to the Directory by its representatives.[37] When, therefore, Malmesbury claimed the Cape and Ceylon, the Directory refused to consider his demands. Nevertheless, such was England's desire for peace that the government was even prepared to surrender the colonial conquests without compensation. Meanwhile, as the result of a ministerial reshuffle of 16 July, Talleyrand had become Foreign Minister. His English connections, his hopes of profitable speculative dealings on the London exchange and his sincere desire for peace all inclined Talleyrand to smooth away difficulties. He and Barras accordingly encouraged Pitt to believe that the French government, in return for hard cash, would not insist on the surrender of the Cape and Ceylon.[38] Pitt consequently did not press the need for immediate concessions on his colleagues, and still reposed considerable faith in the prospects of the triumph of the moderates in Paris.

The precise effect of the *coup d'état* of 18 Fructidor upon the Lille conferences was that Le Tourneur, Maret and Colchen were replaced by Treilhard and Bonnier, who were instructed to present Malmesbury with a virtual ultimatum. It was to the effect that if he had not powers to cede all the English colonial conquests, he was to leave France, and not to return until he had. This new move, so far from being "a raising of the French terms," [39] marked a reversion to the original demands. The Directory had not been informed that these conditions would be unacceptable from the British point of view, and it is clear that the Directors thought that Fructidor would enable them to impose this settlement. The ultimatum was conceived not as a means to end the peace negotiations, but as a way of exacting the full price from an enemy known to be in great difficulty. Malmesbury, having no authority to make the concessions, left Lille on 17 September with little or no hope of return. The resumption of negotiations was finally prevented by the battle of Camperdown. The Directory has always been strongly criticised by English historians for its failure to close with Pitt's offers, but the responsibility must not be borne entirely by the Directors. It was the secret intrigues of French agents at Lille which stiffened the English resistance before Fructidor, and which, after the *coup d'état,* were the cause of French intransigence.

On the other hand, the approval which, under strong provocation from Bonaparte, the Directors gave to the preliminaries of Leoben and the final treaty of

[36] R. Guyot, *Le Directoire et la Paix*, pp. 431–56.
[37] *Ibid.,* pp. 413–15.
[38] Lefebvre, Guyot, Sagnac, p. 363.
[39] H. Rose, *Short Life of Pitt*, p. 143.

Campo Formio, cannot be regarded as indicative of the pacific views of the Directors. It is fairly certain that those treaties would have been rejected by the Directory if its hands had not been tied, and indeed the best interests of France demanded that Bonaparte's policy should have been set aside. The Directors had, in each case, ample room for dissatisfaction. At Leoben, Bonaparte, anxious to monopolise the credit of having concluded peace, speeded up negotiations in order to prevent the official French negotiator, General Clarke, from arriving in time to share the discussions. In the public articles of the preliminaries of peace Bonaparte renounced the left bank of the Rhine, towards the acquisition of which Reubell's foreign policy had been mainly directed, and in the secret articles, by retaining the Duchy of Milan[40] and suggesting the partition of Venice, he definitely disobeyed his instructions for the first time since the inception of the Italian campaign.[41] In addition, it is clear that Bonaparte virtually conceded all that Thugut, the Austrian minister, wished to obtain. The principle of the integrity of the Empire was upheld, access to the Adriatic won, and the surrender by Austria of Belgium and Milan amply compensated for by her acquisition of part of Venice. When the articles of Leoben were read to them three of the Directors—Reubell, Barras and La Revellière—declared they were inacceptable, and the Minister for Foreign Affairs—Delacroix—also reported unfavourably on them. Yet on 30 April 1797 Reubell alone refused to sign the ratification of the preliminaries. The explanation must be sought in two ways—the Directors were compelled to accept Leoben because the French public, acquainted only with the public articles, had received the news with an enthusiasm which it would have been dangerous for the government to have damped, and, moreover, the rejection of the terms would have entailed an admission that Bonaparte's advance into Austria had in actual fact placed him in a very serious military position.[42]

These incidents were paralleled by the negotiations at Campo Formio. Bonaparte withdrew from Austrian territory without waiting for the ratification of the Leoben preliminaries by his home government, and again ignored his instructions. He had been ordered by the Directors to renew the war rather than surrender Venice, and also to insist on the compensation of Austria in Germany. The actual terms of peace, however, conceded most of the advantages to Austria. As a result of the exchange of territory, her position was strengthened both in Italy and Germany,[43] a check was placed on the ambitions of her rival Prussia, and she had the prospect of still further compensations if France succeeded in wresting the left bank of the Rhine from the representatives of the Empire in the projected congress at Rastadt. On the other hand, France deserted her ally Prussia, assumed a share of responsibility for the extinction of Venice, and erected in the Cisalpine Republic an uneasy neighbour whom it would be essential in the future to protect.

---

[40] The Directors wished for the cession of Milan to Austria and the acquisition of the left bank of the Rhine by inducing the Emperor and the German princes to accept compensation on the right bank.

[41] See the important new work by G. Ferrero, *Aventure: Bonaparte en Italie, 1796-1797*, passim.

[42] *Ibid.*, pp. 195-6. Owing to shortage of supplies and lack of co-operation from Germany, Bonaparte had been compelled either to treat with the Austrians or to retreat. He could not have continued the march on Vienna.

[43] Pariset, *La Révolution (1792-1799)*, pp. 369-70.

Once more the Directors submitted, but most unwillingly. They could not afford to forfeit the position they had just won after Fructidor, nor did they wish to see a revival of the European coalition against France, as seemed not unlikely after the failure of the Lille conferences.[44]

The net result of this double surrender on the part of the Directors was to deprive them of the initiative in French foreign policy and to substitute the Italian policy of Bonaparte for that of the natural frontiers as canvassed by Reubell. Moreover, in the years which followed Campo Formio the Directors did much successful work by assimilating the conquered territories in Belgium and on the left bank of the Rhine,[45] by protecting the Italian republics and by exerting further pressure on Great Britain. In fact, for a whole year after Fructidor, French influence on the Continent was virtually unchallenged, and the real reverses suffered by French arms and diplomacy and the revival of the second Coalition must be ascribed not to Directorial incompetence, but to the initiation of the Egyptian expedition—a venture devised by Bonaparte and Talleyrand.[46]

It is less easy to defend the inability of the Directors to secure internal peace and security. Here at least the record of the Directors was one of almost complete failure. This failure, however, only repeated the lapses of monarchical and previous revolutionary governments. Nor should it be overlooked that the task of maintaining public order in the provinces had become immeasurably more difficult under the Directory in consequence of the revival of royalism, the appearance of *chauffage* [bands of roving thieves], and the adoption of conscription (5 September 1798).[47] Conscription was applied at an unfortunate moment—just at the time when the French armies had sustained a series of severe defeats and when the prospect of starvation was greater among the fighting forces than at home. Evasion of the law and desertion both helped to swell the number of brigands, who were able to organise "reigns of terror" in various parts of the country. It is customary to blame the government for having done nothing to face up to these difficulties. A long series of measures designed especially to grapple with brigandage, however, affords little support to this criticism. One of the first acts of the Directory after its acceptance of office was to add a seventh ministry—that of general police—to the six ministries provided for in the constitution, and to institute exhaustive inquiries into the state of the *garde nationale* and the gendarmerie.[48] This investigation revealed defects which were, to some extent, remedied by a law of 17 April 1798 reforming the gendarmerie. Other administrative gaps were filled by the laws prescribing capital punishment for robbery with violence on the high roads and in private houses (15 May 1797), the law enforcing increased penalties against gaolers who connived at the escape of their prisoners (25 September 1797), and the law reforming the personnel of the criminal courts (10 January 1798).[49] It must be

[44] Guyot, *Le Directoire et la Paix*, p. 508.
[45] P. Sagnac, *Le Rhin français pendant la Révolution et l'Empire*, Chap. IV.
[46] See especially E. Dard, *Napoléon et Talleyrand*, pp. 26–30.
[47] A. Vandal, *L'avènement de Bonaparte*, vol. I, p. 18.
[48] M. Marion, *Le brigandage pendant la Révolution*, p. 68.
[49] M. Marion, *Le brigandage pendant la Révolution*, pp. 105, 106, 113.

admitted that these changes did not effect substantial improvement, but it is evident at least that the problem had been taken in hand. Above all, it should not be forgotten that in the Vendée, where political unrest had been so continuously dangerous to previous revolutionary governments, the problem may be said to have been solved by the Directory.

It only remains to summarise the reasons for thinking that the instability of the Directory has perhaps been exaggerated. This political insecurity has been ascribed partly to the Constitution of the year III, and partly to public hostility to the Directors and the general desire for a strong executive government on the eve of Brumaire. Further investigation, however, seems to be required before this line of argument can be regarded as satisfactory.

For, in the first case, there is something to be said for the view that the main constitutional difficulties of the Directors were in the course of time solved.[50] The necessity of having a majority of at least three to two for the transaction of business may have opened the way to differences of opinion among the Directors,[51] but after Fructidor (4 September 1797) the Triumvirate of Barras, Reubell and La Revellière removed this source of weakness. It was not until Reubell retired on 16 May 1799 and was replaced by Sieyès that this solidarity of the Directors was shaken.[52] Similarly, the lack of any power to dissolve the Councils did not seriously hamper the Directors, since resort could always be had to systematic corruption at the annual election of one-third of the Councils or to a *coup d'état*. Although the right of initiating legislation lay with the Council of Five Hundred, the Directors were not deprived of the power of giving effect to their policy, since the machinery of Directorial messages to the Legislative Assemblies proved an adequate substitute. Moreover, the formal absence of the power of initiation often provided the government with ready-made excuses when public opinion showed itself at all critical. Nor was the tenure of the Directory as a whole or of individual members of it really insecure. The life of the Directory was fixed at five years (Article 137)—a period which exceeded that of the Councils by two years and that of the Assemblies of 1791 and 1793 by three. As only one Director retired annually by lot, the political complexion of the executive could not be effectively altered by the Councils except after a wait of three years, and even then only on the unlikely assumption that the majority in the Councils remained stable. Finally, the substitution of three Consuls for five Directors at Brumaire left the form of the executive government very much the same.

Nor can French public opinion immediately before Brumaire be described as actively hostile to the Directors. The prevailing feeling was one of apathy rather than of antipathy. The initial reforming zeal of the revolutionaries had dwindled, people in the provinces had lost interest in electoral devices, and once the tide of victory against the foreigner had turned in favour of France the cry of *"La patrie en danger"* had lost its meaning. Now, in a situation of this kind the government in actual possession of power is not usually in a weak position, and it is doubtful whether in 1799 there was a general feeling in France that the overthrow of the

[50] M. Deslandres, *Histoire constitutionnelle de la France de 1789 à 1870*, vol. I, pp. 305 seq.
[51] Meynier, vol. III, p. 125.
[52] *Ibid.*, vol. II, p. 5.

Directory would do much to improve conditions. Hardly less widespread than apathy was fear—but this fear was of a peculiar kind: it was a fear of extremes, whether royalist or Jacobin. Fortunately for the Directors, the only formidable opposition to their rule came from precisely these two sources. For this reason the Directors had an easy means of prolonging themselves in office by *coups d'état* directed now against the Right, now against the Left. This *politique de bascule* [seesaw political policy] far from being an indication of the essential instability of the government can be regarded as a source of strength. Not only was it effective, it was also consonant with the best interests of the country at large. As the representatives of moderate republicanism, the Directors could in this sense lay claim to a good deal of popular support.

Whether or not Frenchmen were willing on the eve of Brumaire to exchange the republican Constitution of the year III for a military dictatorship cannot be decided with certainty. The difficulties encountered with the Council of Five Hundred at St. Cloud on 19 Brumaire, the cries of *"hors la loi"* [outlaw him] which greeted Bonaparte and the well-known sympathies of the Parisian troops, at least make it clear that the Constitution was still regarded as a bulwark against dictatorship.[53] Bonaparte's military prestige had been somewhat tarnished by his abandonment of the army in Egypt[54] and little was known of his political and administrative ability. As a peacemaker, he still enjoyed the reputation he had gained at Leoben and Campo Formio, but Sieyès evidently thought that he would be willing to accept subordinate political office. Perhaps Vandal got nearest to the truth when he said of Bonaparte, "He came to power by taking advantage of his universal prestige and a gigantic misunderstanding." The theory of an "inevitable" military dictatorship has had a long inning; has not the time arrived when it should be abandoned? France in the autumn of 1799 was economically prosperous, the danger of invasion had already been averted, the reforms of Ramel and Neufchâteau were beginning to bear fruit, and the fear of reviving Jacobinism, dating back to the law of the hostages [July 12, 1799], might easily have been dealt with in the usual way. In religious matters it is difficult to believe the persecution of the priests was any more effective in practice than the measures taken to ensure public order, and although the desire for a restoration of the altars may have been pressing, there was considerable anxiety lest with it there should be associated a return of the church lands.

If Bonaparte had been forty instead of thirty, would he not have remained faithful to his original idea of becoming a Director?

[53] Vandal, vol. I, pp. 279, 396.
[54] Gohier, *Mémoires*, vol. I, p. 174.

A Regime of
Contradictions

DENIS WORONOFF

Denis Woronoff (1939–   ), a graduate of the École normale
supérieure, taught there from 1966 to 1972. At present he is
attached to the French National Center of Scientific Research.
He has written articles on the French metallurgical industry
from 1785 to 1815 and a survey about the Directory, *La
République bourgeoise de Thermidor á Brumaire, 1794-1799*
(1972), from which the following selection is drawn.

When speaking of 9 Thermidor in his memoirs, [the politician of the Directory]
Thibaudeau quotes the remark of an *émigré*, "There are no longer any men in
France, only events." A harsh judgment, but many surely would not hesitate to
apply it to the period from the fall of Robespierre to the accession of Bonaparte; for
history seems to develop in a minor key during this period. In fact, these five years
convey an impression of confused mediocrity, of an interregnum without any
brilliance. In addition, the discredited or abandoned last stages of the Revolution
have found little favor among historians.

Yet this drab pause between two stimulating epochs is essential to understand
the birth of contemporary France. Beyond the incoherencies, pantomimes, and
scandals, one can see the amazing tenacity with which the republican bourgeoisie
sought to keep itself in power. The "respectable people" continuously sought the
"means to conclude the Revolution" . . . in a manner advantageous to themselves. They wanted to define through institutions, society, and ideology the system
that guaranteed and embodied their conquests. That this regime of notables
[influential people] could survive in its original form [the Constitution of 1795] only
by means of expedients does not detract from the interest and modernity of the
attempt. Powerful voices had been stilled. Would it stretch things too much to say
that after the noise and clamor have died away, it is easier to detect a different
language? What is noteworthy in this period is not the sound of lower-class protest,
which, except for certain explosive episodes, reaches us in ever more garbled and

From Denis Woronoff, *La République bourgeoise de Thermidor à Brumaire, 1794-1799* (Paris: Éditions
du Seuil, 1972), pp. 7–8, 222–225. This selection is printed by permission of the publisher. Editors'
translation.

weakened form, but the utterances of moderate politicians, of whom Thibaudeau and La Revellière might be considered the spokesmen, and which typify the new dominant classes in their demands, their contradictions, and even in their banality.

The other sound to which we should listen carefully comes from the provinces. Despite the numerous investigations that have been made of provincial France in these years, it is still difficult to understand, perhaps because research has concentrated too much on the northern part of the country. Paris does retain the initiative and has the last word, but depending upon the issues and the regions we must point out the lags and even discords as much as the agreements in points of view. For the relaxation of revolutionary constraints seems to have released powerful centrifugal forces; in many cases localities obtained their freedom of action. As Richard Cobb recently has written, the country became "communalized" in the year III [1794–1795]. This observation would be quite valid for our entire period [1794–1799]; more than ever, France means diversity.

Finally, all the political jolts, those domestic and foreign "events," should not make us forget a story less known because it was silent, that of the developing social forces in the country. The Directory, an anticlimactic period one might say, is also rich in political and cultural potential, in changes, and in social tensions. In brief, everything is not simply entertainment in this period which has been called frivolous in order perhaps to avoid fully investigating it. . . .

The Directory gave way at the first push. Actually, the regime collapsed primarily under the weight of its own contradictions. It presented the contradiction of a liberal system which could survive only by violating its own legal principles. It also needed war, at least since Fructidor [the coup d'état of September 4, 1797], to satisfy its military contractors and generals and to assure financial resources to the State; but the war reduced its freedom of maneuver and worked to the advantage of its domestic and foreign adversaries.

The Revolution was no more finished than was the war. It was becoming more intense. The blatant domination by the bourgeoisie had created conditions that heightened the consciousness of the common people. In the final analysis, it did not matter much that only a handful of militants at the moment knew how to mount a radical critique of the system. With an impeccable class instinct, the new establishment clearly perceived the danger. This is why the "antianarchist" obsession dominated and even paralyzed the most thoughtful among them. Did the Directory offer full protection in this regard? The weakness of its governmental apparatus resulted in part from its ambiguous nature: the public officials were at the same time employees and elected representatives. As to creating an ideological hegemony which would have insured, better than force, the regime's domination by the notables, the Directory made a very interesting, but hopeless, effort in this direction. Clearly, the anticlerical bourgeoisie was coming to a dead end. Bonaparte was to understand this and draw the logical conclusions. Finally, the opposition could charge, with some justice, that the regime itself fed the current of social subversion. Had it not on several occasions allowed, if not encouraged, Jacobins and even democrats to express their views? These revolutionary spasms were fraught with danger; they threatened to revive a mass ultrarevolutionary political movement.

In addition, the Directory, by the very fact of its imperialist policy, continued to export the Revolution to Europe; and with each step it shook the old regimes already undermined by internal weaknesses. The political and economic reaction against this French expansion is well known. Furthermore, it aroused in the subject countries a nationalist-revolutionary feeling which seemed difficult to direct into channels compatible with the interests of the protector power even when it was not directed against those interests. At the same time, the presence of the occupying power tended to increase antagonisms and invigorate the most traditional sectors of these societies in crisis. But if the foreign policy of the Republic had some contradictory effects, above all it deepened the basic cleavage that opposed revolutionary France to monarchical Europe. So the Directory created implacable opponents on all fronts and made inevitable the birth of a regime that could maintain itself against this two-sided class struggle.

In the light of all this, the longevity of the regime is paradoxical. How was it able to survive? First of all, we should not underestimate the tenacity of its oft-criticized political leaders, who, as exemplified by Barras, fought all the harder because they did not separate their own personal interest from the public interest. So long as there did not appear an alternative solution within a republican framework, these profiteers of the Revolution did not want to relax their grasp on power. Second, the Directory drew strength from the weakness of its opponents. On its left, the mass political movement did not recover from the disaster of the year III [the Thermidorian repression of the Jacobin and democratic movements]. The new regime benefited from the political dexterity of the Thermidorians. Moreover, its police did not cease their manhunt for the former leaders of the great Parisian "days." But these leaders no longer could "enrage" the people, and the movement was extremely fragmented, practically dissolved.

The royalist opposition appeared more formidable. On at least three occasions the Republic was imperiled from that direction: in the Summer of 1795 at the time of the Quiberon episode [a military campaign in Brittany]; between Germinal and Fructidor, year V [March and September 1797], when the counterrevolutionary movement in the legislature threatened to merge with the attempted seizure of power by [General] Pichegru; and finally in the Summer of 1799, when the southwest region was aflame. Yet, this enumeration is a reminder that all these threats were obvious failures. The actions miscarried because of a lack of preparation and coordination, though if they had been better led they could have been fatal to the regime. But such "technical" errors by the royalists bring us back finally to a political explanation—the fundamental heterogeneity of the royalist movement. In all, or nearly all, of their operations, signs of internal division appear: Vendémiaire [the Paris insurrection of October 5, 1795] was exclusively the work of constitutional monarchists; quarrels between Puisaye [commander-in-chief of the expedition] and the absolute monarchists contributed to the defeat of Quiberon; and, finally, the dissension between "feuillants" [moderate royalists] and "white Jacobins" [extreme royalists] in the legislatures of the Directory paralyzed the royalist majority in the year V [1796–1797]. Most important, the royalist camp was weakened by the extreme positions taken by the Pretender [the Comte de Provence, the future Louis XVIII]. A more conciliatory posture would have gained him the support of the majority of the country. Holding to the counterrevolutionary principles of the Manifesto of Verona [June 24, 1795], the monarchy could expect to be restored to power only if France were militarily defeated. This situation left an opening for the Orleanist party; it is very unfortunate that this political tendency under the Directory has not yet been carefully studied.

Finally, among the opponents of the Republic were the foreign armies. The strength of the Directory rested in part on the quality of the military machine forged during the year II [1793–1794]—the talent of the generals, the number and self-sacrifice of the soldiers. But discord among the enemy powers made France's task easier. Prussia's actions during the First Coalition [1792–1797] and the rivalry between Austria and Russia in the Second Coalition [1798–1801] helped the republican government to triumph.

After Brumaire the long denigration of the Directory began. But little by little historians have abandoned the black legend for a more dispassionate approach to the period. Although the regime established by the Thermidorians could not take pride in numerous achievements, it nevertheless prepared a good number of the successes of the Consulate. [The Minister of Finance] Ramel-Nogaret commenced the reorganization of the tax and internal revenue systems. [The Minister of the Interior and then Director] François de Neufchâteau advanced the economic revival and gave the necessary impetus to efforts at innovation. Besides these two frequently mentioned areas, we should add that of the administrative network: the commissioners assigned by the Directory to the departments played somewhat the role later assumed by the Napoleonic prefects. In its last phase, the evolution of the regime in an authoritarian direction and the citizens' apathy regarding electoral matters strengthened the powers of these agents of the government and thereby of centralization. Fragmentary successes of this sort, however, were not enough to increase the regime's standing. They were too fragile—at the mercy of a reversal of the political situation—and too slow to impress contemporaries. For example, the slight beginnings of the cotton industry did not compensate for the lack of growth in traditional textiles, and improvement in farming methods had not yet brought much visible progress. In sum, the reform current of the year VI [1797–1798] had not yet had time to show results. The Consulate inherited some activities already underway and took credit for them. In politics only the short term pays off.

Still the merit of the Directory was not negligible. Despite the final catastrophe it was able to preserve the bourgeois revolution. Picking up where the Constituents had left off, the Thermidorians wanted to finish building the new society that the century had prepared. Circumstances and their own weaknesses prevented them from succeeding. Napoleon will assume this burden. It will be his task "to conclude the Revolution," that is, to reconcile the notables to each other.

8

Who Benefited
From the Revolution?

I N most sports and in some wars there are clear winners and losers, but for many other events in life the outcome is uncertain. This is surely true of the Revolution. Historians disagree about its political results. For example, Alexis de Tocqueville claims that it benefited future tyrants who took advantage of the passion for equality that the Revolution stimulated. But Albert Mathiez argues that the Revolution's most important legacy was the idealism that it inspired in later generations of republicans.

As for the Revolution's social results, Albert Soboul thinks it gave the levers of power to certain strata of the urban and rural bourgeoisie, many of whom were capitalists, and created suffering for most of the rest of society. This point of view is challenged by Albert Cobban, who finds that the Revolution retarded capitalism and profited a diverse group: lawyers, bureaucrats, and others—in general, conservative land-owners from various classes. Darline Gay Levy, Mary Durham Johnson, and Harriet Branson Applewhite look at the Revolution from a different perspective. To them it was a male-dominated movement which at first permitted women to participate in politics, but then repressed their attempts at liberation; after 1799 women were politically and socially no better off than they had been during the Old Regime.

Are all these differences of opinion irreconcilable? Could they be reduced if one made a distinction between long-term and short-term results? If one did not treat the events of the Revolution as a bloc but rather specified which segment of the Revolution had which effects? If one defined such abstract words as "bourgeois," "capitalist," and "class" precisely? Finally, if one studied history less to defend and justify one's own social and political philosophy and more to watch and learn from people as they confront the intractable problems of the human condition?

A Potential Tyrant

ALEXIS DE TOCQUEVILLE

Alexis de Tocqueville (1805–1859) was descended from an ancient noble family of Normandy and pursued a career as a judge, legislator, and man of letters. During the Second Republic he was Foreign Minister for five months. After Louis Napoleon's coup d'état in 1851, he was imprisoned for a time and retired from public service when released. At least two of his works, *Democracy in America* (1835–1840) and *The Old Regime and the Revolution* (1856), are regarded as classics. His subtle point of view in both books is not easy to categorize; and scholars still disagree about whether he was, for example, a liberal aristocrat, a conservative democrat, or a Christian conservative. What is clear is that he detested tyranny.

The French Revolution did not, as has been believed, seek to destroy the sway of religious beliefs. Despite appearances, it was essentially a social and political revolution. Regarding these types of institutions, in no way did it tend to perpetuate and somehow stabilize disorder or to "methodize" anarchy, as one of its leading adversaries has said; but rather it increased the power and rights of public authority. Nor did it, as others have thought, seek to change the character our civilization had until then, nor arrest its progress, nor even alter basically any of the fundamental laws on which our Western society rests. When one separates the Revolution from all the accidents which briefly changed its outward features at different times and in different countries, and when one considers only its essence, then it is clear that the Revolution's sole effect was to abolish those political institutions which for several centuries held total sway over most of the peoples of Europe—institutions which have ordinarily been called by the name feudal—in order to replace them with a more uniform and simpler social and political order having as its foundation equality of rank.

That alone caused an enormous revolution; for not only were these ancient feudal institutions still mingled, interwoven so to speak, with almost all the religious

From Alexis de Tocqueville, *L'Ancien régime et la Révolution* (3rd ed.; Paris: Lévy, 1857), pp. 53–56, 339–342. Editors' translation.

and political laws of Europe, but also these institutions had given rise to a host of ideas, feelings, habits, and customs which were in some way attached to them. A frightful convulsion was necessary to destroy and remove all of a sudden from the social body a portion which was so connected to every organ. That is why the Revolution appears even greater than it was. It seemed to destroy everything, for what it destroyed touched everything and was in some way related to everything.

However radical the Revolution was, it nevertheless introduced many fewer innovations than is generally supposed. . . . What can truly be said is that it has entirely destroyed or is in the process of destroying (for it is still going on) everything from the old society which derived from aristocratic and feudal institutions, everything which was connected in some manner with them, everything which carried in any degree their *slightest* trace. What was conserved from the old society had always been extraneous to these institutions or could exist without them. The Revolution was least of all an accidental event. To be sure, it took the world by surprise. However, it was only the completion of a much longer work, the sudden and violent termination of a task on which ten generations had worked. Even if the Revolution had not taken place, the old social edifice would have crumbled everywhere—in some places sooner, in other places later; instead of suddenly breaking apart, it would have crumbled piecemeal. By a convulsive and painful effort, the Revolution achieved suddenly and without transition, precaution, or regard for anything what would have come about by itself gradually and in the long run. Such was the Revolution's work.

It is surprising that what seems today so obvious remained then so perplexing and obscure to the most clear-sighted contemporaries. "You wanted to correct your government's abuses," Burke said to the French, "but why did you create something new? Why did you not return to your ancient traditions? Why did you not confine yourselves to reviving your ancient liberties? Or if you found it impossible to recognize the worn-out features of your forefathers' constitution, why did you not turn your gaze towards us? Here you would have found again the old common law of Europe." Burke does not perceive what is right before his eyes. It is precisely the old common law of Europe that the Revolution seeks to abolish. He completely misses the point—that is exactly the Revolution's real object and nothing else. . . .

Those who have attentively studied France in the eighteenth century . . . have seen the birth and development in her breast of two principal passions that did not grow up simultaneously and did not always tend to the same end.

One, deeper and more long-standing, is the violent and unquenchable hatred of inequality. This hatred was born and fed by the very sight of that inequality; for a long time it has, by a continuous and irresistible force, impelled Frenchmen to seek to destroy all the remaining foundations of medieval institutions and on the cleared ground to build a society where men are as similar, where social positions are as equal, as is humanly possible.

The other passion, more recent and less deeply rooted, inclined them to seek freedom as well as equality.

Near the end of the Old Regime these two passions were sincerely held and appeared equally vigorous. They met at the opening of the Revolution; at that point they mixed and combined for a moment; by contact they kindled each other and then all at once inflamed the heart of France. That was in 1789, a time of inexperience of course, but also of generosity, enthusiasm, virility, and grandeur, an immortal time, a time men's attention will turn to with admiration and respect long after those who have witnessed it and we ourselves have passed away. Frenchmen were then so proud of their cause and of themselves that they believed that they could be both equal and free. They planted, therefore, free institutions everywhere in the midst of democratic institutions. Not only did they reduce to dust the antiquated legislation which separated men into castes, corporate bodies, classes, and which made their legal rights even more unequal than their social positions, but they also destroyed in one blow those other laws—more recently created by royal power—which had deprived the people of personal freedom and which had put the government alongside each Frenchman as his tutor, his guardian, and if necessary his oppressor. As absolute government fell, so did centralization.

But when that vigorous generation which had started the Revolution was destroyed or became weary, as usually happens to any generation which undertakes such ventures; when, following the natural course of such events, the love of liberty flagged and slackened amidst anarchy and dictatorship in the name of the masses, the bewildered nation began to search gropingly for a master; at this point absolute government found available immense facilities for its rebirth and establishment that were easily discovered by the genius [Napoleon] who was going to continue and destroy the Revolution at the same time.

In fact the Old Regime had contained a host of recent institutions which, not being opposed to equality, could easily fit into the new society and which, however, offered despotism some remarkable advantages. These institutions were again sought and found amidst the debris of all the others. Previously these institutions had created habits, passions, and ideas tending to keep men apart and obedient. They were revived and used. Centralization was plucked from the ruins and restored. As it recoverd, everything which had previously limited its power remained destroyed; and from the depths of a nation which had just overthrown royalty, arose suddenly a power more extensive, exacting, and absolute than any our kings had wielded. Because people thought only of what they themselves saw and forgot what earlier generations had seen, this enterprise seemed extraordinarily bold and an unprecedented success. The tyrant [Napoleon] fell, but what was really substantial in his work lasted; his government died, his administration continued to live; and ever since, any effort to strike down absolute power has succeeded only in placing the head of Liberty on a servile body.

From the beginning of the Revolution to our own time [1850s], the passion for liberty has over and over again died out, then been reborn, then again died out, then been reborn once again. It will continue that way for a long time, always inexperienced and unruly, easy to discourage, frighten, and vanquish, superficial and fleeting. Meanwhile the passion for equality forever resides in the inner recesses of men's hearts. It had entrenched itself there first, and it is attached to our most cherished feelings. While the passion for liberty is always changing appearance in response to events—decreasing, increasing, becoming stronger, weaker—the other is always the same, always aiming at the same goal with the same obstinate, often blind ardor, ready to sacrifice everything to those who will give it satisfaction; and it provides the government wishing to favor and flatter it the habits, ideas, and laws despotism needs in order to govern.

$\mathcal{A}$ll Republicans

ALBERT MATHIEZ

For biographical information on Albert Mathiez, see Chapter 5, entitled "Why Terror in 1793–1794?"

First of all it seems to me, if I am not mistaken, that the French Revolution succeeded only to the extent that it had been prepared: since it was the work of the bourgeoisie, the bourgeoisie was inevitably the first to profit from it. This wealthy and intellectually superior class was bound to triumph over an impoverished and already half-dispossessed nobility, even though the higher element among the nobles had made a considerable effort towards the end of the monarchy to restore itself. It was also bound to triumph over the people, because the people were still illiterate and had no alternative but to seek their own leaders among the bourgeoisie. The bourgeoisie alone had a well enough developed class consciousness to take and keep power.

Furthermore, I am very much struck by the fact that at this time the democratic artisans took up the struggle only on the political level, even when that struggle concerned social and economic demands. The guilds were suppressed. The trade unions did not yet exist. The secret societies of journeymen [*compagnonnages*] were weakened by their divisions. Strikes were prohibited. It was in the political clubs and popular societies, as well as in the communes [municipal governments] and Paris Sections, that the sans-culottes, mingling with the progressive element among the bourgeoisie, strove to defend their own interests. They placed all their hopes in winning political power. In order to take over the State they did not hesitate to resort to riots, which were organized in the political societies and which were successful only because an armed force—the National Guard—worked hand in hand with them. Often the communal authorities also were their partners. For example, the events of July 14, 1789, were prepared by the electoral assembly that had chosen the Parisian deputies to the Estates-General; and that assembly of electors met at the City Hall alongside the official municipal council. Likewise, the insurrection of August 10, 1792, was the work of the Paris Sections and some members of the Commune. The same was true for the coup d'état of May 31, 1793.

After Thermidor the bourgeoisie pulled itself together. It purged the National

From Albert Mathiez, "La Révolution française," *Annales historiques de la Révolution française,* X (1933), 19–24. Printed by permission of the editor of the *Annales historiques de la Révolution française.* Editors' translation.

Guard and soon disarmed it; and the riots, no longer backed by the communal authorities, all failed one after the other. The clubs were closed, and the starving and disarmed masses no longer had focal points or bases of support. They drifted aimlessly. It would have been different if the proletariat of that time had succeeded in forming class organizations instead of borrowing its political organizations from the bourgeoisie. When the sans-culottes lost political power, they lost everything.

But the victory of the bourgeoisie was perhaps too perfect. Mercilessly hunted down by the use of emergency laws, the last of the democrats disappeared or took refuge in embittered abstention from politics. The Thermidorians remained isolated in the midst of a hostile nation.

Most Frenchmen, fed up with politics and crushed by the sufferings of the war, longed only for peace. When voting rights were restored to them, they no longer bothered to fulfill their electoral duties. Politics now interested only the professional politicians. The ordinary Frenchman spoke of public affairs only with irony and disgust. Dictatorship, which had continued in various guises since 1789 and which maintained itself in power by the several coups d'état of the Directory, compelled people to turn inward. Idealism died among royalists as well as among republicans. Egoism replaced generous aspirations. Bonaparte could emerge to reassure and consolidate the interest groups. In the absence of political liberty, he would assure Frenchmen of their individual rights. In the Napoleonic Code, he would sanctify equality, their dearest possession. He would keep most of the revolutionary institutions while at times amalgamating them with those of the Old Regime, which were restored but adapted. His work would prove so solid that it made any total restoration of the past impossible.

The results of the French Revolution in France and Europe were so great that it can be said without exaggeration that a new era began in the history of the world.

France turned out to be greatly strengthened by the destruction of the Old Regime. No state on the globe was more homogeneous. The suppression of separate orders, corporate bodies, and special privileges, the uniformity of the laws and institutions, the decisive spread of the national language infused the country with enormous force. For a long time it was only in France that the all-powerful state reigned over citizens equal in rights.

A significant part of the individualistic program of the physiocrats was fulfilled. Recognized as an absolute, the right of private property permitted Frenchmen the practice of all economic and civil freedoms. The field was wide open for the expansion of capitalism, and it is not by chance that big capitalists were most of the time ardent revolutionaries.

In principle the Revolution proclaimed that it was for peace. It solemnly renounced conquest, and this spontaneous gesture gained it much sympathy abroad. But revolutionary aims clashed too violently with monarchist aims for peace to be preserved. The war changed the terms of the problem; in order to support it, the kings more and more had to adopt French practices. As early as 1794 the King of Spain confiscated the Church's silver plate. The following year he appropriated the revenue from vacant ecclesiastical benefices, which did not stop him from issuing paper money as well. The Holy Roman Emperor was forced to a similar expedient in Austria. From the third year of the war, with his manpower exhausted, he considered ordering military conscription. Pitt's government survived only by loans. Fortunately, the kings dared not decree universal military service (which had saved France) because, as [the contemporary writer] Mallet du Pan put it, they feared their own subjects almost as much as they feared the enemy.

Victory intoxicated the French. Under the pretext of bringing liberty to their neighbors, they brought conquest based upon the old theory of natural frontiers, a theory which they thus rejuvenated. They became a threat to the liberty of Europe. Napoleonic militarism provoked in reaction the birth of nations which had not yet become conscious of their identity.

The clashes of nationalities, which would fill the nineteenth century, were thus the direct result of the French Revolution. Previous wars had been entirely dynastic. The people had played only a passive role. The new wars would be very different, deploying larger and larger armies conscripted according to the French system of military service, a system gradually extended to the whole nation. In 1793, France had 1,200,000 men in arms. It was the first time since antiquity that such a force had been assembled. Never before had so national an army been recruited, one which marched into battle not only to defend its independence, but also to impose its political and religious beliefs on others.

In the course of time, as the nineteenth century progressed, the clashes of peoples would become more and more fierce. By opposing each other, the different nationalisms would move farther apart. But at the beginning such was not the case. The conflict was then more social than political. In every country there was a minority, more or less strong, which sympathized with the French ideal and which hoped, more or less secretly, for its victory. The monarchs were forced to make more and more important concessions to this minority in order to prevent it from increasing and winning over their subjects. Thus, the growth of nationalities was accompanied by a liberal movement that little by little brought down the walls of the Old Regime in the states bordering France. Furthermore, nationalists and liberals were recruited in the same social strata. Both belonged to that enlightened bourgeoisie which had reformed France before serving as a model for Europe.

Although tinged with the Voltairian spirit, the French revolutionaries did not originally harbor any hatred for the Church and even less so for religion. On the contrary, they dreamed of using the clergy to defend their political work. Their union with the lower clergy was close. But the pope's refusal to ratify their religious reforms, the schism of the clergy between those who swore allegiance to the Constitution and those who would not, and the revolutionaries' unsuccessful efforts to restore the broken religious unity pushed them little by little to a policy of conflict with the Church. They eventually secularized the Republic by decreeing the separation of Church and State. Bonaparte's Concordat, designed above all to reassure those who had acquired the nationalized Church lands, could not reestablish the old, intimate union of throne and altar. The registration of vital statistics remained in the hands of civil authorities. Anticlericalism, which had been only a state of mind before 1789, became a program adopted by most liberals throughout Europe.

Likewise, divine right monarchy had suffered irreparable damage from the proclamation of the principles of 1789. The idea of sovereignty had changed its meaning. From the king, it had passed to the people, and the execution of Louis XVI on January 21, 1793, had divested monarchical sovereignty of any supernatural aura. When for the last time Charles X, at his coronation in 1825, was to touch those afflicted with scrofula, this brought forth only derision.[1]

The American Revolution of 1776 had been above all a political revolution. It had respected the privileges of wealth and had established everywhere a regime of limited suffrage. It had not even touched the vestiges of the feudal regime which had survived in some spots. Seigniorial quitrents in New York State, for example, were not suppressed until the middle of the nineteenth century.

The French Revolution was much more thorough. It totally wiped out seigniorial dues and tithes without any indemnity. It nationalized the property of the Church and of the *émigrés*. It altered regulations on commerce and industry from top to bottom. It was imbued almost from the beginning with an ardent egalitarian spirit which reached its peak in 1793–1794. For the first time, in response to necessities more than to theories, the outlines of a social democracy appeared in the world and sought to cross the barrier between thought and action. This premature attempt failed. But it did not disappear without leaving some trace, at least in the minds of men. The de facto collectivism accomplished by the Terrorist regime— price controls, requisitions, the pooling of the nation's entire resources—served as a model to which social reformers for a century after Babeuf could point.

While the Terror frightened to death the bourgeoisie of the nineteenth century, on the other hand it restored the hopes of the partisans of social justice. It played on their imagination like a grandiose myth, generating devotion and sacrifice. The historian Gabriel Monod, in the preface which he wrote to my *Contributions à l'histoire religieuse de la Révolution*, relates that at Nantes, towards the middle of the last century, the woman at whose home he lodged praised her father, who had welcomed the Revolution enthusiastically and who had in his youth defended it against the Vendeans. He had seen with sorrow the Imperial Regime of Napoleon crush the democratic liberties which had been acquired at such great cost. With each new Revolution, in 1814, in 1830, in 1848, he had believed that the ideal Republic dreamed of in 1793 would reappear. At over ninety years of age he died during Louis Napoleon's Second Empire; and at the moment of death, raising his eyes towards heaven with a look of ecstasy, he murmured: "O sun of '93, am I going to die thus without ever again seeing your rays!" This obscure Breton republican was not an exception. Although the sun of 1793, which had illuminated his youth, had disappeared behind the darkened horizon, he had kept its immortal radiance in the depths of his soul.

In the bitter and difficult march towards progress, men need to be reinvigorated by the sun of hope. The revolutionaries of 1789 drew comfort from the memory of the republics of antiquity or the more recent example of the American Revolution, and this sustained them in their fight. They had read Plutarch's *Lives* and, schooled by it in magnanimity, their courage was inflamed, their faith in the Revolution soared! They imitated the heroes of Greece and Rome and, like them, they gave up

---

[1] [The king's touch as a way of healing scrofula was a tradition dating from the Middle Ages.—Eds.]

their lives. That is why they too were heroes. In their turn, they were for their descendants what Aristides, Brutus, and Cato had been for them—that is, martyrs who witnessed by their life and death what devotion to justice and the sacred love of humanity can achieve. French republicans have faithfully preserved their memory, and in our contemporary history, the Revolution has been the wellspring from which they have drawn their example and fortified their faith.

The Triumph of
a New Bourgeoisie

ALBERT SOBOUL

For biographical information on Albert Soboul, see Chapter 6,
entitled "The Revolutionary Common People of Paris."

The Revolution destroyed the feudal aristocracy; it still has to be made clear to what
extent. At the same time it also ruined those sections of the bourgeoisie that were
integrated in one way or another into the society of the ancien regime. The
Revolution made certain the triumph of capitalist economy based on economic
liberty; in this sense, it hastened the ruin of the social categories that were attached
to the traditional system of production. But in the realm of agricultural production,
the resistance of the poor peasantry was such that capitalism could not win a
definitive victory.

The nobility as a social order disappeared. Distinctions between nobles and
commons were done away with. The personal seigneurial rights on which the
dependence of the peasants was based were abolished after the night of August 4,
1789. Above all the aristocracy was hit in its economic basis. Other feudal rights
were finally terminated by the Convention on June 17, 1793. The Revolution
attacked the landed property of the nobility. The former seigneurs had to return the
communal lands that they had seized, and the property of the émigrés was put on
sale in June 1793. As the crisis grew deeper the nobles were gradually excluded
from all public positions, civil or military. Exaggeration should be avoided here,
however. The nobility was not stripped of its lands altogether nor irrevocably. Only
the émigrés had their property confiscated. Many nobles went through the
Revolution without great loss and kept their landed properties. Furthermore,
fictitious divorces and purchases by straw men enabled some émigrés to save or
recover their lands.[1] In this way a certain section of the old aristocracy held on, and
during the 19th century merged with the upper bourgeoisie.

The bourgeoisie of the ancien regime shared the fate of the aristocracy in large
measure. The bourgeois who lived "nobly" on their income from the land saw their

From Albert Soboul, "Classes and Class Struggles during the French Revolution," *Science & Society*,
XVII (Summer 1953), 252–257. Reprinted by permission of *Science & Society*.

[1] On what the émigrés were able to recover of their lands. See A. Gain, *La Restauration et les biens des
émigrés* (1929). [For how the nobility fared, see a later study by Robert Forster, "The Survival of the
Nobility during the French Revolution," *Past and Present*, no. 37 (July 1967), 71–86.—Eds.]

seigneurial dues and rights vanish. Office holders were ruined by the abolition of the sale of offices. The financial upper bourgeoisie received a mortal blow when stock companies and the farming-out of indirect taxes were abolished. It was hard hit too by the disappearance of the [prerevolutionary] Bank of Discount as well as by the resumption of price-fixing and controls. Finally, as a measure of the blows the bourgeois revolution struck at certain sections of the bourgeoisie, we must consider the considerable repercussions of inflation on settled fortunes. The traditional bourgeoisie invested its savings in mortgage loans or the public debt rather than in commercial and industrial enterprises. In 1794, the depreciation of the assignats led debtors to get rid of their mortgage debts at little cost. The consolidation of the perpetual and annuity debts [types of government securities] under the Convention, and the two-thirds bankruptcy under the Directory were additional blows. All these facts account for the rallying of the bourgeoisie of the ancien regime to the counter-revolution. It shared the fate of the aristocracy, whose cause it had taken up.

Just as much as the revolutionary bourgeoisie strove for the destruction of the aristocracy, it obstinately sought the ruin of the traditional economic system, which was incompatible with the expansion of capitalist enterprises. After the Ninth of Thermidor, economic liberty was inaugurated triumphantly on the ruins of the sans-culotte movement.

This had grave consequences for the traditional lower classes. The abolition of guilds by the Constituent Assembly might have seemed democratic, but it hurt the interests of the master artisans. Thus, at the same time that the material conditions of social life were being transformed, the structure of the traditional lower classes was changing. All the conditions were now present for a broad development of capitalist economy, which would necessarily transform the sans-culottes into a proletariat. The artisans and journeymen had a foreboding of their fate. The latter knew that machinery would increase the chances of unemployment, the former that capitalist concentration would mean the closing of their workshops and make wage earners of them. The Le Chapelier law of 1791, prohibiting "coalition" [labor organizations] and strikes, was an effective means of development for the industrial bourgeoisie.

In the realm of agricultural production, where the resistance of the poor peasantry was more desperate, the bourgeois revolution was less radical in its consequences. It made possible the development of a predominant rural bourgeoisie, but it could not completely destroy the rural community and thereby give free rein to the development of capitalist modes of production.

All the peasantry, whether owners or not, profited by the abolition of seigneurial dues and ecclesiastical tithes. The other agrarian reforms of the Revolution served primarily to strengthen those who were already proprietors. Leaving out the city bourgeoisie, who got into their hands a considerable portion of the national[ized] property, the conditions under which it was sold, particularly the auctions, favored the big farmers and the prosperous peasants. The rural bourgeoisie was strengthened and the moat deepened between them and the poor peasantry.[2]

---

[2] Despite some timid attempts in 1793, the bourgeoisie that dominated in the revolutionary assemblies was aware of the need for prohibiting access to ownership for the mass of the peasantry, if industrial

But the last-named did not emerge from the Revolution as badly disarmed in the face of the triumphant bourgeoisie as the urban sans-culottes were. The poor peasantry did not get from the revolutionary assemblies the restoration or reinforcement of the traditional rural community, as it had desired. But the bourgeois revolution did not destroy it beyond repair; it did not brutally do away with the communal properties and collective customs that formed its economic basis.[3] Both lasted throughout the 19th century and have not entirely disappeared yet. The law of 1892, still in force, requires the consent of the peasants of the village for the abandonment of common pasture. The rural community has thus survived, going through a slow disintegration.

Here some distinctions are necessary. In the regions of large-scale farming, where the farmers were active agents in the capitalist evolution of agriculture, the rural community broke up rapidly, not by dissociating into antagonistic classes (the big farmers were generally city capitalists who were strangers to the rural community) but by losing its substance, as it were. The poor peasants who were proletarianized were to furnish the labor force needed for capitalist agriculture and big industry. In small-scale farming regions the evolution was slower. The rural community was sapped from within by the antagonism between the rural bourgeoisie and the poor peasantry desperately defending its customary rights to use fields and woods. Thus two forms of economy clashed, one archaic, the other new and asserting the individualism of the capitalist producers. The struggle was covert but bitter, marked during the 19th century by agrarian disorders of the traditional type, the last of them, in 1848–51, being by no means the least violent nor the least typical.[4]

The bourgeois revolution was consequently unable to eradicate the traditional forms of agricultural production. It could only enact a compromise whose full significance can be measured by comparing the development of French and English agriculture. Undoubtedly the bourgeois revolution accelerated the capitalist transformation of agriculture; but that development was considerably slowed up by the maintenance of collective customs and by the subdivision of ownership and cultivation. The autonomy of the small producers was kept up for a long time, giving the political development of France, especially under the Third Republic, some of its characteristic traits. If enclosure and concentration had been imposed in France as they were in England, capitalism might have triumphed as completely in the realm of agricultural production as in that of industrial production. The obstinate resistance of the landed aristocracy to any compromise with the

enterprises were to be developed. See the report presented to the Convention the 27 Fructidor year II [September 13, 1794] by Lozeau, deputy of the Charente-Inférieure, "On the material impossibility of making all Frenchmen landed proprietors and on the bad effects that this change would entail in any case." (*Moniteur*, Vol. XXI, p. 748).

[3] Nevertheless, the revolutionary bourgeoisie was aware of the need of doing away with communal property and collective customs for the sake of the progress of capitalist agriculture. See in this connection the report of Lozeau in Messidor year II [June–July 1794], "On the need for doing away with communal property and on the principles of property in a free country." (*Bibliothèque nationale*, 8⁰ Le³⁸ 841).

[4] See Albert Soboul, "La question paysanne en 1848," in *La Pensée*, 1948, Nos. 18, 19 and 20; "Les troubles agraires de 1848," in *1848 et les Révolutions du XIXᵉ siècle*, 1948, Nos. 180 and 181.

bourgeoisie forced the latter to deal gently with the peasantry, even with the poor peasantry.

If we now consider the class which led the Revolution, and basically profited from it, we note that it has been radically changed. The traditional predominance within it of the settled fortunes has been replaced by that of those who direct production and exchange; the internal equilibrium of the bourgeoisie has been modified. The bourgeoisie of the ancien regime was not totally destroyed, since those of its representatives who had not emigrated kept their lands; but it lost its primacy. A new money bourgeoisie appeared in the forefront, made up of industrial leaders, and the directors of commerce and finance. Equipping, arming and supplying the armies, sale of the national property, exploitation of the conquered countries afforded business men new chances for developing their enterprises. Speculation gave rise to immense fortunes. The bourgeoisie renewed itself by incorporating those "nouveaux riches" who set the tone for the "society" of the Directory. True adventurers of capitalist society, they gave new life to the traditional bourgeoisie by their enterprising spirit and their flair for taking chances. On a lower rung of the bourgeois ladder, circumstances had allowed many tradesmen or artisans to rise into the ranks of the bourgeoisie. It was from this middle level that the new dominant class was soon to recruit the public servants and the members of the liberal professions. The traits of the new bourgeoisie hardened during the Napoleonic period that fused these diverse elements.

At the end of this sketch, whose only purpose is to stimulate reflection on the history of the Revolution, several points should be stressed for their educative value.

There are laws of historical development, but they can not be reduced to a mechanical schematism, as some have done by a false application of dialectical materialism. Social classes, even when dominant, are rarely homogeneous; the various sections making them up complicate the interplay of classes in the framework of the general development, sometimes causing autonomous secondary currents, such as the sans-culottes in the bourgeois revolution. Only precise social and economic analysis can account for the place in the class struggle of the various social categories, and disclose the contradictions that may appear between political attitude and an economic position. It will not be forgotten, finally, that as the class struggles develop, they affect and transform the classes engaged in them. The bourgeoisie that profited from the Revolution was no longer the same as the bourgeoisie that started it.

These truths may seem self-evident. They deserve to be recalled nevertheless. History is a dialectical movement. If they are not to deform it by schematization, those who engage in studying it must take into account the complexity that makes its richness, as well as the contradictions that give it its dramatic character.

Conservative
Landowners

ALFRED COBBAN

Alfred Cobban (1901–1968) was one of the most eminent
twentieth-century British historians. He studied at Cambridge
University, taught at the University of Newcastle-upon-Tyne
and the University of London, and edited the English journal
History. He wrote an excellent *History of Modern France*
(1957–1965), several works of political theory, and many books
and articles on the Old Regime and the French Revolution. His
writings include *Edmund Burke and the Revolt Against the
Eighteenth Century* (1929), *Rousseau and the Modern State*
(1934), *In Search of Humanity: The Role of the Enlightenment
in Modern History* (1960), *The Social Interpretation of the
French Revolution* (1964), and *Aspects of the French Revolution*
(1968). As the following selection indicates, he was a trenchant
critic who took independent stands on historical controversies.

Looking at the economic consequences of the revolution as a whole, they seem
astonishingly small for such a great social and political upheaval. This is what M.
Soboul, in spite of his acceptance of the theory of the bourgeois revolution, very
frankly recognises. Industrial production under the Directory, he says, was below
that of 1789 in cotton. The woollen and metallurgy industries were stagnating.
Capitalist concentration remained essentially commercial, under capitalists of the old
type, employing domestic labour and combining commercial and banking activities
with the organisation of manufacture. Above all, France remained essentially a rural
country and its old agricultural methods continued unchanged.[1] Most statistics in
this matter are open to question, but, for what they are worth, the figures for

---

From Alfred Cobban, *The Social Interpretation of the French Revolution* (Cambridge, Eng.: Cambridge
University Press, 1964), pp. 77–90, 168–173. All but one footnote included. Reprinted with permission
of the publisher.

[1] Albert Soboul, *Précis d'histoire de la Révolution française* (1962), p. 441.

French commerce in 1825, according to Henri Sée, are hardly greater than those of 1788.[2]

This does not entirely settle the question. There is still one final refuge of theory. Capitalist progress during the revolution must not be exaggerated, says M. Soboul. This is rather an under-statement for what seems to have been a period of serious economic decline. However, he continues, the conditions were none the less brought together for the coming great development of capitalist economy.[3] It may seem that this is all a matter of more or less, and that it does not matter fundamentally to what extent the revolution accelerated the growth of a capitalist economy, so long as it did accelerate it. Similarly, the actual effectiveness of corporative restrictions in 1789, and therefore the importance of the legislation of the revolution in liberating trade and industry from the bonds of the *ancien régime,* is only a matter of degree. The effectiveness of the abolition of internal customs is perhaps least open to doubt.

All this is on the assumption that the revolution represented a step forward in the direction of a more developed capitalist economy. According to prevailing social theory steps in history must always be taken forward. I want to suggest the possibility that, at least in some fundamental respects, it may not have been a step forward at all, but rather one backwards, that instead of accelerating the growth of a modern capitalist economy in France, the revolution may have retarded it.

. . . The evidence in respect of trade and industry is that France was worse off in 1815 than she had been in 1789. After two decades of war this was perhaps only to be expected. More important is the fact that such evidence as we have on the organisation of trade and industry suggests that by and large it remained in 1815 what it had been in 1789.[4] The lack of capital investment, which had been one of the factors holding back French industrial development, continued. In Dauphiné, says P. Léon, those with capital to invest preferred to the certain risk of losses in industry, the gains of speculation and of investment in real estate.[5] The peasantry, which held so much of the productive capacity of the country, was still largely self-sufficient and invested its savings in land, which attracted capital to the detriment of both industry and commerce.[6] France was not to know an industrial revolution—apart from isolated and untypical enterprises in a few areas—before the Second Empire. It is true that the economic history of France is largely unwritten. What I am suggesting is that such researches as have been made give no support to the orthodox theory of the economic effects of the revolution, but on the contrary throw great doubt on it. The revolution, in its economic consequences, seems indeed to have been the kind of revolution we should expect if . . . it was led not by industrialists and merchants, but by *officiers* [officeholders who owned their posts] and professional men.

[2] H. Sée, *L'Évolution commerciale et industrielle de la France sous l'ancien régime* (1925), p. 74.
[3] Soboul, *Précis,* p. 475.
[4] For example, in Lyon, Toulouse, Bordeaux.
[5] P. Léon, *La naissance de la grande industrie en Dauphiné* (1954), p. 370.
[6] F. Crouzet, "Les conséquences économiques de la Révolution à propos d'un inédit de Sir Francis d'Invernois," *Annales historiques de la Révolution française,* no. 168 (1962), pp. 214–215.

A Bourgeoisie of Landowners

It must not be supposed, though Georges Lefebvre did,[7] that I am trying to deny the existence of the French Revolution; I merely want to discover what it was. Professor Reinhard has argued that even if we discard the view that the revolution was against "feudalism," still the struggle against seigniorial rights, against the noblesse and against the privileged classes was central to it.[8] This may have been true in the summer of 1789. Is it true of the next ten years? Seigniorial rights were largely eliminated in 1789, and their elimination was completed by the stubborn resistance of the peasantry, despite the reluctance of the revolutionary authorities in Paris, in the course of the following years. Similarly, noblesse was legally brought to an end—even if only for 14 years—in 1789, as the marquis de Ferrières philosophically observed on 20 June 1790. "Noblesse," he writes, "is already destroyed in fact. The abolition of feudal rights and justice, equality in the division of enclosed land, have given it a mortal blow." Do not write to me any longer as M. le marquis, he instructs his wife; and let my daughter and son-in-law stop being called count and countess. He even asks for his family arms in the local church to be obliterated, though, since Ferrières was a cautious man, only with whitewash.[9] Finally, privileges based on order, heredity and so on were ended by the legislation of 4–11 August 1789. There was no need, then, to continue the revolution to abolish what had already been abolished.

Yet the revolution did continue, and it continued particularly as a struggle against the "aristocrats" and "aristocracy." This was, it is true, a struggle against the counter-revolution, but that is only to say the same thing in different terms. The counter-revolution was led by, and identified with, the aristocrats; it was also a continuation of that *révolte nobiliaire* against the royal government with which the revolutionary movement had begun in 1787–8, and which had been an attempt to set up or—it was believed—revive, aristocratic government. As such it was a political movement, concerned primarily with political power and only secondarily with social privilege. It is not unreasonable, therefore, to expect the opposition to aristocracy also to be mainly political.

An indication of the primarily political nature of the struggle against aristocracy is the actual use of the word. Tom Paine, writing to Edmund Burke from France on 17 January 1790, explains, "The term Aristocrat is used here, similar to the word Tory in America;—it in general means an enemy of the Revolution, and is used without that peculiar meaning formerly affixed to Aristocracy." [10] Nobles could be patriots and if they were such, or often if they were merely discreet and neutral, escaped the label of aristocrats, whereas there were frequent denunciations of bourgeois aristocrats, or, to quote Marat among others, of the *"aristocratie d'argent"* [aristocracy of money].[11] In the Maine, we are told, the term aristocrat was

---

[7] G. Lefebvre, "Le mythe de la Révolution française," *ibid.*, no. 145 (1956).

[8] M. Reinhard, "Sur l'histoire de la Révolution française," *Annales* (1959), p. 557.

[9] Marquis de Ferrières, *Correspondence inédite 1789, 1790, 1791*, ed. H. Carré (1932), p. 212.

[10] *The Correspondence of Edmund Burke*, vol. vi, ed. A. Cobban and R. Smith.

[11] *Cf.* L. G. Wickham Legg, *Select Documents of the French Revolution* (1905), I, pp. 171–5.

employed to designate even simple peasants if they were hostile to the revolution.[12]

The revolution, then, continued as a political struggle against aristocracy—the claim to a monopoly of political power by a small minority of the nation—when the first objectives had been achieved. This is not to assert that it ceased to have any social aims or content, or to deny that removing from power, wealth, influence, and sometimes even life itself, many members, or whole groups, of the socially superior classes, and replacing them in the end with new men—the *"nouveaux messieurs,"* *parvenus,* founders of the "bourgeois dynasties" of the nineteenth century, was a social as well as a political fact.[13]

How far, apart from the removal of the higher noblesse from their positions of wealth and privilege, there was a permanent change of personnel in the upper ranks of society, however, remains speculative. The bourgeoisie proper of the *ancien régime,* like the noblesse with which it was rapidly becoming assimilated, in some cases survived the storms of the revolution and in some cases went under. The *grande bourgeoisie* of finance, such as the Farmers General, suffered severely, but their place was to be taken by others who differed from them only in being a new first generation of financial wealth, instead of the second or third. The bourgeois who had purchased seigniorial dues lost them, but they kept, and probably added to, their estates; and as owners of land profited by the abolition from which they suffered as owners of dues. The bourgeoisie of *officiers,* M. Soboul says, was ruined by the abolition of venality.[14] This is a point which requires investigation. It was an Assembly containing a large proportion of venal officers which carried out the abolition. The abolition was in fact accompanied by compensation and there are indications that the compensation was sometimes profitably invested in the purchase of Church lands. Moreover, many of the former *officiers* seem subsequently to have obtained salaried judicial and administrative positions not dissimilar from those for the loss of which they had earlier been compensated. The open question is how far the expected compensation was actually paid, but even in the upper ranks of the *ancien régime* bourgeoisie it seems likely, that many survived and prospered, or re-emerged after the revolution, to contribute to the recruitment of the new upper class of nineteenth-century France.

Whether many or few survived from the *ancien régime* bourgeoisie is, however, a minor issue. The important question to ask is what essentially was the constitution of the new ruling class of France that emerged from the revolution. I have already suggested that the revolutionary bourgeoisie was the declining one of venal officers, along with members of the liberal professions, rather than the prospering merchants and industrialists. As M. Reinhard puts the point, "It was these lawyers, these doctors, these *officiers* of lower positions, who captured the posts of executive power." [15] For men of business the revolution was less advantageous: socially and politically they received perhaps even less recognition than before the revolution.

---

[12] Paul Bois, *Paysans de l'Ouest* (1960), p. 664, n. 2.

[13] Reinhard, "Sur l'histoire de la Révolution française," p. 561.

[14] Soboul, *Précis,* p. 478.

[15] Reinhard, "Sur l'histoire de la Révolution française," p. 561.

The new Napoleonic élite was one of soldiers and bureaucrats.[16] Georges Lefebvre truly writes of Napoleon that he was essentially a soldier: "His preference was for an agricultural and peasant society; the idea of a society dominated by a capitalist economy was unsympathetic, if not even alien, to him." [17] The effectiveness of his promotion of the economic interests of France, it has been pointed out, is an illusion. Though many historians, and even contemporaries, shared the belief that the industry of Lyon owed much to Napoleon, the Lyonnais merchants did not. One, whose correspondence has been edited, is described as having no words too harsh to use in his criticism of the Emperor and of the toadyism that his policy encouraged.[18] The tendency, which Napoleon shared, to look down on business men, and to exclude them from positions of social prestige or political power, survived well into the nineteenth century. As Michelet said, *"La France n'a pas d'âme marchande"* [France does not have the soul of a shopkeeper].[19]

If the new ruling class was not constituted out of the rising industrial or commercial capitalists, then, how was it composed? Only a few samples have been taken so far, but these, and all other indications, lead in the same direction. An analysis of the 600 *"plus imposés"*—those in the highest tax grade—of the Haute-Garonne [department] in the year X (1801–2) shows that they included in their ranks former nobles and members of *parlements, officiers,* judges and lawyers, but that the new aristocracy of France was above all one of landed proprietors.[20] "It has been said," writes the author of this analysis, "that the First Consul aimed to combine, in the bosom of a new aristocracy, the old noblesse and the industrial and commercial bourgeoisie enriched by the revolution. It seems rather that he aimed to create a new one, whose letters of nobility would be conferred by landed property." [21]

There can be no doubt that the new ruling class was above all one of landowners. These were the local notables. The basis of their wealth and influence was land, their prime aim to increase these by enlarging their estates. Perhaps Taine saw something fundamental in the revolution when he wrote, "Whatever the great words—liberty, equality, fraternity—with which the revolution was ornamented, it was essentially a transference of property; that constituted its inmost stay, its prime motive and its historic meaning." [22] Curiously similar was the verdict of Lefebvre in his earlier, more empirical days. After the abolition of privileges, the nobles and *roturiers* [commoners] joined, he wrote, in the same social class. The new bourgeoisie was one of "propriétaires non-exploitants" [absentee landlords].[23]

This, of course, is one of those broad judgements which can only be given real substance by much detailed research. It raises a host of questions about the changes

[16] M. Reinhard, "Élite et noblesse dans la seconde moitié du XVIIIᵉ siècle," *Revue d'histoire moderne et contemporaine*, III (1956).

[17] G. Lefebvre in *Annales historiques de la Révolution française*, no. 119 (1950), p. 276.

[18] J. Labasse, *La commerce des soies à Lyon sous Napoléon et la crise de 1811* (1957), p. 31.

[19] Cited in R. Bigo, *Les bases historiques de la finance moderne* (1933), p. 4.

[20] P. Bouyoux, "Les 'six cent plus imposés' du département de la Haute-Garonne en l'an X," *Annales du Midi*, t. 70 (1958), pp. 317–27.

[21] *Ibid.*

[22] H. Taine, *Les origines de la France contemporaine: la Révolution* (10th ed., 1881), I, p. 386.

[23] G. Lefebvre, *Études sur la Révolution française* (1954), p. 238.

in ownership of land during the revolution, which cannot at present be answered. Most of the figures for the possession of land before the revolution are robbed of their significance by one simple flaw. The proportions owned by nobles, peasants, clergy, or others, are usually given as percentages of a whole area. Unless we know also how much is good arable land, how much pasture, and how much marsh, woodland or waste, such figures are practically meaningless. The one statement we can safely make is that the proportions of land owned by different classes varied enormously from one part of the country to another; and this doubtless remained true after, as before, the revolution.

It would be interesting to know to what extent, in different parts of the country, the noblesse kept its lands during the revolution, or regained them after temporary loss. It is said that in many departments of the West the noblesse was able to retain or restore its estates almost in their entirety.[24] We know also that there were many purchases of *biens nationaux* [expropriated Church and *émigré* lands] by nobles, sometimes even on behalf of *émigrés*, but we have very little idea what each section of society—aristocracy and upper bourgeoisie, urban middle class, better-off peasants or poorer ones—gained proportionately from their sale. The difficulty of making any reliable estimate is added to by the fact that the initial purchases were often fictitious or speculative, and subsequent sale, especially to peasants, may have changed the whole situation. Whoever they were, many of the purchasers presumably had a sudden accession of wealth through the difference between the nominal and the real price they paid, which resulted from the fall in value of the assignat. We know that wealthy men in the towns purchased a great deal, but we do not know how far the property they kept was urban, and how far rural, since town property is included along with country.[25] Again, did the area of land in large estates, and the number of such estates, increase or decrease? In one department of the West the decline in the number of noble landowners was accompanied by an increase in the size of estates.[26]

How far was the new landed class recruited from its predecessors of the *ancien régime*, and to what extent from new men risen from lower social ranks? Did revolutionary and Napoleonic armies provide entry tickets to the new aristocracy? Was it, to any important extent, a parish-pump aristocracy of local lawyers and business men who seized the opportunity afforded by the troubles of the revolution to accumulate land or houses and promote themselves to the rank of local notables?

Whatever the answers may be to all these questions, the main argument, that this was a revolution which bequeathed to France a ruling class of landowners, remains unaffected. It was, of course, to some extent a different class and type of landowner from that of the *ancien régime*, and one which possessed more political power than its predecessor. If such a class can be called a bourgeoisie, then this was the revolutionary bourgeoisie. If the latter is capable of being interpreted in such terms as these, at least it gives a great deal more sense to the subsequent history of France. We shall not vainly search for a non-existent industrial revolution, in a

[24] Bois, *Paysans de l'Ouest*, pp. 313–14.
[25] *Cf.* Lefebvre, *Études*, p. 232.
[26] Bois, *Paysans de l'Ouest*, p. 320.

country dominated by a landed aristocracy. We shall understand the resistance offered by the landed classes under the Restoration to the attempt of the *émigrés* to come into their own again—now, unfortunately, too often other people's own. We shall see the bourgeois monarchy of Louis Philippe as what its franchise showed it to be—a government by and for landowners.[27] We shall understand the passionate defence of property by the ruling classes of the nineteenth century and their fear of the great centres of urban population, Paris and Lyon. Above all, it will become comprehensible why a revolution should have laid the foundations of such an intensely conservative society as France was to be for the next century and a half. . . .

One object of this study has been to suggest, by providing a positive example, the possibility of an empirical approach to the writing of social history, which will enable it to escape from the rigid patterns of system-makers who have deduced their history from their theories. The relation of social theory to social history should be, it seems to me, similar to the relation of political and economic theories respectively to political and economic history. Each of these theoretical disciplines was evolved after consideration of an extensive range of historical experience. Their terminology is therefore relevant to the task of the historian. A particular weakness of most social theory on the contrary, especially from the point of view of its applicability to history, has been its neglect of historical evidence and its almost exclusive dependence on a small range of contemporary material. This not only means that it has developed a language which is inappropriate to past conditions, it also means that it usually deals either with a static situation or else with one involving only very short-term changes. History, on the other hand, requires perspective, which cannot be achieved by concentrating on the developments of a few months or even a few years.

What has been written on the social history of the revolutionary period has suffered from both these defects. It adopted as its model a sociological theory derived from the circumstances of a later age, and it used for the purpose of historical analysis the events of a mere year or two. This interpretation was then projected backwards and forwards, and the histories of the previous and the following centuries were twisted out of shape by the influence of the same arbitrary pattern. To fit in with the theory, eighteenth-century France had to be envisaged as still basically a feudal society, but one which was to become after the revolution predominantly capitalist and industrial, regardless of the facts. Thus Lefebvre could write of "the terrible conditions into which large-scale industry was going to precipitate the working-class in the course of the following decades" [28]—ignoring the terrible conditions, and numbers, of the poor in 1789, which he himself had described, and assuming the appearance in France of a large-scale industry in the early years of the nineteenth century, which his theory required but the facts, alas, repudiated.

If, on the other hand, we look with an open mind on the society that emerged from the revolution, we will be most struck by the permanent elements in the

---

[27] *Cf.* Sherman Kent, *Electoral Procedure under Louis Philippe* (1937).
[28] Lefebvre, *Études*, p. 261.

French social pattern. We will see a society with many new elements it is true, but bearing on it like a palimpsest the inadequately effaced writing of the *ancien régime*. The whole development of French society appears in a different light if we recognise that the revolution was a triumph for the conservative, propertied, land-owning classes, large and small. This was one of the factors—of course not the only one—contributing to the economic backwardness of France in the following century. It helps us to see that in the course of the revolution the social hierarchy, modified and based more openly on wealth, particularly landed wealth, and political influence, and less on birth and aristocratic connections, was strengthened and re-asserted. Again, it is true that the revolution brought about important humanitarian reforms, and eliminated innumerable traditional barriers to the more unified and politically more efficient modern state: but it also frustrated the movement for a better treatment of the poorest sections of society, both rural and urban, which was manifesting itself in the last years of the *ancien régime*. The agricultural proletariat, says Lefebvre, suffered from the revolution.[29] The charitable activities of the church in the eighteenth century (and these should not be under-estimated) were largely brought to an end; the *biens de charité* were incorporated in the *biens nationaux* in the year II and until 29 fructidor year III [September 15, 1795] went to swell the property of the purchasers of church lands.[30] For the poor, possibly a harsher governmental climate was inaugurated. Whoever won the revolution, they lost.

I am really saying nothing new here, and nothing that the historians in the great revolutionary tradition have not said themselves. But having been said, it has usually been put on one side and forgotten, because the possibility that a revolution of the people—an ambiguous term—might have to be regarded as having had unhappy results for the people themselves could not be contemplated. The revolution was by definition a good thing. If any bad things seemed to be involved in it, then they were not part of it, or did not really exist. The revolution became a Sorelian myth [a slogan calling people to action], as Georges Lefebvre in the end proclaimed.[31] As the heroic age of French republicanism its record must not be sullied. As the mother of revolutions to come, to use M. Guérin's phrase, it was to be treated with filial solicitude. It represented an earlier stage on the road that civilisation had to follow. To see it as in any way a diversion, or even a reversal of the one-way traffic dictated by the laws of a great philosophy of history, was too shocking to consider.

Even when evidence that might have led to a different interpretation of the revolution was adduced, it was forced into the pre-conceived pattern. Lefebvre argues that the economic interpretation of history is given an unduly narrow form when the revolution is regarded as the result simply of the rise of the bourgeoisie. It also came, he says, from the resistance of the privileged to the birth of a new economic order, and the opposition of the least-favoured classes to the coming capitalist society. The grudge of the latter against the aristocracy, he agrees, was not

---

[29] *Ibid.*, p. 260.

[30] G. Lefebvre, *Paysans du Nord* (1924), pp. 738–40. [*Biens de charité* refers to land or other property held by hospitals or other charitable organizations, the income from which was to be used to succor the poor.—Eds.]

[31] Lefebvre, "Le mythe de la Révolution française," pp. 344–5.

only because the feudal order had always oppressed them, but also because the capitalist spirit was penetrating into the aristocracy itself and rendering it more odious. Most of this is true, though it is not the whole truth; but his conclusion is that though in this way the germination of a new social order provoked hostile reactions, at the same time these favoured its triumph. That this view is a little illogical might not matter, but it also assumes that the new social order hypothesised did in fact triumph.

I have tried to show that the social developments of the revolution are capable of a very different and even an entirely contrary interpretation, that it was not wholly a revolution for, but largely one against, the penetration of an embryo capitalism into French society. Considered as such, it largely achieved its ends. The peasant proprietors in the country, and the lawyers, *rentiers* and men of property in the towns, successfully resisted the new economic trends. The latter, in particular, took control of the revolution and consolidated their régime by the dictatorship of Napoleon. "United to what remained of the old noblesse," says Lefebvre, "it [*the bourgeoisie*] constituted henceforth a landed aristocracy powerful enough to hold down, under its economic dictatorship, that rural democracy which it had in part created." [32]

In so far as capitalist economic developments were at issue, it was a revolution not for, but against, capitalism. This would, I believe, have been recognised long ago if it had not been for the influence of an unhistorical sociological theory. The misunderstanding was facilitated by the ambiguities implicit in the idea of the bourgeoisie. The bourgeois of the theory are a class of capitalists, industrial entrepreneurs and financiers of big business; those of the French Revolution were landowners, *rentiers* and officials, including in their fish-pond a few big fish, many of moderate size, and a host of minnows, who all knew that they swam in the same element, and that without the pervasive influence of the social hierarchy and the maintenance of individual and family property rights against any interference by the state, their way of life, confined, unchanging, conservative, repetitive, would come to an end. The revolution was theirs, and for them at least it was a wholly successful revolution.

[32] Lefebvre, *Études*, p. 261.

Women: The Failure of Liberation

DARLINE GAY LEVY, MARY DURHAM JOHNSON, AND HARRIET BRANSON APPLEWHITE

Darline Gay Levy (1939–   ), a historian at Barnard College, has published several articles in the journal *Studies on Voltaire and the Eighteenth Century* and a book, *The Ideas and Careers of Simon Nicolas Henri Linguet* (1975). Mary Durham Johnson (1943–   ) teaches history at Temple University. Her article, "Citizenesses of the Year II of the French Revolution,"[1] is a revised selection from her unpublished doctoral dissertation, "The *Sans-Jupons'* Crusade for Liberation during the French Revolution." Harriet Branson Applewhite (1940–   ), a member of the Department of Political Science at Southern Connecticut State College, has contributed an article to *Studies on Voltaire and the Eighteenth Century*. All three are coeditors of a forthcoming anthology, *The Political Participation of Parisian Women During the French Revolution (1789-1795)*, to be published by the University of Illinois Press; the book will expand at length on the points made in the following selection.

In Everyman's repertory of French Revolutionary characters, the places reserved for women are occupied by at least two familiar political stereotypes. The first is the avenging fury of the Parisian poor, *la tricoteuse* (the knitter). Needles in hand, she is on the scene to consecrate and applaud every act of bloodletting under the Terror; she reigns with King Mob in periodic pillaging and bestial murder. Dickens

From Darline Levy, Mary Durham Johnson, and Harriet Applewhite, "Feminism, Welfare and Subsistence: The Political Activism of Parisian Women During the French Revolution (1789–1795)," *Barnard Alumnae*, LXIII (Spring 1974), 9–12. The entire article is reprinted from *Barnard Alumnae*, Spring 1974 issue by permission of the authors and the editor.

[1] Appearing in *The Consortium on Revolutionary Europe, 1750–1850, Proceedings 1972*, ed. Lee Kennett (Gainesville, Fla.: University of Florida Press, 1973).

immortalized *la tricoteuse* in his portrait of Madame Defarge. He did not exactly invent her—or her politics of blood and vengeance.

The second figure is the bare-breasted Goddess of Liberty, intrepid Amazonian, a larger and purer-than-life embodiment of the Revolutionaries' trinitarian political ideology of liberty, equality, fraternity. Delacroix painted the celebrated portrait of Liberty Leading the People to represent the ideals of the revolutionaries of 1830. Her prototype, however, can be found in the propagandistic art of the late 1790's.

For too long now, these mythologized popularizations have masked a rich, complex historical reality, a small part of which we hope to expose in a portrayal of the Revolutionary woman's politics of liberation. Our survey focuses on two groups of politically active Parisian women. First, in the ranks of an elite practicing a politics of feminism and welfare, we single out middle class liberals (*les femmes à chapeau* in the vocabulary of Paris' laboring poor) who campaigned widely and actively for government-sponsored welfare for the masses, and radical-republicans (*les Amazones* to contemporary sympathizers) who demanded equal political rights for women, including the vote, active membership in Revolutionary institutions, and the right to bear arms and organize their own battalions. Second, among the laboring poor women of Paris, we focus on crowds of *sans-jupons* (working women without fancy petticoats, the wives, sisters, and sometime political allies of the *sans-culottes*), a group permanently politicized on one issue, bread, the eternal question of subsistence; and we treat members and leaders of the notorious Parisian Society for Revolutionary Republican Citizenesses, a *sans-jupon* elite articulating the interests of women of the people.

The commitment of these two groups of ideologues and activists to welfare, feminism, and subsistence amounted to expressions in Revolutionary Paris of a women's politics of liberation: liberation from the tyranny of biological and economic insecurity, and from regimes of social domination and political oppression.

Feminism and welfare attracted a heterogeneous elite of women activists—Etta Palm d'Aelders, Madame Robert-Keralio, Théroigne de Méricourt. We will limit discussion here to one of the most fascinating members of this group, Olympe de Gouges, a butcher's daughter from Montauban, who authors a milestone document in the history of European feminism, a draft for a declaration of the rights of woman and citizeness, and introduces it in the National Assembly in the fall of 1791. Needless to say, no action was taken on her draft, but its publication indicates that Gouges was committed to the task of sensitizing her generation to sexist biases which rendered the Declaration of the Rights of Man and Citizen meaningless for the women of the Revolution.

What is in this draft declaration of the rights of woman and citizeness? The introduction is an outspoken blast against a politics of domination practiced by the Revolutionary establishment: "Bizarre, blind, blown up with learning, and degenerated in this century of enlightenment and wisdom into the crassest ignorance, he [*the Revolutionary male*] wants to govern as a despot over a sex which is in possession of all its intellectual faculties. . . ."

The introduction is followed by a fiery preamble: "Considering that ignorance, neglect, or disdain for the rights of woman are the only causes of public misfortunes and the corruption of governments, [*we*] have resolved to expose in a solemn declaration the natural, inalienable, and sacred rights of woman. . . ."

In one of the seventeen articles in her declaration, Gouges states that the end of every political association is the preservation of the natural rights of *women* and men: liberty, property, security, and above all, resistance to oppression. In another article, Gouges demands universal suffrage, equal access for women to all public offices, and freedom of opinion and expression. In her words, "Woman has the right to mount the scaffold; she must enjoy as well that of mounting the rostrum. . . ."

In other polemic literature, Gouges expresses a real sympathy with a growing French population of the aged, the sick, widowed and orphaned—but she repudiates the poor's most effective political tactic, a street politics of confrontation; and she does not identify with, and cannot give priority to, the *sans-jupons'* principal political objective, guaranteed subsistence. She is guillotined in November 1793 for having hesitated publicly, and at a critical moment in the Revolution, between monarchist, republican, and federal political options for France.

The survey we have made—and we have not presented a full documentation here—suggests the following tentative evaluation of the success of elites practicing feminist and welfare politics.

First, these women activists alienated almost all members of the exclusively male ruling elite. That was only to be expected—complex psychological, social and ideological variables are in play here—but without lines of communication to the establishment, and lacking bases of support there, women practicing a politics of feminism and welfare were courting certain defeat.

Second, cleavages preventing the formation of a united political front, even among the Revolution's politicized women, were developing along the lines of social and economic divisions, divisions pitting an elite of haves against a vast majority of have-nots. What complicates the picture, however, and invalidates any simple analysis of feminine political alignments along modern economic class lines, is a plurality of divisions and conflicts—economic (but pre-capitalist), social and ideological—which splintered this population of have-nots, and the Parisian women in it particularly.

We turn briefly to the second of our two groups here, the have-nots, the *sans-jupon* women of Paris, practitioners of a politics of subsistence.

The fishwives of Paris, the seamstresses, domestics, prostitutes, working girls in government-organized spinning and weaving workshops, and in lace-making and needlework manufactures; the actresses, small shopkeepers, workingmen's wives, laundresses, rag-collectors; the chimney-sweeps, indigent widows and peddlers, composed the *sans-jupon* population of the capital. If it can be said that the *sans-jupons* shared a culture, we would have to define it as a culture of poverty, the culture of laboring poor women.[1]

Insofar as they shared political attitudes at all, the key determinant of the *sans-jupons'* revolutionary politics was the availability, the price and the quality of

[1] [See the illuminating article by Olwen Hufton, "Women in Revolution 1789–1796," *Past and Present*, no. 53 (November 1971), 90–108—Eds.]

staples like soap, candles, sugar, coffee, but bread above all. The bread riot was their single most effective mode of political expression. From their first appearance in the October days of 1789 until their last uprising in May 1795, the politics of the *sans-jupons* remained the same: they demanded the right to life, the security of subsistence.

The *sans-jupons* were most politically effective during the *grandes journées* of the Revolution—the sugar riots of January and February 1792, the food riots of February 1793, and the last stand of the *menu peuple* [common people], the insurrection of Germinal–Prairial Year III (1795). Perhaps the best known of the revolutionary *journées* are the October days of 1789, the "women's march to Versailles." This is a complicated episode in the early history of the Revolution, but what is clear is that a driving force behind the rapid and extensive mobilization of the *menu peuple* of Paris, men and women, is bread scarcity and soaring bread prices. The moment of victory comes on the morning of October 6, 1789, when Louis XVI, besieged by 6,000 armed women and a huge contingent of National Guardsmen, consents to return to Paris, a hostage of the nation. Now, symbolic loaves of bread are loaded onto carts and accompany a striking procession back into the capital. Women are seated on cannon, or in carriages; they wear the revolutionary tricolor. They bear the heads of two murdered royal guards on pikes; but they also stack loaves of bread on pikes, and wave these around. They chant: *nous ramenons le boulanger, la boulangère, et le petit mitron*—we're bringing back the baker, and the baker's wife, and the baker's boy.

In this instance, the women of the people's armed politics of subsistence, an anomic politics, limited as far as the women are concerned to a very narrowly defined political issue, life, pays off. It pays in bread.

The most noteworthy attempt to institutionalize this woman power, and to build upon it to broaden the base and sharpen the focus of *sans-jupon* politics, was led by two women *enragés* [democrats], Claire Lacombe and Pauline Léon. In close alliance with *enragé* radicals, this feminine vanguard drafted declarations of the universal right to life, a right to food, a right to eat bread. Nothing could have been more central in *sans-jupon* mentality and politics. The absolutely essential precondition for liberation, in any of the more exalted and metaphysical senses of the term, is respiration, life, the security of a guaranteed physical existence for oneself and one's family. The Revolutionary Republicans agitated also for totalitarian economic regulation, a general price ceiling or maximum on necessities, a program to update the *ancien regime's* machinery against hoarders, monopolists, and profiteering speculators, "the people's bloodsuckers," in their language. They demanded the exposure and arrest of political suspects—aristocrats, hoarders, speculators, Girondins, Jacobins; they clamored for *cours forcés,* or mandatory acceptance of *assignats* as legal tender; they wanted women placed in high public office and in key administrative posts.

It is possible that if any revolutionary institution was capable of the feat, the Society for Revolutionary Republican Citizenesses, guided by its fully politicized organizers, Léon and Lacombe, could have rallied among the *sans-jupons* a broad base of support for feminist politics and saved Revolutionary feminism from a defeat which its idealistic, isolated elitist exponents were unable to prevent.

Again, the Society might have translated an elite-conceived welfare politics into demands reflecting the acute need among the popular classes for massive government-directed welfare programs; and it might have won *sans-jupon* support for these demands.

Finally, some among the Society's general staff were active in popular societies, political clubs, and in Parisian section politics, and fully capable of serving the *sans-jupons* as a highly organized and experienced nucleus, directing or transmuting economic grievances and demands into *sans-culotte*-supported insurrection.

Capability and political potential, however, do not add up to historical inevitability. The facts are sobering.

Léon and Lacombe, leaders of the Society for Revolutionary Republican Citizenesses, miscalculated the breadth of economic cleavages which divided them and their supporters from other women among the *menu peuple*—prostitutes, sentimental widows, female money-lenders, domestics with ties to former nobility and clergy, flower girls dependent on religious holidays for their income—but most important, Parisian marketwomen. For the marketwomen, the Society-sponsored *general maximum* (government price-controls on all basic foodstuffs, not just bread) and the Society's politics of repression and terror portended economic ruin. The price the leaders paid for their political intransigence was mini–civil war in the fall of 1793, pitting marketwomen in physical combat against Society members.

Then, the open breach in the ranks of politicized *sans-jupons,* that is, the war raging in the streets of Paris between Revolutionary Republican women and the marketwomen, gave the anti-feminist, anti-*enragé* Robespierre and political pragmatists among his supporters their excuse for outlawing the Society, along with all women's political organizations, at the end of October 1793, arresting some *enragés* among the Society's leaders and allies, and placing others under close surveillance. The Jacobin Mountain had launched its campaign to control, if not reverse, the process of *dérapage,* a skidding into radical political democracy, a Rousseauan social egalitarianism, and a program of totalitarian economic regulation. At about the same time, the Government of the Terror took first measures to defuse *sans-culotte* politics in sections, popular societies, and clubs.

Any sober historically grounded assessment of political activism among Parisian women must begin with the recognition that women played a role in radicalizing Revolutionary politics and also contributed to the formation of a permanent Revolutionary ideology. The *sans-jupons* were instrumental in transforming street politics from episodic fraternizations among artisans and lower middle-class Parisians into decisive confrontations between the people and authority over the issue of subsistence. In a larger sense, these confrontations tested the nature and limits of government's obligation to distribute subsistence, and the legitimacy of regimes which defaulted on that obligation. The *sans-jupon* interest-articulators in the Society for Revolutionary Republican Citizenesses restated these gut issues as the principles of an ideology of democracy, social egalitarianism, and social welfare. The *Amazones* and the *femmes à chapeau* politicized the issues of welfare and feminism.

Notwithstanding this imposing claim to a measure of success, the Revolutionary women's liberation movement, as we have defined it here, failed. How? and why?

The politics of subsistence—except when subsistence was given its narrowest expression, the politics of bread—proved politically divisive and ideologically bankrupt, driving women into hostile camps of consumers—those whose lives revolved around daily trips to the market to purchase the family's minimum daily requirements for keeping alive—and producers, wholesalers and retailers of foodstuffs.

Then also, many objectives and demands of our politicized women involved them in competition with men for jobs and other roles conferring status, influence, political power or economic success. The responses of men in power who felt the threat ran the gauntlet from chauvinist and paternalistic abuse and mockery through underhanded maneuvers, to open physical attack and, in a few instances, liquidation.

Then, although women's liberation threatened a male-dominated Revolutionary politics and economy on several fronts, the women's liberation movement did *not*. The Revolutionaries could safely refuse to institutionalize women's basic political rights, secure in the knowledge that women could not organize and sustain a resistance capable of overcoming a permanent inertia backed by armed force. Napoleon simply delivered the *coup de grace* to a moribund feminine politics. His Code Napoléon relegated women to a pre-revolutionary state of tutelage. When he dismantled the Revolution's participatory institutions, the Emperor also erected an elaborate machinery to police bread distribution, thereby defusing the subsistence issue around which the *sans-jupon* women's extra-institutional political mobilization had traditionally occurred. The return of women to the kind of political activism we have been discussing did not occur until the Revolutionary days of 1848.

Select Bibliography

This bibliography includes a selection of some of the more important works on the revolutionary and Napoleonic periods, with preference given to recent publications, especially those with extensive bibliographies. Books marked with an asterisk (*) are paperback editions in English.

1. Aids for Research

An indispensable guide for anyone doing research on the French Revolution is Pierre Caron, *Manuel pratique pour l'étude de la Révolution française* (new ed.; Paris: Picard, 1947). The bibliography in Jacques Godechot, *Les Révolutions (1770–1799)* (3rd ed.; Paris: Presses Universitaires de France, 1970) also is very helpful, especially for revolutionary movements outside France. Another excellent detailed bibliography is in Crane Brinton, **A Decade of Revolution, 1789–1799* (New York: Harper & Row, 1963, orig. 1934). These works will direct one to other guides and bibliographies. A collection of important documents in French is John Roberts and John Hardman (eds.), *French Revolution Documents* (2 vols.; Oxford: Basil Blackwell, 1966–1973); and a similar work with the documents translated into English is John H. Stewart, *A Documentary Survey of the French Revolution* (New York: Macmillan, 1951). To keep abreast of current scholarship on the Revolution, consult the *Annales historiques de la Révolution française*; *The American Historical Review*; *Past and Present*; and the *Revue historique*.

2. General Narratives

Valuable surveys of the Revolution include Georges Lefebvre, **The French Revolution* (2 vols.; New York: Columbia University Press, 1969, orig. 1951), and Crane Brinton, **A Decade of Revolution* (cited in section 1). These two works place the Revolution in its European setting. More restricted to French developments is Albert Mathiez, **The French Revolution* (New York: Grosset & Dunlap, 1964, orig. 1922–1927), exceptionally well-written, very favorable to the Revolution and Robespierre. Much less partisan is James M. Thompson, **The French Revolution* (New York: Oxford University Press, 1966, orig. 1943). The relevant volumes in the *New Cambridge Modern History* are Volume VIII, *The American and French Revolutions, 1763–1793*, edited by Albert Goodwin, and Volume IX, *War and Peace in an Age of Upheaval, 1793–1830*, edited by Charles Crawley (both Cambridge, Eng.: University Press, 1965); they are useful especially for discussions of the lesser-known countries and for nonpolitical subjects. Albert Soboul, **The French Revolution: 1787–1799* (New York: Random House, 1975, orig. 1962) interprets issues in terms of class conflict, a point of view thoroughly criticized by Alfred Cobban in **The Social Interpretation of the French Revolution* (Cambridge, Eng.: University Press, 1968). François Furet and Denis Richet, *French Revolution*

(New York: Macmillan, 1970) is a major work dissenting from some of the ideas of Lefebvre and Soboul. The latter defends the social interpretation in "L'Historiographie classique de la Révolution française," *Historical Reflections/Réflexions historiques,* I (1974), 141–167.

3. The Origins of the French Revolution

An introduction to some of the controversies is John McManners, "The Historiography of the French Revolution," pp. 618–652 in Volume VIII of the *New Cambridge Modern History* (cited in chapter 2). Alfred Cobban, **A History of Modern France, I: 1715–1799* (3rd ed.; Baltimore: Penguin, 1963) contains a pithy survey of the prerevolutionary background; and Albert Soboul, *La Civilisation et la Révolution française, I: La Crise de l'ancien régime* (Paris: Arthaud, 1970) organizes the material around a class interpretation.

An introduction to the issue of the intellectual origins is William Church (ed.), **The Influence of the Enlightenment on the French Revolution* (2nd ed.; Boston: Heath, 1974), with an ample bibliography. On the political impact of the *philosophes* no full-length treatise in English can compare to Daniel Mornet, *Les Origines intellectuelles de la Révolution française* (Paris: Colin, 1933), or Furio Diaz, *Filosophia e politica nel Settecento francese* (Turin: Einaudi, 1962). Joan McDonald, *Rousseau and the French Revolution, 1762–1791* (London: Athlone Press, 1965) evaluates the extent of this thinker's influence; Ralph Leigh, "Review Article: Jean-Jacques Rousseau," *Historical Journal,* XII (1969), 549–565, keenly criticizes McDonald's interpretation. Robert Darnton, "The High Enlightenment and the Low-Life of Literature in Pre-Revolutionary France," *Past and Present,* no. 51 (May 1971), 81–115, provides a fascinating description and analysis. Denis Richet, "Autour les origines idéologiques lointaines de la Révolution française," *Annales: Économies, Sociétés, Civilisations,* XXIV (1969), 1–23, finds the usual bourgeoisie-versus-aristocracy approach unconvincing, as do the articles by William Doyle and Colin Lucas cited later in this section.

A major interpretation of European and American political developments in the late eighteenth century can be found in the first volume of Robert R. Palmer, **The Age of the Democratic Revolution* (Princeton: Princeton University Press, 1969, orig. 1959). Shorter and less persuasive is Jacques Godechot, *France and the Atlantic Revolution of the Eighteenth Century, 1770–1799* (New York: Free Press, 1965). For a debate on the issue of whether there was an Atlantic Revolution at this time, see Peter Amann (ed.), **The Eighteenth-Century Revolution: French or Western?* (Boston: Heath, 1963).

Differing views on economic conditions are presented in Ralph Greenlaw (ed.), **The Economic Origins of the French Revolution* (Boston: Heath, 1958). Marc Bloch, **French Rural History* (Berkeley: University of California Press, 1970, orig. 1931) is a brilliant attempt to describe the leading characteristics of prerevolutionary agriculture. Ernest Labrousse and Fernand Braudel, *Histoire économique et sociale de la France,* II (Paris: Presses Universitaires de France, 1970) is an important synthesis. The massive work by Ernest Labrousse, *La Crise de l'économie française à la fin de l'ancien régime et au début la Révolution* (Paris: Presses

Universitaires de France, 1943) investigates cyclical changes in the French economy. David Landes, "The Statistical Study of French Crises," *Journal of Economic History*, X (1950), 195–211, objects to some of Labrousse's methods of research. George Taylor, "Non-Capitalist Wealth and the Origin of the French Revolution," *American Historical Review*, LXXII (1966–1967), 469–496, is a challenging and influential article.

Ralph Greenlaw (ed.), *The Social Origins of the French Revolution* (Boston: Heath, 1975) presents the issues, with a helpful bibliography. A mine of contemporary information is Arthur Young, *Travels in France during the Years 1787, 1788, & 1789* (Cambridge, Eng.: University Press, 1950, orig. 1792). The most noteworthy of the older treatments of French society is Alexis de Tocqueville, *The Old Regime and the French Revolution* (Garden City, N.Y.: Doubleday, 1955, orig. 1856), very freely translated by Stuart Gilbert. Pierre Goubert, *L'Ancien régime* (2 vols.; Paris: Colin, 1969–1973) reappraises conventional interpretations; the first volume has been translated as *The Ancien Régime: French Society, 1600–1750* (New York: Harper & Row, 1973). Other useful studies on aspects of French society include J. Q. C. Mackrell, *The Attack on "Feudalism" in Eighteenth-Century France* (London: Routledge & Kegan Paul, 1973); John McManners, *French Ecclesiastical Society under the Ancien Régime* (Manchester, Eng.: Manchester University Press, 1960); Robert Forster, "The Provincial Noble: A Reappraisal," *American Historical Review*, LXVIII (1963), 681–691; Franklin Ford, *Robe and Sword: The Regrouping of the French Aristocracy after Louis XIV* (New York: Harper & Row, 1965, orig. 1953); Jean Égret, *Louis XV et l'opposition parlementaire, 1715–1774* (Paris: Colin, 1970); William Doyle, "Was There an Aristocratic Reaction in Pre-Revolutionary France?" *Past and Present*, no. 57 (November 1972), 97–122; Colin Lucas, "Nobles, Bourgeois and the Origins of the French Revolution," *Past and Present*, no. 60 (August 1973), 84–126; Elinor Barber, *The Bourgeoisie in 18th-Century France* (Princeton: Princeton University Press, 1967, orig. 1955); Isser Woloch (ed.), *The Peasantry in the Old Regime* (New York: Holt, Rinehart and Winston, 1970); Jeffry Kaplow, *The Names of Kings: The Parisian Laboring Poor in the Eighteenth Century* (New York: Basic Books, 1972); and Olwen Hufton, *The Poor of Eighteenth Century France, 1750–1789* (Oxford: Clarendon Press, 1974).

4. Political History

A standard brief account of the beginnings of the Revolution is Georges Lefebvre, *The Coming of the French Revolution* (Princeton: Princeton University Press, 1968, orig. 1939). Complex and detailed is Jean Égret, *La Pré-Révolution française (1787–1788)* (Paris: Presses Universitaires de France, 1962). Michel Vovelle, *La Chute de la monarchie (1787–1792)* (Paris: Seuil, 1972) follows in Lefebvre's footsteps. James Murphy and Patrice Higonnet, in "Les Députés de la Noblesse aux États-Généraux de 1789," *Revue d'histoire moderne et contemporaine*, XX (1973), 230–247, carefully distinguish liberal from conservative aristocrats. Ruth Necheles, "The Curés in the Estates General of 1789," *Journal of Modern History*, XLVI (1974), 425–444, looks at an often ignored group. Two outstanding early events in the Revolution are examined in Jacques Godechot, *The Taking of the Bastille: July 14th, 1789* (New York: Scribner's, 1970), and Georges Lefebvre, ** The Great Fear of 1789* (New York: Random House, 1973, orig. 1932). Daniel Ligou, "À Propos de la Révolution municipale," *Revue d'histoire économique et sociale*, XXXVIII (1960), 146–177, deals with a little-studied subject and points out the many forms the municipal revolution assumed in France.

Jacques Godechot, *Les Institutions de la France sous la Révolution et l'Empire* (2nd ed.; Paris: Presses Universitaires de France, 1968) examines the important legislation throughout the period. Robert R. Palmer, ** Twelve Who Ruled* (New York: Atheneum, 1965, orig. 1941) is a fascinating account of the Reign of Terror. Donald Greer has published two admirable statistical analyses, *The Incidence of the Terror during the French Revolution* and *The Incidence of the Emigration during the French Revolution* (Cambridge, Mass.: Harvard University Press, 1935 and 1951). Greer's book on the Terror is ably complemented by James Godfrey, *Revolutionary Justice: A Study of the Organization, Personnel, and Procedure of the Paris Tribunal, 1793–1795* (Chapel Hill: University of North Carolina Press, 1951). For a look at an especially famous case of political justice, consult Michael Walzer (ed.), *Regicide and Revolution: Speeches at the Trial of Louis XVI* (Cambridge, Eng.: University Press, 1974).

Political factions are studied in Michael Sydenham, *The Girondins* (London: Athlone Press, 1961); Alison Patrick, *The Men of the First French Republic* (Baltimore: Johns Hopkins University Press, 1972); Crane Brinton, *The Jacobins* (New York: Macmillan, 1930); and Robert Rose, *The Enragés* ([Carleton, Australia]: Melbourne University Press, 1965).

On the people's role in the Revolution, see George Rudé, ** The Crowd in the French Revolution* (New York: Oxford University Press, 1967, orig. 1959); Albert Soboul, *Les Sans-culottes parisiens en l'an II* (Paris: Clavreuil, 1958), of which there is a good abridged translation, *The Parisian Sans-Culottes and the French Revolution, 1793–1794* (Oxford: Clarendon Press, 1964); Richard Cobb, ** The Police and the People* (London: Oxford University Press, 1972); *Reactions to the French Revolution* (New York: Oxford University Press, 1972); and *Paris and its Provinces: 1792–1802* (New York: Oxford University Press, 1975). Deft analyses of some of the publications of these three authors are Robert R. Palmer, "Popular Democracy in the French Revolution: Review Article," *French Historical Studies*, I (1960), 445–469; and Robert Darnton, "French History: The Case of the Wandering Eye," *New York Review of Books* (April 5, 1973), 25–30. A thorough examination of the end of the Terror is Gérard Walter, *La Conjuration de Neuf Thermidor* (Paris: Gallimard, 1974).

Events after Thermidor are surveyed in Michael Sydenham, *The First French Republic, 1792–1804* (Berkeley: University of California Press, 1974), and Denis Woronoff, *La République bourgeoise, 1794–1799* (Paris: Seuil, 1972). Isser Woloch, *Jacobin Legacy* (Princeton: Princeton University Press, 1970) studies the radical democrats in this period.

The very important international aspects of the Revolution are summarized in Steven Ross, ** European Diplomatic History, 1789–1815* (Garden City, N.Y.: Doubleday, 1969); they receive much fuller treatment in the second volume of

Robert R. Palmer, *The Age of the Democratic Revolution* (Princeton: Princeton University Press, 1970, orig. 1964). Jacques Godechot, *La Grande nation* (2 vols.; Paris: Aubier, 1956) concentrates on the "sister republics" along France's eastern frontier.

The counterrevolutionary movement is treated in Paul Beik, *The French Revolution Seen from the Right*, published in *Transactions of the American Philosophical Society*, n.s., XLVI (1956), part I; Jacques Godechot, *The Counter Revolution* (New York: Harper & Row, 1973, orig. 1961); and Harvey Mitchell, *The Underground War against Revolutionary France* (Oxford: Clarendon Press, 1965). The Duc de Castries studies *Les Émigrés* (Paris: Fayard, 1962).

5. Religious History

A short introduction to the religious problems of the Revolution can be found in John McManners, *The French Revolution and the Church* (New York: Harper & Row, 1970), with a helpful bibliography. A longer survey is André Latreille, *L'Église catholique et la Révolution française* (2 vols.; Paris: Hachette, 1946–1950). Bernard Plongeron, *Conscience réligieuse en Révolution* (Paris: Picard, 1969) examines such questions as the religious historiography, the oaths to the Constitution, and dechristianization. These discussions of Catholicism are supplemented by Burdette Poland, *French Protestantism and the French Revolution, 1685–1815* (Princeton: Princeton University Press, 1957).

6. Social and Economic History

Jeffry Kaplow (ed.), *New Perspectives on the French Revolution: Readings in Historical Sociology* (New York: Wiley, 1965) is a collection of articles for advanced students. Norman Hampson, *A Social History of the French Revolution* (Toronto: University of Toronto Press, 1966) includes political history as well. The books by Rudé, Soboul, and Cobb mentioned in section 4 include much social history. Paris and its people are described in Marcel Reinhard, *Nouvelle histoire de Paris: La Révolution, 1789–1799* (Paris: Hachette, 1971). One important social group is analyzed by Robert Forster in "The Survival of the Nobility during the French Revolution," *Past and Present*, no. 37 (July 1967), 71–86, and in *The House of Saulx–Tavanes* (Baltimore: Johns Hopkins University Press, 1971). Georges Lefebvre's classic *Les Paysans du Nord pendant la Révolution française* (Paris: Colin, 1972, orig. 1924) is ably summarized by Robert R. Palmer in the *Journal of Modern History*, XXXI (1959), 329–342. Olwen Hufton has written a compassionate study, "Women in Revolution 1789–1796," *Past and Present*, no. 53 (November 1971), 90–108. See also Jane Abray, "Feminism in the French Revolution," *American Historical Review*, LXXX (1975), 43–62. On the fate of scholars, see Frank Kafker, "Les Encyclopédistes et la Terreur," *Revue d'histoire moderne et contemporaine*, XIV (1967), 284–295. Other aspects of social life are described in Howard Barnard, *Education and the French Revolution* (London: Cambridge University Press, 1969); Roger Hahn, *The Anatomy of a Scientific Institution: The Paris Academy of Sciences, 1666–1803* (Berkeley: University of

California Press, 1971); and Marvin Carlson, *The Theatre of the French Revolution* (Ithaca, N.Y.: Cornell University Press, 1966). A novel that evokes daily life during the Terror is Anatole France, *The Gods Are A-Thirst* (several editions, orig. 1912). Another novel, long and historically accurate, is Robert Margerit, *La Révolution* (4 vols.; Paris: Gallimard, 1963–1968). The first sections of Tom Kemp, *Economic Forces in French History* (London: Dobson, 1971) provide a straightforward account of economic developments to 1815. An important work with much new material is John Bosher, *French Finances, 1770–1795* (Cambridge, Eng.: University Press, 1970).

7. Military History

A recent survey is Steven Ross, *Quest for Victory: French Military Strategy, 1792–1799* (New York: A. S. Barnes, 1973). Robert Quimby, *The Background of Napoleonic Warfare* (New York: Columbia University Press, 1957), and Matti Lauerma, *L'Artillerie de campagne française pendant les guerres de la Révolution* (Helsinki: Suomalainen Tiedeakatemia, 1956) are excellent, the first dealing with the theory of revolutionary warfare, the second with its practice. Marcel Reinhard's biography of Carnot (cited in section 9) is also recommended. The best study of the revolutionary navy is Léon Lévy-Schneider, *Le Conventionnel Jeanbon Saint-André* (2 vols.; Paris: Alcan, 1901). Arthur Mahan's important work on sea power from 1793 to 1812 is cited in section 10.

8. Regional Studies

Many publications have appeared recently on provincial localities in France during the Revolution. These works are usually marked by sophisticated analyses of social and economic life. On the area north of Paris, consult Olwen Hufton, *Bayeux in the Late Eighteenth Century* (Oxford: Clarendon Press, 1967), and Jeffry Kaplow, *Elbeuf during the Revolutionary Period* (Baltimore: Johns Hopkins University Press, 1964). For the West, see Charles Tilly, *The Vendée* (Cambridge, Mass.: Harvard University Press, 1964), Harvey Mitchell, "Resistance to the Revolution in Western France," *Past and Present*, no. 63 (May 1974), 94–131; and T. J. A. Le Goff and D. M. G. Sutherland, "The Revolution and the Rural Community in Eighteenth-Century Brittany," *ibid.*, no. 62 (February 1974), 96–119. The older historical work by Marcel Reinhard, *Le Département de la Sarthe sous le régime directorial* (St. Brieuc: Les Presses bretonnes, 1935), and a novel by Balzac, **The Chouans* (Baltimore: Penguin, 1972, orig. 1829), are also perceptive. Central France is discussed in Georges Lefebvre, "Urban Society in the Orléanais," *Past and Present*, no. 19 (April 1961), 46–71; Colin Lucas, *The Structure of the Terror: The Example of Javogues and the Loire* (New York: Oxford University Press, 1973); and Régine Robin, *La Société française en 1789: Semur-en-Auxois* (Paris: Plon, 1970). On the South, see François Pariset (ed.), *Bordeaux au XVIIIe siècle* (Bordeaux: Fédération historique, 1968); Thomas Sheppard, *Lourmarin in the Eighteenth Century* (Baltimore: Johns Hopkins University Press, 1971), concerning a village in Provence; and Michael Kennedy, *The Jacobin Club of Marseilles,*

1790–1794 (Ithaca, N.Y.: Cornell University Press, 1973). For eastern France, read Claude Brélot, *Besançon révolutionnaire* (Paris: Les Belles lettres, 1966).

9. Biographies

Brief studies of some of the outstanding figures can be found in James M. Thompson, *Leaders of the French Revolution* (New York: Harper & Row, 1967, orig. 1929), and Robert R. Palmer, *Twelve Who Ruled* (cited in section 4). Longer accounts of leading personalities of the early period include Robert Lacour-Gayet, *Calonne* (Paris: Hachette, 1963); Louis Gottschalk, *Lafayette* (6 vols.; Chicago: University of Chicago Press, 1935–1973), which covers his career to mid-1790 with verve and sympathy; Oliver Welch, *Mirabeau* (London: Cape, 1951); and John Clapham, *The Abbé Sieyès* (London: King, 1912).

The lives of later revolutionary figures are described in Eloise Ellery, *Brissot de Warville* (Boston: Houghton Mifflin, 1915); Hermann Wendel, *Danton* (New Haven: Yale University Press, 1935); Louis Gottschalk, *Marat* (Chicago: University of Chicago Press, 1967, orig. 1927); Louis Jacob, *Hébert* (Paris: Gallimard, 1960); James M. Thompson, *Robespierre* (2 vols.; Oxford: Basil Blackwell, 1935); Norman Hampson, *Robespierre* (London: Duckworth, 1974); Leo Gershoy, *Bertrand Barère* (Princeton: Princeton University Press, 1962); Eugene Curtis, *Saint-Just* (New York: Columbia University Press, 1935); Marcel Reinhard, *Le Grand Carnot* (2 vols.; Paris: Hachette, 1950–1952); Georgia Robison, *Revellière-Lépeaux* (New York: Columbia University Press, 1938); Gerlof Homan, *Jean François Reubell* (The Hague: Nijhoff, 1971); and Jean Garnier, *Barras* (Paris: Perrin, 1970).

10. The Aftermath: Napoleon

The standard survey of the period is Georges Lefebvre, *Napoleon* (2 vols.; New York: Columbia University Press, 1969, orig. 1935). Shorter and less sympathetic to Napoleon is Geoffrey Bruun, *Europe and the French Imperium, 1799–1814* (New York: Harper & Row, 1963, orig. 1938), with an extensive bibliography. Jacques Godechot, *L'Europe et l'Amérique à l'époque napoléonienne* (Paris: Presses Universitaires de France, 1967) briefly treats the Atlantic world and includes a large bibliography. Louis Bergeron, *L'Épisode napoléonien (1799–1815): Aspects intérieurs* (Paris: Seuil, 1972) emphasizes institutional and social history. Jean Mistler (ed.), *Napoléon et l'Empire* (2 vols.; Paris: Hachette, 1968) is an elaborate and well-illustrated collective work.

Among the many biographies are Felix Markham, *Napoleon* (New York: New American Library, 1963), a balanced account, and Vincent Cronin, *Napoleon* (New York: Dell, 1973), admiring and frequently at odds with conventional opinions. Still valuable are such older works as John H. Rose, *Life of Napoleon I* (2 vols.; New York: Macmillan, 1901–1902); August Fournier, *Napoleon I* (2 vols.; New York: Holt, 1911, orig. 1886–1889); and Friedrich Kircheisen, *Napoleon* (New York: Harcourt, Brace, 1932). James M. Thompson, *Napoleon Bonaparte*

(Oxford: Basil Blackwell, 1951) is inferior to the same author's books on the Revolution. Pieter Geyl presents an admirable account of the varying interpretations by French historians in *Napoleon: For and Against* (New Haven: Yale University Press, 1963, orig. 1946).

Few of the many memoirs are of lasting value; among those that are, see especially P. Roederer, *Mémoires* (Paris: Plon, 1942), by a leading administrator; *The Adventures of General Marbot* (New York: Scribner's, 1935, orig. 1891); *Memoirs of Queen Hortense* (2 vols.; New York: Cosmopolitan, 1927), by Napoleon's stepdaughter; Armand de Caulaincourt, *With Napoleon in Russia* and *No Peace with Napoleon* (New York: Morrow, 1935 and 1936); and Madame de Staël, *Ten Years of Exile* (New York: Saturday Review Press, 1972, orig. 1904).

Napoleon's own writings can be sampled in James M. Thompson (ed.), *Napoleon's Letters* (New York: Dutton, Everyman Edition, 1954), and John Howard (ed.), *Letters and Documents of Napoleon* (London: Barrie and Jenkins, 1961). J. Christopher Herold (ed.), *The Mind of Napoleon* (New York: Columbia University Press, 1961) is a collection, taken primarily from his conversations and correspondence, of Napoleon's opinions on various themes.

An outstanding and critical account of a major event in Napoleon's rise to power is J. Christopher Herold, *Bonaparte in Egypt* (New York: Harper & Row, 1962). A classic and favorable work is Albert Vandal, *L'Avènement de Bonaparte* (2 vols.; Paris: Plon, Nourrit, 1902–1907).

Two excellent treatments of the First Consul's reorganization of French institutions are Robert Holtman, *The Napoleonic Revolution* (Philadelphia: Lippincott, 1967), and Jacques Godechot, *Les Institutions de la France sous la Révolution et l'Empire* (cited in section 4). "La France à l'époque napoléonienne" is a long special issue of the *Revue d'histoire moderne et contemporaine*, XVII (1970), 331–920, focusing on social and institutional matters. A handsome and useful volume is Jean Tulard, *Nouvelle histoire de Paris: Le Consulat et l'Empire, 1800–1815* (Paris: Hachette, 1970). Maurice Crosland, *The Society of Arcueil: A View of French Science at the Time of Napoleon I* (Cambridge, Mass.: Harvard University Press, 1967) is an absorbing and important study.

For Napoleonic France's diplomatic history, consult the following: André Fugier, *La Révolution française et l'Empire napoléonien*, Volume IV of *Histoire des relations internationales*, edited by Pierre Renouvin (Paris: Hachette, 1954); E. Kraehe, *Metternich's German Policy* (Princeton: Princeton University Press, 1963); Owen Connelly, *Napoleon's Satellite Kingdoms* (New York: The Free Press, 1969); John S. Watson, *The Reign of George III* (Oxford: Clarendon Press, 1960); the essential work by François Crouzet, *L'Économie britannique et le blocus continental (1806–1813)* (2 vols.; Paris: Presses Universitaires de France, 1958); and Alan Palmer, *Alexander I* (New York: Harper & Row, 1974).

Important works on military affairs include David Chandler, *The Campaigns of Napoleon* (New York: Macmillan, 1966); Vincent Esposito and John Elting, *A Military History and Atlas of the Napoleonic Wars* (New York: Praeger, 1964); Arthur Mahan, *The Influence of Seapower upon the French Revolution and Empire (1793–1812)* (2 vols.; Boston: Little, Brown, 1892); and Geoffrey Marcus, *The Age of Nelson: The Royal Navy, 1793–1815* (New York: Viking, 1971). A fine novel is

Alfred de Vigny, *The Military Condition* (New York: Oxford University Press, 1964, orig. 1835).

Some noteworthy biographies of leading figures of the Napoleonic period are Ernest Knapton, **Empress Josephine* (Baltimore: Penguin, 1969); Walter Geer, *Napoleon and his Family: The Story of a Corsican Clan* (3 vols.; New York: Brentano's, 1927–1929); Georges Six, *Les Généraux de la Révolution et de l'Empire* (Paris: Bordas, 1948); J. Christopher Herold, **Mistress to an Age: A Life of Madame de Staël* (Indianapolis: Bobbs-Merrill, 1962); Owen Connelly's study of Joseph Bonaparte, *The Gentle Bonaparte* (New York: Macmillan, 1968); Carola Oman, *Napoleon's Viceroy: Eugène Beauharnais* (London: Hodder and Stoughton, 1966); Carola Oman, *Nelson* (Garden City, N.Y.: Doubleday, 1946); Hubert Cole, *Fouché* (New York: McCall, 1971); Elizabeth Longford, *Wellington: The Years of the Sword* (New York: Harper & Row, 1970); and Jack Bernard, **Talleyrand* (New York: Putnam's, 1973).

ABOUT THE AUTHORS

Frank A. Kafker is Professor of History at the University of Cincinnati. He received his B.A., M.A., and Ph.D. from Columbia University. Among the many journals to which he has contributed articles are *French Historical Studies, Revue d'Histoire Moderne et Contemporaine, The Historian, Eighteenth-Century Studies, Diderot Studies, Modern Language Review,* and *Studi Francesi.*

James M. Laux is Professor of History at the University of Cincinnati. He holds a B.S. from the University of Wisconsin, an M.A. from the University of Connecticut, and a Ph.D. from Northwestern University. He is the author of *In First Gear: The French Automobile Industry to 1914* and the translator of *The Right Wing in France,* by R. Rémond. His articles have appeared in *French Historical Studies, Le Mouvement Social, Business History, French Review,* and the *Political Science Quarterly.*